Human Rights Transformation in Practice

PENNSYLVANIA STUDIES IN HUMAN RIGHTS

Bert B. Lockwood, Jr., Series Editor

A complete list of books in the series
is available from the publisher.

Human Rights Transformation in Practice

Edited by

Tine Destrooper and Sally Engle Merry

UNIVERSITY OF PENNSYLVANIA PRESS

PHILADELPHIA

Copyright © 2018 University of Pennsylvania Press

All rights reserved. Except for brief quotations used
for purposes of review or scholarly citation, none of this
book may be reproduced in any form by any means without
written permission from the publisher.

Published by
University of Pennsylvania Press
Philadelphia, Pennsylvania 19104-4112
www.upenn.edu/pennpress

Printed in the United States of America on acid-free paper
10 9 8 7 6 5 4 3 2 1

Library of Congress Cataloging-in-Publication Data

Names: Destrooper, Tine, editor. | Merry, Sally Engle, editor.
Title: Human rights transformation in practice / edited by Tine Destrooper and Sally Engle Merry.
Other titles: Pennsylvania studies in human rights.
Description: 1st edition. | Philadelphia : University of Pennsylvania Press, [2018] | Series:
    Pennsylvania studies in human rights | Includes bibliographical references and index.
Identifiers: LCCN 2018015433 | ISBN 978-0-8122-5057-2 (hardcover : alk. paper)
Subjects: LCSH: Human rights. | Social justice. | Human rights and globalization.
Classification: LCC K3240 .H863 2018 | DDC 341.4/8—dc23
LC record available at https://lccn.loc.gov/2018015433

CONTENTS

Preface — vii
    Sally Engle Merry

List of Abbreviations — x

Introduction. On Travel, Translation, and Transformation — 1
    Tine Destrooper

PART I. INITIATIVES BY FORMAL HUMAN RIGHTS NORM-SETTERS

Chapter 1. The Escher–Human Rights Escalator: Technologies of the Local — 29
    Vasuki Nesiah

Chapter 2. Accommodating Local Human Rights Practice at the UN Human Rights Council — 57
    Arne Vandenbogaerde

Chapter 3. Human Rights-Based Approaches to Development: The Local, Travel, and Transformation — 77
    Wouter Vandenhole

PART II. INTERACTIONS BETWEEN SOCIAL MOBILIZATION AND LEGAL CLAIM-MAKING

Chapter 4. Lost Through Translation: Political Dialectics of Eco-Social and Collective Rights in Ecuador — 101
    Johannes M. Waldmüller

Chapter 5. Upstreaming or Streamlining? Translating Social
Movement Agendas into Legal Claims in Nepal
and the Dominican Republic   128
Samuel Martínez

Chapter 6. New Visibilities: Challenging Torture
and Impunity in Vietnam   157
Ken MacLean

PART III. HUMAN RIGHTS PROGRAMS AND THE PROLIFERATION
OF NONCONFRONTATIONAL METHODS

Chapter 7. Rural-Urban Migration and Education in China:
Unraveling Responses to Injurious Experiences   183
Ellen Desmet

Chapter 8. Localization "Light": The Travel and Transformation
of Nonempowering Human Rights Norms   208
Tine Destrooper

Chapter 9. Global Rights, Local Risk: Community Advocacy
on Right to Health in China   229
Sara L. M. Davis and Charmain Mohamed

Afterword. Our Vernacular Futures   251
Mark Goodale

List of Contributors   263

Index   269

Acknowledgments   277

PREFACE

Sally Engle Merry

Human rights are increasingly described as in crisis. Some scholars argue that the system of human rights has become too formalized and professionalized and is therefore too remote from those who need its protection. Others insist that it is a Western ideology that has failed to escape its colonial past. Observers of the contemporary political situation note that some authoritarian governments have threatened or closed down human rights organizations in their countries. The enthusiasm for globalization and a universal order of justice of the 1990s was transformed by the 2010s, in part by the growing inequality generated by economic globalization, including the increasing wealth and cosmopolitanism of the few and the poverty and isolation of the many. In place of a celebrated globalism there is now a rising populist tide that puts nation, religion, and race first—and that poses new kinds of threats to human rights.

But are human rights really on the verge of disappearing? It is certainly the case that many human rights institutions have become more bureaucratic and stodgy and that human rights organizations in many parts of the world are under threat. Yet the appeal of human rights has always resided in the ideal of justice, fairness, and equality that they represent. These remain appealing ideas globally, even if the institutions designed to promote and enforce human rights are in themselves increasingly unable to do so. Recognizing the continuing importance and strength of human rights requires looking for them in different places. These places are not simply the Human Rights Council or the regular meetings of the committees seeking to monitor compliance with human rights treaties, but also the offices of small NGOs and the streets of poor cities. Understanding human rights *in practice* requires looking at the way the ideas they promote have become part of everyday life for many people around the world.

Human rights, in this sense, refer to a set of ideals about how governments should treat their citizens and about how all humans should be treated. These ideals, moreover, have the imprimatur of a global consensus. Although there has been a great deal of sophisticated and valuable scholarship about whether human rights are "effective," measured "effectiveness" is not the only way to evaluate the importance of human rights. After all, we do not judge the value of national laws because they are effective, but because they articulate goals that we would like to make effective. Most—national and international—laws, in fact, have an impact in the absence of sanctions, operating instead on the basis of voluntary compliance with a set of rules and ideas that people (or collectives) come to accept. But they are also routinely violated. Thus, even nation-state law is fundamentally a cultural project, an articulation of a vision of society that many, but not all, aspire to have. Lack of compliance with these laws is not viewed as an indication that the cultural project has failed. We can also think about human rights law and human rights norms in this way.

This book offers new perspectives to think about what human rights are and how they work in the world. It foregrounds the sets of ideas and practices generally labeled as human rights that travel and are transformed as they are appropriated, adopted, and redefined to fit particular social issues and struggles. Elsewhere, I have called the cultural dimension of this process vernacularization. This term refers to the way an idea or norm is redefined and represented in a way that is more or less compatible with the existing social world. This does not mean its meaning is changed entirely (although it may be altered), but rather to the altered mode of presentation. New ideas of gender equality coming from other parts of the world might, for example, be presented through the conventional figures in a familiar genre of a street play or painted on kites that are sold for kite-flying contests so that the kites land in random back yards when the strings break, carrying their message with them. The new idea is dressed in the clothes of the old to render it more understandable, acceptable, and relevant. In time, the human rights idea may altogether lose its grounding in the normative system in which it arose and become part of a different cultural formation.

Yet, framing ideas in human rights terms offers at least three important benefits to social justice activists engaged in "local" struggles. First, the "global" consensus about human rights adds legitimacy to a moral claim made by local actors. Using the human rights language suggests that these are not just ideas from a local community or even country, but ideas that have been created and agreed upon by virtually all the countries of the world.

Whether or not these human rights are implemented, the process of their creation through global debate and agreement provides an important level of legitimacy. Second, calling a social justice claim a human rights claim produces allies. Groups concerned with housing rights, poverty alleviation, educational inequality, racial discrimination in health benefits, and so on, can all join together as advocates of human rights, a process I observed among activists in New York City. Third, describing a particular issue as a human rights one renders this issue legible to a wider audience. For example, in 2008 a group seeking to promote the rights of battered women in New York City family courts turned to a human rights framework to show how the everyday struggle women faced in being heard and not losing custody of their children in court was an instance of a larger justice issue. By translating the difficulties these women faced in court into violations of their human rights, they presented these issues in ways that other justice activists could understand even if they might not have encountered this particular problem themselves.

In sum, the focus on how human rights travel and how they are transformed offers an invaluable corrective to those perspectives locating human rights only in formal institutions and laws. It shows how human rights are embedded in everyday social practice and activism. It challenges the idea that human rights are an entirely Western construct resisted by the postcolonial world by showing how these ideas are appropriated in countries around the world and how the international human rights norms and architecture are shaped by these countries' experiences. And it makes clear that although measuring compliance is important, this is not the only way to assess what human rights do. By examining the human rights system as a social justice ideology with universal aspirations, flexible enough to be reinterpreted and redefined in a variety of contexts and for a broad range of problems, it is possible to develop a more comprehensive and useful understanding of the way human rights work in our contemporary world. This book shows how it is being done.

ABBREVIATIONS

ACT-UP	AIDS Coalition to Unleash Power
BASE	Backward Society Education
BTC	Belgische Technische Cooperatie (Belgian Technical Cooperation)
CAR	Central African Republic
CAT-VN	Campaign to Abolish Torture in Vietnam
CATS	Community Approaches to Total Sanitation
CBO(s)	community-based organization(s)
CCDH	Centro Cultural Domínico-Haitiano (Haitian-Dominican Cultural Center)
CEDAW	Committee on the Elimination of Discrimination against Women
CEL	Compulsory Education Law
CFS	Committee on Food Security
CICC	Coalition for the ICC
CIDR	Centre Intègre pour le Développement des Milieux Ruraux
CMO(s)	community membership organization(s)
CONAIE	Confederación de Nacionalidades Indígenas del Ecuador (Confederation of Indigenous Nationalities of Ecuador)
CPR	civil and political rights
CPRK	Centre Pénitentiaire de Rééducation de Kinshasa (Kinshasa Penitentiary and Reeducation Center)
CRC	Committee on the Rights of the Child
CSM	civil society mechanism
CSO	civil society organization
DRC	Democratic Republic of the Congo
ECHR	European Convention on Human Rights and Fundamental Freedoms

ECOSOC	United Nations Economic and Social Council
ECtHR	European Court of Human Rights
ECUARUNARI	Ecuador Runakunapak Rikcharimuy / Confederación de Pueblos de la Nacionalidad Kichwa del Ecuador (Confederation of Peoples of Kichwa Nationality)
ESCR	economic, social, and cultural rights
EU	European Union
FAO	United Nations Food and Agricultural Organization
FGM	female genital mutilation
FRPI	Patriot Resistance Force
GIPA	greater involvement of people living with HIV/AIDS
HIV/AIDS	human immunodeficiency virus/acquired immune deficiency syndrome
HRBA	human rights–based approach
HRBAD	human rights–based approach to development
HRC	(United Nations) Human Rights Council
HRI(s)	human rights indicator(s)
HRW	Human Rights Watch
IACtHR	Inter-American Court of Human Rights
ICC	International Criminal Court
ICCPR	International Covenant on Civil and Political Rights
ICESCR	International Covenant on Economic, Social and Cultural Rights
ICTJ	International Center for Transitional Justice
ICTR	International Criminal Tribunal for Rwanda
ICTY	International Criminal Tribunal for the Former Yugoslavia
ILO	International Labor Organization
INGO	international nongovernmental organization
LGBT	lesbian, gay, bisexual, and transgender
LRA	Lord's Resistance Army
MOSCTHA	Movimiento Socio-Cultural para los Trabajadores Haitianos (Haitian Workers' Socio-Cultural Movement)
MSM	men who have sex with men
MUDHA	Movimiento de Mujeres Domínico-Haitianas (Haitian-Dominican Women's Movement)
MYWO	Maendeleo ya Wanawake Organisation
NGO(s)	nongovernmental organization(s)

OEWG	open-ended working group
OHCHR	(United Nations) Office of the High Commissioner for Human Rights
OPCV	Office of Public Counsel for Victims
PRSP	Poverty Reduction Strategy Papers
RoV	Republic of Vietnam
SCR	Security Council Resolution
SDI	Shack/Slum Dwellers International
SENPLADES	Secretaría Nacional de la Planificación y del Desarrollo (Ecuadorian National Secretary for Planning and Development)
SIIDERECHOS	Sistema Integral de Indicadores de Derechos Humanos (Integral System of Human Rights Indicators
SNV	Stichting Nederlandse Vrijwilligers (Organization of Dutch Volunteers)
SPSS	statistical package for social science
SR	Special Rapporteur
UN	United Nations
UNAIDS	Joint United Nations Programme on HIV/AIDS
UNCAT	United Nations Convention against Torture and Other Cruel, Inhuman, or Degrading Treatment or Punishment
UNDP	United Nations Development Programme
UNICEF	United Nations Children's Fund
UPR	Universal Periodic Review
VRP	Vietnam Reform Party
WOZA	Women of Zimbabwe Arise
Yasuní-ITT	Yasuní Ishpingo-Tambococha-Tiputini (oil field in the Yasuní national park)

Human Rights Transformation in Practice

INTRODUCTION

On Travel, Translation, and Transformation

Tine Destrooper

In the past decade, the discourse of human rights has increasingly been used by grassroots activists, social movements, and (international) nongovernmental organizations to channel and frame their struggles for social justice. As such, the mandate of human rights expanded de facto beyond the protection of civil and political rights, and also chronic deprivations of economic and social rights are now increasingly being addressed using the human rights discourse (Brysk 2013). When the International Covenant on Civil and Political Rights (ICCPR) and the International Covenant on Economic, Social and Cultural Rights (ICESCR) were adopted by the United Nations General Assembly in 1966, they formally had equal importance. However, in practice, civil and political rights have received more attention than economic, social, and cultural rights, and the evolution toward increasingly addressing socioeconomic injustices, exploitation, oppression, and inequality as human rights issues is a relatively recent one.

This increased attention given to economic, social, and cultural rights made the human rights discourse more relevant and appealing for a broader range of social justice activists in various localities in both the global North and the global South. As a consequence, the group of actors invoking human rights language has been steadily growing and diversifying (Vandenhole and Van Genugten 2015; Moyn 2014). This has entailed a shift in the composition of the so-called human rights community. Governments in the South, grassroots actors in remote communities, members of transnational networks, country officers of international organizations, and even corporate actors all refer to human rights in their attempts to create a sense of legitimacy and recognition, remedy structural inequalities, or seek redress for rights violations.

Because of this, human rights can no longer be considered merely as a matter of international law (if this was indeed ever possible), and neither a focus on violations nor work on the justiciability of human rights adequately represents the broad range of human rights activism that seeks to address the structural factors constraining the enjoyment of human rights (Casla 2014). This volume inscribes itself in a more comprehensive understanding of human rights and considers how governmental, intergovernmental, and civil society actors invoke human rights discourses, and how this vernacularization of the human rights discourse affects the symbolic forms, content, and functionality of human rights at various levels. To do this, the chapters in this volume adopt an actor-centered approach focusing on the practices and priorities of rights users. The notion of rights users adhered to in this volume acknowledges that there is a wide range of ways in which to employ human rights, from the use of human rights language as a tool for explicit and formal mobilization to the invocation of human rights values without direct reference to their legal and institutional grounding.

As several authors have previously demonstrated, rights users' dynamic and decentralized engagement with various aspects of human rights quickly proved that the assumption of a more or less monolithic human rights understanding was, in practice, an illusion, and the adoption of human rights discourses by a growing range of actors resulted in various partial, innovative, or biased articulations of this discourse (see, for example, Goodale and Merry 2007; De Feyter et al. 2011; Arthur 2009). Nevertheless, the current liberal human rights regime remains largely Western-derived, not only in historical terms, but also when looking at rights users' access to and influence on the formal agenda-setting and decision-making processes (Goodale 2009; Vandenbogaerde 2015).

How human rights users around the world engage and interact with human rights norms existing at the transnational level, and how this in turn influences the further development of human rights norms, has been studied by anthropologists, social movement scholars, political scientists, and legal scholars, among others (see, for example, Baxi 2007; Meckled-García and Çali 2006; Gready and Vandenhole 2014; Wilson 2007). In this volume, we bring together scholars from these various disciplines in order to broaden and deepen our understanding both of how these ideas about human rights travel and of how they are translated and transformed along the way. Through an interdisciplinary conversation, we seek to go beyond the question of how interpretations of human rights that emerge at different levels interact with and influence one another. We also explicitly seek to bring power and politics back into the picture, so as better to understand issues of access, knowledge genesis, strategy formation, and exclusions (both of actors and of issues). The volume sheds light on the various ways in which co-opting can happen, and the authors reflect on ways to avoid this. In doing so, the descriptive and empirically grounded chapters also entertain more normative questions about a genuine human rights–based alter-insurgency.

The Localization of Human Rights

For the purposes of this volume, we define the process of human rights localization as the travel, translation, and transformation of human rights across scales (see below). The question about the localization of human rights is an important one to consider for practitioners as well as scholars because it is at the local level that human rights can act as a line of defense against injustice. Consequently, it is there that they prove to be vital or illusory (De Feyter 2007). As such, a concern with localization processes is inherently one that is about more than improving our empirical understanding of these processes; it is also rooted in normative or efficacy considerations regarding the protection human rights (can) offer.

The growing importance of localization studies of various kinds can be at least partly understood in the light of the growing importance of actor-centered approaches to human rights more generally (Nyamu-Musembi 2002, 2005; Pantazidou 2013). Actor-centered approaches study how the concrete experiences and practices of actors on the ground shape the relevance and meaning of human rights in practice. These approaches have multidisciplinary roots and call into question a purely legal understanding and analysis of human rights, promoting instead an analysis of legal principles in terms of their concrete effects in social settings, especially for less powerful groups. Actor-centered approaches pay elaborate attention to local contexts and have become an important subfield within the field of human rights studies. Notions like contextualization (Zeleza 2004), indigenization (Merry 2006a), plurality (Falk 2000), vernacularization (Merry 2006b), inclusive universality

(Brems 2001), and human rights upstreaming (de Gaay Fortman 2011) all point out the importance of considering the realities of local rights holders and how they interact with global, regional, and national norms.

These actor-centered approaches to human rights, in line with legal pluralism and critical legal studies, also emphasize the need for new types of coordination and elaboration of international legal norms. Envisioned is the kind of cooperation and elaboration that acknowledge the imprecision, uncertainty, and instability that characterize the international legal realm, and that is not aimed at erasing normative differences. Instead, it is argued that rendering these differences more visible can be a means to return agency to various groups of rights holders (Delmas-Marty 2006; Baumgaertel et al. 2014). As Halliday and Carruthers (2007) posit, in a globalized landscape it is not the authoritative transnational and global bodies that create norms that they can then impose more or less subtly upon a hapless world. The processes of norm setting, as well as that of norm implementation, always and everywhere involves negotiation between various actors with different interests and differential access to power, and therefore cannot be conceptualized as top-down universalizing undertakings. Also, the groundbreaking work of Simmons (2009) and Goodman and Jinks (2013) is crucial in this regard to understand the agency, both on the side of individual and collective rights users as well as on the side of states, in the process of disseminating human rights norms. And while their focus is on the political and institutional dimensions, this volume shares with that literature a focus on power relations, agency, and processes of travel.

In the remainder of this introduction, I discuss the most pertinent concepts and perspectives regarding travel, translation, and transformation of human rights issues and present the conceptual and theoretical framework for thinking about the nature and impact of localization processes.

Travel, Translation, and Transformation

Previous studies on the localization, vernacularization, or indigenization of human rights have contributed to our overall understanding of how various types of place-based actors appropriate existing notions of human rights, and in some cases also set the agenda for the development of new human rights norms. None of these studies, however, systematically addressed the question of how to conceptualize the process of localization in analytical terms;

most theoretical discussions of how human rights became localized lacked an empirical component, while the wealth of rich empirical studies often lacked a focus on the broader conceptual question of what exactly we talk about when we talk about localization. To address this gap in the literature—and possibly even a gap in perception—in a coherent way, this volume distinguishes, within the process of localization, between two analytically distinct processes: on the one hand, the *movement* of ideas, and on the other hand, the way in which this movement triggers *changes* in the framing, substance, and meaning of the norm under consideration.

We refer to the process of movement as human rights *travel*, a term more neutral than, for example, the notion of human rights circulation, which implies a circularity and equality of the actors involved that renders it difficult to account for power differences. Human rights travel refers to the proliferation of existing norms among rights users (who can invoke them as remedies in their specific situation), transnational and translocal human rights communities (who can invoke the norms as indirect users of human rights), and formal human rights norm-setters (who often foresee various kinds of mechanisms to ensure that "voices from below" can reach them). Beyond this neutral process of movement, the notion of travel inevitably also entails a risk of alienation from their originators, in an attempt to have them picked up by journalists, NGOs, legal counsels, or rights users elsewhere (see Martínez in this volume).

The farther certain understandings of human rights travel, the more liable they are to be translated. This *translation* process is not neutral or merely a technical matter. While traveling through the dense human rights architecture of courts, councils, and counselors, for example, local human rights claims are likely to become translated as more or less unidimensional or technical debates that fit the existing narrative of these institutions (Baxi 2007, 69). Therefore, when international human rights practitioners adopt a certain strategy and language to defend rights holders' interests, their choice to use the frame of human rights entails the constant danger of narrowing social movement agendas in ways that fit the existing legalist imaginary of human rights at the international level—sometimes at the cost of becoming incomprehensible or irrelevant to local rights holders. Thus, when intermediaries repeat claims or norms and translate them in ways that are comprehensible—and acceptable—for other constituencies in the human rights edifice, this does not necessarily adequately reflect these claims' history and context of origin, and always carries the potential for *transformations* or distortions of various kinds. Yet the transformations brought about through this process of translation and reframing are not necessarily a matter of impoverishing comprehensive human rights understandings rooted in rights holders' daily realities (see below). When, for example, rights users turn to human rights language and methodologies to frame their struggles for social justice, thereby appropriating the human rights discourse in a specific way that is relevant for their struggle, they may open up this discourse and propose new concepts and readings.

Translation and transformation are thus two sides of the same coin, and both relate to the changes in substance, strategy, and language that occur when human rights norms move between rights users at various scales and localities. For the purpose of this volume, we use the notion of translation to refer to the act of rendering intelligible and acceptable for other constituencies and audiences a discourse and practice that has its roots in one site (be it local, global, or any of the intermediary or overlapping scales). This act of translation, which involves the conscious or unconscious foregrounding of certain elements of the human rights discourse and the omission or adaptation of others, may in turn result in the transformation of the substance, strategy, or language of certain components of the human rights system. As Waldmüller argues in this volume, apparent translational paradoxes are often enrobed in hidden or open struggles for power, with more powerful actors being more likely to be able to capitalize on these translation paradoxes by promoting—or obscuring—certain agendas in the name of intelligibility. Hence, while processes of translation inevitably involve reductions, erasures, or reinterpretations, it is crucial to acknowledge that the selective treatment of certain dimensions of a concept may be an intentional strategy by more powerful actors seeking to shape the eventual understanding that is likely to result from this translation. In this sense, transformations may be either intended or unintended effects of translations.

While none of these processes is in itself problematic,[1] it is crucial for scholars, activists, and practitioners to improve their understanding of how these processes of travel, translation, and transformation relate to and shape one another. By unpacking the question of precisely which elements are erased and which are added and by whom, the contributions in this volume shed light on the dynamic and interactive dimensions of these processes of travel, translation, and transformation. This undertaking is pertinent in terms of gaining not only a better empirical understanding, but also a normative sense: several authors suggest that negotiating with and including local translations might be the only viable strategy to counter the risk that international human rights norms either become co-opted by powerful actors or exist in a vacuum disconnected from the lives of rights holders.

At the same time, several authors in this volume ask whether there are limits to how much transformation on the basis of "voices from below" the existing human rights architecture can accommodate, and whether there are cases in which risks (of co-opting, fractionalization, or offering less protection, for example) outweigh potential benefits of inclusivity and local ownership. Vandenhole (in this volume) asks, for example, if there is a need to define an "untouchable" normative core that is beyond transformation, and if so, what constitutes such a normative core, how it can be identified, and whether it will ever work as a boundary that cannot be overstepped. Are there good and bad forms of transformation, or should this normative characterization be forsaken altogether? How do we understand the choice of organizations to use human rights language even when claiming rights that are not inscribed in human rights law? If certain permutations by grassroots human rights users are deemed unacceptable, by whom and on what grounds should this be decided? These descriptive and normative questions may be impossible to answer in the abstract. This introduction therefore merely seeks to lay out the framework for addressing these questions in the following empirical chapters.

Upstream and Downstream Travel of Human Rights

Within the broad literature dealing with the question of how human rights norms move between various actors, institutions, and scales, two broad sets of approaches can be distinguished, which will be referred to here as downstream and upstream approaches.

In the mid-2000s, Merry (2006a) introduced the language of *vernacularization*, referring to the adaptation of existing international human rights norms to local contexts by norm entrepreneurs. The concept of vernacularization is rooted in legal anthropology and focuses extensively on ideas, practices, and symbolic forms. Merry argued that when specific struggles in non-Western societies utilize a Western liberal-legalist discourse, local understandings, practices, and symbolisms are applied to these global discourses and lead to a reinterpretation of its core concepts and ideas. Scholars in this tradition (e.g., Nyamu-Musembi 2005; Zeleza 2004) analyze how rights users (and in particular norm entrepreneurs) transform the meaning of rights when they translate the—often otherwise legalistic—human rights discourse into action, thereby shifting the parameters and symbolic forms of the discourse. Also, Ensor's concept of "alternative manifestations" of rights (Gready and Ensor 2005, 265) resonates with this top-down understanding of travel, translation, and transformation.

To some extent, this concern with top-down travel, translation, and transformation can also be found in policy discourses of local ownership and democratic legitimacy and in contemporary discussions on, *inter alia*, developmental, environmental, and transitional justice. These discussions have led to the development of a vast nomenclature (e.g., local involvement, community empowerment, participatory development, civil society partnerships, local ownership, NGO engagement) that alludes to the role of local actors as potentially powerful translators—and legitimators—of global norms and programs. However, as Nesiah shows in this volume, this policy process, while at face value showing some similarities with the concept of vernacularization, is fundamentally different from the process described by Merry, in the sense that the centralized and institutionalized approach limits and shapes the options available to grassroots actors.

In reaction to this downstream understanding of human rights travel, another strand of literature emerged, often referred to as *upstream approaches* (de Gaay Fortman 2011). These upstream approaches study rights "from below," or, in other words, the influence the local has, or could have, on human rights norms and institutions at other scales. Through, for example, advocacy relations between grassroots organizations and actors occupying other positions in the human rights architecture, the experience of local advocates and practitioners can potentially feed back into and shape agendas of international NGOs and international human rights bodies, thereby ultimately reshaping international human rights norms. As Gledhill (2009) argues, an upstream approach to human rights travel is not only, or not in the first place, relevant to study how spontaneous bottom-up action by marginalized rights users might bring about changes at the international level. It also, and more importantly, helps us to understand how rights holders' capacity to make claims and organize, allows them to take greater direct control over the production of their own identities and self-representation.

Authors like De Feyter (2007; De Feyter et al. 2011), Oré Aguilar (2011), and Brems (2001) sought to integrate these upstream and downstream understandings of how human rights travel and transform by proposing a bidirectional framework of analysis. In a downstream perspective, states, for a variety of reasons, adopt human rights instruments, and norms are considered human rights norms because states actors agree on this (Simmons 2009). In an upstream perspective, people shape the norms by drawing on their own understanding of human dignity and social justice. Yet, as de Gaay Fortman rightly stresses, the analytical distinction between downstream and upstream perspectives on human rights should not obliterate that these two processes are strongly interwoven and essentially constitute "two sides of what is basically one process" (2011, 13). In other words, there is an ongoing interaction between downstream and upstream perspectives.

This volume advances the idea that upstream and downstream travels of human rights are part of the same complex process, as well as the idea that this process can be facilitated through adequate institutional provisions. However, we also caution against zealously institutionalizing this kind of bidirectional human rights travel per se. As the chapters in Part I of this volume ask, when certain laws, policies, and procedures are adopted and institutionalized by international human rights bodies in the name of advancing local ownership, what happens to the "local," and how does the local alter in response to this institutionalization of localization at the global level? Can the local ever be accurately represented in remote forums, and if not, what kind of institutional action should be considered to cope with the process of localization? Moreover, as Nesiah remarks in this volume, the assumption behind the institutionalization of localization is often that "if only we get the methodology right, access those who live in remote regions (even in the rainy seasons!), train interviewers, acclimatize researchers so that respondents do not feel uncomfortable about discussing sensitive issues with strangers, we would have good input to rationally formulate good policy—especially if the political context does not fluctuate too much." She warns that the irony at the heart of this understanding is that, through these kinds of institutional provisions and the belief in such a technocratic and managerial approach, human rights issues become politically intelligible and responses democratically legitimate precisely because they are recast as technocratic issues and thus stripped of politics.

In an attempt to expose this bias, the authors in this volume do not only examine how this type of bidirectional travel takes place and can be facilitated, but also consider how human rights, and especially the transformation of human rights, is inherently a struggle in which relative access, influence, and power play an important role. In this sense it is relevant to note that a bidirectional understanding of how human rights travel may in itself be inadequate, to the extent that this perspective continues to rely heavily on the assumption of a single vertical axis that structures information-sharing and, in many ways, continues to be deferential to formal human rights bodies as the primary norm-setters. While the adoption of new human rights instruments is one way of addressing the normative and/or application gaps in international human rights law, this volume is concerned with human rights beyond a legal perspective and therefore also looks beyond new rights and obligations asserted by such a new treaty or declaration. The authors also analyze the political and strategic process that brings these instruments into being, paying specific attention to how issues of access and influence are shaped by actors' relative power.

Moreover, the complex role and position of norm entrepreneurs in upstream, downstream, and bidirectional perspectives needs to be further unpacked.[2] To understand who these norm entrepreneurs are, what their position in civil society is, and how they often travel between various audiences and constituencies, we need to acknowledge that, because scientific, technical, and organizational knowledge is usually required for long-term, high-level human rights advocacy, many grassroots activists eventually become embedded to some extent in the systems of power they seek to influence. Shifts in subjectivity may occur, which place these norm entrepreneurs at a crossroads between various realms of which they are part and between various subjectivities they can adopt interchangeably or sequentially. On the other hand, those norm entrepreneurs for whom this kind of insider positioning is not available (for example, those working on controversial or taboo-laden issues) may sometimes find it difficult to have their voices heard at all. Hence, there may be pressures for advocates to focus on advocating within the local bounds of the permissible and on relationship-building both within their immediate local network and with the human rights community at large. As the chapters by Vandenhole, Destrooper, and Davis in this volume show, this raises questions about the meaning of the very idea of local norms and how these relate to norms existing elsewhere. To answer this question, the volume proposes a more complex understanding of human rights travel, which is referred to as multidirectionality.

Multidirectional Travel and Power Dynamics

Can the metaphors of the vertical and horizontal ever properly convey the complex dynamics of how human rights ideas travel? The various contributions to this volume reveal some of the many ways in which human rights norms can travel through complex, multilayered, and juxtaposed networks of rights users at what could be called the translocal level, and beyond. The case studies show how human rights claims chart a complex landscape as they travel within the human rights field, and how travels and transformations may follow several directions simultaneously and involve similar and different actors, concepts, and ways of referring to them. This type of travel is not characterized by the same vertical power relations that characterize the oft-invoked local-global or top-down, bottom-up continuum, and power should therefore be rendered more visible in our analyses.

Not only power and how it manifests itself across, between, and within various localities, but also the notion of the local per se requires explicit conceptualization (see, for example, Hacking 1999). Various conceptions of the local animate discussions of human rights accountability, and often what is at stake is a debate over what constitutes "the most relevant local" for human rights decision-making and who has access to "the people" to better represent their voices (also see Nesiah in this volume). A first notion of local that is relevant for the chapters in this volume is that of grassroots place-based processes that stand in contrast to the national and the international realm to which local actors may have no easy access or of which they might have no direct experience; a second one adhered to by some authors in this volume is that of local as national processes that stand in contrast to the international processes and institutions of global governance. A sovereignty-defined definition of local would be most closely in line with mainstream human rights language of states as duty bearers, and with the language of international law more generally. However, several authors in this volume suggest that, in order to understand the multilayered and multiple ways in which human rights norms travel, the local interests at stake should not merely be the nation-state register vis-à-vis the global, but should also include the grassroots community register vis-à-vis other grassroots, provincial, national, regional, and international actors. Therefore, rather than taking as a point of reference the doctrinal recognition of the nation-state as the local level, this volume accepts that different notions of local circulate alongside different understandings of human rights norms.

Even if some authors in this volume occasionally employ the vocabulary of top-down and bottom-up, all chapters are inspired by an acknowledgment of the complexity of human rights travel and specifically by the need to account for the many ways in which actors at various places within the human rights architecture do or do not have certain kinds of power at their disposition to steer this travel in one way or another. The focus on power dynamics means that all contributions necessarily contemplate local, international, and intermediate politics of rights, which involve the establishment of hierarchies and the prioritization of values, actors, methods, and claims. The localization of human rights cannot be understood without the broader contexts and constellations within which it takes place (such as political interests and cycles, opportunity structures, strategic alliances, media attention, or donor agendas). As such, the political context co-determines the potential of human rights claims and actions to emerge. And, as Oré Aguilar (2011, 117) notes, "in human rights claims, the degree of 'political space' is measured not only by the existence of an ongoing armed or violent conflict . . . but also by the existence and level of functioning of institutional (civilian) governance structures, decision-making channels, freedom of expression, rule of law and open access to information."

In this sense, limited political space and the relative power of human rights users can also shape human rights–based claims of (in)justice (e.g., see Rottenburg 2009). As the case studies from China by Desmet and Davis and Mohamed in this volume show, activists working in the context of a sweeping crackdown on civil society must be skilled at managing political risks of many kinds. This can influence their strategic choices with regard to the translation of human rights. Chinese activists working on the right to health, for example, showed pragmatism, sophistication, and reasonable caution in the selection of their advocacy targets and tactics and prioritized the opportunity to deliver real and measurable gains for their communities. This is also true for the case study on the Democratic Republic of the Congo (DRC) by Destrooper in this volume, where stark power imbalances and incomplete information shaped the emergence of a local human rights understanding that was devoid of any references to accountability or claim-making. The chapters in Part III of this volume ask how the potential for localization is shaped by the political context within which local understandings emerge, especially in highly restrictive or undemocratic societies. The examples in this part of the volume confound any easy assumptions about what results from the integration of global human rights discourse (often funded by bilateral aid) and local advocacy.

If it is true, then, that "human rights claims originate from a local site" (De Feyter et al. 2011, 14) and that the local is the primary site of struggle, more research is needed that sheds light on the multiple power dynamics both at the local level and between the local, global, and any intermediate or translocal levels. For example, how do local human rights advocates find a balance between hybridization and replication, to use Merry's terms (2006a), or between a confrontational and a cooperative strategy? How does unequal access shape local understandings that can then feed back into the discourse existing at the international level? Is the travel of local understandings of human rights to formal human rights norm-setters beneficial per se, or has the human rights field configured localization in such a way that the upstreaming of local concerns and the participation of local communities in the norm-setting process has become internal to global governance rather than a locus for challenging transnational processes or global institutions?

If human rights are to realize the socially transformative potential they are often claimed to have (Haglund and Stryker 2015; Gready and Vandenhole 2014), power dynamics and their impact need to be better understood (Vázquez 2011).[3] The aim of this volume is precisely to arrive at a more textured and multidimensional understanding of how human rights norms travel and become translated and transformed and how power dynamics play a role in this.

Postcolonial Theory

Both the localization perspective discussed above and actor-centered perspectives more broadly adopt a "users' perspective" on human rights (Brems and Desmet 2014). One can be identified as a human rights user from the moment there is an explicit interaction with human rights—or as a *potential* user if one could legitimately and logically invoke human rights but chooses not to do this (Desmet 2014). To better understand this choice to engage with the human rights architecture or, on the contrary, to refrain from doing so, the perception gap between the limitations of the Western-derived liberal international human rights regime and Southern/subaltern social movements and activists is decisive (Goodale 2009).

Several elements of the current human rights regime are identified by postcolonial scholars as factors explaining the disconnect between these grassroots activists in the global South on the one hand and the international human rights architecture and transnational human rights communities on the other. First, as Waldmüller also argues in this volume, from a Western perspective of law and social studies we tend to overlook the dependency of human beings, and of human rights, on factors such as ecological conditions and the socioenvironmental impacts or conflicts that may follow from them. These human rights *indicators* are highly anthropocentric and shy away from any type of ecosystemic thinking or environmental consideration (Merry 2013). Second, the dominant liberal vision of human rights as individual entitlements—a general orientation that can be observed in most contemporary human rights regimes (Hinkelammert 2004; Pitarch et al. 2008; Jordan 2008)—still tends to neglect the full potential and implications of collective political and civil rights, such as the right to self-determination, and no attention at all is paid to group rights in the highly utilitarian methodology of human rights indicators. Third, any efforts by global human rights bodies to "upstream" local voices formally tend to target rights users in the global South, who often have to somehow maneuver and cope with cunning postcolonial governments, which includes trade-offs between (human, ecosystemic, and other) sacrifices and progressive rhetoric. This means that the existing human rights framework is still strongly pinned on a form of knowledge that is not representative of the world vision of significant groups of rights holders.

Post- and anticolonial scholars (such as Baxi 2007, Mignolo 2000) have examined the importance of decolonizing this type of knowledge and worldview for arriving at a more representative and locally relevant human rights architecture. These scholars' work on the decolonization of knowledge highlights the question, Who is the knowing subject of human rights and who defines problems, agenda, and strategies? As Martínez argues in this volume, asking these questions allows us to sketch an alternative geography of global human rights knowledge exchange, not a Western human rights continent surrounded by non-Western ethical-philosophical islets but two large, and at points connected, global terrains of justice, one liberal, the other distributive. These two systems do not just reflect disparities in regard to who holds the power to define issues, they are also indicative of divergent ways of knowing and seeking remedy. Acknowledging the equal value of these distinct worldviews, accepting that different groups may have their own patterns of producing knowledge and meaning, and refraining from shaping the imagination of the dominated to fit the worldview of the (former) colonizer is crucial for any nonexclusionary form of localization to take place (Quijano 2007, 169). In the absence of such an effort, Western-derived systems of thought continue to operate as ways of gaining access to power, and coloniality lives on in a world in which colonialism as a political order has largely been abandoned. From this viewpoint, the danger of narrowing a collectively devised liberation agenda is not only due to dynamics inherent in the travel of ideas, it is also, and to a large extent, caused by the continuation of relations characterized by coloniality.

In discussing the localization of human rights, this volume explicitly inscribes itself in the conversation on the decolonization of knowledge production and transformation, shying away both from the idea that this exchange is a grim top-down imposition as well as from the idea that it is a networked relation of equals, as the perspective of "law as a network" would propose (Ost and Van de Kerckhove 2002). Rights users, indeed, are no "passive entities who require outside aid" from human rights institutions (Urueña 2012), and human rights may travel through networked relations, but historical, economic, and ideological power relations structure these relations and determine rights users' relative access and influence.

Demanding and Granting Access

Both with regard to travel and to translation and transformation processes, grassroots community-based organizations and social movements can play an important role. However, the extent of their eventual influence will, to a considerable degree, be determined by the access these actors have to other human rights users. This issue of access is particularly important with regard to the formal human rights architecture, to which grassroots rights users often lack easy access. This section discusses the situation both of those who seek access and of those who are in a position to grant access to formal norm-setting processes, as well as considering the many ambiguous positions of "inbetweenness."

The Role of Civil Society

One set of questions underlying this volume concerns which grassroots actors and civil society organizations—as norm entrepreneurs and intermediaries—are most likely to play an active role in the process of human rights travel, translation, and transformation and in which stages of the process. And, relatedly, what determines whether and when grassroots actors are likely to be co-opted and merely paid lip service, versus whether and when they may have actual influence beyond their immediate constituency?

What happens to a social movement's formulations of injustice when these are reframed as rights claims? How do movement leaders and external allies collaborate in identifying what claims are to be given first priority, in redefining these in terms of international legal norms, and in deciding the mix of methods through which these are to be pursued? Does juridification inevitably entail a narrowing of social movement claims? And, if so, does such narrowing signal a shift in movement agendas from socially transformative to reformist aims? How may the very *content* of social justice struggles change when community membership organizations translate liberation agendas into legal terms with the aim of upstreaming them? What is the role of grassroots work, and how can we understand why some grassroots groups deliberately decide not to engage with the human rights discourse?

All these questions are relevant because of some of the tensions shaping this process of demanding access: tensions between grassroots organizations and national or international NGOs, but also among and within these grassroots organizations themselves. As Vandenbogaerde argues in this volume, for example, civil society organizations enjoy unequal access to the Human Rights Council (HRC), and the system reveals a strong bias toward Geneva-based professional NGOs—despite its rhetoric about the participation of actors from the South. Organizations working at the grassroots level outside of Europe or North America, especially, may face multiple challenges in accessing the HRC. These challenges are particularly prominent as the phase changes from the agenda-setting to the standard-setting phase. At the standard-setting phase the number of actors involved increases and the public profile of the discussions is enhanced. While some of the HRC mechanisms can still be involved, civil society organizations do not steer the process any longer in this phase. The debates get more technical, political, and structured, making it easy to sideline organizations that do not specialize in interest representation at the United Nations. Moreover, because only a limited number of actors have access to the HRC, tensions within a network may lead to the network's disintegration and a loss of access for smaller organizations that depended on the network for their representation. This, in combination with several institutional obstacles to free and open participation, means that international NGOs can function as gatekeepers to the HRC, and the possibility of localizing human rights can be hindered by these actors if they decide not to provide access to small, grassroots organizations.

This makes any praise for local ownership, and the institutionalization thereof, seem cynical or at best superficial and suggests that this praise is a matter of paying lip service to consultation and outreach rather than a genuine commitment. Moreover, this institutionalization of mobilization and local ownership, combined with the prevailing focus on legal claim-making, has led to what Martínez in this volume calls a process of juridification, that is, conflicts traveling from a local context to legal forums where they encounter a specific set of pressures and are molded into a specific shape. This process tends to coincide with a process of depoliticization when rights are turned into a matter exclusively for legal experts and rights claimants become alienated from their own struggles (Madlingozi 2010). This juridification can also have positive outcomes, of course, in the sense that the upstreaming of social movement agendas into legal language can open avenues for subalterns to have their grievances heard and that it can transform international human rights professionals' understandings of particular human rights crises. However, at the same time, "the pressure to conform to the needs of international NGOs can undermine the original goals of local movements.... Unfashionable, complex, or intractable conflicts fester in isolation, while those that ... match international issues of the moment attract disproportionate support" (Bob 2002, 44). With this statement, Bob raises the question of whether grassroots actors' attempts at legal reformism can ever take the form of an "alter-insurgency" through which social movements may speak directly to power, whether they are more likely to be co-opted by the powers they seek to contest, or whether they are both things at the same time depending on the context.

The Role of Formal Human Rights Bodies

As several contributors to this volume demonstrate, formal human rights norm-setters can play a role in facilitating the exchange of ideas and the extent to which subaltern voices have access to the institutionalized human rights architecture. Arguably, these human rights bodies themselves also benefit from the participation of civil society in the sense that this participation could facilitate a better understanding of local dynamics and that it enhances the democratic legitimacy of these bodies. The information and legitimacy arguments regarding civil society participation has led to an increased concern with participatory approaches, which can be observed, among others, in the emergence of organizations and procedures aimed at facilitating the participation of civil society through written and oral statements at the sessions of the HRC special procedures. Yet, across the board, human rights institutions have often been charged with being deaf to rights holders' concerns and with advancing the interests of the state or the international community instead.

Moreover, several authors in this volume ask how we should understand the role of formal human rights bodies and, by extension, of governmental actors in the localization process. For one, offering actors from civil society a platform for having their voices heard may foreclose these actors' willingness and ability to "engage in confrontational contestation," and instead opt for negotiation—either with a human rights–violating government or with international institutions that have different priorities. How, one can then ask, do the allegedly inclusive strategies of global actors affect people's agency, their social structures, and their cost/risk-benefit analysis? As Patel and Mitlin argue, "the rights-based approach, with its legal associations, takes the poor firmly into the terrain of professionals and elites, and this terrain influences the solutions that emerge." Hence, there is "real danger that this formality undermines the strengthening of local organizational capacity, shifting momentum away from mass organizations of the urban poor and toward professional lobbying" (2009, 118).

Hence, despite the many efforts and recommendations that have generated more or less comprehensive strategies for addressing the democratic deficit by ensuring meaningful "stakeholder engagement," establishing "participation quotas," measuring "local ownership," graphing the "consultation continuum," and the like, broadly conceived as the turn to "the people themselves," beneficial effects for social justice struggles have not always resulted in practice.

Outline of the Volume

The volume is divided into three parts, each of which highlights a different dimension of how human rights travel and are translated, and how they transform under conditions of unequal power. The contributions in the first part of the volume focus on the efforts of formal human rights norm-setters to facilitate human rights travel, addressing tested strategies and examining their shortcomings. The essays in the second part of the book deal with question of juridification and depoliticization, using case studies from various regions to shed light on the many types of erasure and exclusion that can take place in the process of translation and transformation. The chapters in the third part of the volume then examine cases in which rights users transform the human rights discourse and methods to such an extent that questions arise about the compatibility between local and global discourses.

In the first part, the authors examine the policies of actors like the International Criminal Court (ICC), the HRC, and international organizations adopting a human rights–based approach to development, respectively, to chart the complex landscape traveled by local claims that enter the international human rights architecture. They address the multidimensional set of pressures generated when these formal human rights bodies at the international level invite grassroots actors or community-based organizations to participate in the norm-setting process. As claims move dialectically between micro, meso, and macro levels and become institutionalized in the process, how is the original claim transformed? What can these international actors do to avoid the kind of distortions that do not do justice to the original struggles? And how much transformation can the existing human rights system cope with, before evolving into something else altogether?

Vasuki Nesiah's chapter on the role of the ICC in Uganda and the Democratic Republic of the Congo examines how debates about local ownership and victim ownership have been dominated by a belief in the efficacy of technologies of governmentality, thus portraying local ownership itself as a universal public good that everyone cannot but want. As such, she argues, local ownership moves from dissent against the dominant global order to being its conduit and its symbiotic partner: sanitized, depoliticized, and universally recommended as the rule of no one for/over everyone. Nesiah argues that it is precisely when human rights self-determination became embedded in an interventionist paradigm that it gained traction and acceptance at the international level and that this is the pragmatic acceptance of local ownership that characterizes most initiatives at the global level today.

Arne Vandenbogaerde investigates these ideas about a mere pragmatic dedication to localization in the context of the HRC. His chapter analyses the Declaration of the Rights of Peasants and Other People Working in Rural Areas to show how human rights practice at the local level can be accommodated in the existing global human rights framework. Vandenbogaerde argues that the fact that there currently is a standard-setting process in this domain at all is the result of a long trajectory of advocacy and lobbying at various levels, coordinated by a collective of community and nongovernmental organizations: La Via Campesina. Yet, his article looks beyond the strategies of La Via Campesina itself, and instead asks about the discourse and strategies of the HRC. In his conclusion, Vandenbogaerde challenges the lack of a consolidated or proactive approach toward localization on the side of the HRC and refers to the Food and Agricultural Organization's consultation mechanisms, assessing whether the HRC could learn from this to foster a more genuine type of human rights localization.

Building on this question, the next chapter by Wouter Vandenhole asks how much transformation the international human rights architecture itself can support—and who gets to ask and answer this kind of question. The chapter examines the role of the local and of power dynamics across scales in several development interventions adopting a human rights–based approach. The chapter uses the notion of rights subjectivity to understand some of the ways in which grassroots dynamics can potentially transform human rights–based approaches to development (HRBADs). The final section considers whether there is a need for delimiting the transformation of HRBADs on the basis of grassroots dynamics, both with regard to strategies and with regard to substantive norms, and invites an informed discussion about this question.

The chapters in the second part of the volume shift the focus from the macro level to the meso and micro levels. The contributors to this part of the volume address questions regarding the types of erasure and transformation that take place in grassroots actors' formulations of their own social struggles and claims when they indeed respond to these invitations to feed their struggles back into the international system and discourse. What happens when these activists adopt a human rights discourse and join forces with international or transnational activists who are more systematically embedded in the existing human rights architecture?

Johannes Waldmüller's chapter on ecosocial and collective rights in Ecuador examines how the government of Ecuador invokes human rights, selectively reinterpreted and thus transformed, to push internationally for the regulation of transnational corporations. Waldmüller analytically distinguishes between two components of the transformation process: one whereby the government integrates an international methodology in ways that it claims are locally relevant and another whereby this experience is communicated back to the international level, thus promoting a new international standard. The chapter zooms in on an oft-overlooked component of upstreaming a localized understanding of resistance-related human rights to the international level: some genuinely local understandings become reinterpreted or even erased. Why and how does this occur? Is it ever possible to avoid these erasures completely? And if not, why do power-contesting actors at different scales continue to adopt human rights discourses despite the risk of "erasures"?

The same questions are relevant in the cases studied by Samuel Martínez, namely the Nepalese Kamaiya struggle for emancipation from bonded labor contracts and the struggle for recognition of Dominican citizenship by the Dominican-born people of Haitian ancestry. Martínez focuses on processes of juridification that narrow the content of social movement agendas to the point of distortion, in ways that redefine conflict as matters of law and procedural norms. Martínez analyzes how, in these geographically unconnected and socially dissimilar environments, the original multidimensional activist agenda was replaced by a strategy pursuing legal breakthroughs with regard to one key claim. The chapter considers whether juridification is the cause of this narrowing of multidimensional agendas per se, or whether this evolution has to do, instead, with the fact that the claims were defined deductively through an external actor's analysis of a group's subordination, rather than inductively on the basis of communities and social movement praxis.

The chapter by Ken MacLean looks at the pivotal moment in social movement activism when activists decide—consciously or more implicitly—whether or not to adopt a human rights discourse. This chapter on activism against torture and impunity in Vietnam applies a fine-grained ethnographic lens to weigh the impact of several contextual factors (such as fear of retaliation, lack of material resources, low level of human rights awareness, institutional obstacles, and censorship) in shaping activists' strategies, as well as their human rights subjectivities. MacLean finds that there is a growing number of references to the international human rights framework, as well as a growing number of campaigns that deliberately draw upon human rights treaties and mechanisms, such as the Universal Periodic Review, to challenge the structures that perpetuate impunity nationally and to urge policy reforms to increase police accountability. He sees this as indicative of a growing awareness among activists of these frameworks and of their relevance to human rights activism. A central question in this chapter is what the role of new communication technologies is in shaping this process and the decisions of activists.

In the three chapters that make up the third part of this volume, a different dynamic can be observed, and rights holders and rights users show themselves much more reluctant to engage with the existing human rights framework, choosing a strategy of nonengagement in one case or a strategy of heavily modifying existing human rights methods and concepts in the other two cases. One could read these chapters through the lens of framing theories (e.g., Snow 2004) in that they raise similar interpretive and ideational issues that have shaped social movement theory and research since the early 2000s. Yet they also go beyond these theories by avoiding elite biases, static tendencies, and monolithic descriptions. These chapters close the circle and bring us back to the question raised in the first chapters of this volume, namely about how much transformation to existing norms the international level can accommodate, and who gets to decide this.

In Ellen Desmet's chapter on migration and education in China, rights holders explicitly refrain from engaging with the human rights discourse, partly because of low levels of awareness thereof, partly for fear of antagonizing duty bearers. Desmet analyzes how a rights violation can evolve from an unperceived injurious experience to an actual human rights claim and singles out the contextual factors in each step of this process that keep rights holders from moving toward an actual human rights claim. In doing so, she also addresses the underlying question regarding the relevance of human rights framing in this specific context of far-going social and political restrictions on one's capacity to take action. She finds that in this case low perceptions of agency, risk aversion, and group pressure played an important role in keeping rights holders from engaging with the human rights discourse.

The former also played an important role in the Congolese case studied by Tine Destrooper. This chapter empirically examines the extent to which human rights concepts were present in the Sanitized Villages project in the Kongo Central province and argues that, here too, rights holders and development actors have been slow to embrace the language and methods of human rights, and that, to the extent that they have done so, the discourse on human rights has been stripped of most of its empowering potential. The author asks whether this "light" version of human rights that most respondents adhered to should be understood in the light of their own experiences or whether this understanding, one that supposedly emerged from the bottom up, can actually be attributed to the role played by international organizations and the way in which, in this case, they translated human rights. This chapter underlines the dialectic and multidimensional nature of transformations and challenges straightforward conceptualizations of the local.

The same holds true for the case study by Sara Davis and Charmain Mohamed, which reflects on the experiences of HIV/AIDS activists receiving international attention and support in China. Like Desmet, the authors assert that human rights activism is still largely constrained, leading many HIV/AIDS NGOs to adopt service delivery programs, rather than engaging in critical and open advocacy. Davis and Mohamed, too, ponder the question of whether this type of engagement with service delivery and with rights holders' immediate and practical needs allows for a critical stance on government policy and, if not, what it means when these organizations adopt a human rights discourse, while condoning the actions of, and collaborating with, a human rights–violating government. In the afterword, Mark Goodale draws out and synthesizes a number of themes from the preceding chapters and offers an agenda for future research.

Conclusions

Many chapters in this book are unapologetic about their quest to contribute to more progressive and locally relevant human rights norms. Yet they are not naïve about the challenges and complexities of this struggle. In fact, it is precisely these challenges and complexities that are at the heart of this volume. One of the core challenges addressed implicitly or explicitly by all these authors is how to define core concepts underlying and shaping our discussion. Most contributors agree that foregrounding the contested and imperial nature of current discourses is crucial, and seek to bring power dynamics back into the analysis of how human rights norms travel, become translated, and transform in practice. The contributors address these issues on the basis of thorough empirical work that studies how human rights norms unfold in the hands of rights users as they interact with them within a given territory and historical context. The chapters that follow demonstrate that understanding how human rights travel, become translated, and transform is key to understanding the impact these human rights norms are likely to have in practice. The volume thus underlines the need for a concerted focus on these processes, among both scholars and practitioners, in order to ensure that human rights offer the greatest possible protection in cases of human rights violations.

Notes

1. As Vandenbogaerde argues in this volume, local claims may be unsubstantiated, limited in personal scope, or ill-worded and therefore require revision.
2. Merry (2006a) uses the term *norm entrepreneurs* to refer to the activists, advocates, and practitioners who consolidate international and local discourses and practices.
3. Power at the global, national, and local level, and visible, hidden, and invisible power alike (see Andreassen and Crawford 2013).

Works Cited

Andreassen, Bård-Anders, and Gordon Crawford. 2013. *Human Rights, Power and Civic Action: Comparative Analyses of Struggles for Rights in Developing Societies*. Abingdon: Routledge.

Arthur, Paige. 2009. "How 'Transitions' Reshaped Human Rights: A Conceptual History of Transitional Justice." *Human Rights Quarterly* no. 31 (2): 321–367.

Baumgaertel, Moritz, Dorothea Staes, and Francisco Javier Mena Parras. 2014. "Hierarchy, Coordination, or Conflict? Global Law Theories and the Question of Human Rights Integration." *European Journal of Human Rights* no. 3: 326–353.

Baxi, Upendra. 2007. *Human Rights in a Posthuman World: Critical Essays*. New Delhi: Oxford University Press.

Bob, Clifford. 2002. "Merchants of Morality." *Foreign Policy* (129): 36–45.

Brems, Eva. 2001. *Human Rights: Universality and Diversity*. The Hague: Martinus Nijhoff.

Brems, E., and E. Desmet. 2014. Studying Human Rights Law from the Perspective(s) of its Users. *Human Rights & International Legal Discourse* 8, no. 2, 111–120.

Brysk, Alison. 2013. "Human Rights Movements." In *The Wiley-Blackwell Encyclopedia of Social and Political Movements*, edited by David A. Snow, Donatella della Porta, Bert Klandermans, and Doug McAdam. Hoboken, NJ: John Wiley & Sons.

Casla, Koldo. 2014. "Dear Fellow Jurists, Human Rights Are about Politics, and That's Perfectly Fine." In *Can Human Rights Bring Social Justice: Twelve Essays*, edited by Doutje Lettinga and Lars van Troost, 35–40. Amsterdam: Amnesty International Netherlands.

De Feyter, Koen. 2007. "Localizing Human Rights." In *Economic Globalization and Human Rights*, edited by Wolfgang Benedek, Koen De Feyter, and Fabrizio Marrella. Cambridge: Cambridge University Press.

De Feyter, Koen, Stephan Parmentier, Christiane Timmerman, and George Ulrich, eds. 2011. *The Local Relevance of Human Rights*. Cambridge: Cambridge University Press.

De Gaay Fortman, Bastiaan. 2011. *Political Economy of Human Rights: The Quest for Relevance and Realization*. New York: Routledge.

Delmas-Marty, Mireille. 2006. *Le pluralisme ordonné*. Paris: Seuil.

Desmet, Ellen. 2014. "Analysing Users' Trajectories in Human Rights: A Conceptual Exploration and Research Agenda." *Human Rights & International Legal Discourse*, 9 (2): 111–120.
Falk, Richard. 2000. *Human Rights Horizons: The Pursuit of Justice in a Globalizing World*. London: Routledge.
Gledhill, John. 2009. "The Rights of the Rich versus the Rights of the Poor." In *Rights-Based Approaches to Development. Exploring the Potential and Pitfalls*, edited by Samuel Hickey and Diana Mitlin, 31–46. Sterling: Kumarian Press.
Goodale, Mark. 2009. *Surrendering to Utopia: An Anthropology of Human Rights*. Stanford: Stanford University Press.
Goodale, Mark, and Sally Engle Merry. 2007. *The Practice of Human Rights: Tracking Law Between the Global and the Local*. Cambridge: Cambridge University Press.
Goodman, Ryan, and Derek Jinks. 2013. *Socializing States: Promoting Human Rights Through International Law*. Oxford: Oxford University Press.
Gready, Paul, and Jonathan Ensor. 2005. Reinventing Development? Translating Rights-Based Approaches from Theory into Practice. London: Zed Books.
Gready, Paul, and Wouter Vandenhole. 2014. *Human Rights and Development in the New Millennium: Towards a Theory of Change*. London: Routledge.
Hacking, Ian. 1999. *The Social Construction of What?* Cambridge: Harvard University Press.
Haglund, LaDawn, and Robin Stryker, eds. 2015. *Closing the Rights Gap. From Human Rights to Social Transformation*. Oakland: University of California Press.
Halliday, Terrence, and Bruce Carruthers. 2007. "The Recursivity of Law: Global Norm Making and National Lawmaking in the Globalization of Corporate Insolvency Regimes." *American Journal of Sociology* no. 112 (4): 1135–1202.
Hinkelammert, Franz. 2004. "The Hidden Logic of Modernity: Locke and the Inversion of Human Rights." *Worlds & Knowledges Otherwise* no. Fall: 1–27.
Jordan, Peter. 2008. "Group Rights." *Stanford Encyclopedia of Philosophy*. Stanford, CA: Stanford University Press.
Madlingozi, Tshepo. 2010. "On Transitional Justice Entrepreneurs and the Production of Victims." *Journal of Human Rights Practice* no. 2 (2).
Meckled-García, Saladin, and Başak Çali. 2006. "Lost in Translation: The Human Rights Ideal and International Human Rights Law." In *The Legalization of Human Rights: Multidisciplinary Perspectives on Human Rights and Human Rights Law*, edited by Saladin Meckled-García and Başak Çali. Abingdon, UK: Routledge.
Merry, Sally Engle. 2006a. "Transnational Human Rights and Local Activism: Mapping the Middle." *American Anthropologist* no. 108 (1): 38–51.
———. 2006b. *Human Rights and Gender Violence: Translating International Law into Local Justice*. Chicago: University of Chicago Press.
———. 2013. "Human Rights Monitoring and the Question of Indicators." In *Human Rights at the Crossroads*, edited by Mark Goodale, 140–152. Oxford: Oxford University Press.
Mignolo, Walter. 2000. *Local Histories/Global Designs: Coloniality, Subaltern Knowledges, and Border Thinking*. Princeton: Princeton University Press.
Moyn, Samuel. 2014. "Human Rights and the Age of Inequality." In *Can Human Rights Bring Social Justice?*, edited by Doutje Lettinga and Lars van Troost. Amsterdam: Amnesty International The Netherlands.
Nyamu-Musembi, Célestine. 2002. "Towards an Actor-Oriented Perspective of Human Rights." In *IDS Working Paper*. Brighton: Institute of Development Studies.

———. 2005. "An Actor-Oriented Approach to Rights in Development." *IDS Bulletin* no. 36 (1): 41–52.
Oré Aguilar, Gaby. 2011. "The Local Relevance of Human Rights: A Methodological Approach." In *The Local Relevance of Human Rights*, edited by Koen De Feyter, Stephan Parmentier, Christiane Timmerman, and George Ulrich. Cambridge: Cambridge University Press.
Ost, François and Michel Van de Kerckhove. 2002. *De La Pyramide Au Réseau? Pour Une Théorie Dialectique Du Droit*. Brussels: Publications des Facultés universitaires St.Louis.
Pantazidou, Maro. 2013. "De-Constructing Marginality with Displaced People: Learning Rights from an Actor-Centered Perspective." *Journal of Human Rights Practice* no. 5 (2): 267–290.
Patel, Sheela, and Diana Mitlin. 2009. "Reinterpreting the Rights-Based Approach: A Grassroots Perspective on Rights and Development." In *Rights-Based Approaches to Development: Exploring the Potential and Pitfalls*, edited by Samuel Hickey and Diana Mitlin, 107–124. Sterling: Kumarian Press.
Pitarch, Pedro, Shannon Speed, and Xochitl Leyva Solano. 2008. *Human Rights in the Maya Region: Global Politics, Cultural Contentions and Moral Engagements*. Durham: Duke University Press.
Quijano, Aníbal. 2007. "Coloniality and Modernity/Rationality." *Cultural Studies* 21(2–3): 168–178.
Rottenburg, Richard. 2009. *Far-Fetched Facts. A Parable of Development Aid*. Cambridge: Massachusetts Institute of Technology.
Simmons, Beth. 2009. *Mobilizing for Human Rights: International Law in Domestic Politics*. Cambridge: Cambridge University Press.
Snow, David. 2004. "Framing Processes, Ideology and Discursive Fields." In *The Blackwell Companion to Social Movements*, edited by David Snow, Sarah Soule, and Hans-Peter Kriesi. Malden: Blackwell.
Urueña, René. 2012. *No Citizens Here: Global Subjects and Participation in International Law*. Leiden: Martin Nijhoff.
Vandenbogaerde, Arne. 2015. "The Human Rights Council from Below. A Case Study of the Declaration on the Rights of Peasants." In *Localising Human Rights Working Paper Series no. 1*, edited by Koen De Feyter and Ellen Desmet. Antwerp: Antwerp University Press.
Vandenhole, Wouter, and Willem Van Genugten. 2015. "Introduction: An Emerging Multi-Duty-Bearer Human Rights Regime." In *Challenging Territoriality in Human Rights Law*, edited by Wouter Vandenhole, 1–14. London: Routledge.
Vázquez, Rolando. 2011. "Translation as Erasure: Thoughts on Modernity's Epistemic Violence." Journal of Historical Sociology 24(1): 27–44.
Wilson, Richard Ashby. 2007. "Tyrannosaurus Lex: The Anthropology of Human Rights and Transnational Law." In *The Practice of Human Rights: Tracking Law between the Global and the Local*, edited by Mark Goodale and Sally Merry, 342–368. Cambridge: Cambridge University Press.
Zeleza, Paul. 2004. "The Struggle for Human Rights in Africa." In *Human Rights, the Rule of Law, and Development in Africa*, edited by Paul Zeleza and Philip McConnaughay. Philadelphia: University of Pennsylvania Press.

PART I

Initiatives by Formal Human Rights Norm-Setters

CHAPTER 1

The Escher–Human Rights Escalator: Technologies of the Local

Vasuki Nesiah

Over a decade ago, on October 18, 2007, the International Criminal Court (ICC) established a field office in Bangui in the Central African Republic. This was the fifth field office that the ICC had established outside The Hague. The ICC already had a presence in Kampala, Uganda; Kinshasa and Bunia in the Democratic Republic of the Congo (DRC); and in Apache, Chad. More than simply a local outpost from which to conduct investigations and coordinate logistics linked to the case, these field offices represented the ICC's effort to perform outreach and engender local ownership of its processes (HRW 2008, 99-101). Indeed, the opening of the Bangui office underscored that situating human rights in this two-way vertical traffic was critical to the legitimacy, and the perceived legitimacy, of the court (HRW 2008, 105). The ICC is a standard-bearer for particular ideas about human rights, such as the priority of individual criminal prosecutions in advancing justice and protecting peremptory norms of international human rights. However, it is important to the legitimacy of the enterprise, including the reception of these human rights norms, that these ideas are situated in a two-way traffic (i.e., that verticality is not top-down alone) and that the doctrinal and institutional machinery of the ICC also reflects the norm of local ownership. Thus this bidirectional circulation is internal to the ICC mode of governmentality. For the ICC agenda to travel from The Hague to Bangui, local ownership had to travel from Bangui to The Hague.

This chapter explores how invocations of local ownership facilitate the circulation of ideas about human rights accountability through the work of the ICC and approaches advanced by the human rights community to solicit and facilitate such circulation. Local ownership is central to the language of legitimacy in contemporary human rights. In its most familiar form, local ownership is delivered by place-based social movements and is anchored in its proximity to those victims and witnesses of human rights violations who are most affected by an intervention such as an ICC prosecution, a proximity that is seen to enable contextual relevance and advance participatory processes of international criminal justice and the upstreaming of local ideas. By definition, claims of local ownership appear to ground legitimacy of human rights accountability mechanisms in grassroots realities and processes that stand as counterpoint to the national or international discourse.

Yet, as this chapter argues, invocations of local ownership have charted a more complex landscape, as those claims traveled within the human rights field to the International Criminal Court and the international criminal justice community. As they moved dialectically from micro to macro and then macro to micro, invocations of local ownership have been adopted and institutionalized in how transnational processes and global institutions conduct their work. When certain laws, policies, and procedures are adopted and institutionalized in the name of advancing local ownership in the international criminal justice field, is the local instantiated in some way that is distinct from the global? Indeed, is the local terrain of human rights a place from which we may challenge the global and transnational dimensions of international criminal law? Alternatively, has there been a transformation of how the human rights field configures context and participation so that local ownership becomes *internal* to global governance rather than a locus for challenging transnational processes and global institutions? In the past, the local served to interrupt how particular approaches of human rights traveled (be it vertically or horizontally); today, as I demonstrate in this chapter, there is a machinery of local ownership that facilitates that travel. In this context, does that machinery legitimize global processes to enable the circulation and downstreaming of ideas developed by international institutions and transnational networks? Do the metaphors of the vertical and horizontal properly convey the complex dynamics of how such ideas circulate?

This chapter probes these questions in relation to international criminal law's claim to advance human rights accountability through the work of the ICC. It tracks the circulation and intersection of two families of human rights norms: local ownership of human rights agendas and accountability for human rights violations. As in many families, the relationship between these fields is mutually reinforcing in some instances and antagonistic at others. This chapter tracks these family resemblances and tensions, including their shifting hierarchies and influences, by exploring two cases on the ICC docket. First, it examines how victim ownership of ICC processes becomes scripted through a survey of human rights victims at a pivotal moment in the ICC's engagement in Uganda. Second, it looks at how deferral to ICC jurisdiction regarding the prosecution of human rights abuses becomes incorporated into an affirmation of DRC sovereignty. These two cases reference two conceptions of the local that animate discussions of human rights accountability after the ICC was established: first, the notion of local as grassroots, regional processes that stand in contrast to the national and the international; and second, the notion of local as national processes that stand in contrast to the international and institutions of global governance. Through analysis of these cases, I argue that technologies of governmentality and government have knit local ownership to global governance together in a web of universal human rights values that everyone cannot but want. Thus local ownership moves from dissent against the dominant global order to being its conduit: sanitized, depoliticized, and universally recommended as the rule of no one for everyone.

Local Ownership: The Backstory

The discourse of local ownership and democratic legitimacy is front and center in contemporary discussions of the ICC (De Vos and Kendall 2011). This is a relatively new development in international criminal law, but it is not new to the realm of international institutions. Indeed, local ownership discourse has had a long shelf life in development, environment, and other zones of global governance where, over time, a vast nomenclature has been generated to accompany the theme: local involvement, community empowerment, participatory development, civil society partnerships, accountability, local ownership, and NGO and CBO engagement. Each of these generated its own set of programs (such as capacity development, stakeholder consultations, poverty reduction strategy papers)[1] that then infused a new generation of development initiatives that were "grounded in local realities," advanced "bottom-up" growth, and met new metrics benchmarking "best practices." Yet, if tracked over the course of the twentieth century, it took some time for notions of local ownership to become mainstreamed within the field of international criminal justice. Indeed, the local ownership debates have significantly penetrated the field of international criminal law only in the last two decades (Pouligny 2009).[2] There is a parallel between the increased significance of the norm of local ownership and the rise of human rights–relevant norms as the most dynamic domain for doctrinal and institutional innovation within international criminal law. The legacies of international tribunals and war crimes trials emerging from the Treaty of Versailles (Kramer 2006, 441–45) and the London Charter (Bass 2001) were not about a discourse of local ownership; these of course were trials set up at the initiative of a war's victor and were about prosecuting and perhaps persecuting the defeated, not consulting with stakeholders in Istanbul or Leipzig or empowering local communities in Nuremberg and Tokyo. In some ways the ad hoc tribunals continued that legacy; they were widely criticized for being spaceship-like phenomena in The Hague and Arusha, carrying little resonance with the priorities of local communities where the atrocities they were adjudicating took place. The argument was made that if anyone was being empowered it was international law and lawyers, not victim communities, grassroots justice movements, or local justice processes (Koskenniemi 2002, 34–35).[3] Yet, in contrast to those earlier moments, these criticisms catalyzed significant discussions about legitimacy and effectiveness for the ad hoc tribunals. As the discourse of local ownership began to infiltrate and trouble the settled common sense of global governance, institutions with human rights agendas such as the ad hoc tribunals developed different kinds of responses to these criticisms. The ICTY and ICTR took steps to review their proceedings and develop more extensive outreach initiatives. Legitimacy was no longer about procedural regularities within the four walls of the courtroom but also the politics of how human rights was translated into the local justice vernacular (Merry 2006). Promising bolder institutional experimentation in this direction, the international legal community established hybrid tribunals in Sierra Leone, Timor Leste, and Cambodia. The fact that these debates ran parallel to momentum toward the ICC, and the drafting of the treaty (known as the Rome Statute) that established its mandate, meant that the court that would result was fundamentally shaped by this broader democracy discourse. The most significant doctrinal response to these concerns can be found in Article 17 of the Rome Statute. Article 17, often referred to as the doctrine on complementarity, is the ICC's own homage to local ownership. It is articulated, on the one hand, through self-referral (where cases came into the ICC docket through countries opting in and requesting that the ICC take on the case), and on the other, through the admissibility criterion giving national prosecutors primary jurisdiction (where the ICC takes on a case only if the country concerned is unwilling and unable to take on the case). These doctrinal provisions reflected a normative commitment to local ownership where the global complements rather than upstages national jurisdiction. When sworn into office in June 2003, the then-prosecutor, Luis Moreno Ocampo, argued that the principle of complementarity should shape our assessment of the role of the ICC with our radars trained on the functioning of domestic criminal justice processes rather than the number of ICC trials.[4] Concomitantly, the ICC was advocated for as a sovereignty-enhancing, nonintrusive forum of last resort that was a friendly supplement to national criminal jurisdiction.

In the dominant interpretation of complementarity at that point, global processes for human rights accountability were going to defer to the local; complementarity was going to function like a traffic barrier allowing a safe space for domestic processes for human rights accountability. However, as local ownership became part of the fabric of international human rights norms, legislated into Article 17, institutionalized in field offices, and embedded into the architecture of legitimacy that undergirded the ICC, we also saw a transformation in the work of local ownership claims. While catalyzed by criticisms of The Hague (representing global governance here), the machinery of local ownership emerged from The Hague as an effort to address this crisis in legitimacy and effectiveness. Thus, as detailed further in my discussion of two case studies below, the invocation of local ownership traveled differently (from top to bottom not just bottom to top, as it were), and did a different kind of work (challenging and delimiting the local and enhancing the reach of the global).

In both the cases discussed here, the current work mines one narrow slice of the debate to look at how discussions of local ownership unfold at those very specific moments. It is not a discussion of how the ICC debate has unfolded in these countries outside of those very specific windows. Through analysis of these cases, I argue that technologies of governmentality and government have seamlessly sutured local ownership to global governance. Through this vertical travel from The Hague to the local of human rights victims and witnesses and back again to The Hague, local ownership itself is produced as a universal public good that everyone cannot but want. Thus local ownership moves from dissent against the dominant global order to being its conduit—sanitized, depoliticized, and universally recommended as the rule of no one for/over everyone.

Victim Surveys: Consulting Forgotten Voices

On July 8, 2005 the ICC indicted Joseph Kony on 12 counts of crimes against humanity and 21 counts of war crimes in relation to the actions of the Lord's Resistance Army (LRA) in Uganda. The indictments against Kony (and four other LRA leaders) were issued while the Ugandan government and the LRA were engaged in peace negotiations. The indictments instantly catalyzed heated debate within Uganda as well as the wider human rights community. The ICC was criticized on a number of counts. Some criticized the ICC for being so hungry for its first case that it pursued the LRA while aligning with Museveni, the Ugandan president; in doing this it ignored the human rights violations by government forces and the military and majoritarian policy ambitions of Kampala. The argument was that the ICC indictments represented a collusion between the international and the national at the expense of the local, of those most affected by violations of human rights abuse in the Ugandan war. Framing this question in terms of "international justice v. local justice," Katherine Southwick argued that the ICC's actions were "widely opposed by those groups the Rome Statute is designed to serve: the victims" (Southwick 2005, 113). Others criticized the ICC for formulating prosecutorial priorities in The Hague without coordinating sufficiently with Acholi leaders and peace negotiators to ensure that the timing of the indictments would not run interference with the difficult currents of the peace process (Apuuli 2006).[5] Betty Bigombe, the chief mediator for peace talks, declared the ICC prosecutions "ill timed" and argued that they should have paid more attention to local context (Kakaire 2006).[6] Yet others criticized the ICC for formulating prosecutorial priorities in The Hague without exploring the local restorative justice process known as Mato Oput or other "customary justice" traditions that would be led and "owned" by the Acholi community (Clark 2009, 131).[7] Thus one Acholi leader is quoted saying, "Our people do not see our traditional system here as a form of impunity . . . if Joseph Kony were to be taken away to The Hague or elsewhere to be tried, the Acholi people would not be satisfied. They would not accept that matters would have been concluded. We believe that it is only when rituals of cleansing and reconciliation have been carried out that true justice would have been done" (Southwick 2005, 115). The ICC was also criticized for not doing sufficient outreach to ensure that victims knew about the court and began to appreciate and engage with its mission so that there could be local ownership of ICC actions. The one consistent theme was the argument that the ICC was not giving due regard to the justice priorities of those most affected. Some of these criticisms came from local actors in Uganda (from the Acholi community in particular) and others came from critically oriented international actors.[8] All of these issues were markers of a classic invocation of local ownership to challenge and delegitimize the global and the top-down imposition of human rights norms. Indeed, for many, all of these issues were symptomatic of the structure of global governance—namely, the fact that the ICC's power in determining the justice agenda carried echoes of imperial authority, and its actions in Uganda were advanced with imperial hubris.

Even as this debate continued to rage, a group of international human rights organizations surveyed almost 3,000 individuals in three war-affected districts regarding their transitional justice priorities in order to "represent the spectrum of attitudes and opinions of those most affected by the violence" (Pham et al. 2005, 4).[9] Transitional justice is that subfield of human rights that deals with questions of truth, justice, and reparations for human rights abuses in contexts of conflict and postconflict, and the Uganda debates on ICC indictments soon came to be the central reference in the dominant transitional justice conversation. Soon *Forgotten Voices,* the report emerging from this survey, became one of the most critical anchors of the Uganda peace and justice debates—and indeed, it framed the terms for a new debate about "what victims really want." Arguably, *Forgotten Voices* became the benchmark for constructive intervention and local consultation within the transitional justice community engaged with Uganda in this period. Through fortuitous coincidence with the priorities of the ICC and its advocates, the survey reported that, according to their analysis of the research results, victims did prioritize justice (understood here as prosecution by the ICC); the findings of the survey were that peace and justice were deeply compatible—both in Uganda, as well as in the minds of the surveyed victims. *Forgotten Voices* conveyed that the most affected communities were not as dismissive of ICC actions as the ICC critics; rather, they saw the relationship between prosecutions and the peace process as merely a question of political timing and strategic management of both processes to ensure their complementarities were appropriately synchronized. From this perspective, the ICC actions could not be dismissed as simply the imperial ambitions of the global North; in fact to do so would be to indulge in the racist stereotype that Africans did not want justice, that such noble goals were the province of the ethically sensitive global North. The notion of complementarity invoked by Article 17 of the Rome Statute seeks precisely to invoke that universality in the demand for justice, while also grounding itself in local legitimacy. The victim survey mediates and manages those dual registers.

Victim surveys have become an increasingly common feature of the transitional justice field, a subfield of human rights that sees itself as fundamentally victim-centered in its approach to justice. From Uganda to Afghanistan, large-scale population surveys of conflict-affected regions regarding transitional justice priorities have become an increasingly popular method of accessing victims' voices. Surveys are one example of a broader turn to indicators and other measurement tools within human rights that are embedded in specific logics of power and knowledge (Merry 2011).[10] While scripted as simply a gauge of local sentiment in advancing the human rights norms of local ownership, victim surveys can also become a vehicle for particular human rights agendas to travel in advancing global governance processes. The Ugandan survey formulated questions, deployed researchers who brought back completed questionnaires, entered information, exported and analyzed it with the use of the software Statistical Package for Social Science (SPSS), and developed a narrative report that wrapped itself around those figures to convey victims' voices.[11] *Forgotten Voices* treats victim preferences as defined in advance of answering the survey—in other words, the survey itself was not shaping opinions; the survey was simply an instrument of excavating already defined opinions and priorities. Thus *Forgotten Voices* flags the fact that while it has a structured questionnaire, it uses an open-ended questions format so that victims have the freedom to respond in any way they choose and their report simply "represents the spectrum of attitudes and opinions of those most affected by the violence" (Pham et al. 2005, 4, 7–8). Significantly, the interviewer takes those "open-ended answers" and retro-fits them into a finite set of response options, so that those open-ended answers can be legible to the coding programs that spit out claims about victim preferences: "Response options were given to facilitate the interviewer's recording of the responses" (Pham et al. 2005, 4). This process translates preferences in ways that can be recorded, tabulated, and fed into an algorithm that makes them politically intelligible. Of course, this process is not only rendering those preferences intelligible, but it is also interpolating those "forgotten voices" as rights-holding subjects who can be incorporated within the logic of the ICC conversation. This process of retroactively translating local preferences to a language that can be understood at the international level is how particular human rights agendas can travel in the context of transitional justice. "Victims" become fungible in a universally recognizable currency of human rights in ways that makes it easier for the transitional justice field to leave behind the complex sociopolitical stakes of specific contexts and translate transitional justice blueprints from South Africa to Peru, Uganda to the DRC. This yield is both an effect of the success of the transitional justice field, and a prerequisite for the field to have a recognizable legal and normative logic.

The power of the victim survey as a measurement tool has had an interesting and important role in the development of the field of transitional justice. Historically, truth commissions, reparation programs, and war crimes prosecution initiatives (whether sponsored by international actors or national political elites) have been charged with being unresponsive to victim priorities and needs. Yet from the ICTY to the South African Truth Commission, these institutions have often been charged with advancing the interests of the state or the international community. It is argued that these institutions are subject to elite capture and soon develop their own bureaucratic interests and ambitions, increasingly deaf to victims' voices while advancing initiatives in victims' names. Against this backdrop, those deploying survey instruments saw their work as a way of pulling victims into the transitional justice conversation. Institutions such as the Berkeley Human Rights Center developed methodologies that seek to survey, analyze, and convey victims' voices in a register that is accessible and persuasive to policy makers. In a November 14, 2004 interview in the *Oberlin Review,* Eric Stover, the director of the Berkeley Human Rights Center and coauthor of the *Forgotten Voices* report, says that these surveys yield "data that you collect that you can honestly say reflects the community themselves, not the political leaders that run those communities."[12] He presents this work as a way of escaping politics through expertise so that rather than bickering between different elite players, population-based surveys are motivated by an effort to *just* "ask the people themselves." In this invocation, "the people" becomes another way of invoking the local and establishing local legitimacy. Thus the questions of who is surveyed, how community is defined, who conducts the survey, how questions are framed, what options are presented implicitly and explicitly, how this process solicits and represents local priorities and concerns, the interpretive frameworks through which answers are analyzed, and several other questions of methodology are all deeply political questions—selective, contestable, and high-stakes. Yet *Forgotten Voices* advocates for the survey as an instrument that can rise above conflict by what Stover (in the *Oberlin Review* interview quoted above) described as a methodology of "applying scientific method to these investigations." The description of the survey method and procedures in the *Forgotten Voices* report conveys a similar confidence that if only we get the methodology right, access those who live in remote regions, train interviewers, acclimatize researchers so that respondents do not feel uncomfortable about discussing sensitive issues with strangers, we would have good input to rationally formulate good policy—especially if the political context does not fluctuate too much (Pham et al., 2005, 9–12). The irony at the heart of this understanding of the political is that through the victim survey, debates on topics such as the ICC's role in Uganda are interpolated as politically intelligible to the transitional justice community, even if it is at the cost of politics itself.

These surveys reflect and assert a methodological certainty/belief in survey instruments, and this then becomes the basis for a "data"-empowered political certainty to extend democratic legitimacy to particular initiatives.[13] The survey instruments allow us to escape from the messy dialogical terrain of political conflict while authoritatively weighing in on debates in the human rights community about transitional justice priorities and approaches; the survey instrument translates that conflict into something that can be summoned, appraised, and audited—and in doing so preemptively legitimates the received boundaries of those debates.[14] In fact, here it presents the debate over the ICC indictments and their potential threat to the peace process or their displacing of local justice mechanisms as having been needlessly politicized: "The peace-versus-justice debate in Northern Uganda has become unnecessarily polarized over the controversy surrounding the ICC, and is often put into stark terms of false alternatives between peace and justice. Indeed, the way forward in Northern Uganda should be driven by a comprehensive strategy that integrates the strengths of all mechanisms—formal and traditional—aimed at bringing peace and justice to the region" (Pham et al. 2005, 7). In presenting human rights victims as having priorities and preferences that can be targeted through a finite option set of strategies advancing human rights that are already in circulation in the globally dominant transitional justice discussion, transitional justice institutions present themselves as producing policies that respond to those preferences. Rather than citizens with contested and potentially irreconcilable desires, interests, and human rights commitments, victims become stakeholders with preferences that feed into technocratic decision-making processes. Victim surveys can mediate and ameliorate conflict between contested human rights agendas; in harnessing all potential interventions within the framework of options presented in the survey, the survey instruments can pacify and assimilate critique. Accordingly, *Forgotten Voices* concludes with the following recommendation to the ICC:

> *Implement an outreach strategy that fosters greater awareness among Ugandans of the Court's mandate and mode of operations.* This effort should aim to disseminate more information about the Court and engage the public in dialogue. Such a strategy should also seek to manage the expectations of victims, many of whom believe the ICC can deliver more than it is able. As part of such a strategy, the Court should establish a presence in the North so that people will have regular access to ICC staff. Finally, the ICC should consider holding trials *in situ* to increase public access to its proceedings. (Pham et al. 2005, 42)

In response to the contentious political debates that attended the ICC's LRA indictments, *Forgotten Voices* works to reframe the ICC's role in Uganda as the local justice option in a policy preference set defined by the human rights ideas that were determined as relevant from the perspective of the survey metric. In doing so, the victim survey reframes contentious political debates (with distributive implications for the Acholi in particular and Ugandans more generally) as preferences to be tabulated. In performing this mediation of global governance and local ownership in ways that are formulated as matters of technical methodology (not politics), the survey project naturalizes the ICC's complementarity framework as one that can be seamlessly sutured to local preferences. Victims are rendered as potential consumers of policies formulated to advance their interests—interests represented by the survey.

Self-Referrals: Affirming Sovereignty

In 2004 the Democratic Republic of the Congo (DRC) referred the situation in the DRC to the prosecutor.[15] Later in 2004 the ICC formally opened an investigation, and over the next several years it issued arrest warrants for six people in association with crimes in the territory of the DRC. In July 2007, the ICC issued a sealed warrant for the arrest of Germain Katanga; he was charged with three counts of crimes against humanity and six counts of war crimes, including murder, sexual slavery, and the inhumane treatment of civilians in and around Bogoro in the Ituri region of northeastern DRC. Three months later, the government handed Katanga over to the ICC and he was flown to The Hague for trial, which began in November 2009; in March 2014 Katanga was convicted of five counts of war crimes and crimes against humanity.[16] The human rights community has celebrated this result as advancing accountability for heinous human rights violations. However, the human rights norms at stake in this case were also procedural—thus, as the case unfolded, the human rights norm of local ownership of accountability procedures was debated and the admissibility of this case was contested on that basis. Like the LRA case from Uganda, the Katanga case from the DRC also raises questions about the bidirectional circulation of notions of human rights accountability between the global and the local. However, in this case, the local at stake is not at the grassroots community register (vis-à-vis the national and the international), but at the nation-state register vis-à-vis the global. The sovereignty-defined notion of the local was anticipated in the drafting of the Rome Statute, and this is what gets doctrinal recognition in the article on complementarity. That article, then, also works in circulating a definition of the local that becomes the reference point for the debate on the legitimate forum for accountability for human rights violations that is articulated in the Katanga trial.

Katanga, a former leader of the Patriot Resistance Force (FRPI) and a former general in the DRC army, had been in government custody since March 2005 in connection with the killing of nine UN peacekeepers. He was in the Kinshasa Penitentiary and Reeducation Center (CPRK) for two years awaiting charges when the ICC indictments were issued. Katanga challenged ICC jurisdiction by arguing that there was a presumption of inadmissibility on the basis of Article 17's complementarity doctrine. Given that the DRC had already detained him, he argued that the ICC was violating the requirement that the ICC be only a court of last resort when the state concerned was both unwilling and unable to prosecute. Here Katanga was drawing on the notion of local accountability for human rights, enshrined in Article 17. When Article 17 was drafted, this was seen not merely as a convenient rule of criminal procedure but as representing a more fundamental principle of human rights—with national jurisdiction being a central dimension of the right to self-determination, reflected in the joint first article of both human rights covenants. Thus here the local had a more lofty purchase that drew on place-based struggles for decolonization that shaped the human rights system and inflected questions of human rights universalism with the historical dynamics of North-South politics. These norms were a critical backdrop to the drafting of the ICC, and they became even more prominent in the ICC's first decade, as the prosecutor's indictment portfolio focused exclusively on Africa. Katanga argued that the fact of his CPRK detention was itself proof that the ICC was not operating as the court of last resort where the state concerned was unwilling and unable and that therefore the ICC was, in effect, usurping DRC sovereignty and riding roughshod over norms of local accountability for human rights violations.[17]

The Katanga case was the first case before the ICC where there was a sustained legal challenge on admissibility on the basis of the complementarity doctrine. However, following the argument of the prosecutor, the trial chamber ruled that the case was admissible because the DRC was not investigating Katanga for crimes committed in Bogoro, but for other crimes in Ituri.[18] More significantly, the court argued that since the DRC had itself referred the situation to the ICC, it had clearly conveyed that it was unwilling to prosecute Katanga itself. The DRC did not want Katanga prosecuted domestically, but by the ICC. It concluded that the complementarity test's requirement of an unwilling state was met and that, since the case was admissible, the ICC proceedings could move forward.[19] Thus the entire debate was conducted in ways that framed the notion of local human rights accountability in terms the Rome Statute had launched into circulation.

Katanga's appeal of the admissibility decision sought to foreground the work of the trial chamber in *constituting* the local, rather than just responding to it. This constructionist perspective has significant implications for how we understand the sociopolitical dynamics of how ideas about human rights circulate. Katanga argued that the trial chamber had mistakenly confused unwillingness and inability and that in fact a state could not voluntarily eschew its jurisdictional obligations to prosecute by deferring to the ICC. In similar vein, in the June 2009 edition of *Refugee Rights News*, critics of the ICC's construction of the local raised concerns that the ICC would be encouraging outsourcing, so that it becomes "a court of first, rather than last, resort," while facilitating states that do not want to invest in local criminal justice institutions in violation of their obligations to provide justice for victims of human rights violations. In turn, the prosecutor responded that if the trial court had made such a finding, it would be interfering with the DRC's sovereignty—that is, that it cannot force the DRC to prosecute Katanga, and to do so would be a violation of the human rights norm of local accountability.[20] Thus the ICC claimed jurisdiction in the name of the local.

Different notions of the local circulate alongside different notions of human rights norms. Thus often what is at stake is a debate over what constitutes the most relevant local for human rights decision-making, and who has access to "the people" to better represent their voices. In the Uganda case discussed earlier, advocates of the survey instruments spoke of the victims surveyed as more local than community leaders—the data was, in effect, the voice of the people themselves. We can track different claims about the circulation of human rights ideas by mapping how these claims to local ownership of human rights agendas are anchored at different scales. In the Katanga case, the debate takes place at the nation-state scale on whether the ICC admissibility procedures are a more reliable channel for the human rights priorities of the people represented by DRC sovereignty. What is significant in this episode is not the technical disputes regarding the interpretation of complementarity, but rather the ways that the exercise of ICC jurisdiction itself becomes evidence of a commitment to sovereignty—and the concomitant irony that in this case refusing the referral and encouraging domestic prosecution becomes an unacceptable challenge to sovereignty. An expert study commissioned by the ICC argues, "Voluntary acceptance of ICC admissibility does not necessarily presuppose or entail a loss of national credibility, nor a lack of commitment to the fight against impunity."[21] Rather, it becomes evidence of a state's maturity that it is "prepared to expressly acknowledge that it is not carrying out an investigation or prosecution" (Agirre et al. 2003, 19). Moreover, "[i]n the types of situations described here, [for the state] to decline to exercise jurisdiction in favor of prosecution before the ICC is a step taken to *enhance the delivery of effective justice*" for human rights victims (Agirre et al. 2003, 19). Thus it makes a claim to be "consistent with both the letter and the spirit of the Rome Statute and other international obligations with respect to core crimes" and peremptory human rights norms, and "distinguishable from a failure to prosecute" perpetrators of human rights violations and reneging on the "fight against impunity" for heinous human rights violations (Agirre et al. 2003, 19). According to this argument, then, the DRC is complying with its ICC obligations to ensure that certain crimes are prosecuted by choosing not to prosecute. Through an uncontested ceding of criminal jurisdiction to the ICC, "[t]he duty to 'exercise criminal jurisdiction' should be read in a manner consistent with the customary obligation *aut dedere aut judicare*, and is therefore satisfied by extradition and surrender, since those are criminal proceedings that result in prosecution" (Agirre et al. 2003, 19). In the model of complementarity represented by the Katanga decision and the ICC expert paper, ICC jurisdiction and national jurisdiction of human rights are not in tension. This model of uncontested admissibility ensures that there is always local ownership of human rights accountability procedures.

The DRC's "self-referral" (or what is sometimes referred to as voluntary referrals) was itself courted and encouraged by the ICC.[22] The prosecutor, keen to plunge the ICC into its first case and establish the court's bona fides with the human rights community, had invested considerable energy soliciting this request and making the argument that Article 14 of the Rome Statute was designed precisely for such a deferral of jurisdiction by state parties to the ICC. Indeed, the first three situations on the ICC docket—Uganda, the DRC, and the Central African Republic (CAR)—all entered The Hague through self-referrals by their governments. Rather than solicit these self-referrals, the prosecutor could have supported local criminal justice processes in the name of "positive complementarity,"[23] or he could have initiated investigations himself and applied to the pretrial chamber for permission to launch an investigation. However, he and many other supporters of the ICC (Robinson 2011) were keen that the first situation that the ICC investigates be one where the state requests the ICC—a case, in other words, that represents local ownership of the ICC.

Significantly, in all these cases, the government's referral and the ICC's hospitality toward these requests were not uncontroversial with local human rights groups concerned that these de facto ICC-government partnerships were whitewashing government records and running interference with other local priorities (Schabas 2008). Adam Branch, who sees a real disjuncture between local human rights priorities on the one hand and ICC hospitability to government self-referrals on the other, notes that this hospitality was itself shaped by the ICC's own insecurities regarding its role—insecurities that led to "casting about for a case to prove its relevance and utility" (Branch 2004). In Uganda, as already noted, there was concern that ICC action would damage the peace process, engender an escalation of the war and concomitant human rights violations, and further empower Museveni, his military alliance with the United States in the region, and his majoritarian policies domestically. In the DRC, there was similar concern: that it was the Kabila government that was empowered by prosecutions that targeted his opponents, and indeed that it was the international actors implicated in the resource wars who benefited from a de facto narrowing of the human rights lens (via the Lubunga and Katanga cases) to conflicts between the Hema and the Lendu communities. The focus on individual criminal prosecution and ethnic conflict would distract from calls for action addressing the human rights dimensions of the resource wars, including local control over natural resources—all symptomatic of the long-term structural issues responsible for the acute poverty and land scarcity in the Ituri region and the DRC more generally.[24] Yet accountability efforts are being directed at the world of Lubunga and Katanga, not the resource wars that fuel and exacerbate the human rights crisis in local resource sovereignty, struggles over land, and regional militarization.[25] Most significantly, as the Katanga admissibility hearings conveyed, this global-governance-friendly focus can advance through the international legal framework of complementarity in the name of upholding national sovereignty. In fact, questions of sovereignty become translated into questions of managerial efficiency. The ICC expert paper invokes the language of "burden sharing" and a "division of labor"; in this framing, ICC jurisdiction is presented as so complementary to national jurisdiction that it can benignly displace it.

Local Ownership Redux: The Rule of No One for Everyone

The two windows into local ownership explored here are suggestive of the legitimacy challenges the ICC faces. For some, the concern with these processes is that the odes to local ownership are cynical or at best superficial; thus one witnesses lip service to consultation and outreach, rather than processes that are genuinely committed to local ownership of human rights accountability. However, for us what is more significant is that these windows are also suggestive of how the work of local ownership in the ICC debates is itself troubled. Many of the strategies that were advanced in contesting global governance in the name of local ownership of human rights struggles have become assimilated into the very governance armature they sought to challenge. The advocacy of local ownership and attendant arguments for democratization in the international public sphere were fundamentally political claims, dissenting from the laws, norms, policies, and practices that were embedded in the international criminal law regime. However, in that path from the ICTY and ICTR to the ICC alluded to in the opening pages of this chapter, the advocacy of local ownership also became sanitized and transformed into a universal human rights value in which everyone had an equal stake. Local involvement, community empowerment, civil society partnerships, victim consultations—what was not to like? As the politics are purged from these claims, they become available for absorption into the ICC's institutional performance of an optimistic liberal humanism.

From the liberal humanist perspective, democracy deficits emerge because of institutional inefficiencies, lack of knowledge of best communication practices, and so on; but international criminal law is premised on the interests of humanity, and its media strategy is available for reorganization to address those deficits. Courts may be said to always carry a democracy deficit in that they are not populist institutions; on the other hand, they are seen to advance democratic norms and agendas through prosecutorial priorities and operating procedures that are premised on the interests of the demos. Accordingly, the assumption is that, if local communities were better informed about the ICC's work, they would feel a sense of ownership; advocates perceive the ICC's work as built on a universal humanist currency that transcends class, race, region, gender, colonial history, and the like. Thus for them, the challenge is not legitimacy but communication. To know the ICC is to want to buy into its logic. In this vein, Human Rights Watch recommended that the Office of the Prosecutor "improve efforts to consistently convey to affected communities important information about the office's work" (HRW 2008). Accordingly, the ICC has adopted a range of different ICC initiatives in the name of local ownership. For instance, the 2010 *Outreach* report lists plans for 2011 as including 25 village/town hall–style meetings, 20 gender outreach meetings, 15 school outreach events, radio programs by outreach partners, building networks to increase participation of internally displaced persons in outreach activities, meeting more than double the number of women's groups, and so on (ICC 2010). This expansion of outreach activities is in line with the recommendations of many ICC-friendly INGOs concerned to deepen local ownership–related ICC initiatives with stakeholders. For instance, the Coalition for the ICC (CICC) suggested that as the broader context "has become ever-more fraught," it has made it difficult for the court to just do its work without appeasing the critics through some outreach initiatives (CICC 2015, 3). Thus, the CICC urges the ICC to follow the "accepted best practice" and take steps to enable early outreach to "bolster a positive image" and establish the ICC registry as a source of "neutral information" (CICC 2015, 3). Thus outreach is aimed at producing the ICC as a body whose structure and agenda is not up for political contestation by "affected communities." The CICC says that such measures should be part of a strategic effort to "set the agenda on international justice" without being "a political actor" (CICC 2015, 2). Rather, it is marketed as a neutral actor representing human rights as a public good; standing outside politics, it is a body with universal appeal for local ownership.

Recommendations such as these have generated earnest and fanciful schemes for addressing the "democracy deficit" by "ensuring meaningful stakeholder engagement," establishing "participation quotas," measuring local ownership, graphing the "consultation continuum," and the like.[26] Indeed, there now are organizations that are themselves devoted to maximizing local ownership, which provide training and "how-to" guides in the "democracy for dummies" vein.[27] Organizations like UNDP developed strategies to take their experience in local ownership projects in the development field to support the ICC to "promote dialogue, coordination and victim centered approaches" in advancing the principles of complementarity (UNDP 2012, 12). The former ICC prosecutor, Luis Moreno Ocampo, referenced the ICC's effort to steer a course between the seemingly contradictory goalposts of local ownership and global governance, noting that the "complementary nature of the court" requires recognition of the ICC as "independent and interdependent at the same time"; accordingly, the first initiative he announced was the convening of a "public hearing for a participatory dialogue." Indeed, that inaugural speech was infused with the vocabulary of local ownership and hit all the buzzwords: "consultation," "participation," "diversity," and "dialogue."[28] The overarching theme was that this was not only a court that would seek to have jurisdiction over the world, but that this was a court for and by the world.

It is a telling irony that the currency of the discourse of local ownership gained value in the human rights world in ways that were tied to good governance policy frameworks that are exemplars of the post–Cold War liberal imperium. The focus on local ownership seemed to be most celebrated as an expression of human rights self-determination precisely when it became embedded in an interventionist paradigm that intervenes in the name of human rights. Thus local ownership is reborn not as a challenge to global governance but as its symbiotic partner. It thrives in this double life, carrying the particular in the universal, as both local and global, the subnational and the transnational, a way of being context-specific while being heralded as a globally mobile best practice, an expression of democracy and a project of democracy promotion.

Indeed, an ability to corral and carry these apparently contradictory discursive currents has emerged as critical to gaining traction in the institutional and normative architecture of contemporary global governance.

The Rome Statute was negotiated and passed in the context of this landscape, and Article 17, the article clarifying the doctrine of complementarity, is the most telling embodiment of this ambidexterity. In framing Article 17 as the mechanism managing the tensions between national legitimacy and international governance technologies, it chokes potential challenges to the reach of the ICC by channeling such opposition to the parameters of national-international law complementarity and attendant terms of reference. It also establishes an elaborate institutional edifice to anchor those terms of reference. Thus the Rome Statute details a range of procedures to review the admissibility of any potential case that defines the relationship between the jurisdiction of the court and the jurisdiction of national sovereignty, and ensure that the ICC is exercising jurisdiction only when the state party concerned is unwilling or unable to advance an investigation and prosecution process—all this in the name of advancing local control over human rights accountability agendas and procedures. Thus, Article 17 grants the imprimatur of local legitimacy on this global institutional actor by embodying the claim that the ICC is directed at buttressing, not undermining, the primacy of national courts. In addition, it contributes to that imprimatur by miring challenges to ICC jurisdiction in a range of procedural reviews determining complementarity, and all in a vocabulary about admissibility and jurisdiction that is predicated on the international criminal law regime. Local ownership then is not about grassroots challenges to the dominant global order but a free-floating value of good governance that can be advanced by those at the top of the global governance gravy chain as much as by someone at the bottom of it.[29] This, then, is good governance—the rule of no one for everyone.

This alliance between local ownership and global governance is not without consequences. These consequences include displacing distributive justice questions from international legal concerns with the prioritization of political closure over political accountability. Concomitantly, as local ownership has come to dominate the conceptual and institutional apparatus of human rights, initiatives to harness human rights to support struggles for more radical sociopolitical transformation or even basic economic rights are increasingly disempowered. Moreover, as the transitional justice field has become ever more tied to institutions such as the Security Council, there has been a narrowing of policy agendas, institutional forms, and political vocabularies for justice in ways that have rendered ICC dynamics even more hostile to dissenting and subaltern communities in conflict and postconflict societies.

Conclusion: Governmentality and Governments

Originally the ICC did not anticipate the functional need for field offices such as the Central African Republic office described in the opening paragraphs. The ICC expected that it could conduct investigations and conduct in-country work through short-term staff missions from The Hague. Accordingly, when it submitted its early budgets, the ICC made no provision for field offices. However, there was a growing recognition that this was not satisfactory, and indeed that the functional tasks were but one component of the value of field offices in the interface with local communities. Thus today, a field office is not merely a hub to coordinate its investigations for practical purposes but a platform for community engagement in the name of local ownership.

The Uganda victim survey and the Katanga admissibility debates trace how local ownership can become this potent empty signifier that performs and manages legitimacy for international criminal law's claim to advance accountability for human rights violations. The victim survey and the self-referrals each speak to related, but distinct, dynamics of this process—what I refer to, in shorthand, as the domain of governmentality on the one hand, and governments on the other. The victim survey can be located among a family of instruments, such as the population census and the opinion poll, that seek to study, count, classify, and represent communities and their human rights agendas. There has been a distinctive turn toward measurement practices within the transitional justice field that advance the disciplinary work of modern governmentality in constituting the subject as legible to international human rights law, norms, and institutions. When surveyed, consulted, or enlisted in Ocampo's "participatory dialogue," that subject is also constituted as one who is then poised to "own" the ICC initiative. Here ownership is not a claim to or against the ICC or any particular ICC-referenced agenda, but is the fact of being hailed by the ICC, of being classified by the ICC-referenced local ownership machinery as a stakeholder. For instance, Human Rights Watch defines outreach as "a sustained, two-way 'dialogue' between the court and affected populations," but then goes on to say that the purpose of this dialogue is not for the affected populations to shape the ICC agenda but for the ICC to reach out to the "affected populations . . . to promote understanding about the court's work" (HRW 2008). In other words, local ownership is precisely to establish that populations victimized by human rights violations should cede the terrain of justice to the ICC. One may even say that to own here, is, in fact, to acquiesce in being "governed" by the international criminal law enterprise. Timothy Mitchell's reflections on democracy are apposite here: he notes that one meaning of the term *democracy* is a reference to "ways of making effective claims for a more just and egalitarian common world," just as one sense of local ownership of human rights accountability procedures is of ways of making effective claims on the justice agenda, including challenging institutions that are seeking to narrow that agenda (Mitchell 2011). However, as Mitchell notes, there is also another meaning of democracy: the term "can refer to a mode of governing populations that employs popular consent as a means of limiting claims for greater equality and justice by dividing up the common world" (Mitchell 2011). In our case studies, popular consent to a universal human rights order circulates through instruments of local ownership such as surveys, polls, consultations, and participatory dialogues. In this other meaning of democracy, Mitchell argues that such limits to more subversive claims "are formed by acknowledging certain areas as matters of public concern, subject to popular decision, while establishing other fields to be administered under alternative methods of control" (Mitchell 2011). The international criminal law regime's approach to human rights accountability is precisely an alternative method of control. Here, instruments of local ownership employ popular consent to cede the terrain of justice to the ICC.

If globally mobile instruments of popular consent transformed local ownership claims into technologies of governmentality, we have also seen the subversive thrust of local ownership claims defanged by governments as such. The DRC's abdication of jurisdiction in the Katanga case presents the nation-state not as a counter to global governance but as its conduit. Thus even when the African Union protested the ICC, the pivotal rallying cry for African governments has been the question of head-of-state immunity.[30] The irony of head-of-state immunity being the locus of local ownership claims complements governmentality in channeling local ownership from resistance to governance.

Governmentality and governments provide different windows into that work of local ownership; they suggest that a top-down or vertical account of imperial power relations does not fully capture the dynamic of how local ownership of the ICC is enacted. Rather, the travel of human rights agendas both constitutes and is facilitated by the horizontalized habitus of what Kamari Clark calls "tribunalized violence"; this involves normalizing the legal order represented by ICC justice and the sedimentation of global subjectivities that are framed through the human rights apparatus. The transitional justice field and institutions such as the ICC have been shaped by diverse interests and circumstances; however, the field has cohered into a distinctive project that ends up being compatible with, and even complementary to, the dominant structures and dynamics of global governance. Yet it functions through the performative enactment of local ownership, sovereign rights, civil society participation, and victim consultation. Global governance emerges as not merely a repressive power manifested through the wielding of imperial authority, but a productive power whose reach can be appreciated by how the discourse of local ownership doubles back on itself. Local ownership and sovereignty can operate, through mimicry and alterity, to conform to the structures of global governance. In this sense, local communities are both author and subject of their own constitution in the legal and normative architecture represented by the International Criminal Court.

Acknowledgments

My thanks to commentators at IGLP Doha, at CAICL London and Windsor, the Helsinki Conference on International Law and Empire, and the Third World Approaches to International Law (TWAIL) Oregon workshop. A version of this chapter spun off during its extended gestation process to focus very specifically on a TWAIL perspective on international criminal law, and I am indebted to Asad Kiyani, John Reynolds, and Sujit Xavier for comments on that article (see Nesiah 2016); there is a large overlap between both versions and those engagements inevitably influenced this chapter. Most significantly, however, this version, and its preoccupation with the circulation of human rights norms, developed in conversation with Tine Destrooper, Sally Merry, and others present at the November 2015 workshop on Localizing Human Rights, and I am indebted to all for their input. The comments of Tine Destrooper through successive drafts have been particularly helpful in shaping this final version.

Notes

1. Poverty reduction strategy papers (PRSPs) are required by the World Bank and the IMF in negotiating debt relief conditionalities; while required, paradoxically, they are also presented as ways for member countries and their populations to participate in the formulation

of debt policies. Participation is highlighted as a key dimension through which the PRSPs are produced and for the goals that they are intended to serve. For the IMF description of these initiatives, see http://www.imf.org/external/np/prsp/prsp.aspx. The World Bank has embraced the discourse of participation even more emphatically, with its former head, James Wolfensohn, urging that aid recipients should be "owning and implementing their development strategies" (Pouligny 2009, 6). Accordingly, various World Bank initiatives devote themselves to maximizing participation through consultations, surveys, public hearings, and the like. For instance, the bank established a Global Partnership for Enhanced Social Accountability Consultations (http://siteresources.worldbank.org/INTKAZAKHSTAN/Resources/CA_GPESA_Consultations_Brief_Sept2012_Eng.pdf); similarly, another World Bank Group Affiliate produced a five-point plan for consultation processes (http://blogs.worldbank.org/publicsphere/getting-evaluation-right-five-point-plan).

2. The focus on local ownership has emerged as a central preoccupation for the human rights field and attendant debates regarding the legitimacy of "universal" norms and the voice of local communities (Merry 2006b, 38).

3. Koskenniemi notes, "It often seems that the memory for which the trial in The Hague is staged is not the memory of Balkan populations but that of an 'international community' recounting its past as a progress narrative from 'Nuremberg to The Hague,' impunity to the Rule of Law. This 'community' would construct itself in the image of a 'public time' (in analogy with 'public space') in which it would contemplate its past and give a moral meaning to disasters such as Rwanda or Srebrenica as implying a promise of radiant future" (Koskenniemi 2002, 34–35).

4. "The Court is complementary to national systems. This means that whenever there is genuine State action, the Court cannot and will not intervene. As a consequence of complementarity, the number of cases that reach the Court should not be a measure its efficiency. On the contrary, the absence of trials before this Court, as a consequence of the regular functioning of national institutions, would be a major success" (Ocampo 2003).

5. For instance, Apuuli argued that "the issuing of the arrest warrants seems to have ended all hopes of resolving the conflict peacefully" (Apuuli 2006)

6. Bigombe said the ICC's intrusion severely undermined local efforts to end the war. "'It is now extremely difficult for me to talk meaningfully to the LRA leadership when they know they are being hunted down to be locked up behind bars in Europe,' she said" (Kakaire 2006).

7. See the discussion of Kamari Clark regarding "multiple space of justice" in Uganda, including Mata Oput and the "competing social practices that exist alongside ICC justice mechanisms" (Clark 2009, 131).

8. In fact, some critics also represented a hybrid insider/outsider status—for instance, among the most prominent was Father Carlos Rodriguez, a Spanish priest who spent over two decades in Uganda and worked closely with the Acholi Religious Leaders' Peace Initiative and the Justice and Peace Commission of Gulu Archdiocese. Rodriguez is quoted criticizing the ICC indictments against the LRA as running interference with the peace process and local priorities for ending the conflict: "Nobody can convince a rebel leader to come to the negotiating table and at the same time tell him that when the war ends he will be brought to trial" (Lanz 2007).

9. The report is based on the preliminary analysis of quantitative data collected from interviews with 2,585 residents of four northern districts—Gulu and Kitgum (both Acholi districts), and Lira and Soroti (both non-Acholi districts). The interviews were conducted by teams of trained interviewers led by researchers from the Human Rights Center (HRC), University of California, Berkeley, in partnership with the International Center for Transitional Justice

(ICTJ). Makerere University Institute of Public Health partnered with UC Berkeley in two of the districts. The interviews took place "between April 20 and May 2, 2005, using a structured questionnaire" (Pham et al. 2005, 3).

10. For a more extended discussion of the role of quantitative indicators in the human rights field with particular focus on the representation of women in truth commissions, see Nesiah (2015). The discussion of the turn to measurement in this chapter draws freely from that earlier work.

11. The report identified the following objectives of the survey process: (1) measure the overall exposure to violence as a result of war and human rights abuses in Northern Uganda since 1987, (2) understand the immediate needs and concerns of residents of towns, villages, and internally displaced person (IDP) camps in Northern Uganda, (3) capture opinions and attitudes about specific transitional justice mechanisms, including trials, traditional justice, truth commissions, and reparations, and (4) elucidate views on the relationship between peace and justice in Northern Uganda (Pham et al. 2005, 4).

12. Eric Stover describes this as the central motivation of the population-based surveys that he and his colleagues at the Berkeley Human Rights Center have conducted.

13. On the methodological point, it is worth noting that the 73-page report has only one page listing survey limitations. The limitations cited range from inadequate recall to the possibility that respondents provided answers that the interviewer may find favorable; yet the report urges that these issues were minimized by the structure of the survey and the fact that the ongoing conflict ensured that events were still fresh in people's memory. There was concern that victims may have thought interviewers were government officials, but again the report notes that they addressed this problem by asking for signed consent forms that would have underscored that interviewers were in fact independent actors. In a follow-up 50-page survey report, the same authors have only one short paragraph listing five survey limitations, including geographic scope, fluctuating political context, the inaccessibility of some of those who were to be interviewed, errors by some of those interviewed, and potential discomfort that some of those interviewed may have had in discussing sensitive issues with strangers; the authors note that "this may have affected some of their answers" (Pham et. al. 2007, 13). As discussed further in Nesiah (2015), these modest cautions themselves suggest a breathtaking confidence in the capacity of survey instruments to capture and convey victim voice.

14. As noted in Nesiah (2015), over the last several years a range of imperatives has fueled the widespread turn toward measurement practices in the transitional justice field. This broader trend within human rights is reflective of how this field too has incorporated the disciplinary modalities of modern policy science and its "marshaling of information that constitutes the subjects it then governs. The deployment of measurement technologies in the human rights field can be situated in this larger dynamic of state structures mapping, surveying and administering populations—in their own interest" (Nesiah, ibid.).

15. Situation in the Democratic Republic of the Congo (ICC-01/04), available online at https://www.icc-cpi.int/drc.

16. Germain Katanga was the second person convicted by the ICC. Thomas Lubanga Dyilo, also of the DRC, was the first person arrested under an ICC warrant (in March 2006) and convicted by the ICC (in July 2012).

17. He argued that even if the DRC arrests and investigation were not focused on the Bogoro events that were part of the ICC indictments, he was being investigated for other crimes of comparable gravity, proving that the DRC was not unable to prosecute allegations related to

the events in Bogoro; moreover, even if Bogoro was not cited in his arrest, it was cited in hearings in Ugandan courts regarding his continued detention.

18. Rather than assess prosecutorial will in terms of whether the domestic system was pursuing charges against the same individual for "other crimes of comparable gravity," the ICC ruled in the Lubanga case that it would define the "willingness" criterion more narrowly to reference specificities that "encompass both the person and the conduct which is the subject of the case before the Court."

19. Thus the court concludes that it finds a "clear and explicit expression of unwillingness of the DRC to prosecute this case. It recalls that the DRC did not challenge the admissibility of the case when the warrant of arrest was communicated to it and that as soon as said warrant was unsealed, Germain Katanga's transfer to The Hague was ordered immediately. . . . The Chamber concludes therefore that the DRC clearly intends to leave it up to the Court to prosecute Germain Katanga and to try him for the acts committed on 24 February 2003 in Bogoro."

20. The prosecutor referenced Article 17 (1)(a) to argue that the plain meaning of that provision was that the only relevant factor for the admissibility test was whether the state was taking action; the argument of the court was in effect that it was not necessary for the court to investigate the state's *mens rea* on this. The court is indifferent to a state's motives if it is not prosecuting; just the fact of nonprosecution can trigger admissibility. If the state is in fact prosecuting, the court is interested in whether this is a good faith and feasible prosecution effort in relation to the specific case in question to determine admissibility. The appeals chamber affirmed this argument and held that the Katanga case was indeed admissible, and underscored the prosecutor's argument that the key factor in determining admissibility with attention to complementarity was the activity, or inactivity, of the state.

21. In a sense, the ICC expert paper argues that while the state's *mens rea* may not be relevant for the legitimacy of the ICC's actions, it is relevant in determining that the state is in compliance with its ICC obligations (Agirre et al. 2003, 19).

22. As Fassassi puts it, "in the Democratic Republic of Congo and Uganda cases, the Prosecutor strongly encouraged the states to refer the situation to the ICC" (2014, 52). Indeed, in September 2003, the prosecutor threatened to open an investigation using his Article 15 *proprio motu* powers; within six months, the DRC government made a self-referral under Article 14.

23. The ICC's Office of the Prosecutor defines positive complementarity as "a proactive policy of cooperation aimed at promoting national proceedings" (ICC 2010b, 5).

24. The conflicts of the DRC have a material basis in the struggle over resources, in particular minerals such as cassiterite and coltan and the multinational companies that mine these minerals for use in the computers, cell phones, and DVD players that we all use. With a death toll that matches the number of Jews killed in the Holocaust (some six million deaths over the last dozen years), there are a lot of lives and a lot of dollars at stake.

25. As many have reported, many in the Ituri region were harshly critical of the child soldier charges against Lubanga—partly because Lubanga was not being charged with crimes that were more serious, and partly because many were less critical of his actions vis-à-vis child soldiers. It is a complex history but there are credible reports that many parents had voluntarily given up children as a measure of political solidarity; they had a more complex view of child soldiers, knowing the significance they had had in the ouster of Mobutu (HRW 2008, 127–28).

26. As noted earlier, discourses regarding stakeholder ownership and attendant codes and policies have long been familiar dimensions of the international development landscape (Brynne and Mallet 2005).

27. For instance, the International Association for Public Participation (iap2) presents itself as "the preeminent international organization advancing the practice of public participation" and it does so through developing a series of tools, training programs, and "state of the practice" reports (http://www.iap2.org).

28. In fact, the ICC is now giving rise to further expansion of the local ownership vocabulary—thus, one commentator coins the term "inreach" to describe the process of "obtaining ideas, opinions, and feedback from local populations about their expectations and responses to the transitional justice process." Wendy Lambourne argues that the ICC has incorporated "innovative victim participation provisions and a sophisticated outreach program including action plans adapted to each context in which the Court is operating" (quoted in Lambourne 2010).

29. This extends from the ICC itself to the Security Council. For instance, the Libyan situation came before the ICC through a Security Council referral on February 26, 2011 (SCR 1970). For the victim and defense team, this referral was itself a vote for ICC jurisdiction. *Situation in Libya in the Case of the Prosecutor v. Saif Al-Islam Gaddafi and Abdullah al-Senussi* (https://www.icc-cpi .int/CourtRecords/CR2012_05322.PDF). Here local ownership meant particular notions of "rule of law" that the ICC would safeguard in the name of victims and due process. Thus the Office of Public Counsel for Victims (the OPVC), the designated representatives of victims, was arguing that international institutions such as the Security Council and the ICC were the best champions of local ownership and victims' rights; thus, in their interpretation, the commitment to local ownership that was embedded in the doctrine of complementarity was an argument in favor of admissibility. In contrast, legal argument in support of Libyan jurisdiction advanced the argument that the Security Council referral of the Libyan situation to the ICC was not a military intervention reinforcing intervention—a military intervention driven by NATO's interest in regime change and oil fields. Rather, in the October 9, 2012 open session of the Pre-Trial Chamber's hearing regarding the Libya situation, the questions of referral and jurisdiction implicated in the complementarity debate was situated in terms of the UN's commitment (quoting Ban Ki-Moon) to "the principles of Libyan ownership" (In the case of *The Prosecutor v. Saif Al-Islam Gaddafi and Abdullah Al-Senussi*, 2012). Local ownership, then, is a free-floating principle that even the most powerful body in the world supports by definition. Thus the UN's press release of October 17, 2012, refers to the secretary-general's speech to the Security Council lauding the potential of a partnership between the Security Council and the ICC in championing local justice: "The Court and the Council can support each other in building local justice responses and in strengthening the rule of law."

30. "No charges shall be commenced or continued before any international court or tribunal against any serving head of state or Government or anybody acting in such capacity during his/her term of office. To safeguard the constitutional order, stability and integrity of member states, no serving AU Head of State or Government or anybody acting or entitled to act in such a capacity, shall be required to appear before any international court or tribunal during their term of office" (African Union 2013).

Works Cited

African Union. 2013. "Statement from the Extraordinary Session of the Assembly of the African Union." Addis Ababa: African Union. Accessed June 24, 2016. http://www.au.int/en/sites /default/files/decisions/9655-ext_assembly_au_dec_decl_e_0.pdf.

Agirre, Xabier, Antonio Cassese, Rolf Einar Fife, Håkan Friman, Christopher K. Hall, John T. Holmes, Jann Kleffner, Hector Olasolo, Norul H. Rashid, Darryl Robinson, Elizabeth Wilmshurst, and Andreas Zimmermann. 2003. *Informal Expert Paper: The Principle of Complementarity in Practice*. The Hague: International Criminal Court. Accessed June 24, 2016. https://www.icc-cpi.int/NR/rdonlyres/20BB4494-70F9-4698-8E30-907F631453ED/281984/complementarity.pdf.

Apuuli, Kasaija Phillip. 2006. "The ICC Arrest Warrants for the Lord's Resistance Army Leaders and Peace Prospects for Northern Uganda." *Journal of International Criminal Justice* 4: 179–187.

Bass, Gary. 2001. *Stay the Hand of Vengeance: The Politics of War Crimes Trials*. Princeton: Princeton University Press.

Branch, Adam. 2004. "International Justice, Local Injustice." *Dissent* 51 (3): 22–26.

Brynne, Abra, and Patrick Mallet. 2005. *Stakeholder Consultation Practices in Standards Development*. British Columbia: ISEAL Alliance. Accessed August 4, 2016. http://orgapet.orgap.org/annexes/annex_A4-3.pdf.

Clark, Kamari. 2009. *Fictions of Justice: The International Criminal Court and the Challenge of Legal Pluralism in Sub-Saharan Africa*. Cambridge: Cambridge University Press.

De Vos, Christian, and Sara Kendall. 2011. *Post-Conflict Justice and "Local Ownership": Assessing the Impact of the International Criminal Court*. Leiden: Grotius Centre for International Legal Studies. Accessed August 4, 2016. http://www.grotiuscentre.org/resources/1/Conference%20Report-Final.pdf.

Fassassi, I. 2014. "Understanding the ICC Prosecutor Through the Game of Chess." *Loyola of Los Angeles International and Comparative Law Review* (36)35.

Human Rights Watch. 2008. *Courting History: The Landmark International Criminal Court's First Years*. New York: Human Rights Watch. Accessed August 4, 2016. https://www.hrw.org/sites/default/files/reports/icc0708_1.pdf.

International Criminal Court (ICC). 2010a. *Outreach Report 2010: Public Information and Documentation Section*. The Hague: International Criminal Court. Accessed August 4, 2016. https://www.icc-cpi.int/iccdocs/PIDS/publications/OUR2010Eng.pdf.

———. 2010b. *Prosecutorial Strategy 2009–2012*. The Hague: International Criminal Court. Accessed August 4, 2016. https://www.icc-cpi.int/NR/rdonlyres/66A8DCDC-3650-4514-AA62-D229D1128F65/281506/OTPProsecutorialStrategy20092013.pdf.

Kakaire, Apolo. 2006. "Ugandan Mediator Critical of ICC Indictments." *Institute for War and Peace Reporting*. Accessed June 23, 2016. https://www.globalpolicy.org/component/content/article/164/28551.html.

Koskenniemi, Martti. 2002. "Between Impunity and Show Trials." *Max Planck Yearbook of United Nations Law* 6: 1–35.

Kramer, Alan. 2006. "The First Wave of International War Crimes Trials: Istanbul and Leipzig." *European Review* 14 (4): 441–455.

Lambourne, Wendy. 2010. "Outreach, Inreach, and Local Ownership of Transitional Justice." Paper presented at the International Studies Association Annual Convention. New Orleans, Louisiana, February 17–20.

Lanz, David. 2007. "The ICC's Intervention in Northern Uganda: Beyond the Simplicity of Peace vs. Justice." Medford: Fletcher School of Law and Diplomacy. Accessed May 18, 2016. Accessed August 4, 2016. http://reliefweb.int/sites/reliefweb.int/files/resources/EC66215A0071F156C12573910051D06D-Full_Report.pdf.

Merry, Sally. 2006a. *Human Rights and Gender Violence: Translating International Law into Local Justice*. Chicago: University of Chicago Press.

———. 2006b. "Transnational Human Rights and Local Activism: Mapping the Middle." *American Anthropologist* 108 (1): 38–51.

———. 2011. "Measuring the World." *Current Anthropology* 52 (3): 83–95.

Mitchell, Timothy. 2011. *Carbon Democracy: Political Power in the Age of Oil*. New York: Verso.

Nesiah, Vasuki. 2015. "Icons and Indices." In *Feminisms of Discontent: Global Perspectives*, edited by Ashleigh Barnes and Priya Gupta. Delhi: Oxford University Press.

———. 2016. "Local Ownership of Global Governance." *Journal of International Criminal Justice*, 14, 985–1009.

Ocampo, Luis Moreno. 2003. "Statement Made at the Ceremony for the Solemn Undertaking of the Chief Prosecutor of the ICC, June 16." The Hague, The Netherlands. Accessed June 24, 2016. http://www.iccnow.org/documents/MorenoOcampo16June03.pdf.

Pham, Phuong, Patrick Vinck, Eric Stover, Andrew Moss, Marieke Wierda, and Richard Bailey. 2007. *When the War Ends*. New York: International Center for Transitional Justice and Human Rights Center, University of California, Berkeley. Accessed August 4, 2016. file:///Users/vasukinesiah/Dropbox/Pham%20and%20Vink_When%20the%20War%20Ends_2007.pdf.

Pham, Phuong, Patrick Vinck, Marieke Wierda, Eric Stover, and Adrian di Giovanni. 2005. "Forgotten Voices: A Population-Based Survey of Attitudes About Peace and Justice in Northern Uganda." New York: International Center for Transitional Justice and Human Rights Center, University of California, Berkeley. Accessed August 4, 2016. https://www.ictj.org/sites/default/files/ICTJ-HRC-Uganda-Voices-2005-English.pdf.

Pouligny, Béatrice. 2009. "Supporting Local Ownership in Humanitarian Action." Berlin: Center for Transatlantic Relations (CTR) and Global Public Policy Institute (GPPi). Accessed August 4, 2016. http://www.disastergovernance.net/fileadmin/gppi/GPPiPPR_local_ownership_2009.pdf.

Robinson, Darryl. 2011. "The Controversy over Territorial State Referrals and Reflections on ICL Discourse." *Journal of International Criminal Justice* 9 (2): 355–384.

Schabas, William. 2008. "Complementarity in Practice: Some Uncomplimentary Thoughts." *Criminal Law Forum*, 19 (1): 5–33.

Security Council. 2011. Security Council Resolution (SCR) 1970 (2011). Accessed August 4, 2016. https://www.icc-cpi.int/NR/rdonlyres/081A9013-B03D-4859-9D61-5D0B0F2F5EFA/0/1970Eng.pdf.

Situation in Libya, in the Case of the Prosecutor v. Saif al-Islam Gaddafi, ICC-01/11-01/11-577, International Criminal Court (ICC), December 10, 2014. Accessed August 4, 2016. https://www.icc-cpi.int/CourtRecords/CR2014_09999.PDF.

Southwick, Katherine. 2005. "Investigating War in Northern Uganda: Dilemmas for the International Criminal Court." *Yale Journal of International Affairs* (Summer/Fall): 105–119.

Team on Communications of the Coalition for the International Criminal Court (CICC). 2015. *Key Principles for ICC Communications: Informal Comments to the Registry ReVision Team*. Accessed August 4, 2016. http://www.iccnow.org/documents/CommsTeamInformalCommentsRevision13MAR15.pdf(http://www.iccnow.org/documents/CommsTeamInformalCommentsRevision13MAR15.pdf).

United Nations Development Programme (UNDP). 2012. *Complementarity and Transitional Justice: Synthesis of Key Emerging Issues for Development*. New York: UNDP.

CHAPTER 2

Accommodating Local Human Rights Practice at the UN Human Rights Council

Arne Vandenbogaerde

The emergence of new claims under the guise of human rights is not a novel phenomenon but arguably one as old as the current international human rights framework itself. Since the emergence of the post-1945 human rights framework new rights or standards have been continuously proclaimed. This has led to a surge of human rights treaties, declarations, and mechanisms that cover certain groups, issues, or actors.

The fact that we have such a wide array of treaties and mechanisms would give reason to believe that new standards are not necessary and that we have arrived at an era of implementation of existing norms rather than standard-setting. Yet, in particular at the United Nations (UN) the development of new norms appears never-ending. Some of the new norms under discussion today include the rights of peasants and other people living in rural areas, the right to peace, the right to solidarity, or the rights of the elderly (Human Rights Council 2012b, 2014; UN General Assembly 2010). This, what some would term "inflation" of human rights, has led scholars to discuss the usefulness of new norms (Baxi 2001) and how we can ensure the quality and coherence of such new norms (Alston 1984).

The proliferation of human rights standards arguably lies in the very nature of human rights law as it evolves, or should evolve, when individuals are confronted with new violations (e.g., as caused by globalization processes). As Alston indicated, "the validity and the necessity of a dynamic approach to human rights, as well as the expansion, where appropriate, of the list of recognized human rights, cannot reasonably be disputed" (1984, 607). He adds that:

> [t]he challenge is to achieve an appropriate balance between, on the one hand, the need to maintain the integrity and credibility of the human rights tradition, and on the other hand, the need to adopt a dynamic approach that fully reflects changing needs and perspectives and responds to the emergence of new threats to human dignity and well-being. (ibid., 609)

Such an outlook is grounded in the basic understanding that human rights need to be relevant for individuals in their everyday lives. This starting point has led scholars to identify a need to "localize" human rights (De Feyter et al. 2011). The need for localization implies (1) that international human rights law needs to be interpreted in a locally relevant manner (contextualized), and (2) that the daily realities or local human practice must inform any human rights standard-setting. This chapter adopts this normative position and aims to contribute to the understanding of the extent to which the global UN human rights machinery grants legitimacy to the idea of human rights circulation and transformation. We explore a fundamental element of this process by focusing on how human rights practice at the local level can be accommodated into the existing global human rights framework. We focus on the UN (human rights) mechanisms, as these are currently the only organizations that can enact and proclaim global human rights norms. The UN Human Rights Council (HRC) is the main body within the UN responsible for the promotion and protection of human rights worldwide.

An analysis of how the UN accommodates local human rights practice can be done, among other ways, from a legal, technical point of view, or from an institutional, structural point of view. In this chapter, first I particularly highlight the different manners in which states, civil society organizations, or the UN mechanisms identify certain protection gaps. While agreement on the problems a particular group faces is not always controversial, the way to resolve this most often is. Next I give a brief institutional and political analysis of the HRC's standard-setting processes and mechanisms. Finally, I introduce some ideas regarding how to strengthen the HRC's engagement with local organizations.

Accommodating Human Rights Practice

A Legal Perspective

In this section we will first outline the different potential protection gaps that may exist in human rights law and how the different actors involved identify those gaps. Subsequently, we will discuss the legal, technical solutions to address such gaps.

Identifying the Gaps

It has been indicated that different protection gaps can coexist (International Council on Human Rights Policy 2006). Consequently, the classification of certain human rights issues into certain protection gaps may differ between the different users of human rights such as states, civil society organizations, or UN mechanisms (for a typology of different "users" of human rights, see Desmet 2014). As I will illustrate later on, states or a group of rights claimants often agree on the starting point (the actual human rights violations), yet the perceived solution to the issue often differs.

When new standards are required to enable members of a group to protect their rights more effectively and/or to clarify the obligations of states, one speaks of a normative gap. More generally, commentators have found that a normative gap exists "when a recurrent event (or act or structural factor) deprives human beings of their dignity" (International Council on Human Rights Policy 2006, 7). Others similarly found that "human rights are intended to formally define the thresholds that identify situations in which human dignity is threatened or violated. A normative gap exists when there is no such definition or where the definition is inadequate" (HelpAge International 2012, 2). The identification of a normative protection gap is typically controversial since states—as duty bearers—will often deny the existence of such a gap. Instead, what many states would argue is that there is an implementation gap as existing standards are insufficiently (or not) implemented. For example, currently there is no consensus on the need for a binding instrument concerning the rights of older persons. As indicated by one author, many states "continue to emphasize that the inadequate protection of their [older people's] human rights is caused by an implementation gap, rather than a normative gap, and that as existing norms apply to persons at all stages of life, no new norm-setting process is required" (De Pauw 2014, 236). In certain instances such an analysis can certainly be correct: for example, if no new fundamental rights are claimed for the elderly, one could argue that the core human rights treaties already protect them, in particular because human rights protect the most vulnerable and marginalized in society. The situation is different when claims are made that cannot readily be incorporated into the existing body of law (see, for example, hereunder in relation to peasant rights).

Besides a normative or implementation gap, there can also exist application gaps in international (human rights) law. Such gaps occur when the application or interpretation of *existing* standards is restricted in its scope. A treaty can be restricted, for example, in its material, personal, or temporal scope. The 1951 refugee convention contained, for example, geographic and temporal limitations that resulted in an application gap for certain individuals (UN General Assembly 1951). An additional gap that can be observed is an enforcement gap. Such a gap exists when existing standards cannot be enforced due to the absence of a specific enforcement mechanism.

These gaps can coexist and often it is hard to analytically distinguish between the various types of gaps. This can explain why actors often hold divergent opinions on the existence of a certain gap (International Council on Human Rights Policy 2006, 8). A telling illustration of the potential difference and debates around the identification of the different protection gaps is the case of the declaration on the rights of peasants. Since 2013 the UN has been discussing the adoption of a declaration on the rights of peasants and other people working in rural areas. A UN open-ended working group (OEWG) has been established, which is mandated to draft a declaration on the rights of peasants (Human Rights Council 2012a). The fact that we have such a standard-setting process is the result of a long trajectory of advocacy and lobbying at various levels (provincial, national, international), spearheaded by the transnational agrarian movement La Via Campesina. This movement is rather unique in its capacity to bridge the local and the global and has been extensively studied elsewhere (Borras 2004, Desmarais 2007, Martinez-Torres and Rosset 2010). This movement adopted its own declaration on the rights of peasants in 2008 (La Via Campesina 2009). The substantive starting point of the OEWG has been the Declaration on the Rights of Peasants and Other People Working in Rural Areas that was submitted to the HRC by the Human Rights Council's Advisory Committee (Human Rights Council Advisory Committee 2012). This declaration in turn has incorporated all the provisions of the 2008 declaration of La Via Campesina, and in terms of legitimacy, "this was a strength because that text [the declaration of La Via Campesina] is rooted in the severe discrimination and vulnerability experienced by peasant communities" (Golay 2015, 19). The travels of the declaration of the rights of peasants, from the local Indonesian level up to the HRC, has been extensively documented (Vandenbogaerde 2015a; Golay 2009; Claeys 2013, 2015) and has indeed been described as an illustration of how local claims or human rights practice can travel to the global level through a transnational network (Vandenbogaerde 2015b).

States, civil society, and the UN actors, in particular the Human Rights Council Advisory Committee, all agreed on the facts: farmers, in particular small-scale farmers, are at higher risk of *inter alia* expropriation of their land, forced evictions, displacement, gender discrimination, and lack of social protection (Human Rights Council Advisory Committee 2012). In addition, the various actors involved in the standard-setting all agree that existing human rights (such as the right to food or health) and their concomitant obligations are not being implemented satisfactorily in relation to peasants. Yet, while the various actors agree that there are implementation gaps, they do not agree on the existence of certain normative or application gaps in relation to peasants.

La Via Campesina has asserted that certain normative gaps exist and they have proposed several new, self-standing human rights in their declaration of 2008. Indeed, in order to make the translation of their claims into human rights claims relevant, commentators have argued that La Via Campesina "had to develop an alternative conception of rights that emphasizes the collective dimension of claims; that targets the various levels where food and agricultural governance issues ought to be deliberated; and that provides the tools to fight neoliberalism and capitalism in agriculture" (Claeys 2012, 845). The international nongovernmental organizations (NGOs) that are involved in the advocacy and standard-setting process have also asserted the existence of normative gaps (see, e.g., FIAN International 2013). In addition, the Human Rights Council Advisory Committee explicitly found that there were normative gaps and that in order to protect peasants and other people working in rural areas it was imperative to recognize the new rights contained in the declaration of La Via Campesina (Human Rights Council Advisory Committee 2012, para. 67). In addition to the normative gap, La Via Campesina as well as the other actors that recognize a normative gap also find there is an application gap. This is visible in the fact that in its declaration it claims, for example, the right of peasants to land. Such a right is an existing standard in international law but is applied solely in relation to indigenous people (e.g., ILO Indigenous and Tribal Peoples Convention No. 169).

I have indicated that controversy about the adoption of new human rights is part and parcel of the UN human rights system and that the same pattern of disagreement can be identified in several standard-setting processes. The disagreement between states on the protection gaps in relation to peasants was therefore to be expected. The states that are supporting and driving the process at the UN have recognized a normative gap and the need to recognize new human rights standards on peasants (Human Rights Council 2014, para. 28). States in opposition have voiced familiar arguments by stating, for example, that "a number of UN instruments already focus on realizing the human rights of persons living and working in rural areas. We [the European Union] feel it is more beneficial to take a deep look at these instruments and to use them effectively."[1]

The correct identification of a protection gap can be based on legal arguments. The existence, for example, of an application gap can be determined by looking at the scope of a treaty and the eventual legal practice (case law). Similarly, whether or not there is a normative gap is also relatively straightforward to assess from a legal technical point of view. One simply needs to inquire whether or not the norm in question exists in international law. Yet, resolving the disagreement on whether a nonexisting norm needs to be incorporated in the human rights framework cannot be resolved solely from a legal point of view but will largely depend on one's notion of how human rights should "travel" between duty bearers and individuals. Our starting point of the need to localize human rights does not inform us on how exactly new norms should be developed and accepted. The theory merely asserts the need to take into account local human rights practice in the development of the norms as well as in the interpretation of existing norms.

If one adopts a downstream approach to norm setting (see the chapter by Vandenhole in this volume), then states decide on what norms will be adopted and consequently what standards or claims should be considered a human right. An upstream approach, on the contrary, acknowledges that individuals may shape human rights law in the face of their struggle. Baxi, for example, believes communities and peoples are to be the principal drafters of international human rights (Baxi 2002). Others have argued that the fact that human rights remain largely a discourse of the powerful over the powerless is in itself a violation of human rights, namely the right to define one's own rights (Ife 2010, 126). The tension between the two approaches emerges in the debates around the identification of the normative gaps and how to address these. It arguably also illustrates that both approaches are part of the same process (see Vandenhole in this volume, and De Gaay Fortman 2011).

Addressing the Gaps

There are different ways of addressing the protection gaps identified above. Here we will focus on how to address normative or application gaps in human rights law. We therefore focus on how new claims are accommodated in global human rights practice. Discussing the literature and possible ways of implementation or enforcement falls outside the scope of this chapter.

The adoption of a new human rights instrument is a first manner in which to address normative and/or application gaps in international human rights law. This is often the preferred solution by those actors who have identified a protection gap. A new treaty or declaration can assert new rights and obligations for states or extend the application of certain rights to other groups or individuals. In addition to the potential legal arguments, more strategic arguments also come into play as a new instrument brings with it advocacy and lobbying firepower and often a human rights body specifically mandated to monitor and enforce the obligations set out in the instrument. In this sense, the adoption of a new human rights instrument may also aid in covering the implementation gap, although the choice of hard or soft law instrument may make a difference between having monitoring bodies or not. In any case, a declaration or treaty that reiterates existing rights and standards can also be of strategic or political value.

A second approach to cover normative or application gaps consists in seeking a progressive or extended interpretation of existing human rights norms. Existing human rights standards are then interpreted in such a way that they recognize additional rights or claims. Such extended interpretation is typically sought and achieved through complaints before human rights bodies and courts. Illustrative examples are, for example, the European Court of Human Rights' (ECtHR) protection of certain socioeconomic rights through the civil and political rights provisions of the European Convention on Human Rights (ECHR), for example through Article 8, or the

Inter-American Court's recognition of the collective land rights of indigenous peoples through the individual right to property contained in the American Convention on Human Rights (see Inter-American Court of Human Rights, *Mayagna [Sumo] Awas Tingni Community v. Nicaragua* 2001). A readily noticeable limitation of this avenue to cover protection gaps is the legal uncertainty and the impossibility of overstretching existing rights or treaties. The ECHR, for example, was not drafted and adopted with socioeconomic rights in mind, and therefore its ability to cover those rights remains limited as the ECtHR struggles with expanding its socioeconomic rights jurisprudence. Adopting or recognizing a fundamentally new standard arguably will be hard through a progressive interpretation as one cannot create any new fundamental obligations for the duty bearers under the human rights treaty.

It is striking that typically European and North American states are opposed to the creation of new human rights instruments. Such a pattern of beliefs against new human rights instruments (and consequent provisions) can be found in several standard-setting processes at the UN. The European Union, for example, opposes the formulation and adoption of a declaration on peasant rights, a convention on the rights of older persons, and a declaration on the right to peace. One explanation, certainly, is the fear of being overburdened, as these states typically have already ratified many regional and international human rights instruments. Yet, states do not usually make such a pragmatic argument explicitly, so it is difficult to understand their motivations. However, we have explicit arguments and formal statements that are reiterated time and again, and which argue that there is an implementation gap rather than a normative or application gap or that there is no legal basis for declaring new rights in international law. In the context of the discussions around a draft declaration on the right to peace, for example, states such as Australia, the United States, Canada, and the EU member states have opposed any standard-setting because there is no legal basis for a right to peace in international law (the right has not been recognized previously).[2] If new standards must fit the existing legal framework, then the possibility for new standard-setting is limited. The arguments against new standards are often grounded on the perceived structural constraints of the existing framework. For example, the international human rights law framework is state-centered as it does not impose obligations on nonstate actors such as business actors or NGOs. In addition, it is also predominantly based on the individual, to the detriment of the collective aspects of some issues and rights (see, e.g., Claeys 2013; Stammers 1999). In practice this means that the main drafters (states) of new instruments rely upon agreed language in order to convince and forge consensus among states, which is often the lowest common denominator (see, e.g., Türkelli, Vandenhole, and Vandenbogaerde 2013). The concrete danger is that agreed language could also be a first step in transforming the particular claims that arise from local human rights practice. The existing norms set the direction of the standard-setting and proposals on new human rights or aspects of those rights will typically have to fit into the existing framework (De Feyter 2011, 57). The further local human rights claims travel, the more they are at risk of being transformed and disintegrating into bracketed texts and technical debates (Baxi 2002, 69; see also Martínez in this volume). Yet, such a traveling process is not necessarily bad as local claims may be unsubstantiated, limited in personal scope, or ill-worded and therefore require revision (see hereunder, for example, on the rights of peasants to reject). The subsequent argument is therefore to include local human rights practice into standard-setting without romanticizing the latter.

The provisions of the declaration of the rights of peasants, as originally suggested by La Via Campesina and later by the HRC Advisory Committee, underwent significant changes. This should perhaps be no surprise as the original declaration clearly went to a great extent beyond existing human rights law and contained what could be termed "radical proposals" such as the "freedom to set prices" or the "right to reject" intellectual property rights or patents that threaten biological diversity. Subsequently, at the first session of the OEWG states voiced criticism about the lack of agreed language (Human Rights Council 2014, para. 32).

At the second session of the OEWG that was tasked with drafting the UN declaration, the chairperson presented a revised draft declaration.[3] This revised draft declaration contains considerable language changes in order to make it compatible with existing international human rights law. Article 5(3) of the UN draft declaration, for example, declares that peasants have the right to reject industrial modes of agriculture. This is remarkable, considering that at the first session of the OEWG, states indicated that provisions opposing the industrial model of agriculture should not be in the text (Human Rights Council 2014, para. 37). Scholars have indicated in this respect that it will be difficult for La Via Campesina to "institutionalize subversion" at the UN (Claeys 2012). At the informal consultations between the first and second sessions of the OEWG it also became clear that "[i]t would not be difficult to reach agreement on the reaffirmation of existing human rights; and that finding and using agreed language—including in FAO and ILO instruments—would be helpful in convincing states to recognize certain additional rights of peasants and other people working in rural areas" (Golay 2015, 18). Golay has indicated that agreed language, in particular from the UN Declaration on the Rights of Indigenous Peoples, could help in rephrasing the various provisions containing a right to reject. He argues that a "right to choose and to be protected" could substitute the right to reject and—being based on agreed language— be more acceptable for states (Golay 2015, 25–27).[4] The revised declaration indeed contains such language as it, for example, asserts a right to decide which crops to cultivate (Article 22(2) of the revised declaration). While this certainly may present a politically viable solution, one could argue that a right to choose or to decide may not entirely coincide with the envisaged right to reject (leaving aside the merits of such a right). While the original authors of the declaration may agree with some transformation of their claims, commentators have also warned that this may lead to the demobilization of activists (Claeys 2012, 853). Moreover, the adoption of such agreed language in order to forge consensus may trigger tensions within the transnational advocacy network. International NGOs and affected people may disagree on strategy as the latter may be reluctant to find compromise when the realities of diplomatic negotiation clash with the ideal of comprehensive protection (International Council on Human Rights Policy 2006, 33). Scholars have also noted that it is probably more common for people to adopt human rights frameworks pragmatically and strategically than through conversion or a shift in rights subjectivity (Merry 2006, 44). Consequently, the member organizations of La Via Campesina might as well consider dropping the rights discourse if this turns out to be trivializing their struggle.

Accommodating Human Rights Practice at the HRC: Institutional and Political Perspectives

The choice of a particular forum for the negotiation of any standard-setting process "influences the type of instrument adopted, the range of issues addressed, the legal obligations that are highlighted, and the scope of the supervisory mechanism" (International Council on Human Rights Policy 2006, 36). The status, power, and degree of participation of the various actors involved also changes with the venue (International Council on Human Rights Policy 2006, 36). A discussion of the different advantages and disadvantages of the various international and regional forums from a user's perspective falls outside of the scope of this chapter but certainly merits more scholarly attention. In this section we will briefly discuss the UN HRC's mechanisms ability to take into account local human rights practice when engaging in standard-setting.[5]

In its resolution establishing the HRC, the UN General Assembly acknowledges that NGOs play an important role in the promotion and protection of human rights at the national, regional, and international levels, and that the HRC needs to work in close cooperation with civil society (UN General Assembly 2006, 2–3). Arguably, the HRC itself also benefits from the participation of civil society as this enhances their democratic legitimacy (similar to, for example, the European Union institutions). The legitimacy of civil society actors is thus definitely recognized and the various UN HRC mechanisms allow the formal participation of civil society through, for example, written and oral statements at their sessions.

The agenda-setting stage of (the need for) new standards typically happens through the HRC's mechanisms. The Advisory Committee and the UN special procedures are particularly active in the identification of protection gaps and how to resolve them. The thematic and country-specific individual mandate holders are independent experts. The UN special procedures can tackle human rights issues at the global, national, and local levels, and several studies have documented how these procedures have engaged in norm-setting in the UN. These mechanisms can either lend support to civil society proposals or be engaged directly in the norm-setting process (Golay, Mahon, and Cismas 2011; Nifosi 2005). The special rapporteur (SR) on the Right to Food was, for example, involved in advocating for the need for a new legal instrument on the rights of peasants. Civil society organizations are considered crucial to the work of the various special procedures, in particular in the provision of information and analysis. This has been recognized by scholars (Piccone 2012), as well as by the special procedures themselves (OHCHR 2008, para. 133). The support and input from civil society also grants legitimacy and authority to their work and as such can reduce the criticisms that the various independent experts often receive from states.

The HRC Advisory Committee functions as the think tank for the Human Rights Council (Human Rights Council 2007a, para. 65). Like its predecessor (the UN Sub-Commission on Human Rights), it regularly undertakes standard-setting initiatives. The HRC Advisory Committee, for example, submitted a draft declaration on the right of peoples to peace to the twentieth session of the HRC. Following this submission, the HRC established an open-ended intergovernmental working group to negotiate a draft declaration on the right to peace (Human Rights Council 2012b). The Advisory

Committee, in collaboration with the independent expert on human rights and international solidarity, is also working on a draft declaration on the rights of peoples and individuals to international solidarity (Human Rights Council 2010). Future proposals include a study on the possibility of a World Court of Human Rights (Human Rights Council Advisory Committee 2013).

When they engage in standard-setting the Advisory Committee enjoys close relationships with civil society. NGOs in consultative status with the Economic and Social Council (ECOSOC) are entitled to participate in the official meetings of the Advisory Committee and can deliver written and oral statements at the sessions. Moreover, at its thirteenth session the Advisory Committee decided to hold private meetings in the framework of each of its sessions with nongovernmental organizations and civil society representatives (Human Rights Council Advisory Committee 2014). At the same session it also reiterated that it would "continue the practice of resorting to expertise, such as . . . non-governmental organizations, academics and other relevant stakeholders, in order to inform the Advisory Committee's deliberations and work" (Human Rights Council Advisory Committee 2014, decision 13/8).

A pragmatic reason for the participation of civil society in the work of the HRC Advisory Committee is that the body lacks financial and human resources to gather information and perform research on a wide array of topics. In any case, the official statements are surely put into practice. We have indicated in the previous section that the HRC Advisory Committee has taken into account local human rights practice in relation to the rights of peasants.

Once an issue has arrived at the norm-setting stage, that is, when it has been decided that a new instrument needs to be drafted, a so-called open-ended working group (OEWG) is typically constituted by the HRC. "Open-ended" refers to the access all UN member and observer states, intergovernmental organizations, and nongovernmental organizations with ECOSOC consultative status have to the public meetings of the OEWG. In sum, at the agenda- and norm-setting stage of a standard-setting process, civil society organizations enjoy access to the HRC. However, this access is unequal for a number of reasons.

Standard Setting at the UN: Challenges and Way Forward

Civil society organizations enjoy unequal access to the Human Rights Council (International Council on Human Rights Policy 2006, 24–27) as the system reveals a bias toward Geneva-based professional NGOs. In particular, organizations working at the national and local level (and outside of Europe or North America) may face several challenges in accessing the HRC. In an earlier piece, I have identified four general challenges that local organizations may face when seeking access to the HRC: lack of ECOSOC consultative status, lack of financial and administrative resources, absence of relevant expertise in working with the HRC (including the lack of important informal networks with HRC personnel), and lack of political space or reprisals in the country where they work (Vandenbogaerde 2015a, 49–54). These challenges, in particular the lack of resources, may also present a dilemma for local organizations as shifting resources to advocacy at the global level may require reducing work in the countries where they operate. Given these challenges, grassroots organizations will have to work with international NGOs and build a network to gain access to the HRC. The emergence of such a transnational advocacy network is complex for many reasons; most important, perhaps, is the fact that also within such networks there can be power imbalances. While working relations and views may be perfectly compatible between members of a transnational advocacy network, one can also envisage that the collaboration may create tensions between these actors in terms of strategy and positions to adopt, in particular at the norm-setting stage when consensus needs to be sought. It must be noted that these tension are not only found between grassroots organizations and national or international NGOs but also within these organizations. Many Latin American members of La Via Campesina, for example, hesitated to adopt the peasants' rights idea. Tensions may lead to the disintegration of the network and consequently the access for organizations that do not enjoy observer status at the UN and/or lack the human and financial resources to engage in interest representation at the HRC. International NGOs can thus function as gatekeepers to the UN HRC, and the possibility of localizing human rights can be hindered by these actors if they decide not to provide access to small, grassroots organizations.

In addition to these challenges we find that the space for civil society organizations becomes more restricted as the setting changes from agenda-setting to standard-setting. At the standard-setting stage the setting changes considerably as the number of actors involved increases and the public profile of the discussions changes. When it is clear that a new instrument will be adopted, states take the lead in the process at the OEWGs. While some of the HRC mechanisms can still be involved, civil society organizations do not steer the process any longer. The debates get more technical, political, and structured, making it easy to sideline organizations that are not specialized in interest representation at the UN.

Given the challenges mentioned above as well as the state-driven HRC standard-setting processes, one could argue that the UN HRC should explore options to engage more structurally and proactively with grassroots organizations. Currently, there appears to be no systematic commitment to learn from below. In fact, we would argue that pragmatic reasons predominantly influence the degree and impact of involvement of civil society organizations (see also Vandenbogaerde 2015b).

To a certain extent the UN Social Forum is an attempt at giving greater voice to all the actors involved in human rights protection. Different from other mechanisms, the Social Forum allows for the participation of a wide array of actors including nonaccredited organizations and private actors.[6] One step toward further institutionalizing learning from below would be to reinvigorate the mandate of the UN Social Forum developed under the former Commission on Human Rights. The mandate under the Commission on Human Rights was ambitious, including "to propose standards and initiatives of a juridical nature, guidelines and other recommendations for consideration by the Commission on Human Rights, the working groups on the right to development, the Committee on Economic, Social and Cultural Rights, the specialized agencies and other organs of the United Nations system" (Sub-Commission on the Promotion and Protection of Human Rights 2001, para. 2(c)). The Social Forum survived the 2006 UN reform (which established the HRC) and became a subsidiary body of the HRC, and according to the latter it is "a unique space for interactive dialogue between the United Nations human rights machinery and various stakeholders, including grass-roots organizations" (Human Rights Council 2007b, para. 3). The Social Forum, however, does not have a very specific mandate. The HRC sets the theme for each forum and basically requests the Social Forum "to focus" on a specific issue and to recommend measures and actions to address the issue. The reports are presented at the Human Rights Council but there is no vote on those reports' recommendations. The reports merely inform the Human Rights Council. This purely informative role is being reinforced by the fact that through the UN the Social Forum is delinked from the Advisory Committee. Today, the chair of the Social Forum is no longer a member of the Advisory Committee but a government representative. The UN reform has thus also led to more state control over this mechanism. A strengthening of the mandate of the Social Forum goes some way toward enhancing the participation of grassroots organizations and activists and could thereby contribute to localizing the HRC by giving these organizations and activists a forum for setting—or at least influencing—the agenda of the HRC. Another way of facilitating more participation at the UN HRC would be to create a voluntary fund for grassroots organizations to attend meetings and participate in the UN mechanisms (Advisory Committee, Social Forum, etc.) or in a particular OEWG. Such a fund has been established in the past in relation to indigenous populations. The fund served to assist representatives of indigenous communities in participating in the Working Group on Indigenous Populations of the Sub-Commission on Human Rights. The fund was also used when the declaration on the rights of indigenous people was deliberated (International Council on Human Rights Policy 2006). This, however, would only address the financial challenges that civil society organizations, and in particular grassroots organizations, face.

If the goal were to allow for genuine reverse standard-setting in the field of human rights, the HRC should arguably go further and, for example, develop a mechanism similar to the International Food Security and Nutrition Civil Society Mechanism (CSM) of the UN Committee on World Food Security (CFS) (Vandenbogaerde 2015b). Through this mechanism, which is in fact a UN body, civil society organizations, including grassroots organizations and people most affected by food insecurity, could participate in the work of the CFS. Indeed, CSM members are not observers but actual participants in the CFS and are permanently represented at the CFS Advisory Group.[7] The CSM works through 11 constituencies (such as artisanal fisherfolk or the landless) and 17 subregional groups and has a small secretariat. The setup of the mechanism also has the advantage that decisions are monitored at the local level. The CFS has declared that it is "crucial that the work of the CFS is based on the reality on the ground" (Committee on World Food Security 2009, para. 23). Indeed, former UN SR on the Right to Food De Schutter has indicated that the reform of the CFS "was grounded in the recognition that governments will only manage to make true progress towards food security if they accept to work in a bottom-up fashion, by learning not only from one another's experiences, but also from the experience of those who are on the frontline of combating hunger—the international agencies and the nongovernmental organizations—and the victims of hunger themselves" (De Schutter 2013, 4). De Schutter finds that the reform of the CFS constitutes a new breed of international governance "in which civil society, the private sector, international agencies, are co-authors with governments of international law" (De Schutter 2013, 19). A successful example of such lawmaking are the Voluntary Guidelines on the Responsible Governance of Tenure of Lands,

Fisheries and Forests adopted in 2012 by the CFS. The model of the reformed CFS is, however, not without its problems as states have flagged concerns over the deliberative nature of the CFS (civil society having the same rights as states to substantively participate in the debates),[8] and civil society complains about the corporate capture of the process and mechanism.[9] Moreover, actors such as La Via Campesina have indicated the strain their participation in the CFS and the CSM puts on their organization:

> The movement considers it important to occupy such spaces [CFS], bringing citizens' power into the realm of institutional politics and interacting with governments in a more pragmatic manner to promote its goals. However, it is also aware of the limitations of such politics, given the limited impact that can be made, and the immense resources that are required to be part of such spaces, both human and technical as well as financial, which are difficult for a social movement to bear.[10]

Conclusion

The essential dynamism of human rights inevitably requires a willingness to consider the need to proclaim new human rights and/or increase the scope of human rights protection (Alston 1984). There are various ways one can address such applications or normative human rights gaps. One approach is to draft new standards and adapt a new human rights instrument (be it of a soft or hard law nature). This also has it strategic advantages as it provides an important element to engage in advocacy work. Assessing the effectiveness and usefulness of such newly proposed standards and/or instruments needs to occur on a case-by-case basis, and the point of this chapter was not to offer a normative framework on how to assess such new claims (if this could be possible). Instead, I examined how institutions at the global level, such as the HRC, actively seek to incorporate local human rights practice in their standard-setting process. I analyzed what the potential and shortcomings of the HRC's current institutional provisions are, thereby assessing the potential for the localization of human rights norms on the basis of the human rights claims of individuals and communities.

However, human rights standards should reflect real-life struggles and concerns. In order for this to happen we need—among other things—to install procedures that allow for participation "from below." The UN HRC certainly attaches importance to local human rights practices, and UN HRC mechanisms such as the HRC Advisory Committee or the special procedures allow for the participation of grassroots movements in their work, especially in terms of agenda-setting. Yet grassroots organizations encounter considerable challenges in accessing the HRC in terms of resources, expertise, and the requirement of ECOSOC status. In practice this means that an additional challenge emerges, as they must engage in a network with international NGOs experienced in lobbying at the HRC. This means that the latter organizations exercise a gatekeeper function for issues coming from below. A more consolidated and proactive approach of the HRC to learning from grassroots organizations is therefore warranted and should be explored further. I have indicated several options that could be further explored: from relatively simple ones such as reinvigorating the UN Social Forum or the development of a fund to the more difficult option of the establishment of a mechanism similar to the CSM of the FAO's CFS.

This volume focuses on the mobilization for human rights, in particular how activists adopt the human rights discourse and how this shapes their struggles. This chapter focused on the legal and institutional avenues to bring such struggles to the international level. These avenues currently have their limitations. Consequently, their features should be taken into account when attempting to understand patterns of human rights circulation and transformation.

Notes

1. See EU Statement at the second session of the working group on a United Nations declaration on the rights of peasants and other people working in rural areas (2015), available at: http://www.ohchr.org/EN/HRBodies/HRC/RuralAreas/Pages/2ndSession.aspx (last accessed April 27, 2016).

2. See: Statements made during the first session of the open-ended intergovernmental working group on a draft United Nations declaration on the right to peace. Available at: http://www.ohchr.org/EN/HRBodies/HRC/RightPeace/Pages/FirstSession.aspx (last accessed March 20, 2016).

3. See: Draft UN Declaration on the Rights of Peasants and Other People Working in Rural Areas (Advanced version 27/01/2015), available at: http://www.ohchr.org/EN/HRBodies/HRC/RuralAreas/Pages/2ndSession.aspx (last accessed March 20, 2016).

4. Similarly, Golay has argued that the notion of freedom to set prices contained in the original declaration is best replaced by the already accepted right to a decent income.

5. The other main venue or forum for standard-setting at the UN would be the UN General Assembly.

6. The OHCHR has stated that "the Social Forum shall also be open to other non-governmental organizations whose aims and purposes are in conformity with the spirit, purposes and principles of the Charter of the United Nations, including newly emerging actors, such as small groups and rural and urban associations from the North and the South, anti-poverty groups, peasants' and farmers' organizations and their national and international associations, voluntary organizations, environmental organizations and activists, youth associations, community organizations, trade unions and associations of workers." Available at: http://www.ohchr.org/EN/Issues/Poverty/SForum/Pages/Accreditation.aspx (last accessed March 22, 2014).

7. Participants take part in the work of the committee with the right to intervene in plenary and breakout discussions to contribute to the preparation of meeting documents and agendas, and to submit and present documents and formal proposals (Committee on World Food Security 2009, para. 12.).

8. See: http://globalsoilweek.org/areas-of-work/sustainable-development-goals/the-uns-most-inclusive-body-at-a-crossroads (last accessed March 22, 2016).

9. See: http://globalforestcoalition.org/activists-denounce-agribusiness-take-over-of-un-food-body/ (last accessed March 22, 2016).

10. See: http://viacampesina.org/en/index.php/main-issues-mainmenu-27/food-sovereignty-and-trade-mainmenu-38/1501-gaining-support-for-the-peasant-s-way-la-via-campesina-at-un-s-leading-food-security-institutions (last accessed April 26, 2016).

Works Cited

Alston, Philip. 1984. "Conjuring Up New Human Rights: A Proposal for Quality Control." *American Journal of International Law* 78 (3): 607–621.

Baxi, Upendra. 2001. "Too Many, or Too Few, Human Rights." *Human Rights Law Review* 1 (1): 1–9.

———. 2002. *The Future of Human Rights*. Oxford: Oxford University Press.

Borras, Saturnino M., Jr. 2004. *La Vía Campesina: An Evolving Transnational Social Movement*. Discussion Paper 2004/6, Amsterdam: Transnational Institute Briefing Series http://www.wphna.org/htdocs/downloadsfeb2013/2007%20La%20Via%20Campesina%20TNI.pdf.

Claeys, Priscilla. 2012. "The Creation of New Rights by the Food Sovereignty Movement: The Challenge of Institutionalizing Subversion." *Sociology* 46 (5): 844–860.

———. 2013. "From Food Sovereignty to Peasants' Rights: An Overview of La Via Campesina's Rights-Based Claims over the Last 20 Years." Paper presented at *Food Sovereignty: A Critical Dialogue*, Program in Agrarian Studies at Yale University, New Haven, September 14–15, 2013.

———. 2015. "Food Sovereignty and the Recognition of New Rights for Peasants at the UN: A Critical Overview of La Via Campesina's Rights Claims over the Last 20 Years." *Globalizations* 12 (14): 452–465.

Committee on World Food Security. 2009. Reform of the Committee on World Food Security. CFS:2009/2 Rev.2.

De Feyter, Koen. 2011. "Law Meets Sociology in Human Rights." *Development and Society* 40 (1): 45–68.

De Feyter, Koen, Stephan Parmentier, Christiane Timmerman, and George Ulrich, eds. 2011. *The Local Relevance of Human Rights*. Cambridge: Cambridge University Press.

De Gaay Fortman, Bas. 2011. *A Political Economy of Human Rights: Rights, Realities and Realization*. London: Routledge.

De Pauw, Marijke. 2014. "Interpreting the European Convention on Human Rights in Light of Emerging Human Rights Issues: An Older Person's Perspective." *Human Rights & International Legal Discourse* 8 (2): 235–258.

De Schutter, Olivier. 2013. The Reform of the Committee on World Food Security: The Quest for Coherence in Global Governance. CRIDHO Working Paper 2013/8.

Desmarais, Annette Aurélie. 2007. "La Vía Campesina." *Wiley-Blackwell Encyclopedia of Globalization*.

Desmet, Ellen. 2014. "Analysing Users' Trajectories in Human Rights: A Conceptual Exploration and Research Agenda." *Human Rights & International Legal Discourse*, 9 (2): 111–120.

European Union. 2015. "Statement at the Second Session of the Working Group on a United Nations Declaration on the Rights of Peasants and Other People Working in Rural Areas. Available at: http://www.ohchr.org/EN/HRBodies/HRC/RuralAreas/Pages/2ndSession.aspx (last accessed April 27, 2016).

FIAN International. 2013. General Statement by FIAN International at the 1st session of the OEWG for the Elaboration of a UN Declaration on the Rights of Peasants and Other People Working in Rural Areas.

Golay, Christophe. 2009. "Towards a Convention on the Rights of Peasants." In *The Global Food Challenge: Towards a Human Rights Approach to Trade and Investment Policies*, edited by Sophia Murphy and Armin Paasch, 102–112.

———. 2015. *Negotiation of a United Nations Declaration on the Rights of Peasants and Other People Working in Rural Areas*. Geneva: Geneva Academy of International Humanitarian Law and Human Rights.

Golay, Christophe, Claire Mahon, and Ioana Cismas. 2011. "The Impact of the UN Special Procedures on the Development and Implementation of Economic, Social and Cultural Rights." *International Journal of Human Rights* 15 (2): 299–318.

HelpAge International. 2012. *International Human Rights Law and Older People: Gaps, Fragments and Loopholes*. London: HelpAge International.

Human Rights Council. 2007a. Institution-building of the United Nations Human Rights Council. UN Doc. 5/1.

———. 2007b. The Social Forum. UN Doc. A/HRC/RES/6/13.

———. 2010. Human Rights and International Solidarity. UN Doc. A/HRC/RES/15/13.

———. 2012a. Promotion of the Human Rights of Peasants and other People Working in Rural Areas. UN Doc. A/HRC/21/L.23.

———. 2012b. Promotion of the Right to Peace. UN Doc. A/HRC/RES/20/15.

———. 2014. Report of the Open-Ended Intergovernmental Working Group on a Draft United Nations Declaration on the Rights of Peasants and Other People Working in Rural Areas. UN Doc. A/HRC/26/48

Human Rights Council Advisory Committee. 2012. Final Study of the Human Rights Council Advisory Committee on the Advancement of the Rights of Peasants and Other People Working in Rural Areas. UN Doc. A/HRC/AC/8/6.

———. 2013. Report of the Advisory Committee on its Eleventh Session. UN Doc. A/HRC/AC/11/2.

———. 2014. Report of the Advisory Committee on its Thirteenth Session. UN Doc. A/HRC/AC/13/2.

Ife, Jim. 2010. *Human Rights from Below: Achieving Rights Through Community Development*. Cambridge: Cambridge University Press.

Inter-American Court of Human Rights, *Mayagna (Sumo) Awas Tingni Community v. Nicaragua*, No. 79 (2001).

International Council on Human Rights Policy. 2006. *Human Rights Standards: Learning from Experience*. Versoix: International Council on Human Rights Policy.

La Via Campesina. 2009. *Declaration of Rights of Peasants—Women and Men*. Seoul: La Via Campesina.

Martinez-Torres, Maria Elena, and Peter M. Rosset. 2010. "La Vía Campesina: The Birth and Evolution of a Transnational Social Movement." *Journal of Peasant Studies* 37 (1): 149–175.

Merry, Sally Engle. 2006. "Transnational Human Rights and Local Activism: Mapping the Middle." *American Anthropologist* 108 (1): 38–51.

Nifosi, Ingrid. 2005. *The UN Special Procedures in the Field of Human Rights*. Antwerp: Intersentia.

OHCHR. 2008. *Manual of Operations of the Special Procedures of the Human Rights Council*. Geneva: OHCHR.

Piccone, Ted. 2012. *Catalysts for Change: How the UN's Independent Experts Promote Human Rights*. Washington, DC: Brookings Institution Press.

Stammers, Neil. 1999. "Social Movements and the Social Construction of Human Rights." *Human Rights Quarterly* 21 (4): 980–1008.

Sub-Commission on the Promotion and Protection of Human Rights. 2001. The Social Forum. UN Doc. E/CN.4/SUB.2/RES/2001/24

Türkelli, Gamze Erdem, Wouter Vandenhole, and Arne Vandenbogaerde. 2013. "NGO Impact on Law-making: The Case of a Complaints Procedure under the International Covenant on Economic, Social and Cultural Rights and the Convention on the Rights of the Child." *Journal of Human Rights Practice* 5 (1): 1–45.

UN General Assembly. 1951. Convention Relating to the Status of Refugees, United Nations, Treaty Series, vol. 189, p. 137.

———. 2006. Human Rights Council. UN Doc. A/RES/60/251.

———. 2010. Follow-up to the Second World Assembly on Ageing. UN Doc. A/RES/65/182.

Vandenbogaerde, Arne. 2015a. The Human Rights Council from Below: A Case Study of the Declaration on the Rights of Peasants. UN Doc.

———. 2015b. "Localizing the Human Rights Council: A Case Study of the Declaration on the Rights of Peasants." *Journal of Human Rights*.

CHAPTER 3

Human Rights-Based Approaches to Development: The Local, Travel, and Transformation

Wouter Vandenhole

In a fair amount of recent development policies, programs, and practices, human rights–based approaches to development (HRBADs) have been introduced by international organizations, donor countries, and nongovernmental organizations (Crawford and Andreassen 2013, 2). Contrary to grassroots rights struggles induced from below, the adoption of HRBADs by local development organizations and actors has often, if not always, been induced by external actors, whether donor states, international intergovernmental organizations, or nongovernmental organizations (Hellum et al. 2013, 27). As Ife (2010, 131) argued, in development, "[h]uman rights has traditionally been seen as a top-down discourse and has had difficulty dealing with the contextual, and with ideas of difference and diversity, within its more conventional frameworks." At first sight, HRBADs can thus be seen as a prime example of vertical, largely downstream travel. But is the travel of human rights so unidirectional in HRBADs, and how does transformation play out in the context of HRBADs? These questions guide this chapter.

Notwithstanding more empirical work on HRBADs since the mid-2000s (Gready and Ensor 2005; Hickey and Mitlin 2009), HRBADs remain poorly understood and implemented, and assessments of achievements and success have shown mixed results. Recent scholarship that explicitly factors in power (Andreassen and Crawford 2013) and change (Gready and Vandenhole 2014a) may to some extent contribute to a better understanding of whether the travel of ideas and approaches is multi- rather than unidirectional (and hence whether the notion of travel or circulation is the more appropriate one to use), and whether and how HRBADs transform as part of that travel. What has been less explicitly investigated, though, is how "the local" (Ensor 2005, 255) may affect the ways in which human rights travel and transform. More explicit attention to the local in HRBADs may shed new light on the travel and transformation of human rights in action, but also on how and when HRBADs work (better). Whereas transformation may be welcomed as a token of the flexibility that allows HRBADs to adapt to and be appropriated by the local, it may also entail risks of cooptation if it can be transformed too easily and to too large an extent.

Before I examine HRBADs from a travel and transformation perspective, it is worth recalling that for a long time, human rights diffusion has been seen predominantly as a global and top-down process. In a reaction to that dominant approach, two strands have emerged. Merry introduced the language of vernacularization, that is, the adaptation of international human rights to local contexts (Merry 2006a). Ensor's "alternative manifestations" of rights or a right (Ensor 2005, 265 and 272) may resonate with this idea of vernacularization. A second strand uses the language of "localizing human rights," bottom-up approaches, or "rights from below" to refer to the influence the local has or should have on human rights norms and institutions. Nowadays, there seems to be an increasing awareness that human rights travel or circulate, both vertically (top-down and bottom-up) and horizontally, and between the local and the global. Each of these notions may be problematic and therefore in need of further clarification. In this chapter, I do not seek to give a definite definition of any of these terms, but rather to explain why I use particular concepts. Whereas the top-down, bottom-up binary may be unidirectional and oversuggestive of power inequalities, "travel" or "circulation," while emphasizing multidirectionality, may inadvertently suggest power-neutral dynamics. In line with the conceptual framework presented in the introduction, I use the term "travel" rather than "circulation," because of the latter's association with circularity. The notion of travel accommodates attention for power dynamics, travel directions, and the concept of human rights transformation. The notions of local vs. global, too, may be problematic, since they suggest a binary distinction, while realities may be multipolar. While these are ideal types, they are useful analytical categories.

In what follows, I will first briefly introduce human rights–based approaches to development. Next, I examine the role of the local in human rights travel, analyze the power dimensions in human rights travel and transformation, and use the notion of rights subjectivity to understand some of the ways in which grassroots dynamics can potentially transform HRBADs. A final section considers whether there is a need for delimiting the transformation of HRBADs on the basis of grassroots dynamics, with regard to both strategies and substantive norms.

Human Rights–Based Approaches to Development

Initially, HRBADs were meant to address the gap between development programs and discourses developed mostly in New York (e.g., by the United Nations Development Programme) and human rights programs and discourses developed mostly in Geneva (e.g., by the United Nations' human rights bodies), by mainstreaming human rights into development. A common understanding of UN agencies about the HRBAD was reached in May 2003 in Stamford at the second interagency workshop on implementing a human rights–based approach in the context of UN reform (*Report Second Interagency Workshop* 2003). The Common Understanding is built on three pillars:

1. All programs and policies of UN development cooperation should further the realization of human rights, that is, they should make a positive contribution to human rights.
2. All development cooperation and programming, in all sectors and in all phases, needs to be guided by human rights standards and principles.
3. In particular, development cooperation should be about the capacity development of duty bearers to meet their obligations and of rights holders to claim their rights.

The Common Understanding mentions six human rights principles: universality and inalienability; indivisibility; interdependence and interrelatedness; nondiscrimination and equality; participation and inclusion; and accountability and the rule of law.

The Office of the High Commissioner for Human Rights (OHCHR) has defined a HRBAD as "a conceptual framework for the process of human development that is normatively based on international human rights standards and operationally directed to promoting and protecting human rights" (OHCHR 2006, 15). In the words of Darrow and Tomas, "[a] human rights–based approach represents both a 'vision' of development as well as a way of 'doing' development" (Darrow and Tomas 2005). Central principles of most HRBADs can be summarized in the acronym PANEN, that is, participation, accountability, nondiscrimination, empowerment, and normativity. HRBADs are not purely or even primarily legal, although the normativity principle reflects a clear legal core. Neither are HRBADs meant to draw exclusively on legal strategies and mechanisms, although they may be part of them (see further below on the critique of legalization).

Meanwhile, a good number of international NGOs have also adopted HRBADs. The argument in this chapter will be illustrated with references to ActionAid's turn to a HRBAD, since it has been particularly well documented. ActionAid made a rather radical shift to Southern leadership and introduced changes in its governance structures (Chapman 2009, 169 and 174) in order to turn itself from a traditional international NGO into a federation of affiliated organizations. Together with the adoption of the new structure, it was also accepted that rolling out a HRBAD would happen in a way that was respectful of the local context (Chapman 2009, 169). In other words, it was not taken for granted that a HRBAD would be possible or desirable in all circumstances.

The Local and Traveling of Human Rights Norms

The reference to international human rights standards as the normative basis for HRBADs in the OHCHR definition (OHCHR 2006, 15) suggests that the travel of human rights is understood as downstream and unidirectional. Chapman has pointed out the limitations of top-down travel of human rights, for example, through policy perspectives that focus on international debates without making links to domestic issues (Chapman 2009, 178).

Originally, HRBADs were not intended to stimulate localization of human rights, as explained in the previous section. However, they became part of the localization agenda as soon as nongovernmental organizations and social movements also turned to HRBAs (as documented by Gready and Ensor 2005; Andreassen and Crawford 2013). Conceptually, entry points for a more multidirectional understanding of how human rights norms can travel (starting from the local as well as starting from the global) can be found in two human rights principles characteristic of HRBADs: participation and empowerment. As Ensor has argued, "(t)he emphasis on participation comes closest to acknowledging the need to consider rights in their local context" (Ensor 2005, 255). Such consideration of rights in their local context may occur by simply taking into account the local context when implementing international human rights norms, but it may equally imply rights articulation that differs from the one in international human rights norms (Ensor 2005, 255). In the latter case, it is a small step to consider the impact of that local articulation on international human rights norms and processes.

Accountability, too, may bring in a bottom-up perspective. Typically, accountability allows rights holders to hold their domestic state to account, which already suggests a reverse travel in which rights holders appropriate human rights language to make claims toward the state as the duty bearer. This bottom-up travel is further reinforced by including accountability of all actors, including all external actors who introduce HRBADs, whether states, intergovernmental organizations, or nongovernmental organizations, to the rights holders (Chapman 2009, 174).

The more important question, however, is how travel, in particular from the local to other human rights actors, may transform human rights action. The literature on HRBADs from a change perspective has highlighted that in bottom-up and localized approaches, human rights are primarily seen as struggles rather than as preconceived legal rules. "Human rights as struggle" emphasizes bottom-up travel and embodies the idea of transformation of human rights: it introduces a different starting point (local struggles, not international norms), a different prioritization (processes rather than outcomes), and a different end-goal (change in power relations rather than the implementation of international standards). Hence, the direction in which human rights travels will impact the nature and the process of social transformation (Gready and Vandenhole 2014b, 12–15). If external actors draw in the HRBAD on preconceived human rights norms, they may be concerned mainly with the implementation of these international standards, with little room for different interpretations. On the other hand, if the HRBAD draws on local human rights struggles, the emphasis is bound to be much more on processes, on different interpretations, and on changing power relations.[1] De Gaay Fortman's notion of "downstream and upstream human rights" conveys a similar message on key implications of bottom-up or upstream travel. Downstream approaches are associated with international human rights law (legal norms), while upstream approaches are said to "arise from people's own convictions on concrete freedoms and entitlements relating to their human dignity" (De Gaay Fortman 2011, 13). In other words, the vertical travel dimension also involves major shifts in who produces the norms and what the source ("legitimizing anchor") of these norms is. In a downstream perspective, states adopt human rights instruments, and the norms are considered *human rights* norms because states say so (legal positivism). In an upstream perspective, people shape norms drawing on their own understanding of human dignity. At the same time, De Gaay Fortman rightly stresses that the analytical distinction between downstream and upstream perspectives on human rights should not obliterate that these two processes are strongly interwoven: they constitute "two sides of what is basically one process" (De Gaay Fortman 2011, 13). In other words, there is an ongoing interface and influence between downstream and upstream perspectives although, historically, human rights originated in upstream perspectives.

Power and Human Rights Transformation

The opportunities for human rights transformation in HRBADs through the principles of participation and empowerment (and possibly accountability) do not necessarily always materialize in practice. One should not too readily accept that with participation "room is left within such a policy for local definitions or interpretations of rights" (Ensor 2005, 263). To the contrary, it has been argued that many HRBADs "exclude those already marginalized from decision making, thus doing little to change power structures or dynamics, and making any change achieved less likely to be sustained. Such approaches instead promote a singular focus on policy reform, which often results in advocates being consumed by lobbying and losing touch with constituencies" (Chapman 2009, 166). Others have pointed out that HRBADs may have "neoliberal affinities" (Gledhill 2009, 32), so that "it is important to be realistic about what can be achieved in very unequal societies if the rights of the rich are treated as sacrosanct" (Gledhill 2009, 31). Moreover, it is unclear whether HRBADs have a distinct contribution to make to the understanding of participation and empowerment: Chapman has submitted that the "positive outcomes of rights-based approaches depend largely on linking them with what we have learned about the roles of participation, empowerment, and development alternatives in change processes that focus on transforming power relations" (Chapman 2009, 175). In addition, questions remain regarding the definition and identification of local communities, and of the most vulnerable and marginalized within these communities. Whereas a HRBAD's nondiscrimination principle prescribes that development actors should prioritize the participation of the most marginalized, it has not always been considered strategic to do so exclusively at the local level: "There are times when the most effective way to challenge inequitable power relations and structures is to work with broader groupings of excluded groups or poor communities" (Chapman 2009, 172–173), and not just with a locally affected community. Gledhill warns about the limits of the principle of participation:

> Neoliberal notions of participation empower unequal actors equally, leaving the socially powerful in the dominant position.... It is not realistic to imagine that spontaneous "bottom up" action by poor citizens will be sufficient by itself to bring about changes, but there is everything to be said for measures that enhance their capacity to organize, not merely to make demands, but to take greater direct control in the production of their own identities and of public understanding of their lives and their problems. (Gledhill 2009, 43–44)

This point speaks to the question of transformation of human rights, how power issues may impact on who steers transformation and in which direction, and how to deal with spoilers.

Although it has been argued that "the efficacy of rights analysis for exposing power relationships" is uncontested (Ensor 2005, 263), in practice, HRBADs often have not really paid explicit attention to power and power dynamics, or only at the level of abusive dominant state power. Other forms of power and other power holders, in particular at the local level, have received only limited attention under HRBADs. If HRBADs are to realize the socially transformative potential they are often claimed to have (inter alia by repoliticizing development) (Gready and Vandenhole 2014b, 13), power dynamics and their impact need to be better understood. In the literature on vernacularization and localizing human rights, too, power analysis has not been systematized. A 2013 volume edited by Crawford and Andreassen

LEVELS
Global
National
Local

FORMS OF POWER
Invisible
Hidden
Visible

Closed   Invited   Claimed

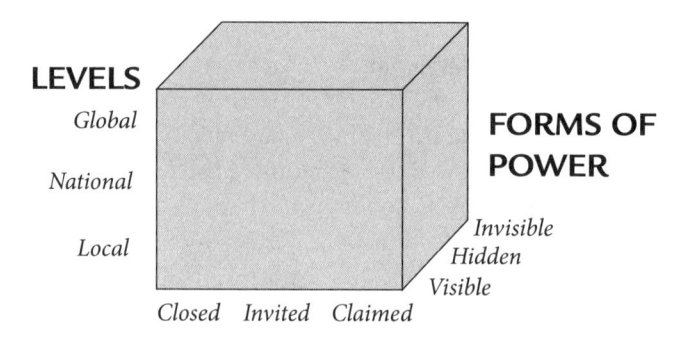

SPACES

Figure 3.1. The power cube.
Source: http://www.powercube.net/analyse-power/what-is-the-power cube/; The Participation, Power and Social Change team at the Institute of Development Studies, University of Sussex. Creative Commons Licence.

that systematically analyzes power dynamics in several NGOs and social movements that adopt a HRBAD fills this gap to some extent. Crawford and Andreassen draw heavily on the power cube developed by Gaventa, which introduces three levels (global, national, and local), spaces (closed, invited, and claimed), and forms of power (visible, hidden, and invisible) (Crawford and Andreassen 2013, 10–11) (see Figure 3.1).

The distinction between visible, hidden, and invisible power may be of particular relevance when studying the travel and transformation of human rights (Crawford and Andreassen 2013, 11–12). First, it helps to analyze the power dimensions that are present at different levels, ranging from the global to the local. Whereas the local is primarily understood within the public sphere of government as the subnational level, the private and intimate level of household and person is not necessarily excluded and should in fact be more explicitly included. The exercise of power at the local level is not confined to the public sphere. Any ambition in HRBADs to meaningfully engage with the local will therefore necessitate much more careful consideration of the private and the way power dynamics play out there. Second, that typology of forms of power draws attention to a dimension that may be most difficult to address and redress, that is, invisible power. Invisible or internalized power relates to socialization and has been defined as "control over the norms and beliefs that shape people's perception of themselves and their possibilities to influence the social, economic and political relationships in which they are embedded" (Hellum et al. 2013, 35). Invisible power may be a key explanatory factor in understanding both human rights transformation and social change, in that it draws attention to the form of power that may be most effective, while being least visible. The concept of invisible power may help us to better understand why rights subjectivity (see further below) remains superficial or nonexistent in some contexts, notwithstanding attempts to roll out HRBADs and hence introduce or reinforce rights subjectivity.

The distinction between closed, invited, and claimed or created spaces is equally useful to understand (the lack of) human rights transformation and social change. Closed spaces leave little space for involvement in decision-making, invited spaces are only open to selected actors, whereas claimed or created spaces have not been offered but rather have been taken (Crawford and Andreassen 2013, 11–12). With regard to HRBADs, closed and invited spaces are least likely to really open up for the local. At the same time, they may be most vulnerable to subversion of HRBADs, since they seem to seriously weaken (in the case of invited spaces) or even compromise (in the case of closed spaces) the key principles of participation and nondiscrimination, and also of empowerment and accountability.

Another analytical distinction that has proven useful to better understand the human rights principle of empowerment is that between power within, with, and over. Empowerment, in the sense of creating rights subjectivity (see further below), may well have to do more with power within than with power over. For example, Women of Zimbabwe Arise (WOZA), a social movement in Zimbabwe that seeks to empower poor women through civic education and community mobilization (Hellum et al. 2013, 31), empowered members "by learning to deal with violence": by changing "members' perceptions of what they can do and achieve," power within was built so that they felt in control when they were arrested by the police (Hellum et al. 2013, 45). This notion of power within complements that of power over in gaining a better understanding of the dynamics in the processes of creation of rights subjectivity, and hence of human rights transformation.

The application in practice of any of these analytical notions has made clear that they are not stable or unchangeable categories, "'closed space' and 'open space' depend on the kind of rights that are claimed, the timing of elections and other political events, and even where claims are made (urban or rural)" (Hellum et al. 2013, 36). The dynamic character of all these analytical notions complicates but also enriches the analysis of human rights transformation in the context of HRBADs.

Grassroots Dynamics and the Introduction of Rights Subjectivity

By introducing a HRBAD, ActionAid and others are said to have reoriented their work toward lobbying and advocacy at the expense of grassroots service provision. Chapman makes a strong call for development actors not to focus exclusively on policy work, but to integrate policy work with grassroots education, development of grassroots leadership, and mobilization work (Chapman 2009, 176). The need for grassroots work has also been echoed more generally. What is required is "advocacy for institutional, legislative and policy reforms, along with cultural changes in society at large, in order to alter existing power asymmetries in favor of the relatively powerless" (Crawford and Anyidoho 2013, 113). But even if HRBADs managed to engage in grassroots work, can they be expected to bring about these cultural changes in society at large?

Another finding is that some grassroots organizations have distanced themselves from a HRBAD. For example, Patel and Mitlin have reported on Shack/Slum Dwellers International (SDI), a grassroots network that mainly focuses on local savings schemes (primarily for women). SDI has challenged the premise in HRBADs that claiming rights from the state helps to address development needs. SDI's reluctance to engage with a HRBAD stems from the pragmatic recognition "that the state has little or no capacity to take control of the development strategies that the federation groups require" (Patel and Mitlin 2009, 120). "State capacity is therefore central to the practical value of a model whereby 'citizens claim and the state delivers'" (Gledhill 2009, 33–34). However, the lack of capacity is not simply a matter of insufficient resources: "the complex layers of informality that make up the life of the urban poor are not easily managed by state bureaucracy" (Patel and Mitlin 2009, 120). In other words, SDI's approach to HRBADs raises important questions about redesigning the roles and responsibilities between the state and civil society, but also about the balance between individualism and the collective (Patel and Mitlin 2009, 110–111).

SDI has a different "understanding of how power operates at the settlement and city levels": they therefore choose not to antagonize the state, but rather to seek to win its heart and mind (Patel and Mitlin 2009, 108). Where does this reluctance to "engage in confrontational contestation" come from? Why do they prefer negotiations over confrontation? Patel and Mitlin identify a couple of explanatory elements: first, the "capacity of people to claim legal rights depends on the level of agency available to them as they negotiate complex social relations and structures" (Patel and Mitlin 2009, 114). Second, "local groups differ from professional NGOs in their assessment of risks" (Patel and Mitlin 2009, 116). When global actors move on, they leave "local actors to deal with the consequences of the campaign, which often include an angry violator whose shaming has made exchanges impossible [footnote omitted]" (Patel and Mitlin 2009, 110). Third, global rights campaigns based on global human rights norms are said to "maintain the position of the poor as perpetual victims, offering them only the roles of supplicant and beneficiary. These campaigns provoke deep frustration and resentment among local grassroots activists, whose roles and contributions are pushed to the periphery of the process" (Patel and Mitlin 2009, 110). Fourth, Patel and Mitlin also warn about risks of disempowerment through processes of legalization and shifts toward lobbying: "the rights-based approach, with its legal associations, takes the poor firmly into the terrain of professionals and elites, and this terrain influences the solutions that emerge." Hence, they see a "real danger that this formality undermines the strengthening of local organizational capacity, shifting momentum away from mass organizations of the urban poor and toward professional lobbying" (Patel and Mitlin 2009, 118). This resentment of confrontation is believed to be rather widespread in the development (cooperation) community (Vandenhole 2014, 125). Likewise, the development (cooperation) community has assigned an increasingly limited role to the state in development (Gready and Vandenhole 2014b, 3–4). So what does all this mean for HRBADs?

Ensor has suggested that taking the grassroots and the (non)appropriation of rights seriously may lead to "a second mode of rights-based practice . . . that offers an alternative process based on constructive engagement with communities" (Ensor 2005, 272). In his view, "when engaging with issues that are closely tied to images of identity, or when recourse to the state is impossible," an alternative process of constructive engagement is needed (Ensor 2005, 272). His point ties in with the debate on whether a HRBAD is per definition confrontational, or whether it can also be more collaborative. Whereas a HRBAD tends to be seen as primarily confrontational, it is not necessarily so (Vandenhole 2014, 125). Whether a local infusion of the global HRBAD narrative is likely to add support for a nonconfrontational, collaborative approach needs to be seriously studied empirically, but it is not unlikely to do so in local contexts where struggles for social transformation are waged in less confrontational ways, or where the state's ability or willingness are in doubt.

So what is the role of grassroots work, and how can we understand why some grassroots organizations have turned their back on HRBADs? Merry has studied how "grassroots individuals take on human rights ideas" (Merry 2006b, 180), that is, how "transnational knowledge of rights" is localized (Merry 2006b, 179). She has found that the "rights framework does not displace other frameworks but adds a new dimension to the way individuals think about problems" (Merry 2006b, 180; compare Merry 2006a, 8). Therefore, transforming subjectivity into rights subjectivity is not so likely to occur as often as assumed, and tends to remain partial (Merry 2006a, 43–44). Merry compares a shift in subjectivity with a conversion, and warns that "it is probably more common for people to adopt human rights frameworks pragmatically and strategically than through conversion" (Merry 2006a, 44).

Limits to Human Rights Transformation?

Several challenges for NGOs that have adopted a HRBAD revolve around the question of how much space there is for human rights transformation in HRBADs, both at the action level (in particular with regard to operational approaches) and in substance. At the action level, NGOs wonder whether they can continue with service delivery. According to some, there is a "false dichotomy between empowerment and political engagement on the one hand, and service provision on the other" (Patel and Mitlin 2009, 121). Others have warned of risks of "blunting the radical edge" when social movements become service providers in partnership with the state (Gledhill 2009, 33). This raises interesting questions of transformation of human rights due to the layered structure of frameworks: a HRBAD does not simply replace preexisting frameworks (such as service delivery in this case), but can be added to these frameworks (compare Merry 2006b, 180). Gready talks about a "layered archeology of approaches" (see Gready 2014, 183). But is there somewhere a threshold beyond which service delivery becomes too prominent and contradicts or undermines a HRBAD?

Merry's work (2006a, 40) on the ambiguous position of translators (i.e., intermediaries who translate international human rights norms into local contexts) is helpful in this regard.[2] Translators are at the same time powerful and vulnerable. That ambiguous position shapes the process of human rights transformation or vernacularization into an approach that is somewhere on the continuum between replication and hybridization. In translation by replication, "[t]he transnational idea remains the same, but local cultural understandings shape the way the work is carried out" (Merry 2006a, 44). In other words, international human rights norms are a given. In hybridization, "symbols, ideologies, and organizational forms generated in one locality [merge] with those of other localities to produce new, hybrid institutions" (Merry 2006a, 46). These notions of hybridization and replication may help in asking questions in a more sophisticated way: When and why does a HRBAD become hybridized by parallel service delivery? When and why does a HRBAD fail to strike a chord because it simply replicates international definitions and approaches, but is completely detached from service delivery?

Merry's findings on the ambiguous position of translators are likewise directly relevant for a better understanding by external actors of what can be achieved by local partners through HRBADs, but also how these approaches may transform in the process of implementation. Translators in this context of externally induced HRBADs will most likely be either local staff and/or local organizations as the implementation partner of the external actor. The position of these local actors as translators will be characterized by a power-vulnerability dynamic: "The translator must walk a fine line between too much replication, in which case the new ideas will lose their appeal to local communities, and too much hybridity, in which case the reforms will lose the support of the global community, including its funding and publicity" (Merry 2006a, 48). This reflects the "paradox of making human rights in the vernacular: To be accepted, they have to be tailored to the local context and resonant with the local cultural framework. However, to be part of the human rights system, they must emphasize individualism, autonomy, choice, bodily integrity, and equality—ideas embedded in the legal documents that constitute human rights law" (Merry 2006a, 49). These insights about the tension between replication and hybridity challenge the often dogmatic embracement of a HRBAD and its normativity by external actors: the latter tend to ignore that the pure and simple replication of international human rights norms and principles might not work with local communities. On the one hand, the insights on the paradoxical position of translators, combined with the earlier finding that rights subjectivity rarely displaces preexisting subjectivity, invite modesty on the part of external actors that seek to roll out a HRBAD. For these actors it is important to acknowledge and accept that the paradoxical position of translators and the only partial rights subjectivity in local communities limit the impact of HRBADs, but also transform HRBADs in the process of being rolled out. On the other hand, the paradoxical position of translators and the partial rights subjectivity raise the question of whether and where to strike a balance between replication and hybridity, or put differently, whether there are limits to transformation of human rights action.

The same question about limits to human rights transformation stands out at the substantive level. Ensor has argued that when organizations introduce a HRBAD, they

> must consider whether they are imposing a version of the "good life" that resonates with their own (often Western, liberal) principles, rather than with the social norms that define the interests of the recipients; whether, indeed, they are knowingly or unknowingly imposing "another form of Eurocentric violence which seeks to normalize a self-serving social vision" [reference omitted]. This is an essential step not only for an intervention to be morally acceptable, but also if it is to be successful in embedding social change. (Ensor 2005, 255–256)

Similarly, Merry has found that "translators are restricted by the discursive fields within which they work. All the translators used human rights discourse, with its reference to international standards and its focus on individual injury and cultural oppression rather than structural violence" (Merry 2006a, 48).

Both authors seem to question the social transformative potential of international human rights norms and principles, and hence open the debate where the anchor of social change strategies is located (i.e., in international legal standards or in "local social forms").[3] For sure, both argue that it is certainly not only located in international legal standards, and that the importance of the local cannot be ignored. This argument begs the question of how much transformation through local infusion the global HRBAD narrative can bear, or in other words, if there is a need to define an "untouchable" normative core that is beyond transformation, and if so, what constitutes that normative core, how can it be identified, and will it ever work as a red line that cannot be crossed? Can an organization use rights language, but not draw on the kind of rights that one can find in human rights law? For example, Women of Zimbabwe Arise (WOZA), a social movement in Zimbabwe that seeks to empower poor women, has asserted "the maternal right to employ 'tough love'" toward the government, that is, the "right to discipline those in power as if they were their children" (Hellum et al. 2013, 39), although such a right is nowhere recognized in human rights instruments. Is such human rights transformation beyond the degree of hybridity that human rights can bear, and if so, why and on which grounds? And what are the implications of this kind of hybridization of the human rights framework?

An even more challenging example may be that of female genital mutilation (FGM). Ensor has argued that "when such a crucial aspect of identity is the target of the intervention, tackling it via prescriptive, judgmental rights language risks closing down opportunities for change" (Ensor 2005, 269). Although from a human rights law perspective FGM is considered harmful, physically and psychologically, it is often (though not always) also part of a rite that marks the transition to womanhood and/or marriageability (Vandenhole 2012). That ambiguity and tension may make it difficult or even counterproductive to simply replicate international human rights standards at the local level, for example, by insisting on criminalization and prosecution. But how much hybridity can human rights (law) bear on this issue? In a recent joint general recommendation/general comment, the Committee on the Elimination of Discrimination against Women and the Committee on the Rights of the Child have argued that "the effective prevention and elimination of harmful practices require the establishment of a well-defined, rights-based and locally-relevant holistic strategy which includes supportive legal and policy measures, including social measures that are combined with a commensurate political commitment and accountability at all levels" (CEDAW and CRC 2014, para. 32). Whereas the acknowledgment of the need for a locally relevant strategy may indicate that some space is left for transformation and hybridity, it is not spelled out what that could mean, and within which limits that should happen. Given the committees' emphasis on the inflexibility or non-negotiability of the substantive international human rights norms in this regard, there seems to be no space for condoning the practice at the level of principle, but only for adapting the responses.

Instead of criminalization of FGM, a local practice in Kenya has been suggested as a more fruitful approach. MYWO, a national women's organization,[4] fears that outlawing the practice will drive it underground rather than root it out. MYWO therefore focuses on awareness-raising and the introduction of alternative initiation rites. These rites are said to maintain the cultural and social significance of female circumcision while doing away with the practice itself (Mohamud, Ringheim, Bloodworth, and Gryboski 2002). This strategy represents a recognition of local communities' traditions and values, and hence is believed to be more effective in addressing FGM. Although the impact of this alternative strategy on international (human rights) practice has been quite limited so far (Vandenhole 2012, 89–90), it could potentially inspire HRBADs in this area by shifting the focus from the introduction of repressive legislation and prosecution to the promotion of alternative initiation rites. But even if alternative initiation rites were to be infused at the global level as an appropriate response to FGM, questions would remain regarding how much transformation the global HRBAD narrative can take, in particular with regard to its anchor in human rights law. To what extent have girls themselves been involved and participated in the development and implementation of these rites? Does the acceptance of the need for initiation rites reflect the acceptance of power relations in local communities, or are girls themselves strongly in favor of these rites? These questions reemphasize points that I made earlier about the importance of participation in human rights travel, but also of systematic power analysis in processes of human rights transformation.

In sum, NGOs that introduce a HRBAD may face a tension between the normativity principle (bringing in human rights *law*) and cultural and religious practices that seem difficult to reconcile with that body of law: child labor; early, child, or forced marriage; unequal gender relations; female genital mutilation, and so on. Should they refrain from "rocking cultural and religious boats" (Chapman 2009, 173)? And more fundamentally, does the basic format of a rights-based approach, in which the individual is the rights holder and the state the duty bearer, stand the test of local relevance and ability to transform without subversion (i.e., in violation of the normative core) on the ground? Gledhill has argued that

> the process of "citizens claiming and the state delivering" will continue to reflect significant differences in the way rights are grounded and in the moral discourses of entitlement that are constructed in different cultural contexts. Even if ideas derived from "advanced liberal" societies in the West actively permeate the public spheres of non-Western countries, they will be resignified by governments and citizens in ways that adapt them to differing institutional arrangements and local understandings. (Gledhill 2009, 34)

In his view, "(i)mportant concerns can therefore be raised about projecting 'rights-based development' as an abstract and universal model that transcends cultural differences and historically specific institutional configurations of state-society relations" (Gledhill 2009, 35). The historical and ideological embeddedness of human rights law may also create its own paradox, in the sense that it may at the same time threaten the local, but also hold a promise for emancipation from forms of oppression (Gledhill 2009, 38). This paradox shows that human rights transformation on a continuum between replication and hybridity raises normative questions on the extent to which human rights transformation can take place without degenerating the very idea of human rights. Is there a core normativity that should be safeguarded from transformation? Are there "good" and "bad" forms of transformation (Merry accepts that some forms of transformation are unacceptable; see the language of "subversion" that she uses: Merry 2006a, 44)? These questions may be impossible to answer in the abstract: it seems to me that in each case, the process of travel and transformation itself may provide some answers, albeit always incomplete and possibly tainted by unequal power relations.

If that is the case, the nature and quality of these travel and transformation processes become of utmost importance. De Feyter's work (2011, 33) on the bottom-up "infusion of best practice or accommodation into regional and international human rights law" may offer some good starting points for further reflection on this. De Feyter focuses primarily on *substantive* transformation, but one could also look at the transformation of *strategies and approaches* such as the HRBADs. How could the global HRBAD narrative be transformed by practices and experiences that originate from the local?

De Feyter has defined localizing human rights mainly as a bottom-up process. He pleads for localizing human rights action and substance of human rights norms, "for the further interpretation and elaboration of human rights norms" (De Feyter 2007, 68). His interest is with allowing human rights to survive and develop into "a global protection tool" as well as with equalizing the relationship between the victims of human rights violations and the human rights movement (De Feyter 2007, 66–67). Clearly, this is about the transformation of human rights. However, he not only seeks to describe what is happening, but also to prescribe what should happen.

Initially, De Feyter and Oré Aguilar firmly defined the itinerary human rights travel had to follow in order to have transformative effects. A chain of actors had to be in place in order to allow local human rights realities to impact on the elaboration of human rights norms. A key role was assigned to the community-based organizations as the first link in the chain (De Feyter 2007, 77; Oré Aguilar 2007). In a subsequent paper on sites of rights resistance, the emphasis on local practice has remained, but the grassroots actor is much more loosely defined than in the 2007 piece. The approach is also less normative and prescriptive (the four links of the chain have disappeared), and there is more emphasis on local accommodation of human rights claims, while the added value of framing claims in human rights language is also dealt with more explicitly. So implicitly, the emphasis seems to have shifted in two ways: transformation is less at the level of standard-setting and more at that of human rights action, and transformation is less globally oriented, but more focused on the local as a site of struggle or resistance (De Feyter 2011). If it is true that "human rights claims originate from a local site" (De Feyter 2011, 14) and the local is the primary site of struggle, future research should be directed to a better understanding of how a balance has been struck at these local sites between hybridization and replication, and between a confrontational and a cooperative strategy, keeping in mind the multiple power dynamics in human rights travel and transformation that were earlier introduced. The next question would be whether these local experiences allow for middle-level generalizations, that is, commonalities that may be instructive in other contexts.

Conclusion

Taking the travel and transformation of human rights seriously in HRBADs, as a form of human rights action, makes eminent sense to improve HRBADs. It may lead to a better understanding of failures and successes of HRBADs; it may bring about a stronger convergence of the human rights and development communities by being less confrontational and less legally normative; and it may infuse the global HRBAD narrative with local practices and hence make it more effective in bringing about change at the grassroots. In other words, the acknowledgment of processes of travel and transformation may "pay off" in the sense that a solid understanding of local social forms may be "used to facilitate change from within" also through a constructive engagement with local power holders (Ensor 2005, 273). This more instrumental acknowledgment of the importance of the local and of processes of travel and transformation echoes De Feyter's concern with improving the local effectiveness of human rights (De Feyter 2011, 37).

But the study of HRBADs through the analytical lenses of travel and transformation may also contribute to a better understanding of these analytical concepts. In particular, when HRBADs are seen as an example of human rights in action, a normative approach seems warranted, in particular with regard to the issue of human rights transformation. It seems that boundaries have to be imposed on the extent to which transformation can occur in order not to subvert the very notion of human rights. Very often, a delicate balancing exercise will be needed between replication (due to the anchorage in human rights law) and hybridization (in order to be meaningful in concrete contexts). Whereas there seems to be a clear need to draw a red line that should not be crossed in any process of transformation, where to draw that red line cannot be defined in the abstract. Drawing that line will need to happen in concrete processes of travel and transformation, hence the need to better understand these processes, in particular by bringing in more explicitly a power analysis.

Notes

1. As explained above, this chapter focuses on externally induced HRBADs. What the change literature has emphasized is that such externally induced HRBADs may be anchored in either the international human rights norms or in local struggles, or in a combination of both.

2. Compare Rottenburg, who has focused "neither [on] the actual development at a particular location nor [on] the construction of a theoretical conceptualization of development . . . but instead on the practices of organizing development cooperation that occur in *interstitial spaces*—neither entirely where the model ostensibly originated nor entirely where it is supposed to be implemented" (2009, xiv).

3. Drawing on Raz, Ensor defines social forms as "shared beliefs, folklore, culture, collectively shared metaphors and the like" (Ensor 2005, 258).

4. MYWO defines itself as "a non-profit voluntary women's organization with a mission to improve the quality of life of the rural communities especially women and youth in Kenya"; retrieved from http://www.mywokenya.org/.

Works Cited

Andreassen, B., and Crawford, G. (Eds.). 2013. *Human Rights, Power and Civic Action. Comparative Analyses of Struggles for Rights in Developing Countries*. London: Routledge.

CEDAW and CRC. 2014. Joint General Recommendation/General Comment No. 31 of the Committee on the Elimination of Discrimination against Women and No. 18 of the Committee on the Rights of the Child on Harmful Practices.

Chapman, J. 2009. "Rights-Based Development: The Challenge of Change and Power for Development NGOs." In *Rights-Based Approaches to Development: Exploring the Potential and Pitfalls*, edited by S. Hickey and D. Mitlin, 165–185. Sterling: Kumarian Press.

Crawford, G., and Andreassen, B. 2013. "Human Rights, Power and Civic Action: Theoretical Considerations." In *Human Rights, Power and Civic Action: Comparative Analyses of Struggles for Rights in Developing Countries*, edited by G. Crawford and B. Andreassen, 1–21. London: Routledge.

Crawford, G., and Anyidoho, N. A. 2013. "Ghana: Struggles for Rights in a Democratizing Context." In *Human Rights, Power and Civic Action: Comparative Analyses of Struggles for Rights in Developing Countries*, edited by G. Crawford and B. Andreassen, 88–119. London: Routledge.

Darrow, M., and Tomas, A. 2005. "Power, Capture, and Conflict: A Call for Human Rights Accountability in Development Cooperation." *Human Rights Quarterly* 27 (2), 471–538.

De Feyter, K. 2007. "Localising Human Rights." In *Economic Globalisation and Human Rights*, edited by W. Benedek, K. De Feyter, and F. Marrella, 67–93. Cambridge: Cambridge University Press.

———. 2011. "Sites of Rights Resistance." In *The Local Relevance of Human Rights*, edited by K. De Feyter, S. Parmentier, C. Timmerman, and G. Ulrich, 11–39. Cambridge: Cambridge University Press.

De Gaay Fortman, B. 2011. *A Political Economy of Human Rights: Rights, Realities and Realization*. London: Routledge.

Ensor, J. 2005. "Linking Rights and Culture—Implications for Rights-Based Approaches." In *Reinventing Development? Translating Rights-Based Approaches from Theory into Practice*, edited by P. Gready and J. Ensor, 254–277. London: Zed Books.

Gledhill, J. 2009. "The Rights of the Rich versus the Rights of the Poor." In *Rights-Based Approaches to Development: Exploring the Potential and Pitfalls*, edited by S. Hickey and D. Mitlin, 31–46. Sterling: Kumarian Press.

Gready, P. 2014. "ActionAid's Human Rights–Based Approach and Its Impact on Organisational and Operational Change." In *Human Rights and Development in the New Millennium: Towards a Theory of Change*, edited by P. Gready and W. Vandenhole, 177–191. London: Routledge.

Gready, P., and Ensor, J. (Eds.). 2005. *Reinventing Development? Translating Rights-based Approaches from Theory into Practice*. London: Zed Books.

Gready, P., and Vandenhole, W. 2014a. *Human Rights and Development in the New Millennium: Towards a Theory of Change*. London: Routledge.

———. 2014b. "What Are We Trying to Change? Theories of Change in Development and Human Rights." In *Human Rights and Development in the New Millennium: Towards a Theory of Change*, edited by P. Gready and W. Vandenhole, 1–26. London: Routledge.

Hellum, A., Derman, B., Feltoe, G., Sithole, E., Stewart, J., and Tsanga, A. 2013. "Rights Claiming and Rights Making in Zimbabwe." In *Human Rights, Power and Civic Action: Comparative Analyses of Struggles for Rights in Developing Countries*, edited by G. Crawford and B. Andreassen, 22–54. London: Routledge.

Hickey, S., and Mitlin, D. (Eds.). 2009. *Rights-Based Approaches to Development: Exploring the Potential and Pitfalls*. Sterling: Kumarian Press.

Ife, J. 2010. *Human Rights from Below: Achieving Rights through Community Development*. Cambridge: Cambridge University Press.

Merry, S. E. 2006a. "Transnational Human Rights and Local Activism: Mapping the Middle." *American Anthropologist,* 108 (1), 38–51.

———. 2006b. *Human Rights and Gender Violence: Translating International Law into Local Justice.* Chicago University: Chicago Press.

———. 2006c. "Human Rights, Gender and New Social Movements: Contemporary Debates in Legal Antropology." http://www.ciesas.edu.mx/proyectos/relaju/documentos/merry_sally.pdf

Mohamud, A., Ringheim, K., Bloodworth, S., and Gryboski, K. 2002. "Girls at Risk: Community Approaches to End Female Genital Mutilation and Treating Women Injured by the Practice." In *Reproductive Health and Rights: Reaching the Hardly Reached,* edited by PATH. Washington: PATH.

OHCHR 2006. "Frequently Asked Questions on a Human Rights-Based Approach to Development Cooperation." New York and Geneva: United Nations.

Oré Aguilar, G. 2007. "The Local Relevance of Human Rights: A Methodological Approach." In *The Local Relevance of Human Rights,* edited by K. De Feyter, S. Parmentier, C. Timmerman, and G. Ulrich, 109–146. Cambridge: Cambridge University Press.

Patel, S., and Mitlin, D. 2009. "Reinterpreting the Rights-Based Approach: A Grassroots Perspective on Rights and Development." In *Rights-Based Approaches to Development. Exploring the Potential and Pitfalls,* edited by S. Hickey and D. Mitlin, 107–124. Sterling: Kumarian Press.

Rottenburg, R. 2009. *Far-Fetched Facts: A Parable of Development Aid.* Cambridge, Massachusetts: MIT Press.

"Second Interagency Workshop on Implementing a Human Rights-Based Approach in the Context of UN Reform." Stamford, USA, May 5–7, 2003. Retrieved from http://www.undg.org/archive_docs/2568-2nd_Workshop_on_Human_Rights__Final_Report_-_Main_report.doc.

Vandenhole, W. 2012. "Localising the Human Rights of Children." In *Children's Rights from Below: Cross-Cultural Perspectives,* edited by M. Liebel, K. Hanson, I. Saadi and W. Vandenhole, 80–93. Basingtoke: Palgrave Macmillan.

———. 2014. "Overcoming the Protection Promotion Dichotomy: Human Rights–Based Approaches to Development and Organisational Change within the UN at Country Level." In *Human Rights and Development in the New Millennium: Towards a Theory of Change,* edited by P. Gready and W. Vandenhole, 109–130. London: Routledge.

PART II

Interactions Between Social Mobilization and Legal Claim-Making

CHAPTER 4

Lost Through Translation: Political Dialectics of Eco-Social and Collective Rights in Ecuador

Johannes M. Waldmüller

It is now commonplace that transformations of substance through the translations of rights and human rights–related assessment methods can occur across scales within countries, regions, and globally. In doing so, circulations and transformations may follow several directions simultaneously and involve similar and different actors, concepts, and ways of referring to them. This, necessarily, touches the local and international politics of rights, which, as it is argued here, must be inherently considered in analyses regarding the "localization" (De Feyter et al. 2011; Goodale 2007; Aguilar 2011), "vernacularization" (Merry 2006b, 2009), "translation" (Waldmüller 2014b; Merry and Wood 2015), and "upstreaming" (De Gaay Fortman 2011) of rights. The politics of rights always involves the establishment of hierarchies and the prioritization of values, actors, methods, and claims. In this way, certain aspects are highlighted, while others (whether purposely or unconsciously) are set aside together with the associated implications. In other words, while some are made visible and others become invisible, human rights–based claims of (in)justice also become transformed.

It is this dialectic process of politics and transformations, inherent to any translation (Vázquez 2011), which this chapter seeks to discern with regard to seemingly contradictory Ecuadorian human rights politics in the recent past. For this purpose I draw on extensive ethnographic fieldwork (including participant observations and over 150, partly repeated, interviews with academics, public officials, representatives of social movements, as well as local and international NGOs) between 2010 and 2015 in the country, focusing primarily on the nation-level implementation of an international methodology for human rights indicators. My role and position has initially been that of an independent academic observer who traced translation processes from UN headquarters to the implementing periphery, where I immersed myself in new cultural, social, and political contexts while gradually establishing lasting relations with my key interlocutors. Later on I became partly more involved, as a lecturer, human rights activist, and occasional consultant in Ecuador, but also as a "translator" of locally translated human rights content back to international levels through my publications and public presentations. I am thus aware that my own gradual involvement and learning co-configure and shape what I discuss as dialectic translations, transformations, and possible omissions.

In the following, I analyze two cases related to extractive industries—one domestic, one international—that are both grounded in the same normative-legal framework of the country. While in the former opponents of a state-led mining project invoke rights of nature, the right to protest, and the integrity of ecosystems and communities, in the latter the government of Ecuador invokes similar rights, selectively reinterpreted and thus transformed, to push internationally for the regulation of transnational corporations. In this process of upstreaming a localized understanding of resistance-related human rights to the international level, something important happens with regard to power inequality: distinctive meanings and notions of rights and rights bearers, in the former case referring to ecosystems and group rights, go by the board and become reinterpreted mainly as claims to financial compensation and political responsibility, as we will see. These "leftovers" do not simply disappear, however. Instead, they become (violently) "invisibilized." This reveals a deeply political and thus power-related dimension of such translational processes. Suggesting a dialectical perspective for analyzing such political transformations, this chapter therefore addresses the residue, or "erasure" (Vázquez 2011), resulting from translating and transforming human rights across scales and actors. Why and how does this occur? Is it ever possible to avoid these erasures completely? And if so, why do power-contesting actors at different scales continue to adopt human rights discourses despite the risk of erasures?

Extractive Industries, Collective Damages, and Regulation

Ecuador, 2014: Soon after the arrest of community leader Javier Ramirez in May 2014, the military violently forced its way into the community of Junín located in the Northern Intag region (Canton Carchi), as previously attempted in September 2006. Its goal was to enforce a dubious law that, under the pretext of the right to national development, permits the national mining enterprise, ENAMI EP, to conduct copper mining explorations in the Junín area for a period of six years. For ten months Javier Ramirez was imprisoned, until his eventual acquittal of the highly political charges of terrorism and sabotage and the reinstatement of his lawful freedom (see Álvarez 2015). He was, nevertheless, later found guilty of certain minor crimes under laws adopted to repress social protest. Between 2006 and 2014, the entire Intag region was militarized and its eco-social resistance movement against the mining project, which had been enduring the struggle for more than 20 years,[1] was undercut by state-led so-called "socialization programs," leading communities to disunite in the face of economic promises and repression. In fact, a campaign of repression and defamation was spearheaded by the former Ecuadorian president, Rafael Correa, who continued to ridicule the protesters for weeks and disseminated incorrect information about them in his weekly TV show (Álvarez 2015).

Yet, all this happened in a country acclaimed for its progressive politics as well as its far-reaching and comprehensive 2008 constitution, including vanguard rights of nature (Gudynas 2009), encompassing legal means to ensure the right to resistance, social protest, and rights to free prior consultation. How can such a blatant discrepancy between international acclamation and domestic politics be explained? Providing an answer becomes all the more troubling in light of the fact that all actors involved claimed similar rights, apparently translating and transforming them in different ways. Around the same time as the violent events in Intag in 2014, Ecuadorian diplomacy in Geneva pushed for the establishment of an international expert working group to elaborate a new binding human rights instrument for regulating transnational corporations.

As I am going to trace here, a driving force behind Ecuadorian diplomatic efforts has been the Chevron-Texaco pollution in the Ecuadorian Amazon and subsequent international litigation cases that Ecuadorians have led against the U.S.-based oil corporation for more than 20 years.[2] Allegedly,

Chevron-Texaco had left major devastation and pollution in their wake in the area of Sucumbíos, causing thousands of cases of severe illness and permanent secondary cultural and social damage within the local population and the ecosystem.[3] Since then, indigenous Amazonian communities had been at the forefront of promoting what eventually became the new national paradigm in 2008—*sumak kawsay* in Kichwa, or *Buen Vivir* ("good living") in Spanish (see Gudynas 2011). Buen Vivir replaced the goal of national development with its adoption in both the constitution of 2008 and subsequent national development plans. It promotes an Andean vision of eco-social progress based on values such as correspondence, complementarity, and reciprocity between humans and nature. However, the Ecuadorian government does have a questionable record of implementing Buen Vivir as an overarching paradigm. Yet this framework also partly informs the Ecuadorian efforts to foster a legal device for dealing with eco-social damage (as in the Amazon) caused by transnational corporations in countries other than where they are registered. However, as we will see, it uses a reduced and selective reading of Buen Vivir that fits its purposes, related to increased mining and extraction activities. In this sense, while the Ecuadorian government advocates individual human rights at the international level, the domestic reality within the country is in stark contrast to these efforts. Here, the government, supposedly acting in the name of development to overcome poverty, becomes an important protagonist of an unlawful and potentially destructive path that subordinates individual rights to the right to development.[4]

Concrete transformations happen by certain ways of translation, which require cautious examination. It is thus far from clear at the outset where, also within governments, the power to shape norm-related discourses and legal regimes of human rights is located. Thinking about micro and macro dimensions of localization requires us to take partial and entire overlaps as well as possible collusions of interests and interpretations into account, as in the example of Latin American and international human rights frameworks and their corresponding methodologies. Therefore we have to ask: How can we approach such complexities of different levels of localization with regard to transformations of human rights? What, ultimately, is each of the human rights envisioned by different actors at different levels in these cases?

In order to address these issues, I will first present the case of human rights indicators—an international methodology for monitoring the human rights situation within countries—that became implemented and thus localized (that is, transplanted from the international headquarters to a national government) in Ecuador mainly between 2009 and 2013. I will then return to the abovementioned paradoxes regarding historical human rights violations in the Amazon, committed by foreign and national companies, and their diverging repercussions for contemporary struggles inside and outside Ecuador. In order to analyze them, let me introduce three crucial, and explicitly political, dimensions to the discussion on localized human rights law, norms, and methods (indicators, for example), which bear particular importance for postcolonial contexts.

First, from a Western perspective of law and social studies we tend to overlook the dependency of humans, and *mutatis mutandis* of human rights, on "socionatural" (Castree and Braun 2001) dimensions (ecological conditions, socioenvironmental impacts and conflicts, etc.). Second, the dominant liberal version of individualized human rights—a general orientation that can be observed in contemporary human rights regimes (Hinkelammert 2004; Tully 2007; Mignolo 2013)—still tends to neglect the full implications of the political and civil right to self-determination, that is, collective or group civil and political rights (Jordan 2008). Third, and more empirically speaking, cases presented under the header "localizing human rights" in fact refer chiefly to postcolonial states, with their emphasis more often than not on the "colonial," rather than on the "post" related aspects. In other words, neither frontiers nor domestic (political and/or economic) power and equality constellations have seen large shifts since independence or proclamation of these states. Although rarely thoroughly reflected, these three elements combined point to the problematic nature of postcolonial governments as duty bearers of human rights and therefore also of human rights translations, transformations, and erasures. The reason is more often than not related to the assumed state ownership of territories, and in particular subsoil territories, which frequently delimit both the full realization of collective civil and political rights and the protection of ecosystems from the outset. These contextual dimensions are therefore also crucial when discussing the Ecuadorian case presented here. Current approaches defining the local level as the "lowest unit of devolving power being appropriate for a particular goal" (Aguilar 2011) have their merit in an analytical sense. However, broader, long-standing, and deeply engrained global—while at the same time local (Merry 2006a; De Feyter 2007)—power structures, for example with regard to human rights as such, should not be overlooked, particularly not when it comes to translations in the context of epistemic violence (Vázquez 2011).

Human Rights Indicators and Varying Levels of Localization

Following long-standing discussions on how to better bridge development and human rights work at the international and local level, the UN OHCHR developed an all-encompassing methodology for human rights indicators (HRIs)[5] between the years 2000 and 2012. These HRIs were designed according to typical management performance indicators (Merry 2016), particularly familiar in the field of public health. They envisioned enabling governments and civil society to monitor the human rights situation in their countries as a requirement for better international assessments during the common Universal Periodic Review (UPR) sessions. At the same time they should lead to improved data recompilation at the national levels. In addition, HRIs were supposed to "mainstream" a human rights focus in national and regional statistics, foster cross-institutional cooperation, and empower citizens to demand government fulfillment of their rights (Waldmüller 2014c).

Generally, HRIs are designed in such a way as to assess each internationally guaranteed human "right to . . ." individually, by means of so-called structural, process, and outcome indicators. Neither ecosystemic thinking nor the environment has a place in the highly anthropocentric and utilitarian rationale of HRIs, which, moreover, foresee no methodology to assess group rights at all (see UN OHCHR 2012). The first two countries to have implemented HRIs were Mexico, starting in 2008–2009, and Ecuador, as of 2009–2010. It should be noted that both countries worked solely with the methodology elaborated by the UN OHCHR, although the regional Inter-American Commission on Human Rights had developed its own, slightly diverging, methodology around the same time (IACHR 2008). While in the Mexican case, the UN OHCHR office elaborated HRIs only at the federal state level, in the case of Ecuador, an attempt was made to implement HRIs for at least 12 selected human rights at the national level at once. The Mexican case resulted in a series of publications, acting as a form of exemplary localization—from the international methodology to implementation guidelines and practice models in Spanish for the entire region—that has been used to counsel and support other countries' experiences with HRI implementations.[6] I will now turn to the case of HRIs in Ecuador. The remarkable effect there with regard to HRIs has been somewhat antithetic to the Mexican case. HRIs were never actually implemented (as of yet), although they acted as very specific "filters" of a local understanding of human rights that was recently promoted at the international level.

Translating Human Rights into Eco-Social Rights

This section briefly recounts the implementation of HRIs in Ecuador, a country in the midst of multiple transitions: having witnessed a serious breakdown of Ecuador's economy and political system throughout the 1980s and 1990s (see Lauderbaugh 2012; Becker 2007; Ayala Mora 1989), former president Rafael Correa's Alianza País has followed a "post-neoliberal" (Macdonald and Ruckert 2009; Bebbington and Bebbington-Humphreys 2011) and "neo-extractivist" path (Veltmeyer and Petras 2014) since 2006–2007. While this path, self-styled as a "citizens' revolution," is characterized by manifold social and environmental conflicts, largely owing to the strict hierarchical top-down homogenization of centralized state governance and increasing legal persecution of political, social, indigenous, and environmental movements (Dávalos 2014b; CEDHU, Acción Ecológica, and INREDH 2011), it is likewise characterized by comparably stable state institutions. These are based on partly nonconformist, novel legal approaches and political concepts. After his landslide victory in 2006–2007, Correa dissolved the national parliament and established the Asamblea Nacional (National Assembly) as well as the Asamblea Constituyente (Constituent Assembly) that elaborated the Constitution of 2008 (see Asamblea Constituyente 2008), still in force today. This constitution is based on the following five pillars: (1) Buen Vivir (good living in harmony) as a state ideology and goal, drawing on the Kichwa indigenous concept and worldview of *sumak kawsay*;[7] (2) "plurinationality" and (3) "interculturality" (both the latter being longstanding indigenous demands); (4) human rights as the highest normative and legal principles together with (5), a global legal novelty, rights of nature (*derechos de la naturaleza*; see Art. 13, 15, 281–285, 304, 318, 410, 413, 423 of the Constitution; Asamblea Constituyente 2008). Importantly, these rights are explicitly placed at the same legal-hierarchical level in the constitution as human rights (Ávila 2011; Acosta and Martínez 2011).

It is against this general backdrop that in the year 2009 Ecuador was the first country worldwide to start implementing human rights indicators at the national level. At the launch of the project, the general aim was to develop HRIs for all human rights equally, but it shifted gradually toward blending them with Buen Vivir indicators in order to continuously monitor the improvement of human rights through public policies. In 2009 a local cross-institutional expert group started to work on human rights indicators as part of larger reforms in the juridical sector. The project's name, SIIDERECHOS (Sistema Integral de Indicadores de Derechos Humanos), emerged soon after. Due to the heavy emphasis on consolidated state planning and investment to bring about Buen Vivir (see SENPLADES 2009, 2013)—understood *inter alia* as the gradual realization and constant monitoring of all human rights, including a few additional rights—SIIDERECHOS was equally embraced by various functionaries at the national Ministry of Justice, Human Rights, and Religious Affairs and the National Secretary for Planning and Development (SENPLADES). Together with the prolific local UN OHCHR office in Quito, in 2011 they set out to promote the already existing methodology of HRIs vis-à-vis the national planning authority, SENPLADES. In early 2012, an initial multiday high-level meeting took place at the UN OHCHR premises in Quito (at which I was present) that assembled all local actors as well as the Latin American regional HRI expert, based in Mexico City.

The role of the regional UN OHCHR HRI expert for Latin America was crucial in terms of "brokerage" (Bierschenk, Chaveau, and Olivier de Sardan 2002; Lewis and Mosse 2006): her task was to mediate between local decision-makers and international experts based mainly at the UN OHCHR headquarters in Geneva. This included reporting on the progress and shortcomings of projects, while forging trust and commitment among local officials in various Latin American countries across cultural contexts. Given this sensitive setting, the lowest common denominator for this brokerage to be successful has been to insist chiefly on technical compliance and methodological rigor. In this way, HRIs become, in a quite unidirectional sense, translated from the HRI methodology of the international headquarters toward local applications but rarely vice versa (e.g., local experiences shaping international designs; see also Waldmüller 2014b, 2014c), which reveals serious weaknesses with regard to the upstreaming of local human rights understandings and methodologies.

In mid-2012, the head of the Ecuadorian Human Rights Sub-Secretariat became responsible for SIIDERECHOS and, as such, the main interface between various data-collecting and processing institutions, SENPLADES (to obtain funding for SIIDERECHOS), the local UN OHCHR office, and national, regional, and international experts. The decisions forwarded by the Sub-Secretariat preceded communication exchanges over several months that hinged on the input of technical experts, for example on the elaboration of a five-year funding proposal to SENPLADES. An important decision was to determine goals and targets for SIIDERECHOS in accordance with the regional HRIs expert.

It soon became clear that the international UN OHCHR methodology of 2012, upon which experts had insisted, would not satisfy the perceived needs of the Ecuadorian civil servants engaged in the project. According to some, the constitution appeared to be "more advanced with regard to rights" than the international human rights framework itself.[8] As SIIDERECHOS was a national project, it was therefore suggested that it should instead monitor and measure any (non)progress with regard to the national/constitutional rights framework (embedded within the international framework) in order to be "useful for any Ecuadorian public authority," as one interlocutor at the statistics department of SENPLADES stated.[9] In other words, it was suggested that the constitutional legal framework should primarily be applied in order to "envelop" international human rights standards—and not vice versa, as initially projected by the UN OHCHR. In late 2012, it was also decided to deviate broadly from the international methodology and to develop structural and process indicators for all assessed rights together, instead of elaborating them on the basis of single rights. This step was justified by highlighting the interlocked nature of human rights that were addressed by various policies prescribed in the national Buen Vivir plans. In early 2013, based on academic input and facilitated by changes in staff at the Ministry for Justice and Human Rights, some influential discussions took place. The former SIIDERECHOS project leader had been recently replaced by a new manager who also supported basing HRIs on the Buen Vivir legal framework of the country. This was inspiring for some consultants, academics, and public officials who argued in favor of adopting a biocentric perspective on SIIDERECHOS, as expressed in Buen Vivir principles, and for others who simply demanded national ownership of the SIIDERECHOS project. Inspired by anti-imperialist rhetoric and the international Yasuní-ITT initiative (see Rival 2012; Le Quang 2016), a biocentric take on international governance got wind in the sails of Ecuador's administration. Perhaps also as repercussion of President Correa's frequent attacks on the Inter-American human rights system, criticisms could suddenly be perceived in the hallways of the ministry that human rights would be overly "anthropocentric," monocultural, reductionist, and, importantly, would not take human-nature relationships and ecosystems sufficiently into account. Both national Buen Vivir plans and discussions about postextractivism have in fact led to the adoption of a strong eco-social, biocentric, or "socionatural" (Castree and Braun 2001) perspective in describing social, political, and economic change as well as possible policy solutions (Waldmüller 2014b). At stake in the resolution of this profoundly epistemological debate was a radically different vision than that of the UN OHCHR: in the international methodology, HRIs are essentially modeled after common development indicators and oriented along mainstream economic models of assessment. In addition, they prescribe a structure and vision of development that follows the approaches of specified development algorithms ("getting the parameters just right") toward a certain desired outcome (see also Apthorpe 1996; Gasper 2000; Merry 2013b). HRIs, as they are currently designed, are in fact highly reductionist: for instance, the question of indigenous, collective, or group rights, or the relationship between governmental realization of economic, social, and cultural rights and the famous obligation to do so "to the maximum of available resources" (Fukuda-Parr and Ely Yamin 2015, 23, 28, 41), which explicitly hints at human-nature interactions, are simply disregarded. Nature, commons, collectives, and all sorts of resources are merely subsumed into this assumed process of change, regarded as subsequent to consciously made choices by humans. This is all the more questionable for a country considered to be a "megadiverse hotspot of fauna and flora" and economically dependent on exploitation and exportation of natural resources (crude oil, mining), agriculture, and fishery products (see Dávalos 2013; Moore and Velasquez 2012).

Given this paramount dependence on nature and its inherent transitions, the Buen Vivir–inspired accusation of anthropocentrism regarding human rights becomes meaningful in the Ecuadorian context. Anthropocentrism is commonly defined as the position "that considers man as the central fact, or final aim, of the universe" and generally "conceiv[es] of everything in the universe in terms of human values" (Watson, 1983, 245). Within and around SIIDERECHOS, it was therefore argued that a biocentric (Agar 1997; Sterba 2011) version of human rights measurement should not be centered on the human individual but should instead take people's encompassing environments as their starting point. This way HRIs became at the same time translated, localized, altered, repoliticized, and essentially expanded by public officials and intellectuals. During this process, human rights parlance was extended to nonhuman, or "Earth beings" (de la Cadena 2010), as in the case of the "vulnerability" of volcanoes or coastal shores. I have analyzed elsewhere (Waldmüller 2014b) how HRI became transformed under the impact of such a state-sponsored biocentric perspective.[10]

For this chapter, however, I am more interested in analyzing the causes that made this particular transformation through localized translation possible. What I am arguing here is that it is associated with the extreme destruction caused by extraction activities in the Amazon decades before the adoption of the current constitution. As previous research suggests (Becker 2011, 2012), the emergence of the Buen Vivir paradigm and rights of nature is, inter alia, linked to the massive pollution caused by Chevron-Texaco in the Ecuadorian Amazon, from which mainly Kichwa indigenous communities have gravely suffered (Rival 2012). It has been the Kichwa community of Sarayaku in the Amazon that—despite not having been directly affected by the destruction left by this U.S. company—is frequently cited as having made one of the earliest references to and descriptions of this paradigm (Viteri 1993, 2002; Altmann 2013a, 2013b). It later found its way, via the detour of international cooperation in Ecuador and Bolivia, into the catalogue of claims issued by the largest indigenous organizations in Ecuador, CONAIE and ECUARUNARI. These claims, linking human rights violations to violations of eco-social dimensions, were eventually taken up by the Constituent Assembly and adopted in 2008. This suggests that in the case of HRIs in Ecuador, a very local, yet long-standing,[11] "vernacularization of human rights" (Merry 2006b, 39)—linking human rights to nature rights and the protection of life—became significant for the way human rights became generally framed in the country.

With regard to HRIs it is important to stress, therefore, that one influential local understanding of human rights is inherently related to indigenous collective rights, self-determination, and an ecological dimension in the sense of protecting human life by protecting natural life and its ecological sources (water, land, food, etc.). However, the current government has assumed a strong role in the litigation between indigenous claimants and Chevron-Texaco, for instance by launching a worldwide campaign against the company.[12] Overall, adopting HRI in Ecuador can be regarded, as I argued here, as a first instance of transformation, facilitated in negotiations between state and international officials (UN staff and international consultants): one of integrating an international methodology that became gradually imbued with local discourses, perspectives, and values until finally the international methodology was itself altered.

In the next section I will show that the shared historical experience for the understanding of human rights norms has equally been promoted back to the international level; it includes a second instance of transformation. The promotion of a new international human rights document (whether a declaration or treaty remains to be seen), as mentioned earlier, can be interpreted as being essentially inspired by rights-based claims with regard to extractive industries. However, some crucial elements of the first transformation of human rights and HRIs to the local level seem to be absent from this second and simultaneous instance of translation back to the international level. In fact, a different translation of human rights took place, again filtered through the government; one that permits government to effectively capitalize on the emerging erasure between the first and the second instance in order to push its own agenda.

Overlapping Transformations, Erasures, and the Postcolonial "Cunning State"

It was stated earlier that transformations through translations of human rights norms, tools, and methods sometimes occur in parallel, partly overlapping and across scales, which involves the—sometimes dirty—politics of human rights. The following sections provide a concrete example of how such processes may play out and offers both a tentative explanation and additional perspective for methodologically approaching such issues.

While concerned institutions of the Ecuadorian administration substantially altered the international HRI methodology during the period of local implementation between 2009 and 2014 and litigation had been continuing against Chevron-Texaco since 1993, the Ecuadorian delegation to the United Nations used its position in the Human Rights Council as of 2014 to push for a new human rights instrument.[13] The legal device envisaged would regulate and sanction the conduct of transnational corporations (see Human Rights Council 2014; de Schutter 2014) operating on foreign territories. More precisely, the goal of this initiative was to generate a political and legal hold over those corporations that violate human rights when extraterritorially active and where the governments of the states where these corporations are registered are not able or willing to pursue legal prosecution. In my view, the Ecuadorian initiative should be seen in the light of the Buen Vivir paradigm enshrined in the Ecuadorian constitution that stipulates, inter alia, rights of nature, food sovereignty (Fairbairn 2010), and rights to free prior informed consultation (Art. 57), including the possibility of withholding consent. As described above, the emergence of this paradigm and its adoption into the constitution can be seen as related to the country's catastrophic experiences with foreign oil companies, which had devastated both indigenous and nonindigenous communities. These experiences have fostered and consolidated the national indigenous movement, which succeeded in becoming an important political actor in the 1990s and even an initial partner of then-President Correa's Alianza País movement (Becker 2011; Walsh 2010; Acosta and Martínez 2009; Gudynas 2011; Altmann 2014). Crucially, Buen Vivir links human rights and well-being to the well-being of ecosystems and the environment. Yet, these aspects were stripped off from the international initiative, permitting the government to capitalize on this erasure both to the detriment of social movements' claims and the substance of human rights themselves.

What Ecuador is pushing for at the international level is a new human rights instrument to enable governments and the international community to regulate transnational corporations that appear "too powerful and cunning to be effectively controlled by their governments."[14] This, in my view, second instance of transformation—the upstreaming of an understanding of eco-human rights protection to the international level—aims at the creation of three main legal devices that, according to its protagonists, should go beyond the Guiding Principles of Business and Human Rights to (1) clarify the question of extraterritorial responsibility, (2) grant all victims access to the national legal system where corporations are based (for claiming compensation), and (3) obligate all implicated parties to establish fair conduct principles respecting priorities according to the legal setup of the country where a corporation operates.[15] Within this parallel process of transforming a shared horizon of affected communities by international extraction business (which became essential for Buen Vivir) into international human rights claims, an important shift occurs.

The main rationale behind this initiative appears to be the creation of a mechanism for international legal recourse that would enable the victims of disastrous business conduct in one country to claim financial redress in the country where corporations are formally based. Beyond questions of legal applicability and feasibility (after all, it's still the local governments that have the obligation to protect their citizens from transnational businesses' wrongdoing; see de Schutter 2014), it is striking that substantial parts of the first instance of transformation, in the case of HRIs, have partly or completely fallen away by this stage. There is no longer reference to rights of nature, to *Pachamama* (Mother Earth), or to the vulnerability of ecosystems and their right to redress, nor to the critique of anthropocentric human rights that would neglect the inherent linkage to territory, water, healthy food, in short life as such, which primarily sustains humans and their conduct. Instead, it is argued that governments are unable to effectively control and regulate the conduct of transnational corporations that they frequently themselves contract. In other words, the semi-parallel circulation of a local understanding of human rights between national and international levels seems to lead to a transformation of substance. This erasure becomes tangible on its way to an economistic translation, spearheaded by government actors, at the international level.

While being based on shared historical experience and political demands emerging therefrom, the divergent paths at different levels of human rights localization in practice is notable. It is therefore necessary to take the context into account for a moment. The case of Ecuador is paradigmatic in this sense for the ambiguous role postcolonial governments tend to play in the era of a "postdemocratic" (Crouch 2004) Anthropocene. Despite its encompassing domestic legal protection framework,[16] the Correa administration has continuously promoted the expansion of frontiers for the extraction of what is called "natural resources." A major example is the withdrawal of the Yasuní-ITT initiative (Burbano et al. 2011) and the subsequent opening of oil explorations in the Amazonian Yasuní national park, one of the most biodiverse places in the world, despite a constitutional prohibition (Rival 2012). As of 2013, faced with declining oil prices and financial obligations to China, the Ecuadorian government began to heavily promote large-scale mining, a complete novelty for the country (Moore and Velasquez 2012). While more than 90 percent of capital investment in Ecuador's nascent mining sector stems from Canadian companies (CEDHU and FIDH 2010, 7), the state itself became highly involved and established its own public national mining company. There is a wealth of documentary evidence to support accusations of persistent human rights violations that have been brought against the large-scale mining activities of Chinese, Canadian, Chilean, and national companies (complex business constructions often make it difficult to identify the exact ownership and funding of mining projects), both in the south (CEDHU and FIDH 2010; Sacher et al. 2015) and north of the country (Waldmüller 2015; Latorre, Walter, and Larrea 2015). In an inherently still colonial world economy—extraction and exportation of natural resources in the global South, import and export of manufactured quality goods in the global North—postcolonial governments tend to act cunningly in a limited margin of maneuvers, which includes trade-offs between (human, ecosystemic, etc.) sacrifices and progressive rhetoric.

In response to these difficulties, social protest has become increasingly criminalized and defenders of human and nature rights are frequently faced with intimidation and violence (Plan V 2015; CEDHU, Acción Ecológica, and INREDH 2011). As mentioned earlier, an important case in point is that of Javier Ramirez, who led the community protests against the governmental showcase mining project in the Intag region (see Álvarez 2015). These projects of increased exploitation of resources are deemed necessary by the government to overcome poverty and achieve national modernization, since, as President Correa famously stated, "we cannot sit like beggars on a sack of gold" (Dávalos 2013). Communal property, indigenous land rights (and claims to land), collective rights, and rights of nature, invoked by anti-extractivism protesters and movements, have thus all become caught in the crossfire of the governmental PR and police apparatus. Social and indigenous protests culminated in violent clashes and countrywide suppression at the end of August 2015 (see Colectivo de Investigación y Acción Psicosocial 2015). As of 2016, it seems that the genuine Buen Vivir paradigm has become virtually voided—yet, human rights in particular have remained a highly contested subject in the country (Waldmüller 2014b), serving as a discursive platform for including all sorts of claims against the government.

How can the international proposal by Ecuador, which draws on local experiences and interpretations, be interpreted while being inconsistent with the business operations launched within the country that are in clear opposition to its own proposal? How can this particular double-localization of human rights be approached in a more analytical sense than simply ascribing it to human rights politics? It seems that the Ecuadorian example falls within the range of what postcolonial scholar Shalini Randeria diagnosed in the case of India (and not for human rights but general politics), that is, a paradigmatic expression of the "cunning state" (Randeria 2007). According to her, states are nowadays not simply weakening or losing sovereignty, as it would seem in the way the Ecuadorian government portrays its situation vis-à-vis international corporations: "The state is not merely a victim of neo-liberal economic globalization as it remains an active agent in transposing it nationally and locally" (Randeria 2003a, 28). Furthermore, states do so, as the author demonstrates through her works, by being "cunning," since they "capitalize on their perceived weakness in order to render themselves unaccountable both to their citizens and to international institutions" (Randeria 2003b, 306). In other words, and as an inverse version of Putnam's well-known two-level game theory (Putnam 1988), governments and public administration seek, for example, to escape international regulations by playing off the demands of their citizens against those of the international community. Applying Randeria's analysis to our case permits acknowledgment of a double twist: Ecuador introduced a new human rights monitoring mechanism that should supposedly assess the compliance of all national public policies with human rights. But instead of making itself a subject of this mechanism, the government incorporated long-standing locally grounded claims to life protection, framed in human rights language, to alter and twist the international methodology to such an extent that it in fact never became implemented in the country. At the same time its earlier role as human rights vanguard permitted the government to push a different, yet entangled, agenda at the international level to help it get a better hold on transnational corporations active in the country. However, instead of pushing for an international working group on, for example, international rights of nature or ecosystemic human rights, the main goal has been (so far) to hold those countries where these corporations are based financially accountable instead of reinforcing the government's own protection mechanism for its citizens.

Seen this way, the local translation of human rights, as inherently anthropocentric, individualistic, and at the same time (but on a different level) fundamentally neglecting an eco-social, or socionatural, dimension of justice, serves the Ecuadorian government to render itself unaccountable (and thus enables it to point to foreign governments for the paying of indemnifications, as in the case of Chevron-Texaco).[17] Given these politics, should international human rights norms therefore abstain from including local translations and transformations altogether? I think such a view would amount to a misconception of the nature of human rights as such, since human rights were neither generated nor are they managed in a space of cultural vacuum. They have, of course, in a sense always been local. The common accusation against the international human rights regime as being overtly individualistic points in this direction. Indeed, human rights have been, and rightly so, criticized for their overtly liberal outlook and propaganda in recent decades, based on a very particular (Western) image of the human in human rights (see Tully 2007; Hinkelammert 2004; Mignolo 2013). This critique cannot easily be dismissed, and negotiating with, as well as including, different local translations seems the only viable strategy in order to forestall cunning governance of governments. Instrumentalized translations of human rights, including transformation of substance and erasure, can indeed serve governments to render themselves unaccountable within a global architecture of resource-based capitalism (Charvet and Kaczynska-Nay 2008) and therefore required "accumulation by dispossession" (Harvey 2003). Neither sensitive vernacularizing nor locally adapting international human rights norms and procedures necessarily prevents this from happening. It is precisely for this reason that it is crucial to unpack all the different layers of circulation and transformation involved in detail, analyzing the reappropriation of human rights and of the upstreaming of such altered human rights practices and discourses.

Final Reflections

It was stated in the introduction that processes of transformation through translation inevitably involve what seem to be losses or erasures. I want to return to this crucial dimension now, since it weaves our two threads of human rights transformations together. The reason is that there is a tragic side story related to the project of the Ecuadorian delegation pushing for a new international human rights instrument, one being truly local, but largely remaining swept under the rug.

In June 2015, at the 29th session of the Human Rights Council in Geneva, Ecuadorian plaintiffs denounced the role of Chevron-Texaco in silencing and criminalizing testimonies and critical voices during this 22-year-long litigation. Around the same time, the Ecuadorian government doubled its efforts at the diplomatic level in Geneva to push for the new human rights instrument it envisioned. NGOs from all over the world and governments allied with the Ecuadorian proposal closely observed and hoped for a breakthrough toward better regulation of transnational businesses.

At the end of May 2015, a political activist explained to me in Quito the moral dilemma facing him and his organization. The issue was the deployment of a delegation of local Shuar community members to Geneva, planned for the following week. The purpose of this delegation was to render public testimony about the case of the indigenous Shuar leader José Isidro Tendetza Antún, whose dead body was found, showing signs of torture, on December 3, 2014 (see Watts 2014). Tendetza had been highly involved in resisting a Canadian-Chinese mining project in the Ecuadorian province of Zamora. After having suffered severe intimidation, he had supposedly been on his way to Lima to denounce the project before the World Summit on Climate Change and to file a complaint against the company before the International Tribunal for the Rights of Nature in the Peoples' Summit, when he encountered his assassins. Already in 2009 and 2013, two other Shuar leaders opposing the mining project in the region had been killed. Yet, the case of José Tendetza is particular insofar as he had been an active plaintiff against the state of Ecuador claiming rights of nature at the Inter-American Commission on Human Rights (Cortes 2015). The examination of the circumstances of his death is a case still pending with the Ecuadorian authorities—it seems that the state itself has become involved in the deadly oppression of protesters and resistance, protecting precisely those transnational corporations on its own (in fact, on illegally appropriated Shuar) territory (Sacher et al. 2015) that it purports to regulate at the international level. My interlocutor's dilemma was linked to the fact that his delegation would denounce the Ecuadorian government in Geneva at the very same moment as social movements from all over the world were expecting to see an important international move from the Ecuadorian government with regard to Ecuador's human rights proposal. The hazard was that the testimony of the Shuar delegation would undermine the global efforts of the Ecuadorian government, spurring its critics to lay the Ecuadorian hypocrisy bare. Should the Shuar delegation be sent? Should, in the context of seemingly almighty transnational businesses and the cunning states complementing them, the greater global good be treated preferentially to the very local case of a severe violation of human rights? These, admittedly, are not easy questions. While they must remain open for now, Tendetza's case of literal erasure points to complex ethical and political considerations that reflections about human rights transformations have to address beyond empirical documentation. The case of José Tendetza, despite having received international news coverage at the time, has remained largely invisible, or rather, has been made effectively invisible by the politics of filtering and surfacing selected human rights violations between local and international levels.

Summarizing the discussions presented in this chapter, two dimensions of translating human rights between local, national, and international levels are crucial to analyzing how human rights become transformed across scales and times. First, assuming that all that becomes global has previously been local (De Feyter 2011, 14), what are counted among human rights cases are always the results of previous filtering mechanisms. These mechanisms include violations, but also new instruments and norms, methodologies, impacting discussions or highlighted cases. Specific state actors and institutions, perhaps particularly in postcolonial and extracting contexts, are crucial in this process, as they tend to play two-level games, playing off local against international politics and vice versa. In addition, the nature of local UN OHCHR offices, as key information filters within an international network, also can contribute to highlighting certain human rights–related aspects, while making others invisible, which inevitably leads to transformations of human rights understandings. This complexity also involves the competition among regional human rights institutions and regimes, as briefly mentioned with regard to different HRI methodologies, especially when it comes to the use of data, methods, and numbers. It also includes international NGOs, which are faced with human rights politics determining the appropriate moment to surface specific information, as in José Tendetza's tragic case. Therefore, while human rights necessarily become translated and localized all the time, the concrete transformation of their substance is always also embedded within broader contexts and constellations, for example, political interests, appropriate moments in time for different actors, media attention, potential allies, funding, and political cycles.

Focusing ethnographically on (1) transformations between various local and international levels of understanding, (2) especially on specific state institutions as main translating interfaces in this process, and (3) erasures or absences of key parts of the local understanding when governments pick them up and transform them seems crucial for analyzing further how human rights law, norms, and methods become shaped across scales, actors, and regions. By doing so, conditions of state dependency on so-called natural resources in a postcolonial setting deserve particular attention. The reason is that local, indigenous, or social movement–related transformations of human rights claims are frequently directed to both governments and the international level of attention at the same time. This involves, therefore, multiple and parallel translations as strategy to gain attention; and translations always bear the danger of erasures. Accordingly, analyses should take these into account, as they are key to unfolding the various scales where transformations through translations take place simultaneously. Also, local UN OHCHR offices would therefore be required to adopt a less purportedly neutral legalistic perspective and a more critical ethnographical position of inquiry, focusing on the cunning politics of both local movements and governments vis-à-vis the international level. This would, furthermore, represent a first step toward opening up for truly local understandings of human rights.

Second, the notion of "cunningness" might help to explain the particular complexity human rights are facing in postcolonial contexts. As of yet, the group political right to self-determination, as it is enshrined in Article 1 of both the International Covenant on Civil and Political Rights (ICCPR) and the International Covenant on Economic, Social and Cultural Rights (ICESCR), has been realized nowhere in the region. Ubiquitous notions of modernization and development still serve postcolonial (read still inherently colonial) states in the appropriation of indigenous territories, and in particular, subsoil territories that remain outside of human rights legislation and are not subject to full collective control by indigenous peoples (Merino Acuña 2014; Schulte-Tenckhoff 2012). Finally, this points to the necessity, when analyzing human rights transformations, of taking into account that selective treatment of local values and tragic fates can always be a possible route while translating substance across scales. Apparent translational paradoxes may actually serve to capitalize on them by pushing or obscuring certain agendas. The question is therefore precisely which parts get erased, which ones added instead, by whom, and whether this occurs intentionally or not. In the case of both HRIs and the international treatment of transnational corporations, ecosystemic considerations eventually became replaced by an economic calculus of compensation. Such a strategic, and less idealistic, approach was later echoed by the social movements' dilemma regarding the delegation's travel to Geneva. Assuming that strategic, instrumental and cunning treatment of human rights politics also impacts the substance of human rights, it therefore remains to be seen whether localizations of human rights can become disentangled from the strategic-utilitarian considerations between cunning states and the "visibilization" of selected human rights violations.[18]

Notes

1. For an overview of the decades-long struggle of Intag communities, see the blog by Carlos Zorrilla (http://www.decoin.org/ [last accessed October 23, 2015]).

2. See the campaign Chevron Toxico (http://chevrontoxico.com/ [last accessed October 22, 2015]) for an overview.

3. According to local plaintiffs, "Chevron-Texaco has polluted more than 450,000 hectares of one of the richest areas of biodiversity on the planet, destroyed the lives and livelihood of its inhabitants, and caused the death of hundreds of people and a sharp increase in the rate of cancer and other serious health problems. More than 60 billion liters of toxic water were dumped into the rivers and streams, 880 hydrocarbon waste pits were dug, and 6.65 billion cubic meters

of natural gas were burned in the open air" (cf. http://chevrontoxico.com/news-and-multimedia/2015/0618-chevron-denounced-before-the-human-rights-council [last retrieved October 23, 2015]).

4. See Kuosmanen (2015) for a philosophical exploration of this complex terrain. In Latin American contexts, the continued scarification of selected individual rights (and rights of nature) for the sake of an envisioned greater good, justified by invoking the right to development, caricaturizes the common approaches and statements by the United Nations to this relationship.

5. The three UNHCHR standard publications on HRI are: UN OHCHR (2006; 2008; 2012—the latter guide provides the most thorough introduction and methodology). In addition, the Mexican UNHCHR office, the first worldwide to implement HRI projects, has published several detailed reports and guides, including accounts of the implementation of various HRIs in the country. These can be found online, at http://www.hchr.org.mx/ (last retrieved April 27, 2015]. The report focusing on Latin America, summarizing all regional field projects, has recently been published by UN ACNUDH (2013). Further essential texts regarding the evolution of the debate, starting with Barsh (1993), who elaborated on the basic scope of measuring human rights, are: Fröberg (2005); Andersen and Sano (2006); Malhotra and Fasel (2005); McInerney-Lankford and Sano (2010); Merry (2011, 2013a); Hines (2005); Welling (2008); Rosga and Satterthwaite (2009); de Béco (2014); Riedel, Giacca, and Golay (2014); Riedel (2007, 2013) and Merry (2016).

6. So far, Brazil, Bolivia, Paraguay, Argentina, and Colombia also have officially begun to implement HRIs without generalizable or homogenous paths, goals, and success (see UN ACNUDH 2013, published in Mexico, for an overview of all regional projects).

7. *Sumak Kawsay*, roughly translated as "living in harmony all together," refers to value-based spiritual, ecological, collective-social, and normative-individual principles that should ensure a sustainable, biocentric, and harmonious way of life beyond material accumulation, extraction of natural resources, and exploitation of humans or nature. *Sumak Kawsay* is officially translated as *Buen Vivir* (e.g., in the constitution), which became gradually co-opted by the government and voided of any overly spiritual and politically transformative content (Gudynas 2014; Oviedo 2014).

8. Personal communication with the SIIDERECHOS manager at the Sub-Secretariat, July 23, 2012 (Quito).

9. Interview, conducted at SENPLADES, January 2012 (Quito).

10. In short, structural indicators became reinterpreted as topographical indicators, that is, focusing first on rights of ecological zones (mountains, bays, beaches, rivers, etc.). In a second step, human interaction with these zones and among humans themselves (mobility) should be assessed as process indicators. Outcome indicators should evaluate potential risks and probabilities for vulnerability (of both humans and nature).

11. On November 3, 2015 the still ongoing litigation process celebrated its 22nd anniversary.

12. See http://lamanosucia.com/ (last accessed October 23, 2015).

13. Together with Bolivia, Venezuela, Cuba, and South Africa.

14. Statement by Pábulo Fajardo, longtime attorney of Ecuadorian plaintiffs in the Chevron-Texaco case, during a public conference on the matter at the Universidad Andina Simón Bolívar in Quito, October 14, 2015.

15. According to a public presentation by the Ecuadorian delegation to the United Nations in Quito, October 14, 2015.

16. As of 2015, Ecuador has signed and ratified all major human rights treaties and declarations.

17. As a matter of course, reality is more complex than what such a simplistic diagnosis could reveal. The case of Chevron-Texaco in Ecuador has been one of particular "cunningness" and criminalization of plaintiffs also by the company itself; see http://chevrontoxico.com/news-and-multimedia/2015/0618-chevron-denounced-before-the-human-rights-council (last retrieved October 10, 2015).

18. Similar to Agamben's *homo sacer* (1997 [1995]), Hinkelammert has insightfully pointed out that human rights always imply not only some form of hierarchy of rights, precisely because of being translated and transformed by governments that have an agenda, but also their rightful violation against violators—the necessary human sacrifice—in order for human rights to be reaffirmed and valid. For the Latin American context, it thus remains necessary to disentangle the link between governments and the (collective) right to development, which appears to commonly trump the human rights of individuals, nature, or certain groups within the national state that become in this sense "sacrificed" in the name of national progress (see Hinkelammert 1999).

Works Cited

Acosta, Alberto, and Esperanza Martínez, eds. 2009. *El Buen Vivir: Una Vía Para El Desarrollo.* Quito: Abya Yala.

———, eds. 2011. *La Naturaleza Con Derechos: De La Filosofía a La Politica.* Quito: Abya Yala.

Agamben, Giorgio. 1997. *Homo Sacer: Le Pouvoir Souverain et La Vie Nue.* Paris: Seuil.

Agar, Nicholas. 1997. "Biocentrism and the Concept of Life." *Ethics* 108 (1): 147–68.

Aguilar, Gaby Oré. 2011. "The Local Relevance of Human Rights: A Methodological Approach." In *The Local Relevance of Human Rights*, edited by K. De Feyter et al., 109–46. Cambridge: Cambridge University Press.

Altmann, Philipp. 2013a. "Good Life as a Social Movement Proposal for Natural Resource Use: The Indigenous Movement in Ecuador." *Consilience: The Journal of Sustainable Development* 10 (1): 59–71.

———. 2013b. "Plurinationality and Interculturality in Ecuador: The Indigenous Movement and the Development of Political Concepts." *Nordic Journal of Latin American and Carribean Studies* 43 (1–2): 47–66.

———. 2014. *Die Indigenenbewegung in Ecuador Diskurs und Dekolonialität.* Bielefeld: transcript.

Álvarez, Pocho. 2015. *Javier Con I - Intag.* https://vimeo.com/142275677?utm_source=email&utm_medium=clip-transcode_complete-finished-20120100&utm_campaign=7701&email_id=Y2xpcF90cmFuc2NvZGVkfDU5MGZhNWVkOWU1MDI4NGNhNTJiNTQxYTg5MWFlNDNmMjk2fDkwNzEwODF8MTQ0NDc2Nzc1M3w3NzAx.

Andersen, Erik André, and Hans-Otto Sano. 2006. "Human Rights Indicators at Programme and Project Level: Guidelines for Defining Indicators: Monitoring and Evaluation." Copenhagen: Danish Institute for Human Rights.

Apthorpe, Raymond. 1996. "Reading Development Policy and Policy Analysis: On Framing, Naming, Numbering and Coding." In *Arguing Development Policy: Frames and Discourses*, edited by Raymond Apthorpe and Des Gasper. London: Frank Cass.

Asamblea Constituyente. 2008. *Constitución Política de La Republica Del Ecuador.* Montechristi. http://www.asambleanacional.gov.ec/documentos/Constitucion-2008.pdf.

Ávila, Ramiro S. 2011. "El neoconstitucionalismo transformador. El estado y el derecho en la Constitutión de 2008." Quito: Abya-Yala.
Ayala Mora, Enrique. 1989. *Nueva Historia Del Ecuador*. Quito: Corporación Editora Nacional.
Barsh, R. L. 1993. "Measuring Human Rights: Problems of Methodology and Purpose." *Human Rights Quarterly* 15 (1): 87–121.
Bebbington, A., and D. Bebbington-Humphreys. 2011. "An Andean Avatar: Post-Neoliberal and Neoliberal Strategies for Securing the Unobtainable." *New Political Economy* 15 (4): 131–45.
Becker, Marc. 2007. "Indigenous Struggles for Land Rights in Twentieth-Century Ecuador." *Agricultural History Society* Spring: 159–81.
———. 2011. "Correa, Indigenous Movements, and the Writing of a New Constitution in Ecuador." *Latin American Perspectives* 38 (1): 47–62.
———. 2012. "Building a Plurinational Ecuador: Complications and Contradictions." *Socialism and Democracy* 26 (3): 72–92. https://doi.org/10.1080/08854300.2012.710000.
Bierschenk, Thomas, J. P. Chaveau, and J. P. Olivier de Sardan. 2002. "Local Development Brokers in Africa: The Rise of a New Social Category." Working Paper 13. Department of Anthropology and African Studies. Mainz: Johannes Gutenberg University.
Burbano, Rafael, Fander Falconi, Carlos Larrea, and Maria Christina Vallejo. 2011. "La Iniciativa Yasuní-ITT Desde Una Perspectiva Multicriterial." Quito: UNDP.
Castree, Noel, and B. Braun. 2001. *Social Nature: Theory, Practice, and Politics*. Malden, MA: Blackwell.
CEDHU, Acción Ecológica and INREDH. 2011. "Informe Sobre Criminalización a Defensores de Derechos Humanos Y de La Naturaleza." In *Informe Sobre Derechos Humanos: Ecuador 2011*, edited by Programa Andino de Derechos Humanos, 141–42. Quito: R. F. Ediciones.
CEDHU and FIDH. 2010. "Large-Scale Mining in Ecuador and Human Rights Abuses: The Case of Corriente Resources Inc." Quito: Comisión Ecuménica de Derechos Humanos / International Federation for Human Rights / Rights and Democracy.
Charvet, John, and Elisa Kaczynska-Nay. 2008. *The Liberal Project and Human Rights: The Theory and Practice of a New World Order*. New York: Cambridge University Press.
Colectivo de Investigación y Acción Psicosocial. 2015. "Informe Preliminar Sobre Las Estrategias Estatales de Control Social Y Represión En El Marco Del Paro Nacional En Ecuador." Quito: Colectivo Investigación y Acción Psicosocial.
Cortes, Paula. 2015. "Human Rights Situation of Leaders and Defenders of the Shuar People in Ecuador." Center for Human Rights and Humanitarian Law. http://hrbrief.org/2015/03/human-rights-situation-of-leaders-and-defenders-of-the-shuar-people-in-ecuador/.
Crouch, Colin. 2004. *Post-Democracy*. Cambridge/Malden: Polity Press.
Dávalos, Pablo. 2013. "'No Podemos Ser Mentigos Sentados En Un Saco de Oro': Las Falacias Del Discurso Extractivista." Quito: INREDH. http://inredh.org/archivos/pdf/las_falacias_del_extractivismo.pdf.
De Béco, Gauthier. 2014. "Human Rights Indicators and MDG Indicators: Building a Common Language for Human Rights and Development Organizations." In *Human Rights and Development in the New Millennium*, edited by Paul Gready and Wouter Vandenhole, 50–70. Oxon/New York: Routledge.
De Feyter, Koen. 2007. "Localising Human Rights." In *Economic Globalisation and Human Rights*, edited by W. Benedek, K. De Feyter, and F. Marrella, 67–92. Cambridge: Cambridge University Press.

———. 2011. "Sites of Rights Resistance." In *The Local Relevance of Human Rights*, edited by K. De Feyter et al., 11–39. Cambridge: Cambridge University Press.

De Feyter, K., S. Parmentier, C. Timmerman, and G. Ulrich, eds. 2011. *The Local Relevance of Human Rights*. Cambridge: Cambridge University Press.

De Gaay Fortman, B. 2011. *Political Economy of Human Rights: The Quest for Relevance and Realization*. New York: Routledge.

De la Cadena, Marisol. 2010. "Indigenous Cosmopolitics in the Andes: Conceptual Reflections Beyond 'Politics.'" *Cultural Anthropology* 25 (2): 334–70. https://doi.org/10.1111/j.1548-1360.2010.01061.x.

De Schutter, Olivier. 2014. "Regulating Transnational Corporations: A Duty under International Human Rights Law." Geneva: UN OHCHR. http://www.ohchr.org/Documents/Issues/Food/EcuadorMtgBusinessAndHR.pdf.

Fairbairn, M. 2010. "Framing Resistance: International Food Regimes and the Roots of Food Sovereignty." In *Food Sovereignty: Reconnecting Food, Nature and Community*, edited by H. Wittman, A. Desmarais, and N. Wiebe, 15–31. Halifax/Winnipeg: Fernwood and Food-First Books.

Fröberg, Ann-Mari. 2005. "Report of Turku Expert Meeting on Human Rights Indicators." Turku/Abo: Abo Akademi University.

Fukuda-Parr, Sakiko, and Alicia Ely Yamin, eds. 2015. *The MDGs, Capabilities and Human Rights: The Power of Numbers to Shape Agendas*. New York: Routledge.

Gasper, Des. 2000. "'Logical Frameworks': Problems and Potentials." Draft Paper ISS. The Hague.

Goodale, Mark. 2007. "Introduction: Locating Rights, Envisioning Law between the Global and the Local." In *The Practice of Human Rights*, edited by Mark Goodale and Sally Engle Merry, 1–39. New York: Cambridge University Press.

Gudynas, Eduardo. 2009. "El mandato ecológico. Derechos de la Naturaleza y políticas ambientales en la nueva Constitución." Quito: Abya-Yala.

———. 2011. "Buen Vivir: Today's Tomorrow." *Development* 54 (4): 441–47. https://doi.org/10.1057/dev.2011.86.

———. 2014. "Buen Vivir: Sobre Secuestros, Domesticaciones, Rescates Y Alternativas." In *Bifurcación Del Buen Vivir Y El Sumak Kawsay*, edited by Attawalpa Oviedo, 23–45. Quito: Ediciones Yachay.

Harvey, David. 2003. *The New Imperialism*. Oxford/New York: Oxford University Press.

Hines, Andrew. 2005. "What Human Rights Indicators Should Measure." Discussion paper. http://www.hks.harvard.edu/cchrp/pdf/Hines_Paper.pdf.

Hinkelammert, Franz J. 1999. "Democracia, Estructura Económico-Social Y Formación de Un Sentido Común Legitimador." In *Ensayos*, 87–130. La Habana: Caminos.

———. 2004. "The Hidden Logic of Modernity: Locke and the Inversion of Human Rights." *Worlds and Knowledges Otherwise* (Fall): 1–27.

Human Rights Council. 2014. "Elaboration of an International Legally Binding Instrument on Transnational Corporations and Other Business Enterprises with Respect to Human Rights." A/HRC/26/L.22/Rev.1. Geneva: UN General Assembly.

IACHR. 2008. "Guidelines for the Preparation of Progress Indicators in the Area of Economic, Social and Cultural Rights." OEA/Ser.L/V/II.132. Inter-American Commission on Human Rights. http://cidh.org/countryrep/IndicadoresDESC08eng/Indicadoresindice.eng.htm.

Jordan, Peter. 2008. "Group Rights." *Stanford Encyclopedia of Philosophy*. September. http://plato.stanford.edu/entries/rights-group/.

Kuosmanen, Jaako. 2015. "Repackaging Human Rights: On the Justification and the Function of the Right to Development." *Journal of Global Ethics* 11 (3): 303–20. https://doi.org/10.1080/17449626.2015.1099050.

Latorre, Sara, Marianne Walter, and Carlos Larrea. 2015. *Íntag, Un Territorio En Disputa. Evualuación de Escenarios Territoriales Extractivos Y No Extractivos*. Quito: Universidad Andina Simón Bolívar and Abya Yala.

Lauderbaugh, George. 2012. *The History of Ecuador*. Santa Barbara: Greenwood.

Le Quang, Matthieu. 2016. "The Yasuní-ITT Initiative toward New Imaginaries." *Latin American Perspectives* 206 (43): 187–99. https://doi.org/10.1177/0094582X15579908.

Lewis, David, and David Mosse. 2006. "Theoretical Approaches to Brokerage and Translation in Development." In *Development Brokers and Translators*, edited by David Lewis and David Mosse, 1–26. West Hartford: Kumarian.

Macdonald, L., and A. Ruckert, eds. 2009. *Post-Neoliberalism in the Americas*. London: Palgrave Macmillan.

Malhotra, Rajeev, and Nikolas Fasel. 2005. "Quantitative Human Rights Indicators—A Survey of Major Initiatives." Discussion paper. March 3, 2005, http://hrbaportal.org/wp-content/files/1237942217malhotra_and_fasel.pdf.

McInerney-Lankford, Siobhán, and Hans-Otto Sano. 2010. "Human Rights Indicators in Development." A World Bank Study. Washington: World Bank.

Merino Acuña, Roger. 2014. "La Política de La Gobernanza Ambiental: Pueblos Indígenas, Cambio Climático Y Ambientalidad." *Revista Andina de Estudios Políticos* IV (2): 99–105.

Merry, Sally Engle. 2006a. *Human Rights and Gender Violence: Translating International Law into Local Justice*. Chicago: University of Chicago Press.

———. 2006b. "Transnational Human Rights and Local Activism: Mapping the Middle." *American Anthropologist* 108 (1): 38–51.

———. 2009. "Legal Transplants and Cultural Translation: Making Human Rights in the Vernacular." In *Human Rights: An Anthropological Reader*, edited by Mark Goodale, 265–303. Malden, MA/Oxford: Wiley-Blackwell.

———. 2011. "Measuring the World." *Current Anthropology* 52 (S3): S83–95. https://doi.org/10.1086/657241.

———. 2013a. "Human Rights Monitoring and the Question of Indicators." In *Human Rights at the Crossroads*, edited by Mark Goodale, 140–53. New York: Oxford University Press.

———. 2013b. "Firming Up Soft Law: The Impact of Indicators on Transnational Human Rights Legal Orders." Lecture given at the Center for Socio-Legal Studies, New York, January 27, 2014.

———. 2016. *The Seductions of Quantification: Measuring Human Rights, Violence against Women, and Sex Trafficking*. Chicago: University of Chicago Press.

Merry, Sally Engle, and Summer Wood. 2015. "Quantification and the Paradox of Measurement: Translating Children's Rights in Tanzania." *Current Anthropology* 56 (2): 205–30.

Mignolo, Walter D. 2013. "Who Speaks for the 'Human' in Human Rights?" In *Human Rights from a Third World Perspective*, edited by José-Manuel Barreto, 44–65. Newcastle upon Tyne: Cambridge Scholars Publishing.

Moore, Jennifer, and Teresa Velasquez. 2012. "Sovereignty Negotiated: Anti-Mining Movements, the State and Multinational Mining Companies under Correa's 21st Century Socialism." In *Social Conflict, Economic Development and the Extractive Industry: Evidence from South America*, edited by Anthony Bebbington, 112–34. New York: Routledge.

Oviedo, Attawalpa, ed. 2014. *Bifurcación Del Buen Vivir Y El Sumak Kawsay*. Quito: Ediciones Yachay.
Plan V. 2015. "Cinco Mujeres Denuncian Al Gobierno." *Plan V*, October 19. http://www.planv.com.ec/historias/politica/cinco-mujeres-denuncian-al-gobierno.
Putnam, Robert. 1988. "Diplomacy and Domestic Politics: The Logic of Two-Level Games." *International Organization* 42 (3): 427–460.
Randeria, Shalini. 2003a. "Cunning States and Unaccountable International Institutions: Legal Plurality, Social Movements and Rights of Local Communities to Common Property Resources." *European Journal for Sociology* 44 (1): 27–60.
———. 2003b. "Glocalization of Law: Environmental Justice, World Bank, NGOs and the Cunning State in India." *Current Sociology* 51 (3/4): 305–28.
———. 2007. "Legal Pluralism, Social Movements and the Post-Colonial State in India: Fractured Sovereignty and Differential Citizenship Rights." In *Another Knowledge Is Possible. Beyond Northern Epistemologies*, edited by Boaventura de Sousa Santos, 41–75. London and New York: Verso.
Riedel, Eibe. 2007. "Measuring Human Rights Compliance. The IBSA Procedure as a Tool of Monitoring." In *Les Droits de L'homme et La Constitution. Etudes En L'honneur Du Professeur Giorgio Malinverni*, edited by A. Auer, A. Flückiger, and M. Hottelier, 251–71. Geneva: Schulthess.
———. 2013. "Global Human Rights Protection at the Crossroads: Strengthening or Reforming the System." In *Der Staat Im Recht: Festschrift Für Eckart Klein Zum 70. Geburtstag*, edited by Marten Breuer, Astrid Epiney, Andreas Haratsch, et al., 1289–1306. Berlin: Duncker and Hublodt.
Riedel, Eibe, Gilles Giacca, and Christophe Golay. 2014. "The Development of Economic, Social, and Cultural Rights in International Law: Introduction." In *Economic, Social, and Cultural Rights in International Law*, edited by Eibe Riedel, Gilles Giacca, and Christophe Golay, 3–48. Oxford: Oxford University Press.
Rival, Laura. 2012. "Planning Development Futures in the Ecuadorian Amazon: The Expanding Oil Frontier and the Yasuní-ITT Initiative." In *Social Conflict, Economic Development and the Extractive Industry: Evidence from South America*, edited by Anthony Bebbington, 153–72. London and New York: Routledge, Taylor and Francis.
Rosga, A. J., and M. L. Satterthwaite. 2009. "Trust in Indicators: Measuring Human Rights." *Berkeley Journal of International Law* 27: 253–315.
Sacher, William, Michelle Báez A., et al. 2015. "Entretelones de la megaminería en el Ecuador: Informe de Visita de Campo en la Zona del Megaproyecto Minero Mirador, Parroquia Tundayme, Cantón El Pangui, Provincia de Zamora-Chinchipe, Ecuador." Quito: Acción Ecológica.
Schulte-Tenckhoff, Isabelle. 2012. "Treaties, Peoplehood and Self-Determination: Understanding the Language of Indigenous Rights." In *Indigenous Rights in the Age of the UN Declaration*, edited by Elvira Pulitano, 64–86. Cambridge: Cambridge University Press.
SENPLADES. 2013. "Buen Vivir Plan Nacional 2013–2017." Quito: SENPLADES. www.buenvivir.gob.ec.
SENPLADES, Secretaría Nacional de Planificación y Desarrollo. 2009. *Plan Nacional de Desarrollo. Plan Nacional Para El Buen Vivir 2009–2013. Construyendo Un Estado Plurinacional E Intercultural*. Quito: SENPLADES.

Sterba, James B. 2011. "Biocentrism Defended." *Ethics, Policy and Environment* 14 (2): 167–69. https://doi.org/10.1080/21550085.2011.578376.

Tully, James. 2007. "Two Meanings of Global Citizenship." In *Global Citizenship Education: Philosophy, Theory and Pedagogy*, edited by M. A. Peters, A. Britton, and H. Blee, 15–23. Boston: Sense.

UN ACNUDH. 2013. "Construcción de Indicadores de Derechos Humanos: Experiencias Regionales." Mexico: UNHCHR.

UN OHCHR. 2006. "Informe Sobre Indicadores Para Vigilar El Cumplimiento de Los Instrumentos Internacionales de Derechos Humanos: 11.05.2006." HRI/MC/2006/7. Geneva: UN OHCHR.

———. 2008. "Report on Indicators for Promoting and Monitoring the Implementation of Human Rights." HRI/MC/2008/3. International Human Rights Instruments. Geneva: UN OHCHR. http://www2.ohchr.org/english/bodies/icm-mc/docs/HRI.MC.2008.3EN.pdf.

———. 2012. "Human Rights Indicators: A Guide to Measurement and Implementation." HR/PUB/12/5. New York and Geneva: UN OHCHR.

Vázquez, Rolando. 2011. "Translation as Erasure: Thoughts on Modernity's Epistemic Violence." *Journal of Historical Sociology* 24 (1): 27–44. https://doi.org/10.1111/j.1467-6443.2011.01387.x.

Veltmeyer, Henry, and James Petras. 2014. *The New Extractivism: A Post-Neoliberal Development Model or Imperialism of the Twenty-First Century*. New York: Zed Books.

Viteri, Carlos. 1993. "Mundos Míticos. Runa." In *Mundos Amazónicos: Pueblos Y Culturas de La Amazonía Ecuatoriana*, edited by Noemi Paymal and Catalina Sosa. Quito: Sinchi Sacha.

———. 2002. "Visión Indígena Del Desarrollo En La Amazonía." *Polis, Revista de La Universidad Bolivariana* 1 (3): 1–6.

Waldmüller, Johannes M. 2014a. "Buen Vivir, Sumak Kawsay, 'Good Living': An Introduction and Overview." *Alternautas* 1 (1): 17–28.

———. 2014b. "Human Rights Indicators and Buen Vivir in Ecuador: A Decolonial Actor-Network Study." PhD Thesis, Geneva: Graduate Institute of International and Development Studies.

———. 2014c. "Human Rights Indicators as 'Development 2.0'?." *Alternautas* 1 (1): 76–87.

———. 2015. "Analyzing the Spill-over Matrix of Extractivism: From Para-Legality, Separation and Violence to Integral Health in the Ecuadorian Íntag." Blog/Journal. *Alternautas*. March 20. http://www.alternautas.net/blog/2015/3/20/analyzing-the-spill-over-matrix-of-extractivism-from-para-legality-separation-and-violence-to-integral-health-in-the-ecuadorian-ntag.

Walsh, Catherine. 2010. "Development as Buen Vivir: Institutional Arrangements and (de) Colonial Entanglements." *Development* 53 (1): 15–21.

Watson, Richard A. 1983. "A Critique of Anti-Anthropocentric Biocentrism." *Environmental Ethics* 5 (3): 245–56.

Watts, Jonathan. 2014. "Ecuador Indigenous Leader Found Dead Days before Planned Lima Protest." *The Guardian*, June 12. http://www.theguardian.com/world/2014/dec/06/ecuador-indigenous-leader-found-dead-lima-climate-talks.

Welling, J. V. 2008. "International Indicators and Economic, Social and Cultural Rights." *Human Rights Quarterly* 30: 933–58. https://doi.org/10.1353/hrq.0.0040

CHAPTER 5

Upstreaming or Streamlining? Translating Social Movement Agendas into Legal Claims in Nepal and the Dominican Republic

Samuel Martínez

What happens to a social movement's formulations of injustice when these are reframed as rights claims? This shift, from political mobilization to legal claims-making couched in human rights norms, has been called variously "juridicalization" (Baxi 2007, 62–67), "juridification" (Eckert et al. 2012, 4), "lawfare" (Comaroff and Comaroff 2006, 26–31), "legal formalization" (Kennedy 2004, 12), "legalization" (Meckled-García and Çali 2006), "legal reductionism" (Campbell 2013), and "verticalization" (Wilson 2007, 355–356). All these concepts refer to the removal of conflicts from a local context and their elevation to legal forums where they encounter a different set of pressures. Critics of these trends coincide in warning of "depoliticization" (Eckert et al. 2012, 4–6): if rights are turned into a matter exclusively for legal experts, then rights claimants can be alienated from their own freedom struggles, creating situations in which "everything is known by the lawyer, nothing is known by the client" (Osiatyński, 2009, 101, quoting Filipino human rights activist Carlos Medina).

While its dangers loom large, depoliticization is not my main concern in this chapter. I ask a subtly different question: How may not just the means but the very *content* of social justice struggles change when community membership organizations (CMOs) upstream liberation agendas into legal terms?[1] Does juridification inevitably entail a narrowing of social movement claims?[2]

And, if so, does such narrowing signal a shift in movement agenda from socially transformative to reformist aims?

Among the positive outcomes of juridification, the upstreaming of social movement agendas into legal language can not only open avenues for subalterns to have their grievances heard but can also transform international human rights professionals' understandings of particular human rights crises. Two-way, North-South dialogues about the very nature of the wrongs assume particular importance as international human rights extends its scrutiny beyond the simpler wrongs of the suppression of dissent, political disappearances, and other government abuses of individuals' prepolitical rights. "While human rights began as a legal defense of the lives and physical integrity of political dissidents and religious or ethnic minorities from the malfeasance of dictatorships," observes Alison Brysk (2013, 2), "its mandate has expanded to chronic deprivations of economic and social rights." If closing "the gap between the defined human rights framework and the people's realities and needs" (Oré Aguilar 2011, 115) seems more urgent than ever, then that is in part because human rights are being stretched to encompass the exploitation and oppression of whole gender, sectarian, ethnic, or national groups. These issues, Shareen Hertel (2006, 263) observes, are often "marked by differences of opinion among activists . . . over the nature of human rights and the best way to protect and promote them."

Yet seeking legal resolution for multilayered, hereditarily entrenched forms of group subordination is also likely to result in just one or two of the most obvious abuses being brought under human rights scrutiny, leaving undergirding citizenship exclusions and distributive injustices undisturbed. This larger architecture of injustice I have elsewhere likened to an onion: "a dense, layered mass of mutually supporting injustices" (Martínez 2011, 55); these complex injustices may be found the world around and are difficult to reduce analytically to one wrong, one perpetrator, and one duty bearer. Not just cultural distance, then, may hinder the translation of hereditary or embodied subordination into human rights legal claims. Also, the collective experience of abuse, the multidimensionality of oppression, and the participation of several identifiable perpetrators all pose challenges to legal reductionism. Behind diverse local justice vernaculars and traditions, strikingly similar injustice scenarios, rooted in comparable colonial histories, may confront peasants, migrants, and racial/ethnic minorities the world over.

One theoretical approach to studying the rights perception gap between international human rights and Southern social movements may be found in South Asian and Latin American anticolonial scholars' and activists' views of the limitations of Western-derived liberal rights regimes. In 1928, the Peruvian neo-Marxist cultural theorist José Carlos Mariátegui wrote of the inherent limits in elite projects of "redemption of the backward and enslaved indigenous race through an outside protective body that without charge and by legal means [seeks] to serve as its lawyer in its claims against the government." Mariátegui dismissed the "liberal, humanitarian, enlightened attitude," which "inspires and motivates 'leagues of human rights,'" as the latest in a succession of efforts dating back to the "wise and detailed ordinances" of Spanish colonial legislation; these, even though "worked out after conscientious study," had, for Mariátegui, all proven "quite useless."[3] Legal reformism, he saw, demobilized afflicted communities and distracted from core political economic issues, chiefly land tenure. It has similarly been asked whether legal reformism is a "counter-insurgency" (Guha 1983)—through which social movements are coopted by power—or an "alter-insurgency"—through which social movements may speak directly to power—or both things.

Perhaps the broadest significance of my chapter, then, is to ask in what ways South Asian and Latin American scholars' calls to *decolonize knowledge* (Baxi 2007; Mignolo 2000; Quijano 2008) may be brought into human rights. Decolonizing human rights knowledge, I contend, starts with broadening the problem of localizing human rights beyond questions of linguistic translation among diverse cultures. Decolonizing equally highlights the question: Who is the knowing subject of human rights? Who defines problems, agenda, and strategies? These questions sketch an alternative geography of global human rights knowledge exchange, not a Western human rights continent surrounded by non-Western ethical-philosophical islets but two large, and at points connected, global terrains of justice, one liberal, the other distributive.[4]

Within human rights studies, efforts to theorize the mismatch between social movement aims and human rights frames remain scattered. Clifford Bob (2002) still stands alone in boldly putting the problem in general terms: "[T]he pressure to conform to the needs of international NGOs can undermine the original goals of local movements.... Unfashionable, complex, or intractable conflicts fester in isolation, while those that ... match international issues of the moment attract disproportionate support" (Bob 2002, 44). More directly pertinent to juridification, Angelina Snodgrass Godoy (2013) calls attention to behind-the-scenes disagreements about the use of human rights tools to advance affordable access to prescription medicines. She observes, "[M]any Central American health activists questioned the primacy of what they refer to as 'curative' medicine, based on the model of biomedical interventions in the individual patient body rather than collective processes to address the social determinants of health" (Godoy 2013, 99). Discussing similar frictions between international and Russian women's rights organizations, Julie Hemment (2004, 816) writes, "The framing of violence against women not only screens out local constructions of events, but it deflects attention from other issues of social justice, notably the material forces that oppress women."

All these examples involve not just disparities in who holds the power to define the issues but divergent ways of knowing and seeking remedy. In a study of postrevolutionary Nicaragua, Maxine Molyneux (1985) distinguishes "strategic" and "practical" logics of gender rights struggle. In common with the researchers whom I have just cited, Molyneux highlights frictions between human rights agenda defined strategically (ibid., 232)—that is, deductively and through an external actor's analysis of a group's subordination—versus practically—that is, inductively, on the basis of CMO social movement praxis (ibid., 233). Human rights allies' strategic approaches may diverge from CMO leaders' practical ways of knowing/changing the world. One way this can happen is when international human rights professionals' strategic aims—such as reinforcing a regime of rights or advancing a particular global campaign—subsume practical aims—of building a holistic activist agenda and developing members' citizenship capacities.

Other human rights theorists differ from Bob in seeing the social process of juridification not as a top-down transfer but rather a path of negotiation between local leaders and national and international human rights professionals, or what Sally Merry (2006a) calls "mapping the middle": How do movement leaders and external allies collaborate in identifying what claims are to be given first priority, in redefining these in terms of international legal norms, and in deciding the mix of methods through which these are to be pursued? For Koen De Feyter (2007; also Oré Aguilar 2011), the localization of human rights is not simply a North-to-South transfer but a two-way street, through which global rights are translated into locally meaningful terms but also international organizations' understandings may be redefined. North-South human rights knowledge exchange is neither a happy "networked relation of equals" (Destrooper 2015, 241) nor a grim, top-down imposition (Merry 2006b, 4). The Nepalese and Dominican case studies on which I focus in this chapter fit better with De Feyter's (2007) vision of localization as a two-way street than with Bob's (2002) view that human rights issues are imposed by international NGOs with little consultation with local activists.

At the same time, social movement CMOs find shrinking alternatives to rights language and legally focused approaches, due to what Sam Moyn (2010, 8) calls the "collapse of other, prior utopias," leaving only the minimalist utopia of human rights as "a global framework for the achievement of freedom, identity, and prosperity" (ibid., 9). Shannon Speed (2007, 176) aptly summarizes this situation:

> There is no escaping the fact that the spread of neoliberalism . . . has taken place in tandem with the spread of other discourses, among them democratization, human rights and indigenous rights/multiculturalism. Precisely as the triumphalist march of neoliberal capitalist democracy moved forward over the ruins of socialist projects and authoritarian governments, rights struggles became the primary form of contestation to state power and social injustice.

Speed echoes widely shared concerns: Is human rights *antithetical* to the neoliberal state, acting as a last line of defense of human dignity against crumbling welfare state protections and harshening capitalist exploitation? Or is it sooner *symbiotic* with the state, confirming the state's role "as the purveyor and protector of rights" (Speed 2007, 178) and politically containing collective demands into the regulatory frame of legal and bureaucratic petitions?

What matters in the end is what works in achieving social movement aims. Viewed from the standpoint of what works, political mobilization and litigation may be less rigid commitments than flexible options. "[T]he 'politics' of setting collectively binding rules" is, after all, inextricably linked to "the 'legalism' of merely using such rules," as cultural anthropologist Olaf Zenker (2012, 139) reminds us in his study of a South African black community's successful turn to litigation in securing legal rights to communal land. In Zenker's view, while politics and law may both contest the existing normative order of rules, each does that through distinctive "codes" and institutional "connectivity." Quite the opposite of contradictory and mutually exclusive domains, then, litigation and politics are subject to "code switching." When litigation does not yield hoped-for outcomes, for example, protest and media may once again take center stage.

These questions exceed what I can speak to conclusively, but the Nepalese and Dominican cases that I compare here point to the same dangers: juridification narrows the content of social movement agendas to the point of distortion and redefines conflict as matters of law and procedural norms. Once resituated on legal ground, dissent can be engaged by state agents in ways that appear productive, instead of by suppressing protest.

"[T]he question of how law relates to more overtly political means of social transformation is," as Eckert and colleagues (2012, 6–7) write, "an empirical matter that requires ethnographic scrutiny." Recognizing that more studies need to be done of how social movement agendas are turned into legal claims, and with what consequences, I compare the juridification process followed by CMOs in two geographically unconnected and socioculturally dissimilar environments in Nepal and the Dominican Republic. The method of controlled comparison that I follow (Eggan 1954), though well established, offers generalizations of only limited certainty about juridification's effects on social movements worldwide. Still, the two cases bear compelling resemblances. Roughly contemporaneously in the late 1990s and early 2000s, the two social movements went through a process of narrowing their justice agenda into legally actionable terms.

In neither was there any necessary link between the adoption of human rights language and a turn to lawfare.[5] Legal action became important in both places only after years of patient rights consciousness-raising and human capacity-building work among the hereditarily derogated groups from which the CMOs' leaders and members were drawn, *kamaiya* bonded laborers in Nepal and undocumented Haitian immigrants and Haitian-ancestry people in the Dominican Republic. Neither group ever renounced their earlier multidimensional activist agenda. Yet both the Nepali and the Dominican CMO leaderships embraced a strategy of pursuing a legal breakthrough, hinging on the ratification of one key claim: emancipation from bonded labor contracts for the kamaiyas, and recognition of the Dominican citizenship of Dominican-born people of Haitian ancestry. Outside experts, national CMO leaders, and governance institutions together pushed action down a legal path, lined with hopes that state acceptance of international human rights norms could trump entrenched custom. These paths, even so, differed strikingly, reflecting fundamental differences in the political space in the two countries. Key events unfolded over a span of months in Nepal while the process ground on for years in the Dominican Republic; litigation was involved only at the start of the kamaiya emancipation story, with mass protests taking center stage at a decisive moment there, while lawyering in both national and international courts was central throughout the Dominican juridification process.

I combine a review of English-language publications on kamaiya activism with findings drawn from my ethnographic research with Haitian-Dominican CMOs to compare the paths traced by juridification processes in these two contexts. Admittedly, my knowledge of the Dominican case is deeper: I speak the Spanish and Haitian Kreyòl languages; have accompanied Dominican CMO staffers to meetings with government officials, the press, and village constituents; and have tracked domestic and international activism on this case over a span of decades. Yet the kamaiya case is well enough documented through the work of other social researchers that I feel it is possible responsibly to bring it into comparison even without knowing the local languages or having observed the situations and events firsthand.

I first give a brief overview of the two cases, then compare them across four sequential phases: the formation of a social movement agenda; juridification; legal reduction; and outcomes. I conclude by considering how De Feyter's theory of localization provides a framework in which the mixed social movement outcomes in both places can be accounted for while also providing the conceptual flexibility needed to encompass important differences in how juridification unfolded in each country.

Overview

Kamaiya Emancipation

In the first few months of 2000, a social movement of *kamaiyas*, bonded laborers in the Himalayan kingdom of Nepal, burst onto the international mediascape and, by July 17 of that year, had won a royal edict nullifying all kamaiya debts and declaring the workers to be free. Thousands of bonded laborers for the first time protested publicly and put forward legal challenges to debts that bound them to landowners. What makes retrospective attention to the kamaiya emancipation story important are its unexpected and even paradoxical outcomes. To the kamaiyas and their Nepali and international allies alike, perhaps the only thing as surprising as how rapidly they won was how incomplete a victory emancipation ended up being. As I describe below, it seems that extracting the kamaiyas from circumstances portrayed to be "slavery" landed many in a situation worse than what they suffered before.

A fatal flaw was breaking bonds between the kamaiyas and their landlords without affirming a compensatory bond to the *land*: without accompanying land reform, becoming landlord-less meant becoming landless.

Haitian-Dominican Statelessness

International concern about the human rights deficits suffered by Haitian immigrants in the Dominican Republic was also initially couched in terms of contemporary slavery.[6] And similarly, a fatal defect of the contemporary slavery diagnosis was how hard it was for these "slaves" to survive without the incomes supplied by their alleged "captors." In mid-1991, Dominican president Joaquín Balaguer retaliated against international human rights monitors' U.S. congressional testimony in favor of imposing trade sanctions on the Dominican Republic, through a decree repatriating all unaccompanied Haitian national minors and elders over 60. This was justified as a humanitarian move, aimed at extracting the most vulnerable, the youngest and eldest migrants, from wretched exploitation on the sugar plantations. Dominican officials quickly overstepped the decree by hustling tens of thousands of Black plantation residents of prime working age onto trucks bound for Haiti. Local NGOs were left to deal with the subsequent humanitarian and legal crisis, which ended only as the Dominicans suspended the expulsions following the overthrow of Haitian president Jean-Bertrand Aristide in late September 1991. The majority of the displaced returned to the Dominican Republic, resuming the livelihoods and ties with neighbors and faith communities on which they had previously depended for survival.

In the late 1990s, consultation between international human rights lawyers and the leaders of Haitian-Dominican social justice CMOs brought statelessness to supplant modern slavery as the leading frame through which international human rights approached Haitian descendants' rights struggles. This shift broadened concern, from a few thousand male seasonal migrants to the hundreds of thousands of Dominicans of Haitian ancestry, female as well as male, whose rights were being put in danger by the Dominican state's claim that the Dominican-born were not Dominican citizens but Haitian nationals. Simultaneously, activist strategy shifted to litigation in national and international courts with the aim of winning a court ruling(s) that could in one stroke invalidate the discriminatory policies of the state. Really, two major shifts—one conceptual, the other methodological—resulted from the international human rights lawyers' entry onto the scene, shifts that together align well with De Feyter's vision of localization as a two-way street. First, international advocates began to consult in-country CMO leaders—perhaps most prominently, MUDHA (Movimiento de Mujeres Domínico-Haitianas) and MOSCTHA (Movimiento Socio-Cultural para los Trabajadores Haitianos)—in setting priorities and strategies of action. This consultation led to a fundamental shift in international perceptions of the situation. At the second, methodological level, a shift to strategic litigation won major rulings between 2005 and 2015 in the inter-American human rights system, dealing unequivocal rejections to the Dominican state's citizenship and migrant rights policies.[7]

The Santo Domingo government has unfortunately responded in ways that mostly run contrary to the greater adherence to liberal legal norms sought through international pressure. Haitian-ancestry Dominicans now face forms of exclusion from state protections that reach more people and are more rigidly codified in law than before international activists took up their cause. Laws, high court verdicts, and bureaucratic measures enacted by all three branches of the Dominican government have given the form of unambiguous legal writ to the exclusion from birthright citizenship of Haitian-descendant children, a practice formerly implemented variably and with imprecise legal foundations. As a result, the basis of anti-Haitian policy today looks less blatantly arbitrary and coercive than before but, in spite of its veneer of procedural normativity, threatens to relegate Haitian descendants more remorselessly than ever to a perpetual outsider civil status.

Social Movement Formation

The Kamaiya Struggle

Kamaiya-led activism did not come suddenly to life in 2000 but had been coalescing since the 1980s.[8] By the time of the restoration of multiparty democracy in 1990 a de facto nationwide social justice CMO, the Shramik Mukti Sangathan (Organization for Laborers' Liberation), had emerged and received international donor support for work on adult literacy and agricultural extension. Finally registered as an organization in 1991, it was given the anodyne name Backward Society Education (BASE), chosen to allay official suspicion that it might be an insurgent or political party organization.[9] BASE's kamaiya founder, Dilli Chaudhari, was awarded the Reebok Human Rights Award in 1994 and the Anti-Slavery International Award in 2002.[10]

The cultural anthropologist Tatsuro Fujikura accompanied the kamaiya protesters on their decisive July 2000 march to Kathmandu from kamaiya homelands in western Nepal and was in prison with kamaiya leaders at the moment when emancipation was declared. As befits an ethnographer, Fujikura does not take for granted what it meant to be a kamaiya. After noting that there were a wide variety of arrangements called "kamaiya" in the far western Tarai districts of Dang, Banke, Bardiya, Kailali, and Kanchanpur, Fujikura (2007, 324) describes the kind of kamaiya agreement that is most easily categorized as bonded labor:

> This type of kamaiya contract involved a person taking a loan, called *saunki*, from another farmer or a landlord and, in exchange, agreeing to work exclusively for the latter as a kamaiya (or sending his son to work . . .). The landlord in turn agreed to provide the kamaiya with a fixed amount of grain or money every year. The landlord also gave the kamaiya one set of clothes every year and guaranteed to provide shelter for those kamaiyas who were landless. Moreover, kamaiyas also had the right to demand additional credits for basic and emergency needs from their employers. These additional loans were added to the *saunki*. In order to leave the landlord, kamaiya had to pay back the *saunki* or find a new employer to do so.

This kind of land/labor/credit arrangement fits the definition of debt bondage in the UN Supplementary Convention on the Abolition of Slavery, the Slave Trade, and Institutions and Practices Similar to Slavery, of 1956: "the status or condition arising from a pledge by a debtor of his personal services or of those of a person under his control as security for a debt, if the value of those services as reasonably assessed is not applied towards the liquidation of the debt or the length and nature of those services are not respectively limited and defined."[11] Particularly troubling was the potentially unlimited duration and at times hereditary nature of kamaiya debts.

What also jumps to more than one observer's eye is what kamaiyas might have had to *lose* by being extracted from bonded labor: allotments of grain and clothing, shelter, access to further credit, and at times a small subsistence parcel of land (Lamichhane 2006, 161). To this, geographer Katherine Rankin (1999, 29) adds that incurring kamaiya debt was for many land-poor rural dwellers the only way to pay for a child's wedding or cover other major expenses. Things like the kamaiyas' and landlords' reciprocal guarantees (Fujikura 2007, 325–26) and the kamaiyas' advantages over destitute others in the labor market (Adhikari 2000) do not mean that the ex-kamaiyas were really free all the time they were in bondage. Taking account of the kamaiya contracts' subsistence guarantees, rather, points to reasons why the kamaiya social movement has traced a broadly inclusive agenda. The kamaiyas know better than anyone how problematic it can be if the negative freedom of severing kamaiya contracts comes without the positive freedoms provided by access to land and schools. The context of Nepal's severe land and resource scarcity makes it clearer still why BASE and other kamaiya CMOs sought freedom from bonded labor contracts on one hand and land redistribution and human capacity-building on the other, as the two sides of a single liberation agenda.

The Haitian-Dominican Social Movement

Similarly, the CMOs led by Haitian immigrants and Haitian descendants in the Dominican Republic have not restricted their activism to the civil and political rights favored by international monitor groups but have instead pursued a broad-spectrum approach. They see the rights abuses, injustices, and social exclusions that confront Haitian nationals and Haitian descendants as interrelated and mutually supportive wrongs. Like layers of an onion, each wrong is a source of other injustices, permits other wrongs to occur, or acts to block the targets of abuse from obtaining protection or redress. And rather than peeling away at just the most obvious rights infringements, these organizations have sought to pierce the onion's core by simultaneously militating for economic development, women's empowerment, cultural revitalization, and constitutional rights (Martínez 2011).

In methods, too, these organizations have less often sought to assemble legal cases than to build their constituents' ability to promote and defend their own rights. The idea is that downtrodden members of the Haitian minority must be prepared to stand up for their rights, whether this involves resisting attempts by authorities to evict and deport them, demanding admission to schools and health clinics, or gaining the literacy skills needed to decipher a property deed or other legal document.

My interviews with Haitian-Dominican CMO staffers suggest that it was the context of struggle and not any prior ideological commitment that brought their organizations to espouse such a holistic vision of rights. The approach was, as Molyneux (1985) would put it, practical and not strategic. As the director of the Centro Cultural Domínico-Haitian (Haitian-Dominican Cultural Center), Antonio Pol Emil, told me, "We understood that, in the context of great misery . . . , the work of organizing was not so easy, because a hungry group neither gains awareness nor, even less, does it organize. . . . For the people to develop consciousness of their reality, it was necessary to help them, even if only minimally, to resolve some of their many problems."[12] Much like the kamaiya-led CMOs, praxis, not theory, led the Haitian-Dominican CMOs to endorse the indivisibility of civil-political and economic, social, and cultural rights.

Juridification

The Kamaiya Mobilization of 2000

The developments that led to kamaiya emancipation in 2000 began when one leader of one branch of BASE, Yagyaraj Chaudhari in the Kailali District, grew tired of BASE's human capacity-building strategy and decided instead to start freeing kamaiyas one by one. Targeting one prominent landlord named Shiva Raja Pant, Yagyaraj met at night over a span of two years with Shiva Raj's kamaiyas. Under the cover of leading evening adult literacy classes, he persuaded the skeptical kamaiyas that they should present a legal challenge to their landlord (Fujikura 2007, 340–41; also Lowe 2001). After asking Shiva Raj repeatedly for a raise in wages and getting no satisfaction, the kamaiyas took their case to their local Village Development Committee asking that he pay minimum wage and cancel their debts. As their demands rose up the administrative ladder, Shiva Raj's kamaiyas gained public support from BASE members, who staged marches, rallies, and sit-ins, accented with camera-friendly theatrics (Fujikura 2007, 342–43; also Lowe 2001). BASE upped the scale by encouraging other kamaiyas to file cases with their districts' administrative offices. In the Kanchanpur

District of western Nepal, government officials, judges, kamaiyas, activists, and landlords outlined a formula that would ultimately emancipate all the kamaiya families in the district. By July 14, some 1,600 kamaiyas had petitioned for freedom (Bales 2007, 101).

In the same month, BASE convened a two-day meeting of kamaiyas and their supporters in the western town of Nepalganj (Fujikura 2007, 343). At that meeting, a dilemma materialized: in speaking to the government, would they be better off maintaining a broad range of demands or narrowing their message to one key demand? Vivek Pandit, a tribal rights activist from India and winner of the 1999 Anti-Slavery International Award, had been invited to serve as facilitator of the Nepalganj meeting and made a crucial intervention on this point. Whereas the cases filed by Shiva Raj's kamaiyas and others had presented a varied menu of demands—better wages, housing, personal security, and cancellation of their debts—Vivek "insisted that 'freedom' was the first and foremost issue for the kamaiyas": "After freedom, other issues could be dealt with. The goal of the movement had to be clearly defined. And the goal was freedom. . . . It was, Vivek suggested, an epic fight between good and evil, as in Hindi movies. . . . The heroes, of course, were the kamaiyas who deserved freedom; the villains were the landlords and the chief district officers who denied them freedom" (343–44). After the Nepalganj meeting, BASE leaders decided to adopt the freedom first agenda and take the movement to the capital, Kathmandu.

The Haitian-Dominican Movement's Turn Toward Strategic Litigation

The holistic issue framing and activism that had been developed by Haitian-Dominican CMOs over the course of the 1980s and 1990s was radical, but it was also being ignored internationally until a new set of allies entered the scene. A pivotal moment was an extended field visit by Berkeley international human rights lawyer Laurel Fletcher and her then-student, Roxanna Altholz, in 1998. On the basis of this visit, they submitted an unpublished report to the Inter-American Commission on Human Rights setting forth priorities articulated by Haitian labor rights activists and plantation-born leaders of Haitian-Dominican CMOs. What mattered to the Dominican-based rights defenders were rights of legal residency for de facto resident immigrants, the right for all workers to organize trade unions freely, women's economic empowerment and right to sexual self-determination, and, above all, the recognition that the Dominican-born were Dominican citizens.[13]

It had for decades been the practice of local-level civil registry officials to issue valid birth certificates to the Dominican-born children of Haitian nationals, even when the latter bore no proof of identity other than the "temporary" identity cards (*carnets temporeros* or *fichas*) issued to seasonal workers by the sugar companies upon arrival from Haiti.[14] As sugar's prospects went from buoyant to depressed, official permissiveness was replaced by growing restrictiveness. By 1990, evidence had emerged that Dominican-born children of Haitian ancestry were being denied birth certificates under the pretext that the Dominican Constitution exempted the children of persons "in transit" from the *jus soli* right to Dominican nationality (Cedeño 1992, 139; CCDH 1997, 16; Lawyers Committee for Human Rights 1991, 13–14).[15]

Fletcher and Altholz were not looking for a case to litigate and only returned to the Dominican Republic to explore legal avenues at the prompting of one of the Inter-American commissioners. Through the intercession of the Haitian-Dominican feminist CMO, MUDHA, they found their test plaintiffs, the girls Dilcia Yean and Violeta Bosico. Even though Yean and Bosico were Dominican-born children of Dominican-born mothers, they were denied late registration birth certificates on March 5, 1997, because civil registry officials said their names "sounded foreign." This set in motion litigation that culminated years later in a landmark Inter-American Court of Human Rights (IACtHR) ruling invalidating the Dominican Republic's exclusion of Haitian-Dominicans from jus soli citizenship. During the court proceedings, it became embarrassingly clear how arbitrary and badly founded in law the official policy was, when government lawyers presented the court at different times with distinct and incompatible lists of official criteria for approving late registration of births.[16]

All along, the fear, shared confidentially by MUDHA's lead coordinator, Sonia Pierre, and others, was that legal confrontation in an international forum would anger the country's political leaders and precipitate a backlash. Enacting cosmetic reforms while changing nothing of substance had for decades been the state's response to negative international human rights reports. Never, during the years-long legal process, did I hear it predicted that the state might respond by developing a whole new policy approach of reactionary juridification. In the years following the *Yean and Bosico* ruling, the state has fought lawfare with lawfare, countering international legal pressure with legal measures containing Haitian descendants' social and economic mobility. At the core of reactionary juridification is the premise that the state can, without contradiction, both promote the rule of law and expand anti-Haitian exclusionism.

Legal Reduction

Divergent Opinions in Kathmandu

Even as protestors converged on Kathmandu, kamaiyas disagreed with each other and with their allies about the right way forward. The Nepalese human rights NGO, Informal Sector Service Center, which had produced the earliest human rights field reports on kamaiya bonded labor in the 1990s, warned the BASE leader, Dilli, not to come to Kathmandu. They said that comprehensive legislation had been drafted and needed to be passed by parliament before the liberation process could begin (Fujikura 2007, 344). It was evident to some that more than official repression and rejection was being risked, namely, that winning an edict of emancipation unaccompanied by land reform and recognition of other entitlements might amount to a Pyrrhic victory. Still, all the political parties fell forward to express support when the marchers arrived in Kathmandu (ibid., 345). Meanwhile, BASE leaders privately disagreed with other NGOs about strategy: "[M]any organizations argued that since the Kamaiya issue was complex, the movement should make many demands, including even the implementation of land-reform measures" (ibid., 344). BASE leaders and Kathmandu-based intellectuals took the line articulated by Vivek at the Nepalganj meeting: "[T]he demand had to be simple and clear, otherwise the movement would not produce any tangible results."[17] The strategy was to be emancipation first, and resolution of the many other rights deficits later. What could not have been predicted was that a hitherto uninvolved actor, the king, was to enter the scene and short-circuit this process.

Legal Reduction by Ruling of the IACtHR

An important contrast with the Nepali story is that no strategic simplification was ever, to my knowledge, consciously adopted by either MUDHA or the international lawyers who supported Yean and Bosico. It was sooner through the Inter-American Court's ruling, rather than the legal reasoning presented by the plaintiffs' attorneys, that legal reduction set in.

An expansive case was presented by Yean and Bosico's legal representatives, led by the Berkeley International Human Rights Law Clinic and MUDHA's lawyer, Genaro Rincón. The commission's original petition cited the Dominican Republic for violating nine articles of the American Convention on Human Rights. Rights to a legal identity and a nationality were always the central issues, for without a birth certificate the girls' names and nationality would have been completely absent from any official register. But the girls' representatives also asked the court to rule on a cascade of other rights infringements that would follow if the girls could not get birth certificates: their right of free mobility within the Dominican Republic would be endangered if they could not get the national identity card, the Cédula de Identidad y Electoral, which every Dominican is required by law to carry; their right to travel abroad would be blocked by their inability to obtain a passport; registering for secondary and postsecondary schools would be precluded; even opening a bank account or getting legally married would be impossible. Fletcher, in a conversation with me before the case went to hearings, expressed hopes for a ruling that would set new precedents not only on the prevention of statelessness but also citizenship, education, mobility, and access to health care.[18]

The ruling of the court traced a middle ground, not troubling the precept that each state holds a sovereign right to set its citizenship rules, even as the court found the Dominican state in contravention of the international legal obligation to protect Yean's and Bosico's rights to a legal identity and a nationality. Narrow and conservative though it was, the court's judgment also made detailed reference to the range and seriousness of the other rights infringements to which Yean and Bosico were being exposed. And the ruling affirmed that thousands of other Haitian-ancestry Dominicans were being wronged in like manner, ordering sweeping corrective steps. Considering that the IACtHR generally advances legal precedent incrementally and not by leaps, this ruling may have been as decisive a victory as could have been expected. The *Yean and Bosico* case was also hailed in international legal circles at the time as the most significant legal ruling on statelessness of 2005.

Even though it was not the intention of either MUDHA or its international legal team to reduce the focus to statelessness and its remedies, the IACtHR judgement in *Yean and Bosico* seems to have had that narrowing effect, a tendency buoyed now by statelessness having become a global cause *du jour*.[19] One worry is that focusing on statelessness, like focusing on modern slavery and its abolition, may be channeling activism onto ground where the state can indefinitely put off responding to other, farther-reaching distributive justice claims.

Outcomes

Kamaiya Emancipation: Snatching Defeat from the Jaws of Victory

Leading contemporary slavery scholar Kevin Bales (2007, 102) describes the climax of the story:

> In parliament discussion had been proceeding on a law that would both free and rehabilitate slaves, but its passage was still months away. In a true democracy, the law would have been moved to the fast track, and public statements would have emphasized that the new law was coming. But in a monarchy like Nepal's there is a way to short-circuit the democratic process, and on July 17 the king ordered, by royal edict, that debt-bondage slavery was abolished. . . . The royal edict said little more than "keeping a family in debt slavery is now an offense, and the debts are now void." It did not include the wording of any new statute, instructions on how the law was to be enforced, any indication of where the funding was coming from, or whether there would be any compensation or rehabilitation for ex-slaves.

Euphoria among the kamaiyas was matched by panic among the landlords. Would freed kamaiyas claim to be the rightful owners of the garden plots and huts that they occupied? Would landlords be legally prosecuted if caught with a kamaiya family on their land? Both fears pointed toward a swift and remorseless response: "On the morning of July 18, widespread forcible evictions began" (ibid., 104).

For most kamaiyas, emancipation was like being dropped from the fat into the fire.[20] Tens of thousands were left without homes or livelihoods and crowded into refugee camps, "homeless, jobless, and hungry" (ibid., 105). Food rations fell to starvation levels and, as the monsoon rains of autumn began, "disease broke out, and people, children in particular, began to die of pneumonia, dysentery, malaria, and encephalitis" (ibid., 105). Looking back, Bales writes, "By 2007, seven years after the abolition of debt-bondage slavery in Nepal, the situation is still dire. The precise numbers are still unclear, but of the forty thousand freed kamaiya families, about two-thirds have never had any help at all. Many have not received an identity card that allows them to claim help and land, while perhaps one-fifth have been given certificates for land to be awarded in the future. One-third are still living in refugee camps" (ibid., 106). "It doesn't have to be that way," Bales (2007, 106–107) adds, noting that a postemancipation program funded by the International Labor Organization had housed 14,000 ex-kamaiyas in western Nepal, 70 percent of whom have been endowed with secure title to farms.

Reactionary Juridification: The Dominican Government's Response

Euphoria triggered by Yean and Bosico's victory in 2005 quickly faded. Far from complying with the Inter-American Court's judgment in *Yean and Bosico*, the state has taken actions that cast a shadow of potential threat over even those Haitian-ancestry Dominicans who had hitherto legally possessed citizenship, assimilated culturally, and moved up the social ladder. People who had passed unperceived into the mainstream are now being detected to be of Haitian ancestry, through inspection of their birth certificates by government officials, and are facing the prospect of exclusion from Dominican citizenship.

Particularly worrying are government moves to strip Dominican nationality retroactively from people who have had valid Dominican papers their whole lives. This has typically occurred when applicants seeking to renew their *cédula* or obtain official replica documents for university enrollment or foreign travel are found through inspection of their birth certificate to be the offspring of an undocumented immigrant (Garcia 2006, 21). Nationality stripping began even before the Dominican Constitution was amended in January 2010 to block citizenship for children of undocumented immigrants. The government claims this power under the Ley General de Migración (República Dominicana 2004, 22), which, in 2004, made it official that anyone not a legal resident is, for the purposes of the law, "in transit" (Baluarte 2006, 28). The Dominican high court (República Dominicana, Tribunal

Constitucional 2013, 99–100), in its *Sentencia 168* of September 2013, sustained the state's contention that the Dominican Constitution's "in transit" exclusion from jus soli has applied to the children of undocumented immigrants all along. This ruling also confirmed the policy of barring the issuance of official copies of birth certificates to anyone whose birth was registered by a parent bearing a nonstandard identity document.

In a move of extraordinary reach, the high court also went beyond the challenge put forward by the plaintiff, Juliana Deguis Pierre, to order the state agency in charge of the nation's civil registry, the Junta Central Electoral (JCE, State Electoral Board) to make an inventory of all "irregularly inscribed foreigners" since 1929 (the year when the "in transit" exclusion was added to the constitution). The court also called upon the presidency and Congress to pass laws resolving the residency status of undocumented foreign nationals as well as two groups of Dominican-born offspring of "illegally" resident foreigners, those inscribed as citizens and those lacking identity documents. This set off a flurry of executive, legislative, and bureaucratic actions, the outcomes of which remain ambiguous and uncertain. Only a few thousand foreign nationals have been issued permanent residency, but nearly 300,000 were to be accorded legal residency for one or two years in spite of failing to assemble all the proofs of employment and residence required for permanent residency. The JCE made public a list of 55,000 names of Haitian-ancestry Dominicans deemed immediately eligible for the *cédula* but has issued the document to very few of these people. What is sure is that the children of unauthorized immigrants born after 2007 will no longer be eligible for birthright citizenship. This future stateless group has gotten little press or activist attention amid the outrage triggered by the prospect of stripping citizenship from tens of thousands of bona fide Dominicans.

Thus it seems that the same rule of law channels in which human rights advocates had invested hope—laws and court verdicts—have been turned to go the opposite direction than that sought by rights liberals, toward entrenching ethnic exclusionism rather than treating all Dominican-born people as equals. It is as if Dominican legislators and presidential administrations took international advocates' strategic translation of Haitian rights claims into liberal constitutional terms and performed a reverse-motion pantomime of that international strategy by recasting anti-Haitian exclusionism in a legally based but antiliberal sovereignty-rights nexus. In keeping with the larger pattern of turning the legal vocabulary and strategies of human rights on its head, this reactionary juridification process culminated with a court decision, the Sentencia 168, explicitly repudiating another court decision, the Inter-American Court's ruling in *Yean and Bosico*.

Conclusion

Important contrasts distinguish the styles and forms taken by legal reductionism in these two cases. The jostling crowds of kamaiya protesters in peasant garb seem a world away from the mountains of paper that soundlessly accumulated in Washington, DC, San José, Costa Rica, Berkeley, New York, and Santo Domingo through competing legal motions in the *Yean and Bosico* case. Fundamental differences in each country's political space are also reflected in the starkly different time horizons of the two cases, kamaiya emancipation having happened rapidly, perhaps even prematurely, through royal fiat, by contrast with the years of lawyering through which a normative focus on the prevention of statelessness would be distilled via the Inter-American Court's *Yean and Bosico* ruling. More importantly still, kamaiya CMO leaders *chose* to simplify their claims around the goal of winning a law or edict that would outlaw kamaiya contracts, while in the Dominican case legal reduction seems to have happened *in spite of* the efforts of MUDHA and its lawyers to seek a more expansive ruling than they got from the Inter-American Court. The Dominican case presents a paradox worthy of scrutiny: juridification narrowed social movement claims to one—preventing statelessness—even as the involvement of human rights lawyers broadened international understandings of Haitian descendants' rights struggles, expanded the evidence base for rights claims, and better aligned the international human rights agenda with the priorities of frontline rights defenders. Claims narrowing was in this case not a conscious strategy so much as an unintended product of the legal process. Uniting both cases, it seems to have been at the very moment when law was pronounced—whether via royal edict or the ruling of a regional human rights court—that the social movement agenda underwent fatal constriction.

That commonality between the two cases points to what might be called the "lawfare conundrum": in passing through the prism of national and international law, can a broad-spectrum activist agenda ever be faithfully and fully upstreamed? Or will translation into a "juridical notion of power" (Prakash 1990, 219) always result in social movement agendas being diffracted into narrow and discrete bands of concern, pushing the multiplicity of oppression's forms and forces out of sight? Behind this dilemma stands the enduring challenge to human rights of structural injustice, wrongs that cannot be blamed on a single legal personality (Young 2011, 45 and 96). In spite of the term's abstract sound, structural injustice is more than an academic concern but mirrors the political dilemma that, according to Fujikura, confronted kamaiya leaders in July 2000: Would narrowing their demands produce a legal breakthrough, on the basis of which they could pursue a full range of entitlements? What precisely gets lost, and under what circumstances this kind of strategic trade-off has proven worth the gamble, are questions ripe for further case-based, comparative study. Everything may hinge on the object and context of struggle. Legal avenues may work well, and work far better than political protest would, where the claim concerns access to specifiable goods or services, such as land rights or prescription medicines (Zenker 2012, 138). Where the object of struggle is injustice that is not just structural but *complex*, consisting of multiple, overlapping, and mutually supportive abuses, unfair exclusions, and prejudices, then litigation may yield positive outcomes only when joined with traditional forms of protest and innovative media appeals.

What stands out also is the "the gap between the defined human rights framework and the people's realities and needs" (Oré Aguilar 2011, 115). This gap was, in the Nepali and Dominican cases, not a conflict between a universalizing human rights and particular local concepts and systems so much as a mismatch between holistic subaltern social justice politics and the reductive techniques of a human rights managerial elite. In no way do I reject the validity or urgency of bringing localized perceptions and idioms of justice into account. Cultural pluralism is a fact. My issue is how the issues raised by local human rights defenders may be made to appear of limited significance when referred to as nothing more than a reflection of localized concerns. Anthropology's habitual particularism falls short when it implies that the tensions between social movement aims and international human rights tactics are nothing more than cultural particularities or problems of linguistic translatability. "Making native informers out of radical critics," writes critical theorist Hamid Dabashi (2015, 130), "is the oldest trick in the outdated Orientalist arsenal." Or as Boaventura de Sousa Santos (2002, 90) concludes, legal pluralism, when described in idiographic particularist terms, "became an analytical device that allowed for thicker descriptions of law in action, while the political challenge it mounted against [the] state . . .

was sidelined." Applying Dabashi's and Sousa Santos's insights to the cases at hand, the interpretive frame of universalism versus particularism shrinks social movements' messages of dissent against human rights orthodoxy to the particulars of culture. That completely undercuts social movements' claims also to be able to say something universal about the human.[21] Gaps often understood to hold between the universal and the particular may also involve conflicts of perspective between politically dominant and subordinate actors. It is not a question of subaltern universals but of the universality of superordinate-subordinate divides.

The question remains open whether the frame of liberal versus distributive justice accurately demarcates the ground for a decolonized human rights. It seems surer to say that in the vastly different local contexts of Nepal and the Dominican Republic, decisions about how to translate social movement agendas into rights claims have weighed two competing visions of justice, one juridical—prioritizing civil/political freedoms, free contracts, and unimpeded geographical, social, and occupational mobility—the other distributive—seeking entitlements to the material and intellectual resources needed to turn liberal rights into effective freedoms. A major asset to De Feyter's "two-way street" concept of localization, then, is that it opens a window on not just the locally, linguistically, and culturally particular but also admits consideration of distributive justice deficits of global scope, which are to date only imperfectly addressed through human rights.

Remembering lastly that juridification was embraced by social movement CMO leaders as an imagined path to breakthrough, Aníbal Quijano's vision of "coloniality" may provide a particularly apt theorization through which to launch a dialogue about decolonizing human rights. Coloniality, for Quijano, is more than enduring racial ideologies and persistent inequalities in trade and military might. It is also "a colonization of the imagination of the dominated" (Quijano 2007, 169), resulting historically from the colonizers' first mystifying "their own patterns of producing knowledge and meaning" (i.e., privileging Western gnosis as a bearer of transhistorical truths) and then instituting Western-derived systems of thought as ways of gaining access to power. Thus coloniality lives on in a world in which colonialism as a political order has largely been destroyed, one micro-process of which is the alienation of knowledge from subaltern subjects by converting it into "evidence" for processing and packaging by legal experts. From this viewpoint, the danger of narrowing a collectively devised liberation agenda seems to increase exponentially with every step that rights claims take from their CMO origins.

That is not to say that other outcomes might not have emerged from juridifying these two rights struggles. The Nepalese king might have been persuaded to hold off from enacting a feel-good emancipation decree until the parliament devised a comprehensive plan that might enable ex-kamaiyas to find alternative livelihoods once their debt contracts were severed. And instead of peppering the state with further lawsuits, the Dominican CMOs and their international backers might have pivoted, after the *Yean and Bosico* victory, to a nonlitigational approach, using social media and traditional media to try to persuade their fellow Dominicans of the rightness of their rights claims. Is the problem, then, juridification? Or is it that juridification played out in ways that, in Molyneux's (1985) terms, were too "strategic"—that is, defined deductively and through an external actor's analysis of a group's subordination—and not "practical" enough—that is, defined inductively on the basis of CMO social movement praxis? Alienating claims from their originators seems necessary—at some point another knowing subject (journalist, monitor, attorney) must pick up other humans' rights claims and repeat these in their own words—yet always carries potential distortions. International human rights practitioners may have no choice other than to proceed with a greater skepticism about the value of sticking to a single strategy and a constant awareness that narrowing social movement aims is a risk inherent in a legalist imaginary of human rights.

Acknowledgments

Funding for various stages of the author's Dominican Republic–based research was awarded by the Carter G. Woodson Institute for Afro-American and African Studies, University of Virginia, by the University of Connecticut Research Foundation, by the William and Flora Hewlett Foundation, US–Latin American Relations Program, and by the Social Science Research Council, Program on Global Security and Cooperation. Secondary-source research on kamaiya emancipation was made possible by a fellowship from Yale University's Gilder Lehrman Center for the Study of Slavery, Resistance and Abolition. The author is, except where duly noted, the originator of this chapter's content and is responsible as well for any remaining errors or omissions. Profound gratitude goes to Tine Destrooper and the two anonymous peer reviewers for their extraordinarily valuable comments on a revised version of this chapter as well as to the participants in the NYU workshop on localizing human rights (November 10–11, 2015), who read and commented on a preliminary draft, with thanks in particular to the workshop's preceptors, Tine Destrooper, Sally Merry, and Koen de Feyter.

Notes

1. Community membership organizations (CMOs) are defined here as a kind of nongovernmental organization, based on grassroots participation and consensus-based decision making.

2. Of the five dimensions of juridification identified by Blichner and Molander (2008, cited in Eckert et al. 2012, 4–5), I am concerned here only with the middle one, "the tendency to solve conflict increasingly by reference to law." This sequentially follows the first two dimensions, "the establishment of a legal order" and "law's expansion and differentiation."

3. "The Problem of the Indian," p. 4, n. 4, 2, 1. In *Seven Interpretive Essays on Peruvian Reality*, https://www.marxists.org/archive/mariateg/works/7-interpretive-essays/essay02.htm.

4. Just who is today's "colonizer" may not be obvious. In his chapter in this volume, Johannes Waldmüller raises the possibility that the Ecuadorian leftist regime of Hugo Morales mimics Spanish colonizers even as it ventriloquizes Amerindian shamans, by pairing public celebrations of *pachamama* with private invitations to multinational corporate extractivists. Such abuses are perpetrated in the name of including collective subaltern voices and propounding a holistic vision of rights, in terms not entirely dissimilar from the decolonization that I advocate here. Coloniality may thus, like the law, come in hard and soft varieties, the domination of international human rights professionals looking very soft when compared with cynical state appropriations of human rights discourse à la Morales.

5. John and Jean Comaroff (2006) coin the term "lawfare" as a shorthand for the tendency of diverse social movements worldwide to turn to litigation by preference over other established forms of political action (e.g., public protest, media and lobbying). The law's focused power sucks energy out of these other avenues of justice-seeking, to the detriment of social movement participants' aspirations to find a voice independently of structures of state power. David Jacobson and Galya Ruffer (2003) earlier discerned that the global expansion of human rights was bringing about a shift toward "judicial agency," in which the pursuit of legal rights claims enables individuals and groups "to bypass traditional democratic forms of political mobilization" (74)

6. The first international denunciation was issued by the Migration Secretariat of the World Council of Churches in 1978, but the report most often credited with first raising international awareness of the plight of Haitian workers in the Dominican Republic is that issued the following year by the Anti-Slavery Society (1979).

7. Besides the case that is discussed in some detail in this chapter, that of *Yean and Bosico v. Dominican Republic*, the Dominican state has seen its migrant and minority rights record challenged in three other cases brought before Inter-American human rights bodies. In the so-called "mass expulsions" case, the Inter-American Court in 2014 awarded remedies from the Dominican state on behalf of Haitian nationals who were expelled to Haiti without due process and for Dominicans of Haitian ancestry who were expatriated in spite of carrying valid legal identity documents identifying them as Dominican citizens (http://corteidh.or.cr/docs/casos/articulos/seriec_282_esp.pdf). In the case of the so-called "Guayubín massacre," the court in 2012 found the Dominican government at fault for the failure of the Dominican justice system to prosecute soldiers implicated

152 Samuel Martínez

in an extrajudicial killing of seven undocumented Haitian migrants in 2000 near the frontier with Haiti (http://www.corteidh.or.cr/docs/casos/articulos/seriec_251_esp.pdf). And in 2010, a petition was filed with the Inter-American Commission for Human Rights (the investigative body of the Inter-American human rights system) on behalf of Emildo Bueno Oguis, a Dominican of Haitian parentage who was barred from joining his wife in the United States solely because the Dominican authorities refused to grant him an official copy of his birth certificate (https://www.opensocietyfoundations.org/sites/default/files/Petition%20Summary-20100601.pdf).

8. The report commissioned by the World Organisation Against Torture (OMCT 2010, 13–16) describes a series of kamaiya uprisings, strikes, and land occupations dating back as far as 1951. See also Cheria et al. 2005, Ch. 4; Dhakal et al. 2000, Ch. 5; GEFONT 2006, 32–35.

9. There were also other, less prominent, kamaiya-led NGOs at work prior to 2000, as well as the allegedly Maoist rebel-linked Tharuwan Mukti Morcha (Tharu Area Liberation Front), credited with having "taken action against feudal landlords as revenge against the exploitation of *Kamaiyas* and their sisters, daughters and wives" (OMCT 2010, 20–22).

10. http://nepalbase.org/chairpersons-profile/

11. https://treaties.un.org/pages/ViewDetailsIII.aspx?src=TREATY&mtdsg_no=XVIII-4&chapter=18&Temp=mtdsg3&lang=en

12. Author's interview, July 4, 1997.

13. Author's interview with Roxanna Altholz and Laurel Fletcher, Berkeley, California, November 16, 2012.

14. Author's interview with MUDHA staffers, May 22, 2002, Santo Domingo; Garcia 2006, 21.

15. "Jus soli" is effectively synonymous with "birthright citizenship." According to Merriam-Webster's online dictionary, "jus soli" is "a rule that the citizenship of a child is determined by the place of its birth" (http://www.merriam-webster.com/dictionary/jus%20soli).

16. Author's interview with Laurel Fletcher, February 4, 2005, New Haven, Connecticut. Also, Genaro Rincón Miesse, the Dominican lawyer representing MUDHA at the IACtHR proceedings, noted, "The civil status registrars do not apply these requirements consistently," registrars in districts where there are few Haitians being more permissive (Inter-American Court of Human Rights 2006, 116).

17. Dilli at the time characterized the change in BASE strategy as a shift from a "project mentality" to a "social movement" (Fujikura 2001, 306). Rankin (1999, 41), in a paper published soon before the events of 2000, writes that BASE "realizes that the potential to overturn the kamaiya system lies first neither in the market nor the law, but rather in gradual consciousness-raising among both kamaiyas and Tharus generally."

18. Author's interview with Laurel Fletcher, February 4, 2005, New Haven, Connecticut.

19. The UNHCR sponsored the first global forum on statelessness in The Hague in September 2014 and, noting that at least 10 million people worldwide remain stateless, in that year also launched a ten-year campaign to eradicate statelessness by 2024 (http://www.unhcr.org/pages/53174c306.html).

20. In the kamaiya-rights activist literature there is agreement that kamaiyas were displaced in the tens of thousands after the emancipation edict, with most of the displaced ending up living like refugees (Cheria et al. 2005, Ch. 5; Chhetri 2005, 40–42). Tim Whyte (in Lowe 2001) adds that uncounted numbers of kamaiyas remain on their landlords' land for lack of anywhere else to go. On the basis of interviews with ex-kamaiyas, economist Jon Kvalbein (2007, 63) concludes "that the *kamaiyas*' dominant strategies right after the abolition were to work for the same landlord for a couple of years as casual workers or to do casual work and live in their own home."

Birendra Giri (2009, 607–608) reports that there are ex-kamaiyas who have renewed their debts with landlords not by moving back as families but by sending their children to work in their place (see also GEFONT 2006, 60–62).

21. As cultural anthropologist Harry Englund (2012, 89) recommends, anthropologists should "consider carefully whether the claims they investigate are best regarded as culturally specific hybrids or . . . entail insights that have more general consequence for theorising human rights."

Works Cited

Adhikari, Bipin. 2000. "Kamaiyas of Nepal: Bonded No More?" *Independent Weekly* (Kathmandu) 10 (23), July 26–August 1, http://www.hrsolidarity.net/mainfile.php/2000vol10no09/705/.
Anti-Slavery Society. 1979. "Migrant Workers in the Dominican Republic." *Anti-Slavery Reporter and Aborigines' Friend (Series VI)*, 12 (6): 11–14.
Bales, Kevin. 2007. *Ending Slavery: How We Free Today's Slaves*. Berkeley: University of California Press.
Baluarte, David C. 2006. "Inter-American Justice Comes to the Dominican Republic: An Island Shakes as Human Rights and Sovereignty Clash." *American University Human Rights Brief* 13 (2): 25–28, 38, http://www.wcl.american.edu/hrbrief/13/2baluarte.pdf?rd=1.
Baxi, Upendra. 2007. *Human Rights in a Posthuman World: Critical Essays*. New Delhi: Oxford University Press.
Blichner, Lars C., and Anders Molander. 2008. "Mapping Juridification." *European Law Journal* 14 (1): 36–54.
Bob, Clifford. 2002. "Merchants of Morality." *Foreign Policy* (129): 36–45.
Brysk, Alison. 2013. "Human Rights Movements." In *The Wiley-Blackwell Encyclopedia of Social and Political Movements*, edited by David A. Snow, Donatella della Porta, Bert Klandermans, and Doug McAdam. Hoboken, NJ: John Wiley & Sons.
Campbell, Tom. 2013. "Human Rights: Moral or Legal?" In *Human Rights: Old Problems, New Possibilities*, edited by David Kinley, Wojciech Sadurski, and Kevin Walton, 1–26. Cheltenham, UK: Edward Elgar.
CCDH (Centro Cultural Domínico-Haitiano). 1997. *Análisis de la situación de inmigrantes haitianos en la República Dominicana*. Santo Domingo: CCDH.
Cedeño, Carmen. 1992. "La nacionalidad de los descendientes de haitianos nacidos en la República Dominicana." In *La cuestión haitiana en Santo Domingo: Migración internacional, desarrollo y relaciones inter-estatales entre Haití y República Dominicana*, edited by Wilfredo Lozano, 137–43. Santo Domingo: FLACSO–Programa República Dominicana and Centro Norte-Sur, Universidad de Miami.
Cheria Edwin, Anita, Nanda Kumar Kandangwa, and Khemraj Upadhyaya. 2005. *Liberation Is Not Enough: The Kamaiya Movement in Nepal*. Kathmandu: ActionAid International Nepal.
Chhetri, Ram B. 2005. "The Plight of the Tharu Kamaiyas in Nepal: A Review of the Social, Economic and Political Facts." In *Occasional Papers in Sociology and Anthropology, vol. 9*, 22–46. Kathmandu: Central Department of Sociology and Anthropology, Tribhuvan University. Accessed via Digital Himalaya: http://himalaya.socanth.cam.ac.uk/collections/journals/opsa/pdf/OPSA_09_02.pdf.

Comaroff, John L., and Jean Comaroff. 2006. "Law and Disorder in the Postcolony: An Introduction." In *Law and Disorder in the Postcolony*, edited by Jean Comaroff and John L. Comaroff, 1–56. Chicago: University of Chicago Press.

Dabashi, Hamid. 2015. *Post-Orientalism: Knowledge and Power in an Age of Terror*. 2nd edition. Piscataway: Transaction Publishers.

De Feyter, Koen. 2007. "Localising Human Rights." In *Economic Globalisation and Human Rights*, edited by Wolfgang Benedek, Koen de Feyter, and Fabrizio Marrella, 67–92. Cambridge: Cambridge University Press.

Destrooper, Tine, 2015. "Reconciling Discourses on Women's Rights: Learning from Guatemalan Indigenous Women's Groups." *Journal of Human Rights Practice* 7 (2): 223–245.

Dhakal, Suresh, Janak Rai, Dambar Chemchong, Dhruba Maharjan, Pranita Pradhan, Jagat Maharjan, and Shreeram Chaudhary. 2000. *Issues and Experiences: Kamaiya System, Kanara Andolan and Tharus in Bardiya*. Kathmandu: Society for Participatory Cultural Education.

Eckert, Julia, Zerrin Özlem Biner, Brian Donahoe, and Christian Strümpell. 2012. "Introduction: Law's Travels and Transformations." In *Law against the State: Ethnographic Forays into Law's Transformations*, edited by Julia Eckert, Brian Donahoe, Christian Strümpell, and Zerrin Özlem Biner, 1–22. Cambridge: Cambridge University Press.

Eggan, Fred. 1954. "Social Anthropology and the Method of Controlled Comparison." *American Anthropologist* 56 (5): 743–763.

Englund, Harri. 2012, "Human Rights and Village Headmen in Malawi: Translation Beyond Vernacularisation." In *Law against the State: Ethnographic Forays into Law's Transformations*, edited by Julia Eckert, Brian Donahoe, Christian Strümpell, and Zerrin Özlem Biner, 70–93. Cambridge: Cambridge University Press.

Fujikura, Tatsuro. 2001. "Discourses of Awareness: Notes for a Criticism of Development in Nepal." *Studies in Nepali History and Society* 6 (2): 271–313.

———. 2007. "The Bonded Agricultural Labourers' Freedom Movement in Western Nepal." In *Political and Social Transformations in North India and Nepal*, edited by Hiroshi Ishii, David N. Gellner, and Katsuo Nawa, 319–51. New Delhi: Manohar.

Garcia, Michelle. 2006. "No Papers, No Rights." *Amnesty International Magazine* (Fall): 20–23, 30.

GEFONT, 2006. *Nepal: Kamaiyas and Interventions (Report on Analysis of the Effectiveness of Interventions for the Release and Rehabilitation of Bonded Labour in Nepal)*. Kathmandu: General Federation of Nepalese Trade Unions.

Giri, Birendra. 2009. "The Bonded Labour System in Nepal: Perspectives of Haliya and Kamaiya Child Workers." *Journal of Asian and African Studies* 44 (6): 599–623.

Godoy, Angelina Snodgrass. 2013. *Of Medicines and Markets: Intellectual Property and Human Rights in the Free Trade Era*. Stanford: Stanford University Press.

Guha, Ranajit. 1983. "The Prose of Counter-Insurgency." In *Subaltern Studies II: Writings on South Asian History and Society*, edited by Ranajit Guha, 1–42. Delhi: Oxford University Press.

Hemment, Julie. 2004. "Global Civil Society and the Local Costs of Belonging: Defining Violence against Women in Russia." *Signs* 29 (3): 815–840.

Hertel, Shareen. 2006. "New Moves in Transnational Advocacy: Getting Labor and Economic Rights on the Agenda in Unexpected Ways." *Global Governance* 12: 263–281.

Inter-American Court of Human Rights, 2006. "Case of the Yean and Bosico Children v. the Dominican Republic, Judgment of September 8, 2005." *Refugee Survey Quarterly* 25 (3): 92–182.

Jacobson, David, and Galya Benarieh Ruffer. 2003. "Courts Across Borders: The Implications of Judicial Agency for Human Rights and Democracy." *Human Rights Quarterly* 25 (1): 74–92.

Kennedy, David. 2004. *The Dark Sides of Virtue: Reassessing International Humanitarianism*. Princeton: Princeton University Press.

Kvalbein, Jon Audun. 2007. *Liberated Bonded Laborers: Are They Better Off? Welfare and Efficiency Implications of an Agricultural Reform in Western Terai, Nepal*. Bergen: Chr. Michelsen Institute.

Lamichhane, Padma Raj. 2006. *Bonded Labour (Kamaiya) in Nepal*. Kathmandu: Trilij Counselling Centre.

Lawyers Committee for Human Rights. 1991. *A Childhood Abducted: Children Cutting Sugar Cane in the Dominican Republic*. New York: Lawyers Committee for Human Rights.

Lowe, Peter. 2001. *Kamaiya: Freedom and Slavery in Nepal*. Introduction and Afterword by Tim Whyte. Kathmandu: Mandala Book Point.

Martínez, Samuel. 2011. "The Onion of Oppression: Haitians in the Dominican Republic." In *Geographies of the Haitian Diaspora*, edited by Regine O. Jackson, 51–70. New York: Routledge.

Meckled-García, Saladin, and Başak Çali. 2006. "Lost in Translation: The Human Rights Ideal and International Human Rights Law." In *The Legalization of Human Rights: Multidisciplinary Perspectives on Human Rights and Human Rights Law*, edited by Saladin Meckled-García and Başak Çali, 11–31. Abdingdon, UK: Routledge.

Merry, Sally Engle. 2006a. "Transnational Human Rights and Local Activism: Mapping the Middle." *American Anthropologist* 108 (1): 38–51.

———. 2006b. *Human Rights and Gender Violence: Translating International Law into Local Justice*. Chicago: University of Chicago Press.

Mignolo, Walter D. 2000. *Local Histories/Global Designs: Coloniality, Subaltern Knowledges, and Border Thinking*. Princeton: Princeton University Press.

Molyneux, Maxine. 1985. "Mobilization without Emancipation? Women's Interests, the State, and Revolution in Nicaragua." *Feminist Studies* 11 (2): 227–254.

Moyn, Samuel. 2010. *The Last Utopia: Human Rights in History*. Cambridge, MA: Belknap Press.

OMCT. 2010. "The *Kamaiya* System of Bonded Labour in Nepal." World Organisation Against Torture, Country Case Study, *Attacking the Root Causes of Torture: Poverty, Inequality and Violence. An Interdisciplinary Study*. http://www.omct.org/files/interdisciplinary-study/ii_b_3_nepal_case_study.pdf.

Oré Aguilar, Gaby. 2011. "The Local Relevance of Human Rights: A Methodological Approach." In *The Local Relevance of Human Rights*, edited by Koen de Feyter, Stephan Parmentier, Christiane Timmerman, and George Ulrich, 109–146. Cambridge: Cambridge University Press.

Osiatyński, Wiktor. 2009. *Human Rights and Their Limits*. New York: Cambridge University Press.

Prakash, Gyan. 1990. *Bonded Histories: Genealogies of Bonded Labor Servitude in Colonial India*. Cambridge: Cambridge University Press.

Quijano, Aníbal. 2007. "Coloniality and Modernity/Rationality." *Cultural Studies* 21 (2–3): 168–178.

———. 2008. "Coloniality of Power, Eurocentrism, and Latin America." In *Coloniality at Large: Latin America and the Postcolonial Debate*, edited by Mabel Moraña, Enrique Dussel, and Carlos Jáuregui, 181–224. Durham, NC: Duke University Press.

Rankin, Katherine N. 1999. "The Predicament of Labor: Kamaiya Practices and the Ideology of 'Freedom.'" In *Nepal: Tharu and Tarai Neighbours*, edited by Harald O. Skar, 27–45. Kathmandu: Bibliotheca Himalayica.

República Dominicana. 2004. "Ley General de Migración, No. 285-04." *Gaceta Oficial* 10291, August 27: 5–46, http://www.seip.gob.do/Portals/0/docs/Migracion/ley.pdf.

República Dominicana, Tribunal Constitucional. 2013. "Sentencia TC/0168/13." http://noticiasmicrojuris.files.wordpress.com/2013/10/sentenciatc0168-13-c.pdf.

Sousa Santos, Boaventura. 2002. *Toward a New Legal Common Sense: Law, Globalization, and Emancipation*, 2nd ed. London: LexisNexis Butterworths.

Speed, Shannon. 2007. "Exercising Rights and Reconfiguring Resistance in the Zapatista Juntas de Buen Gobierno." In *The Practice of Human Rights: Tracking Law between the Global and the Local*, edited by Mark Goodale and Sally Engle Merry, 163–192. Cambridge: Cambridge University Press.

Wilson, Richard Ashby. 2007. "Tyrannosaurus Lex: The Anthropology of Human Rights and Transnational Law." In *The Practice of Human Rights: Tracking Law between the Global and the Local*. Edited by Mark Goodale and Sally Engle Merry, 342–368. Cambridge: Cambridge University Press

Young, Iris Marion. 2011. *Responsibility for Justice*. Chicago: University of Chicago Press.

Zenker, Olaf. 2012. "The Juridification of Political Protest and the Politicisation of Legalism in South African Land Restitution." In *Law Against the State: Ethnographic Forays into Law's Transformations*, edited by Julia Eckert, Brian Donahoe, Christian Strümpell, and Zerrin Özlem Biner, 118–146. Cambridge: Cambridge University Press.

CHAPTER 6

New Visibilities: Challenging Torture and Impunity in Vietnam

Ken MacLean

Visitors to the museum in Phu Quoc enter through the main gate and cross the path that follows the perimeter of the former prison. Two three-meter fences, covered with razor wire, bound the path on both sides, separating it from the prison grounds proper. Visitors pass by life-size mannequins of a Republic of Vietnam (RoV) soldier and his U.S.-trained German shepherd guard dog before moving toward the rows of barracks constructed out of tin, a short distance beyond the inner gate. The former prison covered four hectares of land—then the largest such facility in the country—and it housed approximately 36,000 prisoners in 1972, during the height of the Second Indochina War. Phu Quoc was the primary site where RoV personnel tortured known and suspected "communists." Forty-five *tableaux vivants* are scattered throughout the restored grounds, each of which depicts a different method that the RoV soldiers used to extract confessions and to punish noncompliant prisoners. These methods ranged from "tiger cages" and hand-cranked Magneto devices to apply electrical shocks, to stress positions used to immobilize people during beatings and waterboarding (Hành 2015).

This museum is not unique. Several museums that feature torture exist across the country, most notably Hoa Lo Prison in the capital, where French guards used these techniques on political prisoners during the colonial period.[1] Collectively, these state-supported museums convey a similar message: the nationalist struggle for independence triumphed over those who utilized torture in an effort to stop it. But torture did not end with National

Reunification in 1976. Security services, especially commune-level police, employ many of the same techniques on display in the Phu Quoc museum today. How some Vietnamese antitorture activists challenge the culture of impunity that enables police to employ such practices is the subject of this chapter.[2] The strategies employed take a variety of forms. My focus is upon visual ones, with special attention to the ways in which these representations articulate claims to citizenship and thus specific sets of rights.

The visual objectification of "bodies in pain," Elizabeth Dauphinée argues, enables a wide range of political and ethical projects (Dauphinée 2007, 139). Visual citizenship is among them. According to Jennifer Telesca, visual expressions of citizenship mediate political action. Videos, photographs, and other forms of visual expression do so because they affect people on a visceral level and thus facilitate their desire to challenge the structures and practices that deny them their full sociocultural, economic, civil, and/or political rights as citizens, including state protection from human rights violations. Images, in other words, are readily understood, convey what words often cannot, and provide the affective basis for directed action. Furthermore, according to Telesca, media practices "organize and shape our understanding about ourselves and others as citizenry" in ways that are not reducible to or even captured by legal frames (2013, 339). Legal action is not the sole channel through which people claim citizenship and mobilize the support of others whose rights are already protected, however.

Her argument provides the point of departure for my own. Human Rights Watch (HRW) released a major fact-finding report on police torture in Vietnam in 2014. The report provides summaries of thirty-nine cases that occurred between 2010 and 2014. These documented cases include twenty-eight custodial deaths. Police officials admitted that torture was the cause of death in fourteen of them. The remainder allegedly died of unexplained causes (four), suicide (six), or illness (four). Fourteen more people endured torture while in custody but survived (Human Rights Watch 2014a). The NGO's researchers compiled this dataset primarily using online media sources, which included government-controlled newspapers as well as social media websites and independent blogs. I used this dataset to focus my research into the visual content antitorture activists use to disseminate information, raise awareness, and apply pressure for change. This approach is not without complications. The visual material is "distributed" across spaces (off- as well as online) and appears in multiple interpretive contexts, which affects what the video clips, photographs, and other graphic materials "mean"

(Gell 1998, 221–23). A systematic study of these visual materials is not possible for this reason. Consequently, I limited my analysis to the most widely known and documented cases of torture summarized in the Human Rights Watch report and the emergent forms of antitorture activism related to them.

My initial survey reveals a clear bifurcation in the forms of activism. Local-level claims typically demand retributive justice through court action. Transnational-level claims, by contrast, demand preventive justice through the enactment of national-level reforms in order to bring laws, policies, and procedures into conformity with international practices. So, although both sets of demands call for greater transparency and accountability, they do so using quite different visual vocabularies—entitlement discourse in the case of the former, and human rights discourse in the case of the latter. As a result, there is relatively little interaction between activists working at the local level and the transnational level at present. Nevertheless, the comparison of these visual vocabularies provides important insights into if, when, and why Vietnamese antitorture activists draw upon human rights norms to mobilize support for their respective goals. The next section provides a situation analysis of the torture epidemic in Vietnam. I then present details on the political ecology of human rights documentation online. Two brief case studies follow. The first case study analyzes the local-level media strategies that citizen-journalists use to present visual evidence of police torture to others. The second case study investigates transnational ones. I revisit the implications that the resulting patterns of the (non)adoption of human rights discourse might have on the future of upstreaming and downstreaming relevant norms in the conclusion.

Situation Analysis

Torture and custodial deaths in Vietnam have long been a "public secret," something widely known but not openly acknowledged due to fear of retribution if one speaks out (Taussig 1999). The situation is slowly beginning to change. The government signed the United Nations Convention against Torture and Other Cruel, Inhuman, or Degrading Treatment or Punishment (hereafter UNCAT) in 2013, and the Ministry of Foreign Affairs hosted a workshop in June 2014 to discuss how to implement it upon ratification (Mehta 2014).[3] The National Assembly's Justice Commission went on to hold the country's first public hearing on torture in September 2014. Truong Trong

Nghia, the vice-chair of the Vietnam Bar Association, testified during the hearing. He stated that, although the new constitution (2013) banned torture, the practice "still exists; [investigators] treat suspects like their enemies rather than their equals." "Wrongful verdicts, threats, and torture pose critical threats to the regime itself," he continued; "the [victims'] descendants will hold us responsible" (Tin Nong 2014). The minister of public security, speaking at the same hearing, reported that 23 case of police torture had reached trial between 2011 and 2013, and another 183 officers had been disciplined through dismissal, demotion, or reassignment during this same period for violating investigative procedures (Defend The [Human Rights] Defenders 2014). These statistics only include cases where government officials decided to take action, thus, they are likely to represent only a small portion of the total number of incidents in which police employ torture.

Human Rights Watch asserts this is the case. The NGO released a major report, *Public Insecurity: Deaths in Custody and Police Brutality in Vietnam*, five days after the Justice Commission's hearings ended. The report provided empirical support for allegations that torture is routinely used, geographically widespread, and has grown progressively worse in recent years (Human Rights Watch 2014a). Tran Thi Bich Van, the deputy spokesperson for the Ministry of Foreign Affairs, immediately dismissed HRW's recommendations (Thanh Nien News 2014). Key recommendations included the creation of an independent police complaint mechanism, local-level internal affairs units, a tracking system to address allegations of abuse, and the use of videotape to record interrogations, among others. In her statement, she stressed that "every act of torture or corporal punishment committed during investigative and judicial procedures is strictly treated in line with Vietnamese laws" (ibid.).

The National Assembly ratified the UNCAT in November of 2014. "The ratification of the [UN]CAT is aimed at better ensuring the basis of human rights," stated the chairman of the National Assembly's Committee for External Relations. "Becoming an officially recognized party to the convention would act as a foundation for Vietnam to increase talks on human rights with other countries and international organizations, as well as engaging with the UN human rights bodies," he continued (Tuoi Tre News, October 24, 2014). The prime minister issued an implementation action plan five months later (Thu Tuong Chinh Phu 2015). The plan requires the Ministry of Justice to amend the Penal Code to include torture as a separate charge. (Currently, allegations of torture are framed as either "forcing evidence or testimony" or "applying corporal punishment.") The plan also calls on relevant ministries and agencies to prevent such practices, to hold officials accountable when they occur, and to educate the public about their legal rights and protections as set out in the revised Criminal Procedure Code. Vietnamese antitorture activists welcomed these changes, but they maintain that the plan fails to sufficiently address the institutionalized arrangements that perpetuate impunity, especially at the commune level where police receive the least training and are subject to little oversight by their superiors. They pointed out that poor communication along the administrative chain of command reduces the vertical oversight needed to prevent torture and to respond to it when it occurs. Government ministries also remain "stove-piped" so horizontal information sharing and coordination across them is often difficult as well. Both problems limit the ability of officials to interact effectively with the police, public security agencies, the Supreme People's Procuracy, and the Supreme People's Courts, among other relevant bodies. One nationally known writer, turned torture activist, opined that for these reasons, "there are more and more coffins going sightseeing around town with each passing day" (Vo Thi Hao 2014). The funeral processions that enable the coffins to go "sightseeing" increasingly serve as the vehicle for impromptu protests against police brutality, torture, and custodial deaths. The protests and the often violent response to them by police now garner significant press coverage, including in the state-run media, which is further raising awareness that local, seemingly isolated tragedies are in fact a national problem.

A number of factors limit the ability of people engaged in different types of antitorture projects to combine their efforts to create a broad-based social movement, however. First, police torture and custodial deaths frequently go unreported. Accounts by citizen-journalists sometimes appear online, but rarely receive substantial mainstream coverage in the state-managed press of Vietnam unless violent protests occur. Second, recent government action, summarized above, has created a national framework for challenging impunity with regard to torture, but the reforms related to investigative procedures, while somewhat improved, remain problematic. For example, Circular 28, issued in 2014 and entitled "Regulating the Conduct of Criminal Investigations by the People's Public Security," states that police officials must "comply with the Constitution and laws [and] respect the interests of the State, human rights, and the rights of legitimate interests of offices, organizations, and individuals" (Bộ Công An 2014). Yet, the circular increases the role commune-level police can play in preliminary investigations, even though they have the least training and resources at their disposal and are the most likely to commit torture. Furthermore, the circular undermines due process protections by granting police excessive discretion in determining which defense activities are appropriate and which are subject to penalty, such as "carrying out activities that prevent or cause difficulties to investigation work such as . . . preventing [someone from giving] a statement, disclosing secrets . . . or filing baseless complaints or petitions" (Article 38) (Human Rights Watch 2014b). Third, activists involved in transnational antitorture campaigns are able to engage with like-minded international NGOs and politically engaged diaspora groups. These organizations, while they rely upon the information activists inside the country provide them, are rarely able to directly carry out advocacy-related work on the ground.

Fear of retaliation, lack of material resources, low level of human rights awareness, institutional obstacles, and censorship, among other obstacles, thus limit the ability of antitorture activists from collaborating and coordinating their efforts. Instead, they largely conduct their activism in parallel streams, which prevents these nascent networks from crafting a coherent human rights framework for action. Nevertheless, the activist practices I feature later in the chapter do provide valuable insights into the reshaping of human rights subjectivities, particularly claims to citizenship, in visual form. The next section describes the context in which these activists operate.

Digital Context

Vietnam developed a robust system of surveillance, a combination of bureaucratic procedures and networks of informers, to monitor its citizens during the socialist era. Both practices remain in use, but Internet surveillance has largely supplanted them. Reporters Without Borders, an NGO that monitors freedom of the press globally, consistently ranks Vietnam as an "Enemy of the Internet" due to the tactics security services use to limit expression online (Reporters Without Borders 2015). These tactics typically consist of a combination of technical measures that restrict connectivity, for example, malware to track usage, denial-of-service attacks to prevent access to banned websites, and vaguely worded laws, such as "the abuse of democratic freedoms," which grant prosecutors immense discretionary powers (Civil Rights Defenders 2015). Another NGO, Committee to Protect Journalists, similarly places Vietnam in the top ten of the most repressive countries with regard to freedom of expression (2015). Nevertheless, the number of Internet users continues to explode, rising from approximately 200,000 in 2000 to 39 million in 2014, making it "15th in the world, 6th in Asia, and 2nd in Southeast Asia," respectively (Civil Rights Defenders 2015). Facebook is by far the most popular social media platform with an estimated 30 million monthly active users. YouTube is third, after Google+ (Viet Tan 2015); tweeting is not widely used. Overseas groups, such as the Vietnam Reform Party (VRP), which is banned inside the country, note that Facebook and other social media platforms help "nudge state media" to cover stories they otherwise might not; "introduce an element of accountability" into the public sphere; expand "political space" for expressing ideas; and "expose Party skeletons" (Viet Tan 2015, 5–6). VRP also publishes how-to-books to help bloggers work around the country's firewall, maintain anonymity, and protect their data from government-created malware (Open Technology Fund 2014). These trends indicate how difficult it has become for Vietnamese security services to police the Internet in general and to suppress the growth of online activism in particular. Nevertheless, nearly everyone writing on human rights issues continues to use pseudonyms to protect their identities, though this too is beginning to change among people involved in antitorture activism.

The development of Web 2.0 technologies, which enable user-generated content, has greatly facilitated the growth of "citizen-journalism" (*bao chi cong dan*) in Vietnam. This type of reporting is relatively new, but a number of citizen-journalist groups now provide a forum for people to publish news stories, analyses, and op-eds outside the state-controlled media. Formed in 2009, *Dan Lam Bao* (The People Do News), a crossover between a blog and a social network site and maintained by anonymous members inside the country, is among the most prominent of these groups. It is also unusual. *Dan Lam Bao*, which relies predominantly on volunteers rather than donations, publishes stories authored by ordinary people who report on local events. (Its mission statement: "Every person is a warrior of information"). The authors, although they frequently and explicitly refer to human rights (*nhan quyen*) in their stories, rarely discuss the alleged violations in legal terms or reference the international mechanisms created to respond to them. The government banned the site in 2012, stating that its contributors publish rumors, fabricate stories, misrepresent the country's leaders, and encourage activities challenging the Communisty Party and the state (Van Phong Chinh Phu 2012). Despite the ban, the site remains very popular. *Dan Lam Bao* went online in 2010. By 2012, the site received approximately 150,000 page views per day according to one of its editors (Crispin 2012).[4] *Quan*

Lam Bao (Officials Do Journalism), also banned in 2012, is a similar site, but focuses on "insider" accounts of government corruption, something state-owned media are rarely permitted to do, except for low-level cases. Legal and moral language figure prominently in these accounts (MacLean 2012). *Dan Luan* (People Discuss), another site for citizen-journalism, solicits stories, photographs, and videos on a wider range of issues, though political ones predominate. Torture is a common topic. A keyword search pulls up more than one hundred stories. Most of them concern either specific cases of police torture, including custodial deaths, or the ratification of UNCAT and obstacles to its implementation. Still other sites feature individual bloggers, who have gained (inter)national audiences because they publish information the government regards as threatening state interests, a vague charge that potentially covers any articles that are critical of official policies (Kerkvliet 2015; Freedom House 2016).

Regardless of genre, nearly all of the major citizen-journalist sites maintain a Facebook page and many of them administer a YouTube channel as well. Increased access to these sources of information facilitate the ability of "netizens" to create and maintain hyperlinked digital archives that enable viewers to quickly read about a staggering array of human rights stories. A growing number of the accounts explicitly reference international human rights frameworks, such as the International Covenant on Civil and Political Rights and, more recently, the UNCAT. Some of these accounts also include lengthy translations of the relevant sections, which they use to analyze domestic laws and to critique the government when its agencies failure to honor the country's human rights commitments. This trend suggests that there is growing awareness of these frameworks and their relevance to human rights activism.

Not surprisingly, smartphones are a critical tool for citizen-journalists and contribute to this trend. Thirty-six percent of the country's mobile users own smartphones, which has dramatically expanded the number of people who can "return the state's gaze" (*sousveillance*) by taking photographs and videos of police conduct (Do Anh-Minh 2014).[5] The ability of smartphone users to deter police violence and to provide evidence when it occurs, while clearly effective in some instances, has its limits, however. Ben Brucato, whose research focuses on this issue, points out that such claims are based on a number of questionable assumptions—namely, the spread of cellphone-based documentation will lead to a "reduction in use-of-force incidence," "promote accountability," and "provide incentive for improved self-regulation" (Brucato 2015). But without reliable data it will remain impossible to determine whether increased documentation results in these desired outcomes. Furthermore, cellphone documentation photos and videos capture the "visceral nature" of the violence in visual terms, but fail to convey the context to interpret them accurately, according to Brian Schaefer and Kevin Steinmetz. Web 2.0 site design compounds this problem, they explain. The sheer volume of content online can make it very difficult to find the visual evidence, for example. Hypertext also encourage viewers to click on successive links, which reduces the time spent on a given page and thus the attention given to the accompanying text. These problems, they explain, often neutralize the political effectiveness of the "message" (Schaefer and Steinmetz 2014). The next section explores some of the possibilities and limits of visual documentation by Vietnamese citizen-journalists operating at the local level. The documentation fuels popular demands for retributive rather than preventive justice, the focus of activists engaged in transnational forms of antitorture activism. I feature their work in the section that follows this one.

Posting Torture Online

The citizen-journalists involved in antitorture activism often utilize a globalized hybrid visual form to articulate demands for justice: self-produced videos. A Vietnamese-language YouTube search for "police beating people" in Vietnam results in thousands of Vietnam-specific hits, as does "death while in police custody." The most heavily watched one, at the time of writing, has received more than 3.6 million views to date. Nearly six minutes long, the clip features a riot that ensued after security forces blocked a funeral procession for a man who purportedly committed suicide while in police custody (Welcome to Vietnam 2014). Alleged suicides are typically attributed to hanging and electrocution. Such cases are now so common that some land rights activists reportedly have prepared living wills attesting that they are in "good physical and mental health and have no intention of committing suicide should they be arrested by the police" (Human Rights Watch 2014a, 3).

Cellphone videos used to document such violence can be categorized into different subgenres of countersurveillance of security forces. The most common ones involve encounters with traffic police, who are notorious for extracting bribes for real and imagined moving and registration violations. Assault and battery by the police is a common response to people who dispute the charge and/or refuse to pay a bribe. Clips of popular protests, most of them prompted by illegal land seizures, form another common genre. These videos feature security forces, including riot police, charging and beating unarmed people as a way to break up nonviolent protests. A growing number of videos consist of a photomontage of torture victims, including the corpses of people who died in custody, with soundtracks. A video entitled "Police Beat a Person to Death, Where Is Justice?" (Công an lại đánh người đến chết, luật pháp ở đâu?) is one such example (Mặc Lâm. 2012). The video consists of a montage of photographs of battered bodies and protests, such as the one described above. Excerpts from phone interviews with BBC-Vietnam, Radio Free Asia, and other overseas news agencies conducted with people willing to speak about such cases provide a running narrative. Currently, it is not known who shot the photos or how the images entered the public domain. Regardless, the seven-minute video accumulated more than 351,000 views between May 2012 and December 2012, when it was removed.[6]

The viewer comments on the web pages that prominently feature visual evidence of torture reveal some patterns. These patterns are suggestive rather than definitive for the reasons I mentioned at the beginning of the chapter. The number of pages that refer to specific cases of police torture, even when limited to a small number of nationally known ones where the victim died and legal action occured (e.g., Ngô Thanh Kiều), number in the thousands. Despite this limitation, I identified three broad patterns in the comment sections, which provide some insight into how readers interpretively frame the broader structures that reproduce impunity. Interestingly, these patterns do not appropriate universal human rights norms as part of their critiques.

The widely viewed video "Police Beat a Person to Death, Where Is Justice?" is again instructive in this regard. Some viewer comments stress the underlying causes of criminal behavior among the police force as a whole, suggesting that they view them as systemic rather than the actions of the particular individuals caught on film. One person wrote that there are three requirements to join the police force: "be really stupid, in good physical health, and view the people as enemies." (Security forces and official media often use this term, "enemies," to describe people they regard as a threat to state interests.) "Vietnam has laws, but only uses policeman's clubs," another states. But many of the comments rely upon vernacular concepts. For example, some of the commentators assert that police are "uncultured" (*thieu van hoa*), meaning that they are not sufficiently educated or trained. Others stress a lack of "morality" (*dao duc*), a concept that has its etymological roots in the Confucian concept of "virtue." Still others locate the problem in the failure of the police "to sympathesize" (*thong cam*) with the people, a longstanding and fundamental ideological principle the Communist Party instructed all of its cadres to wholeheartedly embrace when interacting with "the masses." Such comments employ the Communist Party's own moralizing language to critique its failings to protect "the people" (MacLean 2013). The political system also comes under attack. One person, using the government's own discourse against itself, writes, "the institutions of dictatorship" are the single biggest cause because they combine the legislative, judicial, and executive branches of government into a "single entity"—the party/state—which "makes oversight ineffective and creates opportunities for people to pay protection money when cases of torture and police brutality occur."

It is difficult to determine why the authors of these comments do not reference universal human rights norms. Space limitations matter. The format, which preserves anonymity, probably contributes to the kinds of language they use, which is typically judgmental rather than analytical in nature. And, of course, not everyone who writes a response is conversant in these norms. Nevertheless, the visual materials embedded in these stories are important for several reasons.

First, the images provide evidence of the myriad ways police inscribe violence on people's bodies, which is vital because real-time monitoring (e.g., videotaping interrogations) does not occur. Photos of extensive bruising, fractured bones, battered faces, and bloody bandages thus provide visual proof to challenge officers, who deny they are responsible for these outcomes, as well as their superiors, who resist or refuse to hold them accountable. The photos are particularly important in the case of custodial deaths, as the images help the victims to "speak" postmortem. For example, perhaps the two most widely circulated images of the custodial death were taken during the victim's autopsy (Human Rights Watch 2014, 29). The images are tightly cropped, forensic in nature, and feature the severe contusions on his legs where police beat him for extended periods of time and his partially removed skull revealing where the officers delivered the blow that killed him. Such images attest to the "facticity" of the allegations of torture, which as I mentioned police commonly dismiss as being self-inflicted (Radio Free Asia 2014). Indeed, the Ministry of Public Security recently disclosed that 226 people died while in detention between 2011 and 2014 due either to "suicide" or excessive "strenous exercise" (ibid.).

Second, the proliferation of such videos and the graphic images they contain not only document the widespread nature of such practices, but the growing confidence of civil society organizations (CSO), such as Mang Luoi Blogger Viet Nam (Network of Vietnamese Bloggers). More than two dozen CSOs, many of them unregistered because they work on human rights–related issues and are thus illegal, regularly post material on official policies as well as specific cases of police brutality and torture on this site (and elsewhere). Some of the material is idiomatic in nature, moralistic in tone, and employs name-and-shame techniques to advocate for change.

Diaspora groups assist these efforts, multiplying the impacts of citizen-journalism in a variety of ways. I discuss this issue at greater length in the next section where I detail how some groups engaged in transnational forms of activism utilize universal human rights norms to promote preventive justice by pressuring the government to bring its laws, policies, and procedures into conformity with international practices. Here, it is important to note that they disseminate accounts (including in English and French translation) through their organizational networks, hold public demonstrations, submit petitions to government officials, provide financial support, and offer technical assistance to bypass the Internet firewall, maintain anonymity, and so on. The Overseas Support for the Free Journalist Network in Vietnam, for example, lobbies international actors to provide protection for bloggers inside the country, especially those in detention or jail. These groups also serve as information sources for international NGOs, such as Amnesty International and Human Rights Watch, which advocate on behalf of a wide range of social justice activists who are at risk or are known to have been tortured while in detention.

Third, the photos embedded in these videos provide visual content for digital archives that aggregate information on government repression, including police brutality, torture, and custodial deaths. Hay Bao Ve Nguoi Bao Ve Nhan Quyen (Defend the [Human Rights] Defenders), an NGO that styles itelf as the "last line of defense," is one prominent aggregator for such cases. The site, which is largely self-funded, contains an archive of more than one hundred different defenders (primarily bloggers and land rights activists) and victims, such as people who died while in police custody. The people involved in maintaining the site, unlike the citizen-journalism ones discussed, explicitly frame their work within international human rights discourse. They cite both the UN Declaration on Human Rights (1948) and the UN General Assembly's Declaration regarding human rights defenders (1999) to justify advocacy efforts to "end intimidation, harassment, arbitrary detention" and secure the release of people imprisoned for exercising their right to freedom of opinion and expression (Defend The [Human Rights] Defenders 2014). These archives, as they grow in scope and breadth, offer insights into systemic patterns of repression, make comparative analyses across cases and local forms of advocacy possible, and serve as a critical resource for people researching these issues.

Citizen-based monitoring of torture is not without risks, however. "Stealth torture," for example the use of stress positions and solitary confinement in harsh and degrading circumstances, rarely leaves physical evidence of brutality and is consequently very hard to document (Rejali 2003, 153).[7] Police commonly use stealth torture on people with international profiles, such as prodemocracy dissidents, antiestablishment religious figures, human rights activists, and bloggers, for this reason (Amnesty International 2013). By contrast, ordinary people are subject to physcially brutal forms of torture, typically to extract confessions. Increased pressure on the government to comply with UNCAT and thus hold officials accountable could have two unintended effects. First, the pressure could prompt police who use torture to adopt practices that do not leave visible traces on prisoners' bodies to avoid detection. Second, compliance monitoring, because it does not happen in real time, "can hide as much as it reveals," according to Tobias Kelly, a torture expert. He points out that "the everyday practices and structural inequalities that produce torture are downplayed in favor of a focus on formal processes and procedures" (Kelly 2009, 779). If this occurs, citizen-based monitoring will find it difficult to push for the changes needed to address the broader factors that are contributing to the increased use of torture nationwide and impunity more generally.

Human Rights Claims Making

Rights claims constitute a "paradoxical form of power" in liberal states, according to Wendy Brown. The measures put into place to safeguard specific categories of personhood from continued injury, such as protections and entitlements, are contingent upon the ability of members of the group in question and their advocates to perpetuate their identity claims to "victimhood." This process, she points out, "casts the law in particular and the state more generally as neutral arbiters of injury rather than as themselves as invested with the power to injure" (Brown 1995, 27). What frequently remains intact are the very activities that produce injury and suffering in the first place. By definition, authoritarian states are illiberal, and thus do not evince the same paradox. Yet, human rights activism in such settings can contribute to it by pressuring states to recognize some categories of "victimhood," such as ordinary citizens that warrant state protection, but not others, such as dissidents. Several transnational antitorture campaigns in Vietnam have emerged, and they offer a case in point.

The actors inside and outside Vietnam involved in these campaigns increasingly frame their claims within dominant rights discourse. Their growing involvement in the Universal Periodic Review (UPR) process exemplifies this development. Created in 2006, the UPR is a state-driven process carried out under the auspices of the UN Human Rights Council (HRC). The UPR requires each state to report on what actions it has taken to fulfill its human rights obligations. "Relevant stakeholders," such as NGOs and human rights defenders, are also permitted to submit their own reports and recommendations for the state to take into consideration. Vietnam completed its first UPR in 2009, and all ten of the civil society organizations that submitted information were international ones. By 2014, twenty-three of the forty-eight submissions were Vietnamese-led CSOs, signaling not only a significant growth in the number of CSOs working on human rights issues but their increased willingness to speak out despite the risk of possible retaliation.

Interestingly, the HRC elections coincided with the UPR process. Vietnam was elected for the 2014–2016 term, receiving 184 out of 192 votes despite its poor human rights record. Some of the diplomats at the UPR meeting did voice their criticisms, however. Much of it centered on two issues that have bearing on the increase in police torture. First, the government declined to initiate reforms to prevent the politically motivated imprisonment of people who peacefully exercise their fundamental human rights, as set out in international law. Second, the government refused calls to release people detained without charge or trial. People who find themselves in either situation are often denied prompt legal representation, which leaves them particularly vulnerable to torture. Vietnam's vice-foreign minister dismissed the criticism, stating that it was "a pity that some of the comments were based on a lack of objective information" (Radio Free Asia, February 5, 2014).

The HRC elections prompted some CSOs to engage in new forms of human rights advocacy. For example, Nguyen Ngoc Nhu Quynh of the Vietnamese Blogger's Network helps coordinate events nationwide to bring other bloggers and human rights activists together to discuss international and domestic policies. She was one of the co-organizers of the 2014 Right to Know Campaign, which sought to reduce people's fears about openly discussing important policy matters and asking high-ranking officials to account for their actions. (The Vietnamese version of the campaign slogan, "*Duoc biet la quyen cua cong dan*," translates as, "It's our right as citizens to know.") "Our network believes that free access to information helps people exercise their rights as citizens of the country," she said during a telephone interview with Radio Free Asia. "Today, I say, 'I want to know'—and I have the right to know—because society cannot develop if people don't know about the policies that govern their lives, especially policies that affect the survival of their country" (Radio Free Asia, September 2, 2014). She received the 2015 Civil Rights Defender of the Year award from Civil Rights Defenders, an NGO previously known as the Swedish Helsinki Committee for Human Rights, for her efforts.

Later that same year, twenty-seven CSOs, the Vietnamese Bloggers Network among them, launched the We Are One: 2015 Human Rights, Freedom and Democracy for Vietnam Campaign with this goal in mind. The campaign calls on citizens to organize petitions, hold nonviolent demonstrations, and engage in hunger strikes (Democratic Voice of Vietnam 2015). More prominent activists have formed delegations to meet with local government officials in the country's major cities, relevant UN staff, and foreign diplomats (An Nguyen, September 2, 2014).[8] Their goal is to convince the government to comply with special rapporteurs, treaty bodies, and UN member states' recommendations through the UPR process by calling on foreign governments (1) to place human rights conditionalities on all trade agreements; and (2) to vote against Vietnam's reelection to the HRC. A combination of economic and diplomatic pressure, its organizers argue, will "urge the Vietnamese government to conduct itself with accountability, transparency, and integrity, and to uphold the responsibilities and obligations pursuant to the international human rights treaties it has ratified and the Universal Declaration of Human Rights" (Network of Vietnamese Bloggers 2015). Seven members of the U.S. House of Representatives provided support for this initiative by introducing the Vietnam Human Rights Act of 2015 (House of Representatives 2015) to the House Committee for Foreign Affairs. The goal of the bill is "to promote freedom, human rights, and the rule of law as part of United States–Vietnam relations" (ibid.). The visual elements of the We Are One campaign reinforce these messages regarding citizens' rights. The logo is generic and culturally neutral, that is, it contains no Vietnamese-specific elements beyond the URL (Voice of Vietnam Tieng Viet News Outlet 2015). Notably, "We" is a word cloud, an image composed of words on a subject—in this case the text of the Universal Declaration of Human Rights—that vary in size according to their frequency and importance. The campaign's organizers also call on people to wear white shirts on International Human Rights Day (December 10) to indicate solidarity with its goals. The visual gesture provides a low barrier to participation because the shirts are blank and thus do not express an unequivocal political massage. By contrast, people involved in the new Campaign to Abolish Torture in Vietnam (CAT-VN) take a less "safe" approach.

CAT-VN members (human rights organizations, community-based groups, religious organizations, and individuals) similarly employ claims-making language that is instantly recognizable to international audiences, and they present clear benchmarks for determining progress toward eradicating torture. They also engage in rights awareness activities that also put themselves at direct risk on- and offline. CAT-VN maintains an online platform for visualizing people who, because they are imprisoned, disappear from view. To help prevent this from happening CAT-VN regularly posts news on prison conditions, updates on prisoners of conscience and rights defenders, first-person testimony from torture survivors, and media reports—all of which include photographic and video evidence to provide "proof" of torture in its varied physical and mental forms.

A growing number of well-known activists as well as intellectuals, Catholic priests, and Buddhist monks are using cellphone images to create protest photos that circulate online as well. Each person holds a piece of paper with one word written on it; when arranged in order, the slogan appears: "Resist Acts of Violence [Brutality] and Torture." Some lesser known antitorture activists have created similar images. In both cases, the participants make no effort to hide their identities, which suggests that police torture has become a human rights violation that is now possible to protest openly online. This is not true offline, however. Leading members of the Network of Vietnamese Bloggers organized a series of "human rights cafés" during 2014. These events provided opportunities for interested persons to learn about basic human rights principles, the kinds of violations occuring, local responses to them, national laws, and international mechanisms. The April café focused on police killings and UNCAT. The bloggers wore matching T-shirts. The image included an outline of an officer beating a pair of outstretched hands with a truncheon and an English- rather than Vietnamese-language caption: "Stop Police Killing

Civilians." "Justice for All" is emblazoned on the back of the shirt. Ironically, local police proceeded to assault and then briefly detain the organizers and several family members of victims of prior abuse (Dan Lam Bao 2014).

Translation

Several obstacles prevent human rights discourse—regardless of whether it is articulated in local (idiomatic) or global (universal) terms—from gaining more institutional traction in Vietnam. First, "socialist legality" (i.e., rule through decrees) still shapes the limits of official human rights discourse in contemporary Vietnam. According to legal scholar Bui Thiem, socialist legality continues to privilege sovereign interests over individual ones, conflates citizens' rights with human rights, and subordinates judicial independence to political and economic expediency (Bui 2014, 77–100). Globalized human rights discourse thus has little legitimacy within the government. The country does not have a National Human Rights Commission, for example. Popular understandings of human rights norms are largely limited to politically active intellectuals and a small number of civil society organizations that have connections with overseas NGOs and diasporic groups. But arguments for a more "law-based state" are slowly gaining acceptance in Vietnam, both conceptually as a legitimate topic to discuss, and an institutionalized form of practice as a component of good governance. Nevertheless, socialist legality remains dominant, and it significantly restricts the ability of people to exercise their constitutionally guaranteed civil and political liberties. Indeed, politically motivated charges, such as "undermining national unity" and "abusing the rights to democracy and freedom to infringe upon the interests of the state," remain the two most common charges security services use to suppress demands for both. Second, the process of juridification, that is, the proliferation of formal laws as opposed to decrees under the law, additionally constrains rights-based approaches, states legal scholar John Gillespie (2013, 672–701). Instead, he explains, personal connections with "power brokers in government agencies—such as judges, procurators, and police officials—rather than legal norms and procedures, [remain] the most effective means of protecting their clients" (ibid., 679). Both factors help explain why there are so few cause-laywers litigating cases when officials are alleged to have commited human rights violations.

Cause lawyers push for incremental and technical improvements to the legal system at a national level. Some of them, approximately twenty in total, actually seek to reform the system by challenging the interpersonal networks that perpetuate the status quo. Vo An Don, often referred to as "the people's lawyer," is one such person. Several of his lawsuits, especially the one regarding a custodial death due to police torture, have garnered country-wide attention (Nguoi Lao Dong 2016). (A number of the officers involved received prison sentences, which the court later reduced.) Such cases remain the exception to the rule and are thus beyond the scope of this chapter, which focuses on bottom-up and top-down efforts to challenge impunity through activism rather than the institutionalization of a human rights–based approach at the national level. Such a human rights–based approach would seek to combine retributive and preventive justice in an integrated fashion, something the culture of impunity that exists in Vietnam currently does not permit.

Conclusion

"Torture is the calculated infliction of pain, but it is also an emblem of state power," according to Stanley Cohen. "To talk about torture is not just to talk about pain but to enter into a complex discourse on morality, legality, and politics" (1993, 23). Legal discourse, which dominates discussions about torture, has its limits, however. According to Tobias Kelly, we still remain largely unwilling "to listen, to see, to name, and take responsibility for what is in front of us" with regard to torture (2011, 4–5). The "problem of recognition" (ibid., 4), as he puts it, is readily apparent in contemporary debates regarding the need for enhanced interrogation techniques, the complicated and highly bureaucratic forms of "proof" of torture immigration officials demand during the asylum process, and so on. This chapter examined the problem of recognition in the context of Vietnam. The country's government is only beginning to acknowledge the severity of the epidemic and to take steps to address it. But these steps are largely policy-based and procedurally oriented. As Kelly notes, such steps are necessary, but also problematic. "Legal discussions of torture tend to break down into arguments about due process and the rule of law," he explains, which means that "the suffering of specific individuals and the intentions of particular perpetrators melt into the background" (Kelly 2011, 5). Not surprisingly, people directly affected by police torture (e.g., victims and their families), as well as those advocating on their behalf, find the legal, policy, and administrative reforms important, but not sufficient. Visual strategies of documentation are critical to them, as they enable these actors to mobilize different publics to take action when the security services, judicial system, and/or political representatives fail to hold perpetrators accountable.

This chapter highlights some of the ways Vietnamese involved in antitorture initiatives formulate and implement such projects at the local and transnational scales. These nascent projects, I argued, articulate citizenship claims in different ways and make their appeals to different publics as part of their efforts to ensure compliance with the prohibitions against torture through a combination of "moral suasion and reputational costs" (Niezen 2010, 12). They predominantly take the form of entitlement claims, that is, demands for justice in the case of the former, and rights claims, that is, demands that the state protect basic human rights in the case of the latter. Consequently, these projects operate quite differently, as my comparison shows. For example, local efforts are decentralized because citizen-documentation takes place on a case-by-case basis, and thus has no national leadership structure. Additionally, such documentation also takes a diverse array of visual forms. However, a number of Vietnamese-language websites now aggregate these materials, which includes visual evidence of police torture, into digital archives. By contrast, the transnational campaigns are highly centralized and have a clear leadership structure. Moreover, the organizers make strategic use of English-language content, visuals included, to reach an international audience with the explicit goal of involving them in their advocacy efforts. These campaigns deliberately draw upon human rights treaties and mechanisms, such as the UPR, to challenge the structures that perpetuate impunity nationally and to urge policy reforms to increase police accountability. Both antitorture projects are slowly beginning to intersect with one another because they share a common concern: eradicating torture and impunity. But the degree to which digital media will further facilitate the upstreaming and downstreaming of relevant human rights norms remains an open question.

Notes

1. The Phu Quoc Museum is somewhat unusual, however. The province hosted the 2014 Miss Vietnam beauty pageants and the contestants visited the museum as part of the competition, which visually linked the commodification of the female form with the commodification of torture.

2. The Vietnamese translation of "impunity" is "to go unpunished," and it carries similar connotations to the English.

3. Manfred Nowak, the former UN Special Rapporteur on Torture, was one of the distinguished guests. A number of civil society organizations were present as observers as well.

4. Current figures are not available.

5. Larry Diamond, a political sociologist and coordinator of the Center on Democracy, Development, and Rule of Law, goes so far as to call smartphones one of several "liberation technologies" (Diamond 2012, 3–17).

6. A summary of the video, which includes some photos taken from it, is available at http://danlambaovn.blogspot.com/2012/05/cong-lai-anh-nguoi-en-chet-luat-phap-o.html. (Accessed April 24, 2016).

7. Some of the *tableaux vivants* at the torture museum in Phu Quoc feature these techniques.

8. Several of the organizers traveled to the National Assembly to deliver a signed letter regarding the campaign, but security services closed the building and arrested some members of the delegation.

Works Cited

Amnesty International. 2013. *Silenced Voices: Prisoners of Conscience in Viet Nam*. London: Amnesty International Publications.

An Nguyen. 2014. "Vietnamese Netizens Demand 'Right to Know' in Online Campaign." *Radio Free Asia*. September 2.

Bộ Công An. 2014. "Thông Tư: Quy Định Về Công Tác Điều Tra Hình Sự Trong Công An Nhân Dân," Số 28/2014/TT-BCA (July 7, 2014).

Brown, Wendy. 1995. *States of Injury: Power and Freedom in Late Modernity*. Princeton: Princeton University Press.

Brucato, Ben. 2015. "Policing Made Visible: Mobile Technologies and the Importance of Point of View." *Surveillance & Society* 13 (3–4): 455–473.

Bui, Thiem. 2014. "Deconstructing the 'Socialist' Rule of Law in Vietnam: The Changing Discourse on Human Rights in Vietnam's Constitutional Reform Process." *Contemporary Southeast Asia: A Journal of International and Strategic Affairs* 36 (1): 77–100.

Civil Rights Defenders. 2015. *"We Will Not Be Silenced": Bloggers and the Human Rights in Vietnam*. Stockholm: Civil Rights Defenders.

Cohen, Stanley. 1993. "Talking about Torture in Israel." *Tikkun* 6 (6): 23.

Committee to Protect Journalists. 2015. "10 Most Censored Countries." https://cpj.org/2015/04/10-most-censored countries.php. Accessed December 7, 2015.

Crispin, Shawn. 2012. "Vietnam's Press Freedom Shrinks Despite Open Economy." September 19. https://www.cpj.org/reports/2012/09/vietnams-press-freedom-shrinks-despite-open-economy.php. Accessed May 24, 2016.

Dân Làm Báo. 2014. "Nha Trang: CA Triệt Phá Cà-phê Nhân Quyền, Đánh Người Tàn Bạo (Cập Nhật)." April 19. http://danlambaovn.blogspot.com/2014/04/ca-pha-buoi-ca-phe-nhan-quyen-tai-nha.html. Accessed May 24, 2016.

Dauphinée, Elizabeth. 2007. "The Politics of the Body in Pain: Reading the Ethics of Imagery." *Security Dialogue* 38 (2): 139–155.

Defend the [Human Rights] Defenders. 2014. "About." http://www.vietnamhumanrightsdefenders.net/about. Accessed March 30, 2016.

Democratic Voice of Vietnam 2015. "Open Letter to the United Nations' Human Rights Council and Its Mechanisms Concerning Vietnam's Human Rights Abuses and the People's Human Rights Campaign for 2015." March 10. http://dvov.org/2015/03/20/open-letter-to-the-united-nations-human-rights-council-and-its-mechanisms-concerning-vietnams-human-rights-abuses-and-the-peoples-human-rights-campaign-for-2015/. Accessed February 20, 2016.

Diamond, Larry. 2012. "Liberation Technology." In *Liberation Technology: Social Media and the Struggle for Democracy*, edited by Larry Diamond and Marc Plattner, 3–17. Baltimore: Johns Hopkins University Press.

Dill, Nandi. 2013. "Notes from the Field: An Interview with Fred Ritchin." *Humanity: An International Journal of Human Rights, Humanitarianism, and Development* 4 (3): 393–402.

Do, Anh-Minh. 2014. "36 Percent of Vietnam's Population Owns a Smartphone." *Tech in Asia*, September 16. https://www.techinasia.com/36-of-vietnams-population-now-uses-smartphones-but-where-are-the-mobile-services. Accessed December 22, 2015.

Freedom House. 2016. "Freedom on the Net: Vietnam." https://freedomhouse.org/report/freedom-net/2015/vietnam. Accessed March 30, 2016.

Gell, Alfred. 1998. *Art and Agency: An Anthropological Theory*. Oxford: Clarendon.

Gillespie, John. 2013. "The Juridification of Cause Advocacy in Socialist Asia: Vietnam as a Case Study." *Wisconsin International Law Journal* 31 (3): 672–701.

Hoang, Duy Angelina Huynh, and Trinh Nguyen. 2015. *Vietnam's Social Media Landscape*. Washington, D.C.: Viet Tan.

House of Representatives. 2015. "Vietnam Human Rights Act of 2015 to Promote Freedom, Human Rights, and the Rule of Law as Part of United States–Vietnam Relations (H. R. 2140)." https://www.congress.gov/bill/114th-congress/house-bill/2140. Accessed April 18, 2016.

Human Rights Watch. 2014a. *Public Insecurity: Deaths in Custody and Police Brutality in Vietnam*. New York: Human Rights Watch.

———. 2014b. "Vietnam: Police Reforms Fall Short, Door Opens for Future Accountability" (August 20). https://www.hrw.org/news/2014/08/20/vietnam-police-reforms-fall-shor. Accessed April 18, 2016.

Kelly, Tobias. 2009. "The UN Committee against Torture: Human Rights Monitoring and the Legal Recognition of Cruelty." *Human Rights Quarterly* 31(3): 777–800.

———. 2011. *This Side of Silence: Human Rights, Torture, and the Recognition of Cruelty*. Philadelphia: University of Pennsylvania Press.

Kerkvliet, Benedict. 2015. "Regime Critics: Democratization Advocates in Vietnam, 1990s–2014." *Critical Asian Studies* 47 (3): 359–387.

Mặc Lâm. 2012. "Cong An Lại Đánh Người Đến Chết, Luật Pháp Ở Đâu?" May 17, 2012. *Dân Làm Báo*. http://danlambaovn.blogspot.com/2012/05/cong-lai-anh-nguoi-en-chet-luat-phap-o.html. Accessed April 18, 2016.

MacLean, Ken. 2012. "Enacting Anti-Corruption: The Reconfiguration of Audit Regimes in Contemporary Vietnam." *positions: asia critique* 20 (2): 595–625.

———. 2013. *The Government of Mistrust: Illegibility and Bureaucratic Power in Socialist Vietnam*. Madison: University of Wisconsin Press.

Mạng Lưới Blogger Việt Nam (The Network of Vietnamese Bloggers) https://mangluoiblogger.blogspot.com. Accessed February 20, 2016.

Mehta, Pratibha. 2014. "Remarks by the UN Resident Coordinator and UNDP Resident Representative at the Workshop on the Convention Against Torture." June 6. http://www.vn.undp

.org/content/vietnam/en/home/presscenter/speeches/2014/06/06/remarks-by-un-resident-coordinator-and-undp-resident-representative-ms-pratibha-mehta-at-the-workshop-on-the-convention-against-torture-cat-.html. Accessed February 20, 2016.

Người Lao Động. 2016. "Tin Mới Nhất: Luật Sư Võ An Đôn." http://nld.com.vn/luat-su-vo-an-don.html. Accessed May 24, 2016.

Nguyễn Hành. 2015. "Rùng mình chứng kiến những mà tra tấn tàn ác ở nhà tù Phú Quốc." *Dân Trí*, April 21. http://dantri.com.vn/xa-hoi/rung-minh-chung-kien-nhung-man-tra-tan-tan-ac-o-nha-tu-phu-quoc-1062218.htm. Accessed July 22, 2015.

Niezen, Ronald. 2010. *Public Justice and the Anthropology of the Law*. Cambridge: Cambridge University Press.

Open Technology Fund. 2014. *Internet Access and Openness: Vietnam 2013*, 83–95. Washington, D.C.: OTF.

Radio Free Asia. 2014. "Vietnam Slammed at UN Rights Review for Jailing Critics." February 5.

Rejali, Darius. 2003. "Modern Torture as a Civic Marker: Solving a Global Anxiety with a New Political Technology." *Journal of Human Rights* 2 (2): 153–171.

Reporters Without Borders. 2015. "The Enemies of the Internet: Vietnam." http://surveillance.rsf.org/en/vietnam/. Accessed December 7, 2015.

Schaefer, Brian, and Kevin Steinmetz. 2014. "Watching the Watchers and McLuhan's Tetrad: The Limits of Cop-Watching in the Internet Age." *Surveillance & Society* 12 (4): 502–515.

Taussig, Michael. 1999. *Defacement: Public Secrecy and the Labor of the Negative*. Palo Alto: Stanford University Press.

Telesca, Jennifer. 2013. "Preface: What Is Visual Citizenship?" *Humanity: An International Journal of Human Rights, Humanitarianism, and Development* 4 (3): 339–343.

Thanh Nien News. 2014. "Vietnam Shrugs Off US Rights Group's Report on Police Abuse." September 18. http://www.thanhniennews.com/politics/vietnam-shrugs-off-us-rights-groups-report-on-police-abuse-31313.html. Accessed April 20, 2016.

Thủ Tướng Chính Phủ. 2015. "Kế Hoạch Triển Khai Thực Hiện Công Ước của Liên Hợp Quốc Về Chống Tra Tấn và Các Hình Thức Đối Xử Hoặc Trừng Phạt Tàn Bạo, Vô Nhân Đạo Hoặc Hạ Nhục Con Người." Quyết Định Số 364/QĐ-TTg. March 17.

Tin Nóng. 2014. "Nghiên Cứu Biện Pháp Làm Giảm Tình Trạng Nhục Hình, Bức Cung." September 12. http://tinnong.thanhnien.com.vn/phai-doc/nghien-cuu-cac-bien-phap-lam-giam-tinh-trang-nhuc-hinh-buc-cung-5685.html. Accessed August 27, 2015.

Tuoi Tre News. 2014. "UN Convention Against Torture Submitted to NA for Ratification." October 24. http://tuoitrenews.vn/politics/23512/un-convention-against-torture-submitted-to-na-for-ratification. Accessed March 12, 2016.

United Nations General Assembly. 1948. "Universal Declaration of Human Rights." December 10. http://www.refworld.org/docid/3ae6b3712c.html. Accessed May 24, 2016.

———. 1999. "Declaration on the Right and Responsibility of Individuals, Groups, and Organs of Society to Promote and Protect Universally Recognized Human Rights and Fundamental Freedoms." March 8. https://documents-dds-ny.un.org/doc/UNDOC/GEN/N99/770/89/PDF/N9977089.pdf?OpenElement. Accessed May 24, 2016.

Văn Phòng Chính Phủ. 2012. "Về Xử Lý Thông Tinh Có Nội Dung Chống Đảng và Nhà Nước." Công Văn Số 7169/VPCP-NC, September 12.

Viet Tan (Vietnam Reform Party). 2015. "Social Media Landscape." March 23. http://viettan.org/IMG/pdf/Viet_Tan_-_Vietnam_s_Social_Media_Landscape_March_2015_.pdf. Accessed April 20, 2016.

Voice of Vietnam Tieng Viet News Outlet. 2015. "Phát Động Chiến Dịch Vận Động Nhân Quyền Cho Việt Nam." December 3. http://www.voatiengviet.com/content/phat-dong-chien-dich-van-dong-cho-nhan-quyen-vietnam/2677478.html. Accessed April 20, 2016.

Võ Thị Hảo. "Ai Bảo Kê Cho Tra Tấn." 2014. *Radio Free Asia*, November 2. http://www.rfa.org/vietnamese/blog/who-protect-the-torture-11022014120006.html. Accessed August 24, 2015.

Welcome to Vietnam. 2014. "Bạo Loạn Đã Xảy Ra Ở Móng Cái Khi Một Dân Thường Bị Công An Phương Đánh Chết 2." October 18. . https://www.youtube.com/watch?v=HQNvJzvhO28. Accessed September 17, 2015.

Xuân Nguyên. 2015. "Vân Nạn Công Dân Bị Chết Ở Nơi Tạm Giam, Tạm Giữ." *Radio Free Asia*. November 29.

PART III

Human Rights Programs and the Proliferation of Nonconfrontational Methods

CHAPTER 7

Rural-Urban Migration and Education in China: Unraveling Responses to Injurious Experiences

Ellen Desmet

Since the mid-1980s, the exponential growth of China's megacities has attracted an increasing number of migrants from the countryside. These rural-urban migrants face a range of challenges regarding access to, and quality of, compulsory education for their children. This chapter assesses the impact of rights consciousness on parents' and children's perceptions of, and strategies to deal with, these challenges in a district of Chongqing Municipality. The educational situation of migrant children in Chongqing gives rise to various human rights issues, which have been repeatedly flagged at the international level. Only in hypothetical situations, however, were some of the claims of parents couched in human rights language. Moreover, the strategies adopted were not conceptualized as human rights actions. This chapter tentatively identifies some factors that may explain this limited relevance of human rights discourse and strategies in addressing the educational situation of migrant children in Chongqing.

Quite a different picture of legal mobilization emerges when one does not focus on settings where using the law is part of rights holders' standard response as it is, for example, in legal aid centers (see Gallagher 2006), or on institutions, whether governmental or nongovernmental, that (are likely to) disseminate human rights ideas (Liu, Hu, and Liao 2009; Davis and Mohamed, in this volume). In the chapter by Davis and Mohamed in this volume on right-to-health advocacy in China, for instance, both the actors and the context differ substantially from the present case study. Their chapter examines how members of right-to-health community-based organizations participated in a training program in which human rights advocacy was explicitly promoted, and the authors analyze the impact of such programs. Both with regard to actors (Chinese health rights activists) and context (human rights advocacy training), human rights were already "present" in that setting. By contrast, this chapter focuses on a situation that raises questions from a human rights perspective, but where there was no indication of the circulation of human rights concepts before engaging in the fieldwork. The persons interviewed in the context of this research were parents and children confronted with an unfavorable educational situation, not activists. They did not form a community organization or social movement, but dealt with their situation as individuals, at times supported by social connections (though these were with, e.g., their employer or a teacher, not with other parents). It was found that in this setting, human rights were only hypothetically and marginally mobilized.

These findings may point to a risk of overestimating the relevance of law in general, and human rights in particular, for common people in settings where these concepts are not predisposed to play a role. In this sense, the results of this case study are in line with research by Engel and Engel (2010) on personal injuries resulting from traffic accidents in north Thailand, which showed declining relevance for both state and nonstate law in how people dealt with these injuries. Their conclusion, that "[t]he dog that does not bark is precisely the phenomenon we need to study and explain" (Engel and Engel 2010, 161), is supported by this study.

This project constituted a pilot study within a broader research program on the localization of human rights.[1] Although in recent years empirical approaches have increasingly been adopted in human rights research in China (see, e.g., Liu, Hu, and Liao 2009; Davis and Mohamed in this volume), more interdisciplinary research is still required. In particular, there is "need for more research that pays closer attention to the experiences and practices of ordinary citizens" (Svensson 2012, 685). Regarding the education of rural-urban migrant children in particular, much research has been based on legal and documentary analysis, with less empirical research (but see Wang 2008; Wenbin 2009; Chen 2010; Pong 2015). This research project aimed to contribute to filling these gaps.

After sketching the theoretical frameworks on which this chapter builds, the methodology employed is briefly discussed. The following section explores the multiple dimensions of accessing education in the city for both urban and rural-urban migrant children. Thereafter, the chapter describes the limited circulation of (human) rights concepts among parents and children, and analyzes how parents and children deal with education-related (human rights) problems. In conclusion, the chapter identifies some tentative explanatory factors for the limited occurrence of human rights language and strategies.

Theoretical Frameworks

The main theoretical framework of this research is the "localizing human rights" approach, as developed by De Feyter (2007, 2011). This approach starts from the understanding that for human rights to be effective, they must be relevant at the local level. Localization implies taking the human rights needs as formulated by local people (in response to the impact of economic globalization on their lives) as the starting point, both for the further interpretation and elaboration of human rights norms, and for the development of human rights action at all levels ranging from the domestic to the global (De Feyter 2007, 68).

Vandenhole (2012) has shown that the localizing human rights approach is also applicable to children's rights, such as the right to education considered here. Other studies examining human rights "from below" were also built upon in the development of this chapter (e.g., Merry 2006a; Merry et al. 2010; Goodale and Merry 2007).

The localization process has been disentangled by Oré Aguilar (2011) into various tracks (Figure 7.1). Track 1 explores why and how people articulate their claims on the basis of the human rights framework. Track 2 concerns the translation of these claims into human rights action. In track 3, local communities and their support networks employ strategies aimed at obtaining responses from administrative, policymaking, or judicial actors at the local, national, and/or international level. Track 4 examines (1) the impact of these responses on the local community and (2) the consequences for international or regional human rights norms, practices, or institutions. Finally, track 5 analyzes "whether and how global human rights norms enhanced by local experiences have the power to transform similar realities of human rights transgression or deprivation" (Oré Aguilar 2011, 139).

In this case study, no explicit human rights actions or disputes were identified. The analysis in this chapter therefore focuses on whether and why a transformation took place from an unperceived injurious experience to a (human rights) claim. This corresponds to track 1 of the localization process.

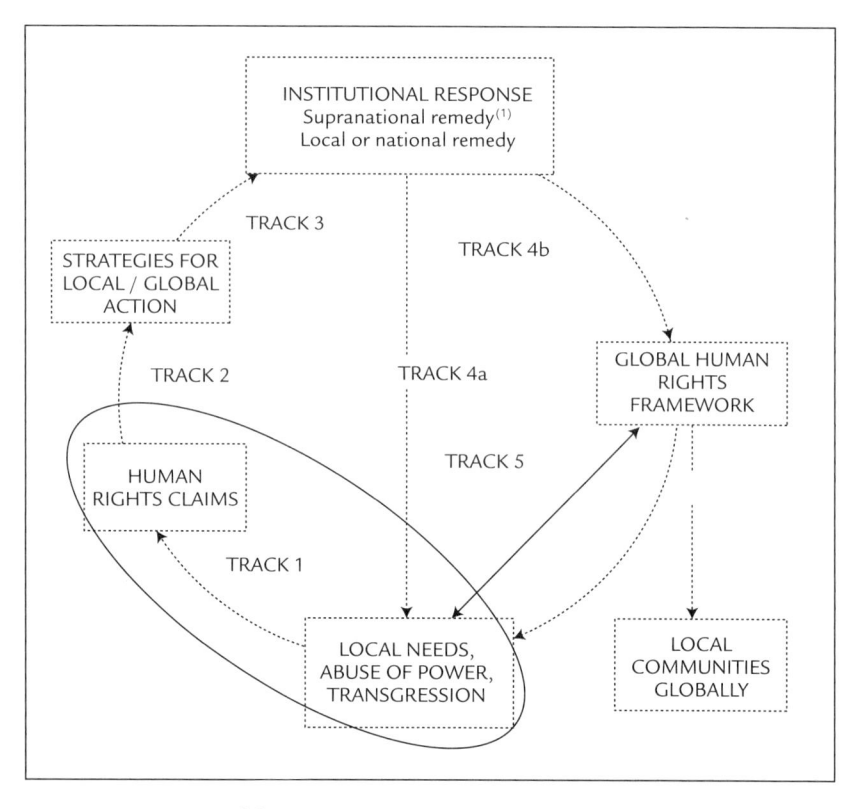

Figure 7.1. Situation of the case study in the localization framework. See Oré Aguilar (2011, 131).

To operationalize the process of arriving from a local need or transgression to a human rights claim (track 1), the theoretical framework on the emergence of disputes developed by Felstiner, Abel, and Sarat (1980) was employed.[2] In this framework, experiences not initially perceived as injurious may later become perceived as such (*naming*). A perceived injurious experience becomes a grievance when a person attributes that injury to the fault of another individual or entity (*blaming*). A grievance may then be voiced to the person or entity believed to be responsible, asking for a remedy (*claiming*). When such a claim is rejected, a dispute emerges. When there is a dispute, one party may decide to resort to a legal regime. The concept of "legal mobilization" then describes "the tendency for various individuals and groups to define their problems as legal ones and to take them to some legal regime for help or settlement" (Merry 2012, 72).

Applying this transformation perspective to human rights research leads to distinguishing between human rights–based and other instances of naming, blaming, and claiming. When based on, or inspired by, human rights, an injurious experience would be perceived as such because it would be considered a human rights violation. The entity that is perceived to be a human rights duty bearer in the situation concerned would be blamed, and a claim using human rights language would be formulated, insisting on the accountability of that duty bearer.

Finally, this research adopts a users' perspective on human rights (Brems and Desmet 2014). An individual is identified as a human rights user from the moment there is an explicit interaction (engagement) with human rights. It is also interesting, however, to explore why people who could invoke human rights have not taken this step, that is, to extend the field of enquiry toward *potential* users of human rights (Desmet 2014, 137). This is the approach adopted here: parents and children were asked about their (children's) educational situation, without prior knowledge about their knowledge of, and engagement with, human rights. As will be seen, some respondents invoked a kind of human rights language, whereas many did not. Four empirical categories of (potential) users may be distinguished (Desmet 2014, 129–131) (see Figure 7.2). Parents and children can be considered as (potential) "rights claimants," that is, those who (may) invoke human rights. Another category

Direct human rights users	Indirect human rights users
Rights claimants — *invoke*	Supportive users — *support*
Rights realizers — *give effect to*	Judicial users — *impose*

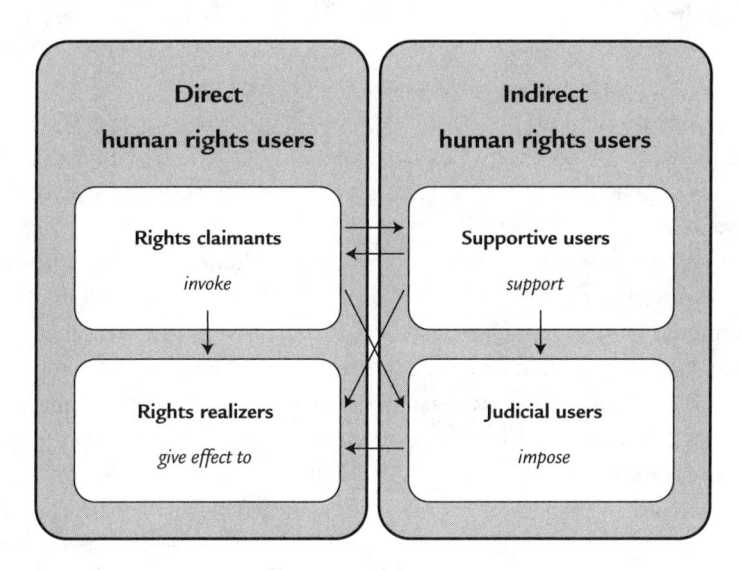

Figure 7.2. Categories of human rights users.

of direct users is "rights realizers," who give effect to human rights. Indirect users of human rights are either "supportive users" (e.g., NGOs, national human rights institutions, UN treaty-based bodies) or "judicial users," who impose the implementation of human rights (e.g., courts and tribunals).[3]

Methodology

This chapter builds on a collective effort by a gender-balanced team of researchers from Chongqing University and the University of Antwerp.[4] Fieldwork was mainly conducted in May and June 2013 in the Shapingba District of Chongqing Municipality by the Chinese team members, employing a multiplicity of data collection methods (interviews, focus group [FG] discussions, direct observation, and document analysis).[5] The conversations with parents and children were taped and transcribed in Mandarin, translated into English by professional translators, and checked for accuracy by the main interviewer. The data analysis for this chapter was carried out by the author with the support of NVivo. The preliminary findings were discussed in seminars at Chongqing University, the University of Antwerp, and New York University in 2014 and 2015.

Overall, 65 persons participated in the research. Of the 33 parents (P) involved, the majority were rural-urban migrants (25 persons, or 76 percent). In order to be able to make comparisons with the situation of urban parents, eight urban parents (24 percent) were also interviewed. Although a gender balance was originally envisaged, only 10 fathers (30 percent) could be engaged in the research. Furthermore, 24 children (C) between 10 and 14 years old participated in the research.[6] Here, there was a balance between migrant and urban children, as well as between boys and girls. A specific topic guide for children was developed and additional ethical issues were considered (Alderson and Morrow 2011). Finally, a limited number of other stakeholders (O) were interviewed, mainly from the governmental and educational sectors, to contextualize the research findings and obtain policy information. Confidentiality was guaranteed and respondents' names were only accessible to the Chinese research team. Some research participants expressed a certain discomfort when asked to evaluate a school or government policies. In these cases, stressing confidentiality proved to be important.

Guanxi (personal social connections) turned out to be critical for finding research participants. The various ways of accessing the field all started from the personal networks of the Chinese research team: (1) via governmental institutions, that is, the neighborhood committee and the Shapingba District Education Commission, (2) via school personnel and activities, and (3) via direct personal relationships.[7] This confirms that in China, "gaining access to ... interview participants is most convenient when using one's social network" (Liang and Lu 2006, 163). A possible consequence of accessing participants through the Chinese senior researcher's personal network may be the fact that more mothers than fathers were involved in the research.[8] Furthermore, the interviewees recruited via direct personal relationships (the third way of access identified above) were mostly urban persons, since the researchers did not know many migrant people personally, as "life is separated." We sought to account for these biases by mentioning them explicitly and using all the different ways of access.

Access to Quality Education in China

A Multidimensional Problem

Compulsory education in China is free and comprises six years of primary school and three years of junior middle school (Art. 18 Education Law 1995; Art. 2 Compulsory Education Law [CEL] 2006). It should be realized "regardless of gender, nationality, race, status of family property or religious belief, etc." of the children concerned (Art. 4 CEL 2006). State responsibilities have been decentralized (Art. 7 CEL 2006): the governmental institution responsible for education at the level of Chongqing is the Chongqing Education Commission; for the Shapingba District, it is the Shapingba District Education Commission. This decentralization results in important differences in the implementation of the Central Government's educational policies between provinces, cities, and even districts (Chunli 2006, 51; Pong 2015).

In China, access to public services, such as education, is determined by household registration (*hukou*).[9] For urban children, this implies that only children whose *hukou* is located in the enrollment area of a certain school are entitled to enroll in that school for free ("proximity principle"). Parents and children indicated three reasons for preferring a school outside their enrollment area: (perceived) quality of education, distance,[10] and safety. Urban (and migrant, see below) parents who prefer a school outside their enrollment area usually circumvent the proximity principle by paying a fee for their children to be admitted to their school of choice: the "school selection fee" or "sponsorship fee" (*zexiaofei* or *zanzhufei*). This practice goes against the legal prohibition on charging fees in the implementation of compulsory education.[11] Nonetheless, many research participants reported the ongoing practice of school selection fees being charged and paid. The amount of this fee is variable, depending most importantly on one's *guanxi* (see below). Personal connections with a schoolteacher or director can considerably reduce the fee, creating inequalities between well-networked persons and others.

The *hukou* of rural-urban migrant children and their parents usually remains in the countryside, because changing *hukou* to the city is expensive, administratively burdensome, and implies giving up some benefits (most importantly land in the rural area). Regarding the access of these nonlocal-*hukou* children to compulsory education in urban areas,[12] a clear policy evolution is noticeable. At first, the access of migrant children to urban schools was discouraged; later, it was made financially more burdensome than for urban children (Dong 2010). Since 2006, local governments have been legally obliged to provide migrant children with "equal conditions for receiving compulsory education" (Art. 12 CEL 2006).

To realize migrant children's access to compulsory education, local urban governments designated certain primary and junior middle schools as so-called "allocated schools" (*dingdian xuexiao* or "schools for children coming from rural-urban migrant households").[13] Migrant children are then expected to enroll in these schools, which receive financial support from the local government for accepting such students. Because local governments are reluctant to designate "top" schools as allocated schools, the latter are generally (perceived as being) of a lower educational quality. Moreover, such a segregated system encourages stigmatization and contributes to an inferiority complex in migrant families. Consequently, migrant parents frequently resorted to paying a school selection fee, so that their children would be allowed into a nonallocated ("better") school.

In research, most attention has—rightly—been paid to policies regarding the access of rural-urban migrant children to compulsory education in the city. However, various challenges appear to be similar for both urban and migrant children: parents with money and/or *guanxi* can afford to pay the school selection fees, and thus have their children admitted to a "better" school, whether this is a school outside their enrollment area (for urban children) or a nonallocated school (for migrant children). In addition, within the urban population, inequalities exist as regards access to high-quality schools, based on financial resources and personal connections. Many things happen under the radar and in contravention of state laws and policies. There is also a great deal of variation, for instance, in the amount of the school selection fee, which creates or enhances socioeconomic inequalities and fosters insecurity.

A Limited Circulation of (Human) Rights Concepts

Legal consciousness, referring to "the way individuals experience and understand the law and its relevance to their lives" (Merry 2012, 71), is difficult to assess. Familiarity with, and understanding of, rights terms were only probed for toward the end of the interviews and focus group discussions, to avoid hypothesis guessing. Overall, many people "had heard of" terms like "rights," "human rights," "children's rights," or "right to education." Often, however, they were unable to formulate an understanding of these concepts. In this sense, there seemed to be a discrepancy between a general, more implicit rights awareness (e.g., talking about discrimination toward migrants) and the ability to give a description of specific legal concepts.

The main channels through which migrant parents and children had heard about (human) rights were the newspapers and TV. Urban children also mentioned the Internet and books as sources of information. Rights consciousness seemed to be positively correlated with the level of education. Since the urban parents in the case study had enjoyed a higher level of education than the migrant parents,[14] their level of rights consciousness was also higher. Hereinafter, the answers to questions probing for familiarity with the terms "rights," "human rights," "children's rights," and "right to education" are presented.

To begin with, the terms "rights" (权利, *quanli*) and "power/authority" (权力, *quanli*) are homophones: they are pronounced in the same way, but written differently. When parents and children were asked about the concept of "rights," they therefore could not know on the basis of the pronunciation whether the interviewer was referring to "rights" or "power." In the first instance, the interviewer observed how the term *quanli* was intuitively understood by the respondent. Thereafter, the interviewer probed more specifically for the respondent's understanding of the "rights" meaning of the term. Three situations could be distinguished, across both urban and migrant parents and children. Although the sophistication of understanding was clearly greater with *some* urban parents and children, no clear line could be drawn on the basis of migrant status.

Some parents and children said they were not familiar with the term *quanli*, or did not know what it meant. This may have been out of genuine ignorance, especially in the case of migrant persons in our sample, who had completed fewer years of formal education. In some cases, however, a concern to avoid sensitive subjects seemed to be underlying the "I don't know" response. Finally, the unfamiliarity may also be partially due to the fact that *quanli* is not a traditionally Chinese term. As Svensson (2002, 82) notes, "the Chinese language had no clear equivalents to 'rights' and 'human rights' before the creation of the neologisms *quanli* and *renquan*." The term *quanli* was first used in the sense of "rights" in the translation of Henry Wheaton's work *Elements of International Law* in the mid-19th century (Angle 2002, 3).

The majority of parents and children interpreted the term *quanli* immediately as referring to "power/authority." *Quanli* was said to mean, for instance, "prestige, social position, and privilege" (migrant children in FG4), or "the government and those businessmen" (urban child C17). A migrant mother (P18) said: "I have nothing to do with [*quanli*]. It is for those who are in power."

Finally, some parents and children gave their reflections on the term *quanli* as referring to "rights," often after some further explanation by the interviewer. An eleven-year-old urban boy described "rights" as "the freedom of a person. What one can do in a given context. It represents one's dignity" (FG3-4). Although some linked "rights" to "duties" (urban P13), one urban father (P9) had the following point of view: "I never really thought about rights, also not for my child's education, I think the most important thing for me is to be happy." Migrant workers were rather pessimistic as regards the relevance of the concept of rights for them, as expressed by a migrant father (P6): "What rights can someone like a migrant worker have? We have no rights." Similarly, a migrant mother (P15) stated: "We common people have no rights, it's up to the leaders."

As regards the content of *quanli* (rights), a migrant girl (C0) interestingly expressed a conception of the right to a remedy, saying that "when your right is injured, you may have compensation." Given the focus of the research on education, others related the content to education, such as P4-M: "I am a migrant worker, being employed in the city; my children have the right to go to a local school." An urban boy (C17) referred to his right to participation when asked whether he had rights at home and in school: "I guess so. Sometimes my advice is required."

From a linguistic perspective, it is not surprising that respondents associated *quanli* more rapidly with "power" than with "rights." As well as *quanli*, the Chinese language contains many phrasal combinations in which *quan* carries the meaning of power. By contrast, *quanli* (rights) is the only Chinese term with this meaning, without synonyms. According to Cao, this "linguistic and conceptual ambiguity and multiplicity may reveal the ambivalence towards the notion and practice of rights in modern Chinese society. It may be symbolic of the struggle of the rights notion in contemporary society as a whole" (Cao 2006, 43).

The term most commonly used to denote "human rights" in Mandarin is the neologism *renquan* (*ren* = individual human being; *quan* = right) (Svensson 2002, 82). The term *renquan* was used earlier in the Chinese language to refer to natural rights, with a meaning broader than the way "human rights" has been used in the West since the Second World War (Svarverud 2001, 142). Since 2004, Article 33 of the Chinese constitution provides that "the State respects and protects human rights."

In general, there was a lack of ability to provide a personal understanding of the concept of human rights. One of the reasons thereof may be that "[h]uman rights work in China today is ... more of an issue between the Chinese government and foreign governments than an issue between the government and its people" (Svensson 2002, 311). The same eleven-year-old urban boy (FG3-4) who provided an eloquent description of rights" said about "human rights": "Human rights refer to one's freedom and dignity. If one has no human rights, it is like a dead body walking." Other persons mentioned "the right to be happy or not to be happy" (migrant P15) or linked human rights to food and shelter (migrant P16) or the freedom of the press (urban P17).

A teacher in an allocated primary school (O8) associated the notions of "equality, autonomy, and democracy" with human rights. According to her, the topic of human rights "is treated in the mandatory lessons." This claim was not validated by other findings. During a follow-up interview in September 2014, the director of allocated primary school A said: "We do not mention human rights in the classroom. The concept of the human rights of foreign countries is different." According to him, children's rights were not mentioned in class either. In the courses on the Chinese legal system, pupils are taught about what good behavior is according to the law. This includes protecting the environment and speaking Mandarin well (the latter raising questions from a minorities' rights perspective). One chapter of a textbook on legal education was entitled "Using Law to Protect Yourself," telling pupils how to protect themselves when they face bullying.

For the research participants, the most familiar rights term appeared to be *ertongquanli*, rights of children. In patriarchal ideology, children are regarded as "dependents and the property of men" (fathers), pointing to a strong hierarchy (Liu et al. 2009, 530). Nevertheless, as a consequence of the one-child policy, children receive a lot of (parental) attention and risk being spoiled. The fact that children are so valuable and unique may also explain an increasing awareness of, and interest in, the rights of children.

When the concept of *ertongquanli* was introduced during the conversations with the research participants, the link was not made between "children's rights" and "human rights." "Rights of children" were generally perceived as less sensitive, whereas the concept of "human rights" was more immediately associated with political, civil, and other more "difficult" rights in the Chinese context. In English-language scholarship, in contrast, the concept of "children's rights" has generally become understood as referring to the "human rights of children" (e.g., Invernizzi and Williams 2011; Vandenhole et al. 2015).

In relation to *ertongquanli*, various (both urban and migrant) interviewees responded that they had never heard of the term, although many others did have some ideas on the rights of children. When asked what kind of rights children have, a well-educated urban mother (P14) answered: "As human beings, they are born to be equally treated and to have the right of freedom. They deserve to be protected and respected and kept away from any danger." According to a migrant boy (C3), "[c]hildren have some right to do things that cannot be interfered with by others," pointing to the negative obligations linked to rights. An urban boy (C17) referred to the "Law of the People's Republic of China on the Protection of Minors."

Various interviewees emphasized the protective aspects of children's rights. A well-educated urban mother (P14) said, for instance: "Children, unlike adults, are underdeveloped in their minds and self-discipline. But they sure do have rights. Since they are unable to practice their rights to protect themselves, they should be paid more attention, and they deserve more protection in a legal way. Society is obliged to provide such safety and protection to our children." This reflects a limited view of children's capacities, focusing mostly on protection without recognizing children's agency.

Child abuse has been a serious area of concern in China. Especially in the domestic sphere, child abuse has long been insufficiently perceived as a social problem meriting public concern, but was rather seen as strong (but admissible) discipline (Qiao and Chan 2005). It has also been reported that child abuse has been triggered by the failure of a child to achieve educational excellence (Qiao and Chan 2005). This was confirmed by a migrant father (FG1-6): "[W]hen it comes to his studies, I don't give him too much pressure, not like some parents, who when their children's marks are not that good, might scold them, or even beat them." This indicates the high pressure that is put on children in relation to education. The fact that corporal punishment is still quite prevalent and not always problematized is illustrated by a migrant father (P18), who said: "[My daughter] is very self-disciplined. But sometimes we physically punish her. Frankly, she survived a lot of the punishments." According to a school director, one can now observe "corporal punishment in a disguised form," e.g., asking a pupil to stand up the whole time, despite the fact that any form of punishment is prohibited.

Awareness of the problematic nature of violence against children seems to be growing, however. When migrant boys in a focus group discussion were asked whether they were happy with their school, they answered affirmatively: "The environment of the school is good. The education quality here is good. *And teachers here won't practice physical punishment to students*" (emphasis added). A migrant boy (FG4-1) had learned from TV "that people will call 911 to stop the parents if they beat up their children. Some of the parents may be put into prison" (referring, however, to the American context). A migrant mother (P0) testified about her child's awareness of her right not to be abused: "[S]ometimes when my daughter is naughty, we will scare her, but then she will say: 'You are mistreating a child!' Nowadays, children have a quite strong sense of self-protection." In a similar vein, a migrant father (P21) noted: "My child always complains: 'You hit me, I will sue you for abusing me!' whenever I punish her," even when something small occurs. Since the girl threatens with "suing for abuse" with respect to minor issues, it is probably intended as a joke. Nevertheless, it is an indication that this child is aware that it would not be acceptable if her parents abused her, and that there are avenues (going to court) that are in principle available to redress such a situation. An urban girl (FG5-3) said this more explicitly: "For instance violence at home, children can go to court then. . . . Right?"

In English, the term "education" may refer to both "schooling" and "parenting." In Chinese, the same confusion exists in relation to the term *jiaoyu*, which can equally mean "education at school" and "parenting/raising children." This complicated the questions that aimed to gauge perceptions in relation to the duty bearers of the right to education.

When asked what the right to education meant to them, some respondents mentioned the system of nine-year compulsory education. Another migrant father (P4-M) interestingly made the link with his own (unrealized) right to education: "Children have the right to receive better education. As for adults like us, even if we want to learn and study, we have no chance." According to another migrant parent (P8), the right to education "means that if my child cannot go to a school in this enrollment area, I could go to the Education Commission." An urban, well-educated parent (P14) showed a more sophisticated understanding of the right to education, indicating the government as the duty bearer: "[C]hildren, they are born to have the right to receive education. In this sense, somebody should have the duty to provide education to the children. So, the government is obliged to provide equal, accessible, and the best education to our children."

Interestingly, the way access to education is currently realized in China, namely on the basis of school performance via the system of quotas and competitive examinations,[15] impacted on how the right to education itself was perceived by some interviewees. A 13-year-old urban boy (C17) stated: "The right to education means [that] those who have better scores can go to a better school and receive a better education. [T]hose who don't have good scores go to an average school to receive an average education. . . . If one works hard, one deserves better education." A similar line of thought was observed in the answer of a migrant mother (P3) to a question on children's rights: "[C]hildren have the right to choose their favorite school. He is a diligent child, so he wants to go to a better school. *If he isn't, it doesn't matter to what kind of school he goes*" (emphasis added). A well-educated urban father (P9) provided a more nuanced view, pointing to the need for education to be tailored to the capacities of each child.

In conclusion, various parents and children had a certain degree of understanding of some rights concepts. The above description should not obscure the fact, however, that the level of rights consciousness among many parents and children was low. What role did rights consciousness then play in the various stages of the transformation process from an unperceived injurious education-related experience to the adoption of a particular strategy?

Perceiving and Responding to Education-Related Problems

Naming and Blaming

Some migrant parents positively evaluated the policy of allocated schools for migrant workers' children in urban areas. Other migrant workers, however, identified the restrictive character of the *hukou* policy as injurious and explicitly linked this to discrimination and inequality in educational opportunities.

Urban interviewees were—not surprisingly—generally more satisfied with their children's education. Frustrations shared by urban and migrant parents included the quality of meals and the poor equipment and infrastructure of schools. Other problems mentioned only by urban respondents included the huge amount of homework and the pressure on children, the overpopulation of classes, the lack of good teachers, and impressions of corruption.

The transformation from an unperceived injurious experience to a perceived injurious experience (*naming*) seems to result from an interplay between contextual (see below), socioeconomic, and sociopsychological factors. More specifically, a frame of reference based on the countryside, fear of reprisals, a low self-image, the absence of "positive" *guanxi*, and a low rights consciousness includes factors that—alone or combined with one another and/or the contextual factors—seem to reduce the probability that an injurious experience will be perceived as such. Being familiar with certain legal concepts, such as discrimination, thus enhanced the probability of an injurious experience being named as such.

The transformation of a perceived injurious experience into a grievance occurs "when a person attributes an injury to the fault of another individual or social entity" (Felstiner, Abel, and Sarat 1980, 635). The majority of the parents[16] did not blame a specific person or entity for their problem, but immediately resorted to another strategy, namely toleration or self-help (see below). This may be because they considered ensuring a good education for their children to be their parental duty, and not an obligation of the government. As such, various parents felt that paying fees formed part of their parental duties. A political climate where the government is not to be criticized and there is lack of a tradition of publicly expressing criticism (Chen, Desmet, and De Feyter 2016, 60) are factors not conducive to attributing an injury to a governmental actor.

Even if one wants to blame another individual or entity, one needs to know who is responsible. Some migrant parents said that they did not know to whom they should report their issues. In a few cases, they received some help from teachers to that end (*guanxi*). Other migrant and urban parents explicitly identified "the government" or the Shapingba District Education Commission as being responsible.

How to explain these findings? Blaming involves a two-step process: (1) external attribution and (2) identification of the individual or entity deemed responsible. First, "people who blame themselves for an injury are not likely to make claims against others" (Coates and Penrod 1980, 660). If one does not attribute the cause of an injurious experience externally, but considers, for instance, that the problem belongs to the realm of parental duties, one will not blame other persons or entities. Second, knowledge is needed with regard to who is responsible. This may be influenced by the level of rights consciousness and education (and thus migration status) as well as by government communication on this matter. Social connections (*guanxi*) may act as a mediating factor.

Toleration, Self-Help, or Claiming

Three types of parental strategies were identified as responses to grievances (cf. Yngvesson, 1976): toleration (not undertaking any action),[17] self-help, and claiming. There was a gap between actual and hypothetical behavior: when probed about actual responses to injurious education-related experiences in the past, toleration prevailed. When asked about a hypothetical situation, parents were more assertive, mentioning self-help and claiming more frequently.

For the purposes of this chapter, "self-help" is defined as strategies employed by parents to improve the educational situation of their child, without claiming this from official actors (the government or the school). This often concerned trying to have their children admitted to a "better" (in the case of migrant parents, nonallocated) school. Four broad subcategories of self-help emerged from the data: (1) changing *hukou*, (2) paying money—usually the school selection fee, (3) using one's personal connections (*guanxi*), and (4) "going public" (e.g., going to the press or posting a complaint online), the latter subcategory only mentioned by the parents as a hypothetical possibility.

Claiming refers to voicing a grievance to the person or entity believed to be responsible, thereby asking for a remedy (Felstiner, Abel, and Sarat 1980, 635). The possibility of claiming is enshrined in Article 9 of the 2006 Compulsory Education Law, which provides that "[a]ny social organization or individual may expose or complain about any violation of this Law to the relevant state organ." For the purposes of this chapter, a local claim qualifies as a human rights claim when it satisfies three criteria (De Feyter 2011, 20): (1) the claim uses human rights language (although there can be a fusion with local concepts of justice), (2) it identifies a duty holder (the state or another agent), and (3) it insists on accountability from the duty holder. This chapter thus supports the view that a certain rights language should be observable when speaking of human rights practice. Otherwise, it is difficult to gauge the added value of the concept of human rights, as people may be inspired by other concepts (such as social justice) when engaging in (human rights–like) practices. Research participants did not formulate actual human rights claims, only hypothetical ones (see below).

A few instances of claiming without using human rights language were identified, involving either teachers or the office of the Shapingba District Education Commission where petitions are received. Parents did not report going to the petitioning office at district level (or only once, hypothetically).

When voicing their concerns to teachers, both migrant and urban parents seemed reluctant to ask for concrete remedies. In a few instances, there was contact with the Shapingba District Education Commission, the local governmental duty bearer as regards the right to education. The research participants did not conceptualize these actions as human rights actions, however. Moreover, the outcome was disappointing; no actual support or remedy was obtained. For instance, a migrant parent (P23-F) related:

> I called the Shapingba District Education Commission, they asked me to call another number. But no one answered this number. That's negligent! They don't care about the policy! All they want is for us to pay the money. . . . I think we migrant workers are neglected all the time! I know there's nothing we can do about it. I called the Education Commission, but no one answered.

Various migrant and urban interviewees hypothetically indicated that they would go to the Education Commission if a school would not accept their child. Some linked this to their child's right to education: "I am a migrant worker, being employed in the city, *my kids have the right to go to a local school*. If this happened, I would definitely go to the Education Commission to reveal it" (P4-M, emphasis added). The question arises, however, as to whether the parent would realize this intention. Other persons told how they planned to approach the Education Commission, but in the end decided not to do so.

Giving effect to national policy on this matter, the Chongqing municipal government established an education supervision system in 2010. In 2012, it became obligatory to publicly announce the educational supervisor's name and telephone number and the school under his supervision as well as his main responsibilities, which included receiving and verifying complaints. During research visits, this announcement of the educational supervisor's existence and responsibilities, via a notice hanging on the main gate of primary and junior middle schools, was indeed observed. Although this seems an interesting route for expressing complaints, this avenue was not mentioned in the interviews or focus group discussions. During follow-up visits in September 2014 to two allocated primary schools (A and B), both directors confirmed that their school's supervisor had not received any complaints. In the view of one director (school B), there were two reasons for this absence of complaints: first, the director himself acted as a mediator, for instance in conflicts that were not handled well by the teacher; and second, people tend to think that "complaining has no use," since in reality complaint procedures are perceived not to work. The school's supervisor did, however, regularly visit the school to attend some courses and "give suggestions."

Which factors seemed to influence the type of strategy preferred or actually adopted? In many cases, the identification of a responsible person or entity (*blaming*) was immediately followed by the expression of a feeling of powerlessness, especially by migrant parents. This led to a perception of the impossibility or uselessness of claiming. A migrant mother (P1), for instance, had never thought about going to court, "because we think the government is in charge and has the final say in these issues." Urban interviewees shared this feeling of powerlessness, albeit somewhat less fatalistically.

The relative absence of claiming in relation to injurious educational experiences was also related to other factors. One factor was the fear of negative consequences for the child or the parent (risk-benefit assessment). When his son broke his arm in primary school, one father (P4-M) said: "I could sue the school in the court and we can be paid by the insurance company and probably by the school. But considering that my son is still going to the school, we let it go." In contrast to most other parents, P4-M demonstrated an awareness of possible legal strategies, but did not use these, giving in to the unequal power relations at the local level between the school on the one hand, and himself as an individual parent with a child who still has to go to that school on the other. Another aspect of the risk-benefit assessment came into play when the assessment of probable benefits did not outweigh the efforts. For instance, an urban mother (P17) did not report the overpopulation of classrooms and the poor school infrastructure to the school or the governmental department because possible reactions to this would not benefit her own child any more, who would have graduated by then.

Another factor restraining parental claim-making was not wanting to make a fuss about little things. There was also a negative group dynamics effect. Parents did not organize, but dealt with their problems at the individual level (see also below). The final elements explaining the absence of action (self-help or claiming) were a low familiarity with rights concepts and the lack of financial resources and *guanxi*.

Additional Explanatory Factors

In addition to the elements identified above in relation to the specific stages of the transformation process, what additional, contextual factors may tentatively be identified to explain the limited occurrence of claiming and the limited use of human rights language by parents and children in relation to injurious education-related experiences in Chongqing?

The political context co-determines the potential of human rights claims and actions to emerge. As noted by Oré Aguilar (2011, 117), "[i]n human rights claims, the degree of 'political space' is measured not only by the existence of an ongoing armed or violent conflict . . . , but also by the existence and level of functioning of institutional (civilian) governance structures, decision-making channels, freedom of expression, rule of law and open access to information." In China, especially the latter elements of freedom of expression, rule of law, and access to information are often problematic. Nevertheless, the general limited political space cannot be the only explanatory factor for the lack of human rights claims and actions in this case study, since in other places and cases in China, human rights mobilization has significantly increased in recent decades (Svensson 2012, 686; see also Davis and Mohamed in this volume).

Another factor is that the interviewed parents did not mention the presence of, or interaction with, "supportive users," organizations or individuals who could support them in invoking their right to education or other human rights. At the level of Chongqing, no organizations were identified that worked on education for migrant children from a human rights perspective. In Beijing, in contrast, Pong (2015) has observed an increased involvement of civil society as regards the educational situation of migrant children. At the international level, various supportive users have spoken on the right to education of the children of rural-urban migrant workers in China.[18] The respondents did not show any awareness of these evolutions at the national and international level. This absence of supportive users implies that it becomes more difficult for local needs and claims to be "translated" (Merry 2006b) into human rights language (cf. Liu, Hu, and Liao 2009).

A possible explanatory cultural contextual factor for the low occurrence of claiming and the limited relevance of human rights is that the "naming, blaming, and claiming" process goes against Confucian values and perspectives: "One of the most pervasive worries about Confucianism is that the practice of claiming one's rights is conflictual. That is, it both reflects a breakdown in social harmony and is a cause of further social strain" (Tiwald 2012, 249–50).[19] This seems to be reflected in the concern of parents "not to make a fuss about little things" (see above). One of the effects of the capacity-building program described in the chapter by Davis and Mohamed (this volume) was that the activists engaged in a more collaborative relationship with local government actors. Here, parents were reluctant to engage in human rights claims and actions, either in a conflictual or in more cooperative ways. This may at least partially be caused by the fact that there is no social movement of (migrant) parents in the Shapingba District of Chongqing to protest against education-related inequalities. The grievances, as well as the few claims and actions, remained at the individual level. According to political opportunity/political process theory, three essential elements influence the emergence and development of social movements: (1) insurgent consciousness, (2) organizational strength, and (3) political opportunities (Cragun and Cragun 2010). The element of "insurgent consciousness" can be linked to the chain of naming, blaming, and claiming. For a social movement to emerge, it is necessary that persons who share a grievance join forces to establish, or become members of, a movement. This has not been the case here, in contrast to the community-based organizations that mobilized around the right to health (cf. Davis and Mohamed in this volume).

Conclusion

This chapter examined education-related experiences of social exclusion in the context of internal migration in Chongqing, China. It assessed how rural-urban migrant workers and their children responded to such injurious experiences, and whether human rights played a role therein. The findings of the case study deepen our understanding of the process leading from transgressions to (human rights) claims. From a transformation perspective, this process was operationalized in the stages of naming, blaming, and claiming. Similar contextual and socioeconomic factors (especially migration status, education, and *guanxi*) played a role in each of the three phases, whereas the sociopsychological dynamics seemed to differ for each phase. As regards the types of strategies adopted, the transformation perspective was broadened to include toleration and self-help, in addition to claiming. Within the category of self-help, possible actions included changing *hukou*, paying (prohibited) fees, mobilizing *guanxi* and (hypothetically) "going public" (to the press or online). Only a few instances of actual claiming were reported, and none of these used human rights language.

This case study shows that there is great potential to unravel more carefully the dynamics at play between a local experience of abuse and the formulation of (human rights) claims. It also demonstrates that the actual relevance of human rights may be much reduced if one does not consider settings where human rights are "destined" to play a role (e.g., through their inclusion in a capacity-building program), but instead one researches a case without prior knowledge regarding the circulation of human rights concepts in that setting.

Notes

1. University of Antwerp, Law and Development Research Group, "Localising Human Rights," https://www.uantwerpen.be/en/research-groups/law-and-development/research-program/localising-human-rights/.

2. For another application in children's rights research, see Godoy (1999).

3. Within the scope of the research project (compulsory education in the Shapingba District of Chongqing), no court cases were found addressing the right to education of rural-urban migrant workers' children.

4. The team was composed of Jingrong Chen, Shisong Jiang, Xi Chen, Dongmei Liu, and Hanbing Ai (Chongqing University), Koen De Feyter and Ellen Desmet (University of Antwerp).

5. On the methodological framework and challenges, see Chen, Desmet, and De Feyter (2016, 45–63).

6. The broader research included a focus on the transition from primary to junior middle school, which explains the age range of the participating children (grades five or six of primary school and grade one of junior middle school).

7. For more information on how this differential access impacted the research proceedings and findings, see Chen, Desmet, and De Feyter (2016, 61–62).

8. This may also have to do, however, with the fact that children's education is traditionally considered a female area of concern in Chinese society. In the discussion of the research findings, "M" stands for male and "F" for female.

9. See generally Zhu (2003); Wing Chan and Zhang (1999).

10. A school outside the enrollment area may be geographically closer.

11. Article 2 CEL 2006.

12. See generally Chunli (2006); Montgomery (2012).

13. In 2014, after the completion of the main phase of fieldwork, new policies on the proximity principle and *hukou* reform were adopted. The term "allocated schools" is being gradually deleted and does not seem to be used anymore in recent policies. In practice, however, migrant children continue to be "allocated" to a school. For more information, see Chen, Desmet, and De Feyter (2016, 118–125).

14. There was a clear difference in the level of education of migrant and urban parents. The majority of the urban parents had enjoyed higher education. In contrast, fifteen migrant parents had dropped out during primary school, ten had finished junior middle school, and only one migrant father went to senior middle school.

15. The new policy adopted in January 2014 by the Central Government, however, abolishes the examinations in the transition from primary to junior middle school.

16. No "blaming" or "claiming" was observed in the interviews and focus group discussions with children.

17. In the literature on dispute management, various concepts have been used to indicate an absence of action. They include "endurance," that is, enduring a state of conflict, as a phase in the dispute process (Merry 1978, 903); "avoidance," that is, limiting the relationship with the disputant (Felstiner 1974, 70), which can be a way of managing or ending a dispute (Merry 1978, 903); and "lumping it," that is, "ignoring the dispute, by declining to take any or much action in response to the controversy" (Felstiner 1974, 81), which is a way of ending the dispute since one gives up one's rights (Merry 1978, 903). None of these concepts was deemed to accurately describe the situation observed in this case study, which concerns the stage *before* an actual dispute emerges: the grievance is not expressed to the party deemed responsible, and thus not rejected. No actual dispute exists, nor is any form of self-help undertaken. The concept of "nonaction," proposed by Yngvesson (1976, 368), was not deemed appropriate either, because it is used there to refer to a "period of assessment, in which the circumstances surrounding a deviant act, and the history of the individual, his or her ties in the community, and the consequences in the community of a formal reaction to the grievance are considered and weighed against one another." The absence of action in the present case study did not seem to include a similar period of assessment, but was due to other factors, as elaborated below. Therefore, it was decided to use the concept of "toleration," in the sense of a reluctant form of tolerance, to indicate the absence of action toward a grievance in relation to the educational situation of children in Chongqing.

18. See UN Committee on Economic, Social and Cultural Rights (2014), UN Committee on the Rights of the Child (2013), and UN Special Rapporteur on the Right to Education (2003). This chapter does not aim, however, to carry out a human rights evaluation of Chinese educational legislation and policies.

19. The impact of Confucianism in current Chinese society is a matter of debate. According to some, "Confucianism is making a comeback. . . . The Chinese government has started to

promote Confucianism very explicitly" (Deklerck et al. 2009, 398). As a matter of fact, however, it has also been argued that "[t]he People's Republic of China . . . is hardly a Confucian society any longer" (Svensson 2000, 202).

Works Cited

Alderson, Priscilla, and Virginia Morrow. 2011. *The Ethics of Research with Children and Young People: A Practical Handbook*. London: Sage Publications.

Angle, Stephen C. 2002. *Human Rights in Chinese Thought: A Cross-Cultural Inquiry*. Cambridge: Cambridge University Press.

Brems, Eva, and Ellen Desmet, eds. 2014. "Studying Human Rights Law from the Perspective(s) of Its Users." *Human Rights and International Legal Discourse* 8 (2).

Cao, Deborah. 2006. "Key Words in Chinese Law." In *Images in Law*, edited by Anne Wagner and William Pencak, 35–50. Aldershot: Ashgate.

Chen, Guibao. 2010. "Access to Compulsory Education by Rural Migrants' Children in Urban China: A Case Study from Nine Cities." *Educational Research* 1 (10): 512–519.

Chen, Jinrong, Ellen Desmet, and Koen De Feyter. 2016. *The Right to Education of Rural-Urban Migrant Households in Chongqing, China*. Localising Human Rights Working Paper Series no. 3. Antwerp: University of Antwerp.

Chunli, Xia. 2006. "Migrant Children and the Right to Compulsory Education in China." *Asia-Pacific Journal on Human Rights and the Law* 2: 29–74.

Coates, Dan, and Steven Penrod. 1980. "Social Psychology and the Emergence of Disputes." *Law and Society Review* 15 (3–4): 656–80.

Cragun, Ryan, and Deborah Cragun. 2010. *Introduction to Sociology*. Tampa: Blacksleet River.

De Feyter, Koen. 2007. "Localising Human Rights." In *Economic Globalisation and Human Rights*, edited by Wolfgang Benedek, Koen de De Feyter, and Fabrizio Marrella, 11–40. Cambridge: Cambridge University Press.

———. "Sites of Rights Resistance." In *The Local Relevance of Human Rights*, edited by Koen De Feyter, Stephan Parmentier, Christiane Timmerman, and George Ulrich, 11–39. Cambridge: Cambridge University Press.

Deklerck, Stijn, Ellen Desmet, Marie-Claire Foblets, Joke Kusters, and Jogchum Vrielink. 2009. "Limits of Human Rights Protection from the Perspective of Legal Anthropology." In *Facing the Limits of the Law*, edited by Eric Claes, Wouter Devroe, and Bert Keirsbilck, 375–414. Berlin: Springer.

Desmet, Ellen. 2014. "Analysing Users' Trajectories in Human Rights: A Conceptual Exploration and Research Agenda." *Human Rights and International Legal Discourse* 8 (2): 121–41.

Dong, Jie. 2010. "Neo-Liberalism and the Evolvement of China's Education Policies on Migrant Children's Schooling." *Journal for Critical Education Policy Studies* 8 (1): 137–60.

Engel, Madeline H., and Jaruwan S. Engel. 2010. *Tort, Custom, and Karma: Globalization and Legal Consciousness in Thailand*. Stanford: Stanford University Press.

Felstiner, William L. F. 1974. "Influences of Social Organization on Dispute Processing." *Law and Society Review* 9 (1): 63–94.

Felstiner, William L. F., Richard L. Abel, and Austin Sarat. 1980. "The Emergence and Transformation of Disputes: Naming, Blaming, Claiming." *Law and Society Review* 15 (3–4): 631–54.

Gallagher, Mary E. 2006. "Mobilizing the Law in China: 'Informed Disenchantment' and the Development of Legal Consciousness." *Law and Society Review* 40 (4): 783–816.

Godoy, Angelina Snodgrass. 1999. "'Our Right Is the Right to Be Killed': Making Rights Real on the Streets of Guatemala City." *Childhood* 6 (4): 423–42.

Goodale, Mark, and Sally Engle Merry. 2007. *The Practice of Human Rights: Tracking Law between the Global and the Local*. Cambridge Studies in Law and Society. Cambridge: Cambridge University Press.

Invernizzi, Antonella, and Jane Williams. 2011. *The Human Rights of Children: From Visions to Implementation*. Burlington, VT: Ashgate.

Liang, Bin, and Hong Lu. 2006. "Conducting Fieldwork in China: Observations on Collecting Primary Data Regarding Crime, Law, and the Criminal Justice System." *Journal of Contemporary Criminal Justice* 22 (2): 157–72.

Liu, Meng, Yanhong Hu, and Minli Liao. 2009. "Travelling Theory in China: Contextualization, Compromise and Combination." *Global Networks* 9 (4): 529–53.

Merry, Sally Engle. 1978. "Going to Court: Strategies of Dispute Management in an American Urban Neighborhood." *Law and Society Review* 13 (4): 891–926.

———. 2006a. *Human Rights and Gender Violence: Ttranslating International Law into Local Justice*. Chicago Series in Law and Society. Chicago: University of Chicago Press.

———. 2006b. "Transnational Human Rights and Local Activism: Mapping the Middle." *American Anthropologist* 108 (1): 38–51.

———. 2012. "Legal Pluralism and Legal Culture: Mapping the Terrain." In *Legal Pluralism and Development: Scholars and Practitioners in Dialogue*, edited by Brian Z. Tamanaha, Caroline Sage, and Michael J. V. Woolcock, 66–82. Cambridge: Cambridge University Press.

Merry, Sally Engle, Peggy Levitt, Mihaela Şerban Rosen, and Diana H. Yoon. 2010. "Law from Below: Women's Human Rights and Social Movements in New York City." *Law and Society Review* 44 (1): 101–128.

Montgomery, Jessica L. 2012. "The Inheritance of Inequality: Hukou and Related Barriers to Compulsory Education for China's Migrant Children." *Pacific Rim Law and Policy Journal Association* 21 (3): 591–622.

Oré Aguilar, G. 2011. "The Local Relevance of Human Rights: A Methodological Approach." In *The Local Relevance of Human Rights*, edited by Koen de Feyter, Stephan Parmentier, Christiane Timmerman, and George Ulrich, 109–146. Cambridge: Cambridge University Press.

Pong, Myra. 2015. *Educating the Children of Migrant Workers in Beijing: Migration, Education, and Policy in Urban China*. London and New York: Routledge.

Qiao, D. P., and Y. C. Chan. 2005. "Child Abuse in China: A Yet-to-Be-Acknowledged 'Social Problem' in the Chinese Mainland." *Child and Family Social Work* 10 (1): 21–27.

Svarverud, Rune. 2001. "The Notions of 'Power' and 'Rights' in Chinese Political Discourse." In *New Terms for New Ideas: Western Knowledge and Lexical Change in Late Imperial China*, edited by Michael Lackner, Iwo Amelung, and Joachim Kurtz, 125–146. Leiden: Brill.

Svensson, Marina. 2000. "The Chinese Debate on Asian Values and Human Rights: Some Reflections on Relativism, Nationalism and Orientalism." In *Human Rights and Asian Values: Contesting National Identities and Cultural Representations in Asia*, edited by Michael Jacobsen and Ole Bruun, 199–226. Richmond, Surrey: Curzon Press.

———. 2002. *Debating Human Rights in China. A Conceptual and Political History*. Lanham; Oxford: Rowman and Littlefield.

———. 2012. "Human Rights in China as an Interdisciplinary Field: History, Current Debates and New Approaches." In *Handbook of Human Rights*, edited by Thomas Cushman, 685–701. Oxon/New York: Routledge.

Tiwald, Justin. 2012. "Confucianism and Human Rights." In *Handbook of Human Rights*, edited by Thomas Cushman, 244–254. Oxon/New York: Routledge.

UN Committee on Economic, Social and Cultural Rights. 2014. Concluding Observations on the Second Report of China. UN Doc. E/CN/12/CO/2.

UN Committee on the Rights of the Child. 2013. Concluding Observations on the Combined Third and Fourth Periodic Reports of China. UN Doc. CRC/C/CHN/CO/3-4.

UN Special Rapporteur on the Right to Education. 2003. Mission to China. UN Doc. E/CN.4/2004/45/Add.1.

Vandenhole, Wouter. 2012. "Localising the Human Rights of Children." In *Children's Rights from Below: Cross-Cultural Perspectives*, edited by Manfred Liebel, 80–93. New York: Palgrave Macmillan.

Vandenhole, Wouter, Ellen Desmet, Didier Reynaert, and Sara Lembrechts, eds. 2015. *Routledge International Handbook of Children's Rights Studies*. Oxon: Routledge.

Wang, Liangjuan. 2008. *Ethnic Migrants, Social Networks, and Education Access: Membership Capitalization in Beijing*. University of Hong Kong, unpublished.

Wenbin, Li. 2009. "Empirical Research on the Factors Affecting the Provision of Compulsory Education to Rural Migrants' Children." *Jianghan Forum* 7: 15–8.

Wing Chan, Kam, and Li Zhang. 1999. "The *Hukou* System and Rural-Urban Migration in China: Processes and Changes." *China Quarterly* 160: 818–55.

Yngvesson, Barbara. 1976. "Responses to Grievance Behavior: Extended Cases in a Fishing Community." *American Ethnologist* 3 (2): 353–73. https://doi.org/10.1525/ae.1976.3.2.02a00100.

Zhu, Lijiang. 2003. "The Hukou System of the People's Republic of China: A Critical Appraisal under International Standards of Internal Movement and Residence." *Chinese Journal of International Law* 2 (2): 519–65.

CHAPTER 8

Localization "Light": The Travel and Transformation of Nonempowering Human Rights Norms

Tine Destrooper

The premise of this volume is that human rights need to be locally relevant if rights users are to consider them as a resource in their struggle against injustice. Broadly speaking, this "localization" can occur in two ways. Rights holders and rights users can *interpret* existing human rights norms in ways that increase their local relevance and that make it relevant to frame local concerns in human rights terms, or they can seek to *shape* the international human rights framework in ways that render it more reflective of their realities. The contributions in this volume seek to better understand how human rights norms circulate between and within different groups of rights users, and how they are transformed during this process. The authors implicitly or explicitly assume that for either of these processes—travel or transformation—to happen, all parties involved should actively and explicitly engage with the human rights framework in some way, for example by adopting approaches or discourses rooted in the human rights framework. In this chapter, I ask whether we can speak of human rights travel and/or transformation in cases where rights users are engaged in a struggle that is conceptually similar to the struggle for human rights, but are not explicitly referencing the human rights framework.

I explore this issue on the basis of a case study from the field of development because the interventions of international organizations that adopt a human rights–based approach (HRBA) to development are a potentially important avenue for exposing rights holders to human rights norms. I use the case of the Sanitized Villages project in the Kongo Central province of the Democratic Republic of the Congo (DRC) to assess whether and to what extent such an HRBA affects rights holders' interest in, and potential for, engaging the international human rights discourse to address threats to their human rights, in this case, their right to water and sanitation. While HRBAs are not the only mechanism that can facilitate the travel and transformation of human rights, on the ground these interventions have often been one of the primary ways in which rights holders are exposed to human rights discourses.

The Bidirectional Localization of Human Rights

The question about the localization of human rights is an important one for practitioners as well as for scholars to consider because it is on the local level that human rights can act as a line of defense against injustice. Consequently, it is there that they prove to be vital or illusory. There is therefore a normative as well as an efficacy argument to make for studying and facilitating the localization of human rights. According to De Feyter (2006), localization can be seen as a two-way highway, where we can analytically distinguish between two processes: one whereby existing international human rights norms are translated, appropriated, and used in the local struggles of individual and collective rights holders and one whereby local and practice-based human rights claims inspire the further development of international human rights norms (also see Oré Aguilar 2011, 112).

This notion of bidirectional human rights localization is rooted in two distinct but related actor-centered approaches to human rights. First, it builds on Sally Merry's groundbreaking work on vernacularization, which contends that for existing human rights norms to become effective they need to be situated within local contexts of power and meaning by norm-entrepreneurs and that they need to be implemented on the basis of a vernacularized consensus (Merry 2006; Levitt and Merry 2009). Second, it builds on the literature about upstreaming practice-based human rights understandings, which focuses on the potential of local rights holders to shape the international human rights architecture through participation and consultation (de Gaay Fortman 2011). The localization perspective proposes to integrate these top-down and bottom-up dynamics, thus foregrounding the agency of rights holders in making the human rights discourse and methods more relevant for the most disempowered and vulnerable groups.

For the purposes of this volume, I take the localization perspective one step further and supplement the attention to the bidirectional top-down, bottom-up travel of human rights with a more multidirectional understanding of how human rights norms travel and become transformed. This multidirectional understanding highlights the many ways in which human rights norms can travel between various communities of rights holders and rights users at the "trans-local" level. It does not presuppose the same vertical power relations that are implicit in the language of bidirectionality or in the idea of a local-global continuum. Human rights travel, then, can be seen as the many ways in which norms move through complex, multilayered, and juxtaposed networks of rights users, ranging from rights holders in remote communities across the globe to human rights practitioners within the global human rights architecture and from norm setters on the international level to grassroots community-based organizations working on local issues.

Both the understanding of localization as a bidirectional process and the multidirectional interpretation that I propose here are rooted in legal pluralism and critical legal studies, which acknowledge that imprecision, uncertainty, and instability characterize the international legal realm and that these conditions require new types of coordination and elaboration that do not aim at erasing normative differences, but that, instead, seek to make differences visible and thereby give agency to various groups of rights holders (Delmas-Marty 2006; Baumgaertel et al. 2014). As Halliday and Carruthers (2007) argue, in a globalized landscape it is not the authoritative transnational and global bodies that create norms that they can then impose more or less subtly upon a hapless world. The process of implementation always and everywhere involves negotiation between those who create global norms and those who implement and appropriate them, and it should therefore never be conceived of as a top-down, universalizing undertaking. This chapter also draws on ordered pluralism's premise of "law as a network" (Ost and Van de Kerckhove 2002), but argues that power relations need to be accounted for more explicitly to allow for an analysis of how some actors in the network may have more access and influence than others. A networked understanding of international human rights norms that also pays attention to power differences can play a role in countering the tendency of international human rights law to transform people into "passive entities who require outside aid" from human rights institutions (Urueña 2012, 3). Urueña argues that the preconceived notion of human suffering, which is implicit in human rights norms, impedes rights holders from expressing their unique—individual or collective—experience, thereby depriving them of their individual agency (see also Mutua 2001).

It is beyond the scope of this chapter to analyze the complex, dynamic, and mutually constitutive relations between these various actors in the network or to determine their relative power, access, and influence. Instead, what I am interested in here is the extent to which, within one node of the network, rights users engage the human rights discourse or turn to human rights methodologies in their struggle for justice. Before reflecting on which partners and mechanisms would be required for human rights norms to develop in ways that take rights holders' own input into account, we first need to ask whether rights holders themselves see the benefit of invoking the human rights framework, and how they do this.

Sanitized Villages in Kongo Central

This chapter relies on new empirical material from a case study in the Kongo Central province of the DRC to examine whether and how various rights users (both rights holders in remote rural villages and human rights–based development actors) rely on a human rights discourse and human rights–inspired methods in their struggle for clean drinking water and adequate sanitation infrastructure. I focus on the Sanitized Villages project, a component of the Sanitized Villages and Schools project, which seeks to implement small, cost-efficient changes to improve rights holders' access to clean drinking water and to improve the sanitation facilities in rural areas. The project is officially administered by the Congolese government, which also initiated it in the early 1990s.[1] However, in practice, UNICEF, because of its financial and organizational weight, plays a dominant role in the development and implementation of the project.[2]

Preconditions for Grassroots Activism

The reason it is relevant to consider this human rights–based project in the context of human rights travel and transformation is the importance of local ownership, community-based approaches, participation, and empowerment, which are supposed to be mainstreamed throughout the lifecycle of the project and which, in many ways, can be interpreted as a precondition and stepping-stone for grassroots organizing and activism. According to the project description of the Sanitized Villages project, interventions take place only in response to a community's explicit request and, before any intervention takes place, rights holders are required to set up community structures and working groups (e.g. the Comité Village Assaini) that will take the lead in the development and implementation of a project strategy. The members of this committee are moreover supposed to be different from the ones holding traditional positions of power in the village, in order to avoid a situation in which working groups become a replica of existing power structures. The role of these working groups goes from taking the initiative to join the program to analyzing the community's situation and needs, and from proposing solutions and actions to carrying out these actions with the support of an implementing partner (UNICEF DRC n.d.; Ministère de la Santé Publique 2011). The project invites rights holders to hold regular meetings to define their position and to negotiate with government, UNICEF, and other project partners that come to the village to assist with the installation of wells and sanitation infrastructure.[3] As such, the requirement that rights holders organize and manage the intervention as a community has the potential to catalyze certain types of grassroots activism, partly because it installs the community structures and dynamics that can facilitate this, partly because rights holders develop transferable skills. While these provisions are insufficient to speak of grassroots activism or social movement activism per se, they can enable this.

Preconditions for Human Rights–Based Activism

In addition to being relevant for studying grassroots mobilization, this case is also relevant for studying the travel and transformation of human rights, and specifically for studying how a human rights–based approach to development shapes this travel and transformation. UNICEF's influence on the development of the project is one of the main factors that could undergird human rights–based activism. UNICEF was one of the first UN programs to commit to human rights–based programming, and its Executive Directive 98-04 made the HRBA a cornerstone of all its actions (UNICEF 1998). Moreover,

UNICEF, together with the UN Development Program (UNDP), was one of the frontrunners operationalizing the HRBA (Russell 2010; Nyamu-Musembi and Cornwall 2004; Gysler 2012). To date, UNICEF's headquarters and specifically its division for Water, Sanitation and Hygiene (WaSH) continue to formally adhere to the HRBA.

This approach is normatively based on international human rights standards and substantively seeks to promote and protect these by analyzing inequalities that lie at the heart of development problems. While there are different interpretations and strands of HRBAs, several principles run through all of them. The UN Common Understanding (UN 2003) as well as academic literature (Gready 2008; Gysler 2012; Nyamu-Musembi 2005) emphasize the centrality of participation, inclusion, accountability, equality, nondiscrimination, transparency, and empowerment, as well as the strengthening of duty bearers' and rights holders' capacities as core principles of HRBAs. The approach suggests an interpretation of human rights that allows for the valorization of local voices and stresses the need for openness and contextualization. From a localization perspective, it is relevant to remark that while there is no formal obligation to consult rights holders in the UN Common Understanding of the HRBA (UN 2003), the references to participation, inclusion, and local ownership implicitly invite the consultation of rights holders at various stages of the intervention. There is, moreover, widespread agreement among development practitioners and scholars that the voices of rights holders should be taken into account when planning interventions (Nyamu-Musembi 2005; Merry 2006; Gready 2008). From a theoretical point of view, as well, consulting rights holders is a pertinent component of responsive planning.[4]

The adherence of UNICEF, a pivotal partner in the Village Assaini project, to the HRBA is not the only component that would explain or facilitate human rights–based interventions in this project. The HRBA became an important conceptual framework for development cooperation across the board in the last decade, for UN programs as well as for other development actors, and it is adhered to by several Congolese NGOs (e.g., Centre Intègre pour le Developpement des Milieux Ruraux, CIDR), international organizations (e.g., UNDP), and bilateral development programs (e.g., the Belgian Technical Cooperation, BTC) that operate in the region. Rights holders have thereby been exposed to the basic principles and methods of an HRBA and could potentially interact with some components of it when organizing.

Fieldwork Methods

The fieldwork for this chapter was carried out in the spring of 2014 based on a mixed-method case study design and was supplemented with findings from ongoing anthropological fieldwork in the coastal region of Kongo Central. Together with a fellow researcher from the region, Pascal Sundi, and interpreters, I carried out interviews ($n = 37$), focus groups ($n = 9$), and direct observations in nine villages spread over the three administrative districts of Kongo Central.[5] In each village, we carried out semistructured qualitative interviews with village elders ($n = 9$), rights holders ($n = 16$), organizers ($n = 3$), and local health officers in charge of implementing the program ($n = 9$). These interviews probed for the presence of human rights principles and methods during the project planning and implementation and gauged how rights holders and project partners perceived these principles. For the structure and analysis of the interviews and focus group discussions, I relied on the Sage Qualitative Research Kit (Kvale 2007; Barbour 2007).

In addition, several interviews ($n = 9$) were held with UNICEF officers in Kinshasa, the national capital, and Matadi, the provincial capital. These interviews probed for the importance of the human rights framework in shaping programmatic decisions, as well as for the existence of formal and informal feedback mechanisms that could facilitate the sharing of local understandings with actors at other scales. The goal of the interviews was twofold: first to assess whether human rights were an explicit inspiration for Sanitized Villages and, second, to gain a better understanding of potential multidirectional travel and transformation processes.

Mid-ranking government officials from the Ministry of Health involved in this program ($n = 2$) and the program officer of a project partner (SNV) were also interviewed. Interviews with rights holders were carried out in Kikongo (with the assistance of an interpreter) or in French. Expert interviews were carried out in French or English. Names of interviewees and villages are not disclosed to protect the identity of participants in this research.

Last, I relied on qualitative discourse analysis to analyze the program documents about the Sanitized Villages project specifically and about UNICEF's HRBA more generally.[6] Using multiple sources of information in this way allows for the triangulation and crystallization of information (Richardson 2000, 934; Ellingson 2009).[7] While this qualitative research methodology does not guarantee external validity or generalizability, it allows for an in-depth understanding and can shed light on dynamics that may also be relevant for other cases.

The next section of the chapter sheds light on the presence of human rights principles and methods both in the practice of rights holders on the ground and in the practice of the human rights–based development actor, in this case mainly UNICEF.[8]

Relevance of Human Rights on the Ground

Development Actors' Engagement with the Human Rights Framework

In a previous publication (Destrooper 2015), I examined the rhetorical and practical relevance of the HRBA on the ground in the Sanitized Villages project. This study was built around twelve indicators derived from the UN Common Understanding of an HRBA (UN 2003). These included general concerns (such as the extent to which the project seeks to further human rights or the extent to which human rights are a guiding principle for interventions) as well as more specific concerns (such as the extent to which attention is paid to the development of sustainable strategic partnerships or to participation as both a means and a goal of development). This study showed that some dimensions of the HRBA served as guiding principles for project partners, but that the rhetorical attention to some dimensions of the HRBA did not always entail foregrounding of human rights principles in concrete interventions.

According to interviewees in UNICEF's country office, this is partly because there is no credible pressure from headquarters to implement elaborate consultation processes regarding the right to water and sanitation, and partly because national and provincial staff did not consider such consultation rounds relevant when working with the Sanitized Village groups in the Kongo Central province, where rights holders often have no formal education, no prior exposure to human rights discourses, and—in the opinion of these interviewees—no interest in seeing this project as anything beyond the provision of clean drinking water and sanitation facilities. Because of the lack of credible pressure or incentives, project partners' utilization of human rights discourses and methodologies was limited.

Accountability, for example, an issue that is crucial from a human rights point of view, was markedly absent from the discourse. Rights holders argued during interviews that they had nowhere to go to complain about fraud and other types of misconduct that, in practice, interfered with their right to water. Many rights holders expressed a feeling of resignation and powerlessness when discussing the lack of mechanisms for reporting problems, sharing information, and seeking redress. When we discussed this with a local health officer, he argued,

> You have to look at these people, their level of education, what they need. They need pumps. They need clean water. They need toilets. I don't need to ask them. I know. I am a doctor. I know that village and its needs. . . . Besides, no one is interested [in talking about rights]. . . . What I am asked is how many pumps we have installed. So that's what we do, we install as many pumps as possible. . . . In the end, it's only the pumps that matter.[9]

In addition to being entirely devoid of references to accountability, duty bearers, or the potential to claim rights, this statement indicates that there were no provisions to consult rights holders about their strategic interests or their development priorities regarding the right to water—allegedly because people in this project are not in a position to reflect on these abstract issues. UNICEF country officers seemed to share this interpretation and did not request that local health officers install this kind of consultation or awareness-raising programs regarding human rights, nor that rights holders' participation in the decision-making about programmatic concerns was facilitated.[10] In the few cases where rights holders were consulted about their priorities, these consultations did not have a human rights focus, but dealt only with practical concerns and were infrequent and ad hoc.[11]

Findings were also mixed with regard to participation, another crucial element of the HRBA. While respondents often initially stressed the participatory dimension of interventions, they were considerably more critical about the *nature* of this participation once the conversation progressed. Focus groups showed that in none of the villages in this case study was the decision to join made by the community members. Instead, the Local Health Office signed them up. Moreover, none of the participants in the focus groups—invariably members of the Village Assaini working group—had been involved in the development of the intervention plan or in any kind of human rights–based evaluation. Interviewees and focus groups indicated that their only participation consisted of providing manual labor and local material resources during the execution of the project, which—unsurprisingly—they did not experience as empowering. In none of the villages did the rights holders have the opportunity to participate in the strategic decision-making.

In sum, fieldwork showed that the HRBA is implemented in a markedly "light" way and that substantive attention to human rights principles was limited, partial or even nonexistent. Rights holders participated in and were consulted about certain practical aspects of a program that was otherwise passed on to them top-down, but there was no platform or phase in which they could comment on or participate in the broader decision-making, nor was there explicit attention to the accountability of duty bearers. Project partners like UNICEF mostly also neglected other dimensions of the HRBA, such as the empowerment of rights holders to claim their rights, the empowerment of duty bearers to live up to their obligations under international law, or the attention to inclusivity or local ownership. What is interesting about this case study is that, despite the lack of attention for the human rights component of the project on the side of the project partners, rights holders themselves did express an interest in certain components of the human rights framework.

Grassroots Engagement with the Human Rights Framework

When discussing the issue of human rights, most participants were eager to confirm that they knew that water was a human right and that they had learned a lot about their rights since the start of the project. However, as the conversation progressed and interviewees felt more at ease, the rhetoric often became more critical, and when probing what respondents referred to when they mentioned they had learned a lot about their rights through this project, one woman replied, "They told us once that the fact that water is a right means that water is life. We need water and therefore we have a responsibility for providing it, and they asked us if we understood this."[12]

"*L'eau, c'est la vie*" [water is life], the slogan of the national water authority, was cited repeatedly in response to questions about how people understood their right to water, as were other marketing slogans that hardly showed overlaps with the discourse on human rights, duty bearers, or rights holders. No one in the nine villages interpreted the concept of a duty bearer or of a rights claim in ways that reverberated with the mainstream understanding of these notions under international law. However, the fact that respondents did not identify the state as a duty bearer (as could be expected in a human rights–based discourse on water) did not mean that they did not engage the notion of a duty bearer in other ways. In fact, respondents often insisted that they considered various other actors to be formal human rights duty bearers, most notably UNICEF, development NGOs, corporate actors active in the region, and—for historical reasons—the Belgian state. The most common—and remarkable—interpretation of the duty bearer concept, though, was that right holders themselves were responsible and should therefore be held accountable for ensuring their right to water. However, the initial focus on the individual and collective responsibility of rights holders did not mean that respondents were uninterested in the structural dimension of their struggle or in calling this a human rights problem.

The study of a particular village where the Dutch Technical Cooperation (Stichting Nederlandse Vrijwilligers, SNV) became involved is significant here. In this village, the quality of hygienic installations had deteriorated rapidly after installation because villagers did not feel ownership. Because of this, the SNV, one of the project partners, initiated a pilot project. During the SNV's first visit to this village, the facilitator talked *with* people, rather than *to* people, and overall villagers did most of the talking. The formal goal of the visit was to assess how local ownership of the sanitation infrastructure could be improved. Formally there was no goal of focusing on human rights, only a more pragmatic concern with ensuring that infrastructure worked and would be maintained. Nevertheless, the fact that rights holders perceived this as a space to talk freely and that the SNV facilitator was willing to work with any issue that rights holders considered relevant prompted rights holders to also invoke human rights language and to discuss some issues that went beyond their immediate needs and that could be seen as dimensions of an HRBA (such as issues of accountability or inclusivity).

This interest in the HRBA—at least in certain components of it—is interesting in itself, considering the argument of UNICEF country officers and the local health officers that rights holders were concerned only about their immediate needs. If this group had indeed only cared about its immediate practical needs, the SNV discussion would have focused solely on the lack of resources that interfered with their capacity to maintain the infrastructure. However, while acknowledging the importance of this problem, the group also spontaneously referred to the responsibility of others—in the first place UNICEF and the local health officers—to foresee these resources. Rights holders further insisted that they should be able to communicate with those actors whom they saw as duty bearers, or *responsables*.[13]

This would require a kind of participation that is currently not in place, namely rights holders' participation in their own interest representation and not merely in the practical execution of projects. More specifically, rights holders discussed how practical interventions could be occasions for raising awareness and developing transferable skills that would help them develop agency, which would also be vital after the installation of sanitation infrastructure. In the absence of these skills, rights holders felt entirely dependent on other actors. As one woman argued during a focus group, this dependency made the project and the rights holders extremely vulnerable, because there was no way for rights holders to take action, demand resources, or even seek protection against abuse of power by, for example, the Local Health Office.[14] Thus, rights holders themselves identified a lack of relevant skills, a lack of access to decision-makers, and a lack of meaningful participation—rather than a lack of resources—as the fundamental causes of a lagging ownership. This interpretation is in line with a human rights–based—rather than a needs-based—analysis of their situation, even if the language of human rights was not explicitly used.

Travel, Transformation, and the Emergence of "Light" Human Rights Norms

The Omission of Certain Dimensions of the HRBA

Several factors explain why the engagement of rights users—both project partners and rights holders—with a human rights discourse is relatively low. UNICEF supplements arguments about output indicators, competing paradigms,[15] lack of clear implementation manuals,[16] logistical obstacles,[17] and political challenges[18] with an argument about the rights holders' alleged lack of interest in such an approach. However, since there were never systematic consultations with rights holders on strategic matters, it is hard to sustain UNICEF country officers' claim that rights holders did not express an interest in the HRBA and that this was the reason for scaling it down. Our fieldwork suggests that the decision to opt for a scaled-down version of the HRBA that did not refer to duty bearers, accountability, or rights claims was based on a top-down assessment by the country office, rather than on rights holders' own voice.

Apart from general questions about accountability that this raises, this nonengagement with key dimensions of the HRBA and the nonchalant use of human rights language also meant that rights holders were not exposed to a potentially empowering human rights discourse in the context of this project, but only to a severely restricted interpretation thereof. This is significant, since the dimension and reach of this project means that it could potentially serve as an important channel for raising awareness about human rights and how they can be relevant in the local context—especially when considering the limited number of alternative avenues rights holders have at their disposal to obtain this kind of information.

At the same time, the absence of certain components of the HRBA (such as accountability and the role of duty bearers) in the project makes the fact that rights holders nevertheless refer to these components all the more significant, and suggests that an HRBA should not a priori be considered irrelevant in concrete technical interventions and that some components of the human rights discourse might have more local resonance than UNICEF officers argued. In addition, the SNV intervention also suggested that rights holders are capable of, and interested in, proposing complex situation analyses and long-term solutions relevant to them. When consulted in an open-ended manner, rights holders expressed nuanced views regarding their access to water and regarding the strategies that are needed to achieve this, most notably with regard to access to *responsables*—a dimension currently entirely absent from the discourse of project partners. Thus, while rights holders were not given the resources to rethink this notion of *responsables* along the lines of *legal* duty bearers, when it came to guaranteeing their access to water, they insisted on the importance of identifying actors that had an *ethical* responsibility. This raises the question of what the relation is between these two notions of legal duty bearer and *responsable*, and of how rights holders would understand the notion of a legal duty bearer if they had been systematically presented with a human rights discourse. More specifically, would they, under such conditions, propose a broader understanding of the duty bearer notion, in line with the *responsable* concept?

The Travel of Scaled-Down Human Rights Understandings

Several scholars who see localization as a process along the bidirectional top-down/bottom-up axis emphasize the importance of avenues for sharing information between grassroots rights users and norm setters on the local, national, regional, and international levels. International governmental and nongovernmental organizations can play a crucial role in facilitating this exchange of information and ideas. Especially for organizations adopting an HRBA (which, according to the UN Common Understanding [2003] is concerned with top-down/bottom-up interventions, local ownership, and the empowerment of rights holders), the installation of mechanisms for exchanging information should be a priority. In this case, there has been little attention to informing rights holders about the human rights framework or seeking their input. To the extent that they exist, participation and consultation mechanisms do not facilitate, or even allow for, the sharing of information on strategic concerns or interpretations of rights holders that could lead to a reformulation of the HRBA or the human rights framework more generally.[19] Instead, rights holders' practical concerns are sometimes shared as if they were strategic concerns, which creates the impression that no proposals for structural change are being made by these rights holders. However, these proposals are there, and the implicit redefinition of the duty bearer notion can be read in that sense.

The fact that international partners have put no structures in place to share rights holders' concerns for structural change in a nuanced manner is not per se problematic. As I specified at the beginning of this chapter, vertical relations are not the only ones that can facilitate the travel and transformation of human rights norms. Rights holders, at least in theory, have other opportunities to share their contextualized understandings of human rights through horizontal and complex networks that could potentially counterbalance the *invisibilization* of their strategic interests that takes place in relations with international donors and partners.[20] This is a promising idea in that it emphasizes the agency of every actor in the network. Yet, it also raises questions about what happens when local understandings, which are at least partly based on deficient information about the human rights architecture (reaching rights holders in the context of formal human rights–based development interventions), then start to circulate through these networks. When looking at some elements of the human rights understanding that our respondents developed in the context of this Sanitized Villages project (which claimed to be human rights–based but omitted several crucial elements from its approach and emphasized individual responsibility and market dynamics in their stead), this problem becomes clear: the idea that "right to water" refers to the individual's responsibility (rather than that of the state) or that not the state, but UNICEF is a human rights duty bearer, both pose challenges in terms of accountability within the current human rights architecture.

As set out in the theoretical section of this chapter, actor-centered approaches to human rights are often grounded in a normative concern with increasing these rights' potential to protect the most vulnerable rights holders. However, what this case suggests is that, while human rights norms inevitably travel and transform when rights holders engage them in their specific situation, this transformation is not per se empowering for rights holders if it is not grounded in a sound understanding of the existing human rights architecture and the ways in which this architecture can be used to support local struggles. Development interventions that adopt an HRBA are often characterized by power imbalances (especially regarding access to information, resources, and institutions), which place rights holders at a significant disadvantage and raise questions about how much scope rights holders actually have to develop a genuinely localized interpretation, in this case, of their right to water or, more generally, of a human rights–based approach.

This case study therefore underlines the importance of explicitly analyzing where local human rights norms come from and under what conditions they have been formed. If this transformation happened in conditions of notable power imbalances and incomplete information, we need to ask what the impact is of integrating these local human rights understandings, and whether it might not impoverish and undermine existing protections. Ignoring how power imbalances and lack of adequate information may have shaped local understandings of human rights entails the risk of eulogizing these interpretations, even if they may be rooted in power inequalities and incomplete information. Moreover, these "light" understandings (for example of the legal accountability of formal duty bearers) can easily be coopted by those seeking to legitimize their own agenda by referring to "local voices."

In this particular case, there is a whole range of human rights methods, instruments, and norms that these rights holders do not refer to, not necessarily because they are not relevant in this context, but because rights holders have had no (or very limited) exposure to them. This means that the translations and transformations happening in this context are not necessarily triggered by local norm entrepreneurs who have a sound understanding of international, regional, national, and local dynamics and who seek to integrate these. Rather, the local—and in practice scaled-down—understanding of human rights norms should, in this case, be ascribed mainly to the limited and biased information that was presented in the context of the Sanitized Villages project.

Moreover, the transformation that takes place here is not just a transformation of the *substance* of the right to water, but also and above all, of the *methods* that can be used to ensure this right. Specifically, we see that one of the most important elements of the human rights toolbox, claim making, is not considered at all in this context—at least not vis-à-vis the formal duty bearer that is the state. Even if rights holders called water a human right, they did not refer to the idea that this right could be claimed. The omission of this crucial component of human rights methods from this localized version of the right to water can be partly explained by the local understanding of a state, one that considers the state as the *Dieu sur terre* (God on Earth), and which renders claim making or accountability mechanisms virtually unthinkable (Destrooper and Sundi 2016). Partly, this omission also has to do with the fact that rights holders' first (and in many cases only) exposure to the human rights discourse has taken place in the context of development projects like this one, where donors and partners are often restricted in what they can say and how far they can go in politicizing the issue because they are also technical partners of the government. This is especially true in the case of multilateral or bilateral development programs, which makes it difficult to speak of duty bearers' obligations or the potential for rights holders to make a claim.

The fieldwork suggests that it is important to take into account the circumstances in which human rights transformations take place, and to be explicit about the impact of power imbalances on local actors' human rights understandings. We need to ask whether "local understandings" should per se be considered the most legitimate source for further developing human rights norms at the international level, even if these local understandings are rooted in incomplete information about the current human rights architecture and the protections it can offer.

Conclusion

This volume explores how human rights transform when they travel. In this chapter, I suggested that both travel and transformation are shaped by the power inequalities surrounding them and that we need to take these power dynamics explicitly into account to better understand why certain local understandings emerge and what they mean for the rights holders proposing them. Specifically, I explored what happens when—a light version of— human rights rhetoric first finds its way to local rights holders' struggles in the context of development interventions that are formally human rights–based, but that present rights holders with a watered-down understanding of what human rights are and how they could be relevant in their struggle, in this case the struggle for clean drinking water and adequate sanitation infrastructure. Following Hannerz's (1992, 100) notion of the "unfree flows of meaning," I argue that, in this context, rights holders are likely to develop an understanding of their human rights that is devoid of any reference to claim making, holding formal duty bearers accountable, or politicizing development. This is so because the understanding of rights holders is more likely to have been shaped by the position of international actors (in this case, UNICEF) than vice versa—despite the increasingly networked structure of the human rights architecture. Thus, rights holders' "light" understanding of human rights and accountability should not be interpreted as a sign of their lack of interest in a more structural approach to issues of water and sanitation, but might, rather, be attributable to the lack of sound information about relevant human rights tools, concepts, and methodologies.

Integrating the conceptualizations and priorities of rights holders more explicitly into the development of human rights–based development projects—through vertical, horizontal, or other forms of travel and transformation—is not just a matter of ensuring the implementation of paradigms that are developed on the transnational level. It can also be a means to ensure that these rights holders' concerns set the agenda for future norm development, not just on the translocal level, but also, for example, on the regional or the international level. Yet, in this context, it is difficult to overestimate the importance of a genuine multidirectional dialogue and of awareness-raising campaigns by actors that are not constrained by political calculation as much as some of the actors in this case study. In the absence of grounded awareness-raising campaigns, the upstreaming and sharing of a "light" interpretation of both human rights norms and human rights methods risks impoverishing the existing human rights framework while, at the same time, giving this scaling down an air of legitimacy because it is based on "voices from below."

Acknowledgments

This research has been funded by the Interuniversity Attraction Poles Programme initiated by the Belgian Science Policy Office, more specifically the IAP "The Global Challenge of Human Rights Integration: Towards a Users'

Perspective" (www.hrintegration.be). The chapter was written during a fellowship at the Center for Human Rights and Global Justice at YNU's Law School and the Wissenschaftskolleg zu Berlin. The author wishes to thank Pascal Sundi, Richard Lumbika and the Université Kongo for facilitating the fieldwork, Koen De Feyter and the participants in the Localizing Human Rights workshop for comments on earlier version of this paper, and Carey Harrison for his elaborate language revisions.

Notes

1. For political reasons, both the USAID's support for the program and the program itself were discontinued from the late 1990s until 2006.
2. Government contributes less than 1 percent of the program funding. The rest of the resources come from bilateral and multilateral aid, and are largely coordinated by UNICEF (Ministère de la Santé Publique 2011).
3. For an overview of all project partners, see Destrooper 2015.
4. Although "participation" in the Common Understanding refers to the broadest possible process of including rights holders, there are several ways in which participation can be conceptualized and implemented to facilitate consultation. While both participation and consultation of local rights holders are pinned on the assumption that the input of these rights holders is valuable, neither is empowering in itself, and there is no simple causal or direct relation between both terms.
5. Villages were selected in collaboration with the Human Rights Research Center at the Université Kongo, in order to ensure a diverse set of actors as well as accessibility of the villages.
6. Strategic documents issued by the UNICEF headquarters included UNICEF 1998, 2005, 2008, 2011, 2012b, 2013a, 2013b; WaSH—UNICEF Division for Water, Sanitation and Hygiene 1999, 2005, 2006, 2010. Operational documents issued by the UNICEF DRC country office included the medium-term strategic plan (UNICEF DRC 2012a), the situation analysis (UNICEF DRC 2012b), the agreement between UNICEF and the DRC (UNICEF DRC 2012c), press releases by UNICEF DRC's WaSH division, the PPP manual, programming info, and other relevant project documents. In addition to this, I used an existing analysis of UNICEF's human rights–based approach (UNICEF 2012a) and the Action Research (WaSH DRC 2013).
7. Crystallization is a more complex process than triangulation, whereby the researcher borrows from several disciplines—in this case political science, sociology, legal studies, and anthropology—and uses a variety of methods and perspectives to arrive at a deepened understanding of social reality. The goal is to better understand the empirical reality through the subjectivities of interviewees.
8. When we speak of "local voices" or "voices from below" here, we reject an understanding that places the global above the local or that sees local constituencies as uniform and static units organized around a shared culture. We argue that local realities can be a fertile ground for promoting human rights and development, but that it is the interplay between the transnational process and the practices of local users that in the end holds the potential of making universal human rights norms and development programs relevant for users.

9. Interview with local health officer in Village 6.

10. It should also be noted that local health officers usually are medical professionals, with little experience or expertise in the organization of inclusive consultation processes, and that they are not trained on this in the framework of the Sanitized Villages program.

11. The program documents foresee that the village committee takes the lead in each step of the intervention, which implies that they should be consulted by the Local Health Office and the technical assistants, especially in the early phase of the process.

12. Focus group in Village 3, statement by a member of the Comité Village Assaini.

13. The notion of duty bearers is absent as such. Instead, people referred to the broader category of "*responsables*" (see Destrooper and Sundi 2016).

14. Focus group in Village 4, statement by the treasurer of the Comité Village Assaini.

15. Headquarters have begun to pay more attention to these paradigms in operational and strategic documents. This eliminates any strong incentive for country offices to implement an HRBA on the ground and generates conflicting sets of priorities. Because of this, country offices have not always actively engaged with the HRBA, and instead continue to use this rhetoric while in practice structuring their interventions along the lines of, for example, market-based approaches to sanitation.

16. Guidelines developed by UNICEF headquarters in the early 2000s, for example, were either not concrete or the paradigm shifts they entailed were difficult to implement due to UNICEF's decentralized structure (see Destrooper 2015 for an overview). Because of this lack of operationalization, country offices were not required to report on their achievements with regard to the HRBA.

17. Several contextual factors explain why an HRBA is difficult to implement: one of them is the remoteness of rights holders' communities and poor communication and transportation infrastructure.

18. UNICEF's WaSH Division in the DRC argues that the conceptualization and implementation of the project is the responsibility of the DRC government and that, moreover, it cannot impose a requirement, for example, to adopt the HRBA, since it is not itself involved in the implementation. This logic of nonactorship is based on the idea that it is UNICEF's responsibility to facilitate the DRC government's ownership of the program and that it should therefore not take the lead itself.

19. See, for example, the role of rights holders in the building of wells and the U-Report infrastructure that links actors from the local, provincial, national, and regional levels through an SMS system (Destrooper 2015).

20. *Invisibilization* is used here in analogy with the notion of "silencing," to refer to a process in which a power imbalance allows one (group of) actor(s) to actively make the interests or demands of another (group of) actor(s) invisible.

Works Cited

Barbour, Rosaline. 2007. "Doing Focus Groups." In *The Sage Qualitative Research Kit*, edited by Uwe Flick. Thousand Oaks, CA: Sage.

Baumgaertel, Moritz, Dorothea Staes, and Francisco Javier Mena Parras. 2014. "Hierarchy, Coordination, or Conflict? Global Law Theories and the Question of Human Rights Integration." *European Journal of Human Rights* 3: 326–353.

De Feyter, Koen. 2006. "Localizing Human Rights." Discussion paper 2006/2. Antwerp: Institute of Development Policy and Management.
De Gaay Fortman, Bastiaan. 2011. *Political Economy of Human Rights: The Quest for Relevance and Realization*. New York: Routledge.
Delmas-Marty, Mireille. 2006. *Le Pluralisme Ordonné*. Paris: Seuil.
Destrooper, Tine. 2015. "An Analysis of the Human Rights–Based Approach to Development: UNICEF's Role in the Village Assaini Program in the Bas-Congo." In *The Global Challenge of Human Rights Integration. Towards a Users' Perspective*. Edited by Koen De Feyter and Ellen Desmet. Antwerp: Antwerp University Press.
Destrooper, Tine, and Pascal Sundi. 2016. "A Praxis-Based Understanding of New Duty-Bearers: Examining Contextual Realities in the DRC." Paper presented at Human Rights in Practice Series, Center for Human Rights and Global Justice, New York, April 2015.
Ellingson, Laura L. 2009. *Engaging Crystallization in Qualitative Research*. Thousand Oaks, CA: Sage.
Gready, Paul. 2008. "Rights-Based Approaches to Development: What Is the Value-Added?" *Development in Practice* 18(6): 735–747.
Gysler, Manuel. 2012. "Strengths and Challenges of a Human Rights–Based Approach to Programming in the Water and Sanitation Sector." Paper presented at Nadel-Mas Cycle. Zurich: ETH.
Halliday, Terrence, and Bruce Carruthers. 2007. "The Recursivity of Law: Global Norm Making and National Lawmaking in the Globalization of Corporate Insolvency Regimes." *American Journal of Sociology* 112(4): 1135–1202.
Hannertz, Ulf. 1992. *Cultural Complexity: Studies in the Social Organization of Meaning*. New York: Columbia University Press.
Kvale, Steinar. 2007. "Doing Interviews." In *The Sage Qualitative Research Kit*, edited by Uwe Flick. Thousand Oaks, CA: Sage.
Levitt, Peggy, and Sally Engle Merry. 2009. "Vernacularization on the Ground: Local Uses of Global Women's Rights in Peru, China, India and the United States." *Global Networks* 9(4): 441–461.
Merry, Sally Engle. 2006. "Transnational Human Rights and Local Activism: Mapping the Middle." *American Anthropologist* 108(1): 38–51.
Ministère de la Santé Publique. 2011. *Villages et Écoles Assainis, Source de Vie: Eau, Hygiène et Assainissement pour le Congo Rural*. Last consulted February 9, 2015. http://www.ecole-village-assainis.cd/fr_programme-eva-fonds-et-financement.html.
Mutua, Makao. 2001. "Savages, Victims and Saviours: The Metaphor of Human Rights." *Harvard International Law Journal* 21(1): 201–245.
Nyamu-Musembi, Celestine. 2005. "An Actor-Oriented Approach to Rights in Development." *IDS Bulletin* 36(1): 41–52.
Nyamu-Musembi, Celestine, and Andrea Cornwall. 2004. *What Is the Rights Based Approach All About? Perspectives from International Development Agencies Institute of Development Studies*. Sussex: Institute of Development Studies.
Oré Aguilar, Gaby. 2011. "The Local Relevance of Human Rights: A Methodological Approach." In *The Local Relevance Of Human Rights*, edited by Koen De Feyter, Stephan Parmentier, Christiane Timmerman, and George Ulrich. Cambridge: Cambridge University Press.
Ost, François, and Michel Van de Kerckhove. 2002. *De la Pyramide au Réseau? Pour une Théorie Dialectique du Droit*. Brussels: Publications des Facultés Universitaires St. Louis.

Richardson, Laurel. 2000. "Writing: A Method of Enquiry." In *Handbook of Qualitative Research*, edited by Norman K. Denzin and Yvonna S. Lincoln, 923–949. Thousand Oaks, CA: Sage.

Russell, Anna. 2010. "International Organizations and Human Rights: Realizing, Resisting or Repackaging the Right to Water?" *Journal of Human Rights* 9(1): 1–23.

UN. 2003. "The Human Rights–Based Approach to Development Cooperation: Towards a Common Understanding among UN Agencies." *Interagency Workshop on a Human Rights–Based Approach*, Stamford, USA.

UNICEF. 1998. *Guidelines for Human Rights-Based Programming Approach: A Human Rights Approach to UNICEF Programming for Children and Women: What It Is, and Some Changes It Will Bring*. New York: United Nations Children's Fund.

———. 2005. *The UNICEF Medium-Term Strategic Plan, 2006–2009 Investing in Children: The UNICEF Contribution to Poverty Reduction and the Millennium Summit Agenda*. New York: United Nations Children's Fund.

———. 2008. *UNICEF Handbook on Water Quality*. New York: United Nations Children's Fund.

———. 2011. *Medium-Term Strategic Plan*. New York: United Nations Children Fund.

———. 2012a. *Global Evaluation of the Application of the Human Rights–Based Approach to UNICEF Programming*. New York: United Nations Children's Fund.

———. 2012b. *UNICEF Strategic Plan 2014–2017. Realizing the Rights of Every Child, Especially the Most Disadvantaged*. New York: United Nations Children Fund.

———. 2013a. *Analysis of the Medium-Term Strategic Plan 2006–2013. A Data and Results Companion to the End of Cycle Review*. New York: United Nations Children's Fund.

———. 2013b. *Revised Evaluation Policy of UNICEF*. New York: United Nations Children's Fund.

UNICEF DRC. 2012a. Country Program Document 2013–2017. Kinshasa: UNICEF DRC.

———. 2012b. *Matrice Résumée de Résultats*. Kinshasa: UNICEF DRC.

———. 2012c. *Plan d'Action du Programme de Pays 2013–2017 Entre le Gouvernement de la République Démocratique du Congo et le Fonds des Nations Unies pour l'Enfance*. Kinshasa: UNICEF DRC.

———. n.d. Ecoles Assainies et Villages Assainis. Last consulted February 10, 2015. http://www.unicef.org/drcongo/french/wes_846.html.

Urueña, René. 2012. *No Citizens Here: Global Subjects and Participation in International Law*. Leiden and Boston: Martin Nijhoff.

WaSH—UNICEF Division for Water, Sanitation and Hygiene. 1999. *Towards Better Programming. A Water Handbook*. New York: United Nations Children's Fund.

———. 2005. *Sanitation and Hygiene Promotion: Programming Guidance*. New York: United Nations Children's Fund and World Health Organization.

———. 2006. *UNICEF Water, Sanitation and Hygiene Strategies for 2006–2015*. New York: United Nations Children's Fund.

———. 2010. *Sanitation Marketing in a CATS Context: A Discussion Paper*. New York: United Nations Children's Fund.

WaSH DRC—UNICEF Division for Water, Sanitation and Hygiene in the Democratic Republic of the Congo. 2013. *Rapport Final de l'Enquête ECRIS Réalisée dans le Cadre du Programme Nationale Ecole et Village Assaini en République Démocratique du Congo*. Kinshasa: UNICEF DRC.

CHAPTER 9

Global Rights, Local Risk: Community Advocacy on Right to Health in China

Sara L. M. Davis and Charmain Mohamed

Since the current Chinese leadership took office in 2013, human rights advocacy has become increasingly challenging for domestic advocates. Hundreds of human rights lawyers have been arrested (Jacobs and Buckley 2015; Human Rights Watch 2016). Even previously tolerated forms of activism, such as for women's rights, have become high-risk: for example, as BBC News reported on April 15, 2015, five young women's rights activists, now called the "Feminist Five," were detained on suspicion of "picking quarrels and provoking trouble" (Zeng 2015). Though they were released on bail after an international outcry, the five women remain under close surveillance. In January 2016, the *New York Times* reported that the internationally respected Zhongze Women's Legal Counselling and Service Centre had been closed by authorities, apparently for receiving foreign funding. In 2017, the passage of an Overseas NGO Law has further hindered the financing and operations of both overseas and domestic Chinese NGOs (Shi-Kupfer and Lang 2017).

Working in the context of this sweeping crackdown on civil society and rights activists, Chinese rights activists must be skilled at managing political risks of many kinds (Chinese Human Rights Defenders 2011). They must manage to mobilize collectively in a context where even announcing a public event may result in abrupt police orders to cancel it. The politics of language are ever more difficult to navigate; while China's constitution formally recognizes human rights, and a number of activists call themselves "rights defenders" (*weiquan renshi*), censorship of many rights-related topics is sweeping.

(For instance, in July 2017, the *New York Times* reported that all social media mentions of the death of Nobel Peace laureate and dissident Liu Xiaobo were blocked by Chinese censors [Qin 2017].) Activists must be judicious at prioritizing in a context where widespread abuses result in a steady flood of urgent community demands, where litigation can result in criminal charges against plaintiffs, and where advocacy targets can often retaliate with impunity.

Furthermore, Chinese rights activists must navigate these risks with little hope of support from outside the country, thanks to a growing "human rights deficit" (De Gaay Fortman 2011) in which international human rights mechanisms lack enforcement powers, and in which China's global power continues to grow. As the *Guardian* reported in March 2014, Chinese rights activist Cao Shunli died in detention after petitioning for the right to participate in the UN periodic human rights review process. China increasingly uses tactics of intimidation to silence critics at the UN Human Rights Council (Wee and Nebehay 2015). In response to the increasingly restrictive climate, which has prompted condemnation from the UN High Commissioner on Human Rights (UN Office of the High Commissioner for Human Rights 2016), and for a range of reasons including security concerns for Chinese partners, some international organizations have chosen to tread carefully in expressing public solidarity (Cohen 2016). Since support from outside China is not always accessible, domestic advocates must increasingly manage these risks on their own.

In this context, the vernacularization of international human rights discourse becomes a delicate task. A few well-known rights advocates may still receive international attention, but that is unlikely to penetrate China's vast interior and reach local activists.

A rich social science literature explores how a diverse and resilient Chinese civil society has emerged and grown over the past decades, despite increasing government restrictions (Economy 2004; Human Rights in China 2015; Wu and Chan 2012; Gadsden 2010; Hildebrandt 2011; Mertha 2009; Saich 2000; Shieh and Deng 2011; Spires 2011; Teets 2009; Turner 2004; and Simon 2013). This chapter builds on that literature to discuss observations from training provided over two years by a U.S.-based NGO, Asia Catalyst, to small Chinese community-based groups working on the right to health—some of them with little formal education. The training program, CBO Catalyst, was designed in consultation with Chinese health rights activists. It aimed to support the emergence of effective right-to-health activists who could place themselves within a global movement; to embed human rights governance principles in their practice; and to improve the effectiveness of their advocacy skills. These skills were used by program participants to position themselves in nuanced ways in relation to government actors.

Right to Health Advocacy

Human rights are rooted in international law, and law can be used by marginalized people(s) to advocate against political domination (Eckert 2006). Human rights law is also a political advocacy tool used to influence agencies and actors outside the court system (De Gaay Fortman 2011; Goodale 2007, 2013; Oré Aguilar, 2011). Advocacy on the right to the highest attainable standard of health also has some specific characteristics.

Health is a scientific and technical area, and advocates must establish expertise and fluency in medical and technical languages. Many HIV activists are "knowledge-breakers" who leverage their scientific knowledge to "crack open the doors of the citadels of science, market, and governance" (Chan 2015, 7). For example, the AIDS Coalition to Unleash Power (ACT-UP), an international direct advocacy group formed in 1987, used a right-to-health analysis, scientific expertise, and public protest to press the U.S. Federal Drug Administration to speed approval of HIV treatments (Crimp 2011). Some members of ACT-UP subsequently formed the Treatment Action Campaign, which developed even more advanced scientific expertise to advocate for treatment access. This established a role for people living with HIV as experts speaking on behalf of their communities; AIDS activism contributed to new forms of citizenship in some countries (Robins 2006). Subsequently, the Joint UN Programme on HIV/AIDS (UNAIDS) also articulated the principle of the Greater Inclusion of People with AIDS (GIPA) as promoting "the rights and responsibilities of people living with HIV, including their right to participation in decision-making processes that affect their lives" (UNAIDS 2007).

Thus, people living with HIV and what the World Health Organization names the HIV "key populations" (men who have sex with men, sex workers, transgender people, and people who inject drugs) have formed formal national, regional, and global networks to share information and advocate collectively. These include the Global Network of People Living with HIV (GNP+), the Global Network of Sex Work Projects (NSWP), and the International Network of People Who Use Drugs (INPUD), and their respective regional and national member networks; as well as numerous regional, national, and international networks of men who have sex with men (MSM) and transgender people. Health governance mechanisms such as UNAIDS and the Global Fund to Fight AIDS, Tuberculosis and Malaria encourage this mobilization, as they rely on processes of consultation with these networks in many ways (Davis 2015).

Right-to-health advocacy, the rubric under which we group diverse individual and collective advocates around the rights of people living with and vulnerable to both communicable and noncommunicable diseases, have emerged in part out of this global movement for treatment access by people living with, and vulnerable to, HIV (Mann et al. 1999). While they have sometimes used litigation, many have focused their efforts on lobbying global, national, and local health agencies and health financing mechanisms, using human rights standards among other advocacy tools. As in other human rights spheres, right-to-health advocacy also relies on the work of vernacularizing "messengers," especially international AIDS activists, who actively translate global human rights laws and concepts into locally acceptable language (Merry and Stern 2005; Merry 2006; Levitt and Merry 2009).

The social, cultural, and linguistic skills used in both domestic and transnational networking become critical for advocates who seek to inspire others to engage in advocacy, especially in high-risk settings (Chua 2015; Goodale 2013; McAdam 1986). Thus, many community-based advocacy networks ground their work in national identity and culture, while also seeking the support and approval of larger, more powerful international health and human rights NGOs that can provide access to funding and to global agencies (Cheng 2011; Bob 2005, 2009). Through these advocacy relationships, the experience of local advocates sometimes feeds into and shapes the agendas of international NGOs and may ultimately reshape global human rights norms (Youde 2009; De Feyter et al. 2011). In one recent example, advocacy by the Global Network of Sex Work Projects helped to persuade Amnesty International to take a position in favor of decriminalization of sex work, despite public advocacy by powerful international critics of that position (NSWP 2016).

Because of the legitimacy conveyed on these networks by UNAIDS and international health financing mechanisms, HIV-related network-building has been a critical site for mobilization in China. There has been greater space for right-to-health advocacy than exists on some more "sensitive" issues.

In the three decades since the first person was diagnosed with HIV in China, while the country's economy and society have transformed, a generation of Chinese AIDS activists have emerged to challenge the state on its top-down management of the epidemic. At an elastic period—first of expanding, then of sharply contracting public space for advocacy—an informal, largely unregistered Chinese civil society has sprouted. Right-to-health advocacy in China now includes diverse groups working on such issues as HIV, hepatitis B and hepatitis C, food safety, chronic diseases, and more. While these groups are not formally collected under a broader right-to-health movement conceived as such, they sometimes find ways to informally share or borrow experiences and tactics.

However, as discussed in this chapter, their advocacy remains constrained. Two well-known AIDS activists, Dr. Gao Yaojie and Wan Yanhai, were among those who first blew the whistle on Chinese state-run for-profit blood collection and the transmission of HIV to thousands of Chinese villagers in the 1990s. Both now live outside of China. During the civil society crackdown following the appointment of President Xi Jinping, some right-to-health advocates came in for public attacks. While Chinese authorities have been more tolerant of right-to-health advocates than of those who advocate on many other human rights issues, the limits of this advocacy are actively policed, and Chinese community-based organizations must learn to navigate them in order to survive.

Capacity Building for Right to Health Groups

About Asia Catalyst

Asia Catalyst was founded in New York in 2007. It has staff in New York, where it is registered as a U.S. nonprofit organization, as well as in Beijing and Bangkok. With an annual budget of under $800,000, the organization focuses on promoting the right to health through partnerships with community-based organizations (CBOs) and peer-based networks of people living with HIV and key populations in China and Southeast Asia. Though the co-authors' work on this chapter was pro bono and not supported by funding, the project discussed in this chapter was funded by the U.S. State Department Bureau of Democracy, Rights and Labor and the Ford Foundation. Asia Catalyst receives funding from two other donors considered "politically sensitive" in China, the National Endowment for Democracy and Open Society Foundations, as well as from many donors who are not considered sensitive, such as the Levi Strauss Foundation and Swedish International Development Assistance.

The co-authors of this chapter have at different times been executive directors of Asia Catalyst.[1] This paper draws on written reports on the program by external evaluators, and on our own observations in managing the program (Asia Catalyst 2011, Asia Catalyst 2013; Asia Catalyst, Korekata AIDS Law Center, and Thai AIDS Treatment Action Group 2013).

As long-time human rights practitioners (who are, however, not living with HIV themselves), Asia Catalyst staff, including the authors, have wrestled with the practical, political, and ethical challenges of this work. We consulted with current and past program managers to solicit their recollections of the program, including relevant critiques, which are incorporated below. We seek to use Asia Catalyst's experience with the CBO Catalyst program to contribute to the literature on the circulation and transformation of human rights.

This chapter focuses on three areas: first, how the program fostered an environment for diverse participants to build a network; second, how the program's training in strategic planning sparked deeply localized right-to-health advocacy; and third, how program participants drew on these two skills to build relationships with officials.

Consultation and Development of the CBO Catalyst Program

From its inception in 2007 as an all-volunteer project, Asia Catalyst provided a variety of types of support to Chinese health and human rights NGOs. This included fundraising for and technical support to a legal aid center for people living with HIV in Beijing; training a sex worker–led NGO in human rights documentation and advocacy; coaching drug user–led NGOs in strategic planning and advocacy; and co-researching reports on HIV and human rights with Chinese NGOs. In 2008, when several Chinese AIDS activists were threatened by police and national security agents in advance of the Beijing Olympics, Asia Catalyst responded to requests to organize emergency fellowships that placed Chinese AIDS activists at larger international AIDS NGOs and U.S. law firms until after the Olympics. Asia Catalyst also organized a film festival in New York, Comrades, to screen lesbian, gay, bisexual, and transgender (LGBT) films that had been prohibited in China.

At this early stage, Asia Catalyst programs and partners in China were identified through informal social networks and consultation. More public or broad-based consultations with Chinese partners on health and human rights were both logistically beyond a small NGO's capacity and politically risky.

During this same period in the mid-2000s, the fast-growing but relatively new world of Chinese AIDS activism was riven by factional struggles between charismatic leaders and their supporters. Allegations of corruption and abuse were widespread. A public rift arose between, on the one hand, "service delivery" AIDS NGOs that accessed funding from the Chinese government and its close funding partners, and, on the other hand, underfunded NGOs that engaged in more openly critical advocacy.

In 2009–2010, after the disruption in activism caused by the Beijing Olympics, Asia Catalyst consulted informally with a number of Chinese health rights activists about how to learn from the organization's early experience. Activists raised a number of concerns, and some even said that they feared that China's nascent right-to-health movement was at risk. A few Chinese activists urged Asia Catalyst to build a network: a cohort of health rights groups that could work in coalition together. This was an intriguing recommendation, though Asia Catalyst staff and board expressed doubt as to whether this was an appropriate role for an international NGO. Other Chinese AIDS activists urged more systematic development of tools to train CBOs in capacity-building. However, they warned Asia Catalyst that current capacity-building programs offered to NGOs in China by other larger international NGOs and funders were too "foreign" in orientation and style and had not been adapted to reflect Chinese culture, to suit the limited educational background of many CBO staff, or to address the practical challenges of the restrictive operating environment. Finally, Asia Catalyst was urged by some Chinese activists to develop a program that would encourage and promote empathy among activists, and to address what they described as ethical weaknesses and abuses in the civil society sector; these were seen as deriving in part from the restrictive operating environment, and in part from a broader context in which corruption was widespread.

The primary question that plagues human rights practitioners is usually: *What works?* The short history of human rights is littered with failed advocacy campaigns. What exactly is the "capacity" that so many human rights programs seek to "build" in civil society? For the activists consulted in Asia Catalyst's planning process during 2009–2010, the answer appeared to be that they sought training that could combine planning and advocacy skills with the social skills needed to build domestic advocacy coalitions. The CBO Catalyst program, which Asia Catalyst developed in 2010 in response to this input, aimed to deliver these specific types of "capacity."

The CBO Catalyst program promoted stronger network-building among CBOs, emphasizing the values of "participation, empathy, grounded-ness, and diversity." It also brought together a small cohort of CBO staff for a nearly year-long series of weekend trainings that used peer-based learning strategies. Asia Catalyst worked with local staff in developing the CBO Catalyst training materials to translate them into Chinese, to make them as simple as possible, and also to make them accessible to persons with disabilities. The training materials explicitly linked democratic NGO governance principles to human rights standards. In addition, the materials emphasized strategic planning skills, using a logic model as a tool for developing short-term plans linked to a long-term vision of fulfillment of the right to health in China.

From 2011 to 2013, Asia Catalyst piloted the CBO Catalyst program, holding eight workshops for two cohorts of ten participants each. In July 2014 an Action Assembly brought all the graduates of the program together to form advocacy coalitions (Lin 2014). The following sections discuss how the program worked in practice to build their network and to strengthen their ability to plan advocacy, while grounding both in the pragmatic and local application of human rights concepts and principles.

Vernacularization through an "Imagined Community"

A number of elements of the Asia Catalyst program promoted a sense of shared values among diverse participants from across the vast geography of China, grounding their local problems in a larger "imagined community" of global right-to-health activists with a shared history and language (Anderson 1991).

First, the selection process aimed to manifest the principles of transparency and openness in the program's implementation. Calls for applications were circulated through email networks and websites, and posted on Asia Catalyst's own website in English and Chinese. The several dozen applications each year came from organizations in 14 provinces, autonomous regions, and municipalities (including Tibet). They reflected CBOs working on a range of issues, including HIV/AIDS, lesbian gay bisexual and transgender (LGBT) rights, rights of persons with disabilities, rights of people with hepatitis B and C, food safety, and right to health of ethnic minority groups. Many applicants were referred by organizations that had previously had some contact with Asia Catalyst, so applicants were likely self-selecting in their comfort level with human rights discourses; but most had no previous experience of formal training in international rights standards.

Applicants completed "intake" questionnaires in Chinese, which asked about their current management and advocacy practices. Asia Catalyst staff reviewed the applications and requested references from a shortlist. Semifinalists were invited for telephone interviews, both to assess the organization's capacity to absorb and benefit from the training and to weed out groups that in practice lacked staff or volunteers.

The diversity of the participants that resulted became an important element of the CBO Catalyst program, as it contributed to the development of the idea of a "movement" linking diverse actors across immense geographic distances, and to the development of empathy and understanding. Most participants had not met before the program began. There were significant differences in socioeconomic class and education levels, ranging from a Beijing man who had studied film at the Sorbonne, to a former schoolteacher who had been fired when she contracted HIV and went on to form a support group for people living with HIV, to a former sex worker. This hodge-podge of identities and marginalized constituencies gradually forged an "imagined community" of Chinese right-to-health activists who began to find commonalities in their different experiences.

The workshop community was explicitly framed as extending beyond China's borders by Asia Catalyst's trainers, who spoke about the experience of international AIDS activists, positioning this program as part of a global history. This narrative began with advocacy led in the United States by the AIDS Coalition to Unleash Power (ACT-UP) in the 1980s, continued through the emergence of an African treatment access movement in the late 1990s, and continued with the growth and global spread of the harm reduction movement in Asia in the 2000s. The trainers also discussed how human rights principles of transparency and accountability begin with activists' own behavior at home: for instance, how Gandhi had begun a national movement for Indian independence by organizing villagers to sweep their own village paths (Constitutional Rights Foundation n.d.). For the participants, seeing trainers from the United States, Europe, and China working together also created a visual representation of transnational activism. This "imagined community" was reinforced by the locations of trainings, which were organized in different locations around the country in order to make travel times equitable for all. Workshops sometimes incorporated visits to participants' home offices, reinforcing the message of solidarity.

While the program began with a brief overview of human rights standards and the global history of health rights activism, subsequent sessions focused less on international human rights mechanisms than on the practicalities of mobilizing staff, volunteers, and donors around shared plans of action, including organizational plans and advocacy plans. Participants were also drilled in the skills of meeting facilitation and conflict resolution, as well as in practical communication skills, such as quick five-minute "elevator pitches" to officials and donors. They were encouraged to adapt content to their local context and to become "norm entrepreneurs" (Sunstein 1996). In between each training session, participants were assigned tasks to implement what they had studied in their home organizations and required to schedule calls with peers to debrief on the experiences. This not only served as an evaluation exercise to check whether or not the participants had mastered workshop content, but also helped the program participants to form closer bonds. Finally, they were repeatedly encouraged to reflect collectively on what worked, what did not, and why.

Over time, the quality of these discussions changed: while many participants initially began by showcasing only their successes, they were pressed to be more specific and to speak frankly about the pragmatic challenges in, for instance, strategic planning, territorial rivalries between CBOs, or coping with unreceptive local officials. The explicit encouragement to work collaboratively during the course of the training program also helped to build experience in teamwork.

Mark Goodale describes human rights training in Bolivia as teaching a new form of "human rights subjectivity" that is both personal and "translocal" (Goodale, 2007). Similarly, Lynette Chua has noted that LGBT activists in Myanmar bonded "by creating a new collective identity linked to human rights discourse; the social interactions intrinsically involved in vernacularization also strengthen old bonds and forge new ties, forming social networks that enable activists to get around the restrictions on collective organizing in Myanmar" (Chua 2015, 327).

One of the concerns that had been raised by Chinese activists consulted by Asia Catalyst in 2009–2010 had to do with the fragility of national networks of right-to-health activists, who were competing for funding and for political space in a highly restrictive environment. The CBO Catalyst program aimed to build a collective identity among participants, while also encouraging them to vernacularize the content of the program by testing and refining it in micro-local contexts.

At the end of the year, participants were invited to apply to continue for a second year as assistant trainers. Three assistant trainers did continue into the second year, contributing to further revisions of Asia Catalyst's training materials based on their experience. After passing an exam, the assistant trainers were formally certified as trainers of the CBO Catalyst curriculum. They went on to deliver the training to others, thus removing the international "messenger" and completing the vernacularization process.

Localizing Advocacy Skills Through Strategic Planning

A second component of the program trained participants in strategic planning. It engaged in vernacularization of human rights discourses by examining examples of successful right-to-health advocacy and developing strategic thinking through use of logic models.

Here, Asia Catalyst trainers drew on a curriculum developed jointly by Asia Catalyst, the Thai AIDS Treatment Action Group (TTAG), and a Chinese group, the Dongjen Center for Human Rights Education (Dongjen). The curriculum, *Know It, Prove It, Change It: A Rights Curriculum for Grassroots Groups*, was made up of three volumes: *Know It: The Rights Framework*, which explains human rights standards applicable to health; *Prove It: Documenting Rights Abuses*, which explains how to conduct human rights documentation related to the right to health; and *Change It: Ending Rights Abuses*, which explains how to plan and implement human rights advocacy campaigns (Asia Catalyst, Korekata AIDS Law Center, Thai AIDS Treatment Action Group 2013). All three volumes were developed through field workshops with Thai and Chinese right-to-health activists and included both narrative sections and training exercises. All three were also published in Chinese, English, and Thai.

The CBO Catalyst program drew on the third volume, *Change It*, to train participants in the basics of problem analysis, campaign planning, community consultation, lobbying, and other relevant skills. The program used examples of successful right-to-health advocacy from China and elsewhere in Asia, such as successful global advocacy for harm reduction services by the Thai Drug Users' Network, and a media campaign to highlight HIV-related discrimination by a Chinese rights NGO, Justice for All. Program participants frequently demanded more China-specific content and case studies. As one former program manager commented, "Sentiments of Chinese exceptionalism tend to be strong generally—which the program anticipated and made part of the curriculum" (Dang 2017).

In addition, participants were drilled extensively in the use of logic models for strategic planning: a one-page template with boxes and arrows that sequentially link resources, immediate programs, short-term outputs, medium-term outcomes, and a long-term vision of the right to health. This approach aimed to ground aspirational visions of human rights fulfillment with measurable milestones and achievable results. While the abstract form of the logic model was initially obscure for participants with less formal education, this was addressed through framing the sequential stages of the logic model in terms of linear increments of time (the long-term vision was 20 years away, the medium-term outcomes 10 years away, the outputs should be achievable in one or two years, and the immediate programs should be completed within the current year).

Participants were again encouraged to use human rights principles of transparency and accountability: to do planning collaboratively at their home offices and in consultation with the communities they served, including all staff and volunteers, down to the office administrative staff or janitors. Again, this approach aimed to break down hierarchies and to ingrain the human rights principle of equality in the practices of CBOs. One Asia Catalyst program manager commented that while the human rights concepts, such as right to health, were not especially novel to participants, "the concept of meaningful participation, involvement of community and staff into decision-making, is a bit different from Chinese culture [where] the leader or the person with authority makes the decision. Most participants accept[ed] the ideas, but it [was] difficult for some" (Shen 2017). Similarly, she noted, human rights concepts differ from more traditional concepts of "doing good for others" as promoted in Buddhism. Nonetheless, another program manager argued,

> Democratic systems and participation seem to still be a difficult sell to some groups. . . . I think right to health is generally accepted. Communities understand . . . that some rights are unlikely to be implemented without communities taking it up, making their voices heard. Especially where those communities already face considerable discrimination, including criminalization. (Durant 2017)

At the end of the CBO Catalyst program, participants worked either individually or in pairs to develop and present draft advocacy plans to the cohort and a visiting human rights expert. Using a voting model, participants themselves decided which three or four of their programs would receive micro-grants, with organizations working in partnership receiving slightly larger grants.

The training in strategic planning was identified by a number of workshop participants as the most valuable takeaway from the program. In the words of one participant, "The new work approach is like 'computer software': having the right 'software' has allowed us to work more effectively" (Lin 2014). Others emphasized feeling empowered and mobilized around a clear direction, less "chaotic," and less susceptible to external pressures: "This strategic plan gave me and our staff a clear idea of what we wanted to do, and helped give us a sense of independence—distinct from donors" (Lin 2014, 11).

While the advocates may have felt more independent and less susceptible to external pressure, though, the advocacy projects voted by CBO Catalyst participants as most likely to succeed tended to be those that operated within the confines of advocacy considered allowable and safe. These "most likely to succeed" projects used existing mechanisms to press for incremental changes that could deliver pragmatic results for community members. The result of this highly localized and specific approach to human rights advocacy was that most of the CBO Catalyst projects were micro-local in focus, and none explicitly challenged existing power structures. There was never any suggestion, for instance, that advocates might demand the right to choose their political representatives through a democratic vote, or to form an alternate political party.

Scaling Up and Managing Risk

Intriguingly, though, in a few cases, the micro-local right-to-health advocacy projects quickly scaled up to address provincial-level or even national concerns. There was, for example, a joint effort between two participants, which led to a successful campaign to reduce the cost of hepatitis B medication in 11 pharmacy chains in Chengdu City, Sichuan Province. This campaign targeted national-level policymakers to urge them to issue official directives that would set maximum price limits for hepatitis B medicines. The advocates successfully persuaded a local government department to drive and monitor this change. Based on the success of the project, the partners were planning to address other medical pricing issues at the time of writing.

Another example of scale-up came from a representative of the Henan Province Women's Network Against AIDS, who worked with a national Women's Network Against AIDS/China and the International Labor Organization China Office on a project that tackled discrimination against people living with HIV in healthcare settings through educating doctors and nurses in two hospitals in Henan and Anhui Provinces. The initiative was later complemented by a national workshop on the problem of discrimination by healthcare workers.

Perhaps the most prominent advocacy project to come out of an Asia Catalyst human rights cohort training, this one bringing together activists from around China and Southeast Asia, was a landmark lawsuit by a gay man who successfully sued a Chinese clinic for giving him electric shocks to change his sexual orientation. A Beijing court required the clinic to repay $560 for costs incurred by the plaintiff and ordered a national search engine, Baidu, to remove the defendant's ads for "gay conversion therapy." Speaking to the *New York Times*, the plaintiff, Yang Teng, said "It shows [gay people] that we don't need to be cured, and when things like this happen and we look to protect our rights from being violated, we can get a fair result" (Levin 2014).

In these and other cases where advocacy scaled up, advocates had to carefully manage political pressures. The tensions and challenges in managing Chinese political pressures played out repeatedly in the CBO Catalyst project.

Asia Catalyst's organizational emails were frequently intercepted by security agents, as evidenced by internal information that circulated externally, and by repeated, blatant attempts to hack office computers through virus-infected emails. Some workshop participants were visited at their offices, and even at their homes, by police with questions about Asia Catalyst and the CBO Catalyst program. On one occasion, the police advised CBO Catalyst participants to cancel a scheduled workshop. Asia Catalyst staff and workshop participants struggled to persuade police and other critics that its capacity-building work, even if supported in part by U.S. government funding, was itself operating independently.

This linked to one explicit critique of Asia Catalyst's work with Chinese activists, as a program manager summarizes, "That Asia Catalyst endangers younger, more inexperienced activists by our mere interaction with them ... but also by giv[ing] advocacy subgrants to do ... advocacy work that we might not be willing to do ourselves" (Durant 2017).

It is perhaps ironic, then, that while the trainers' relationship with the Chinese state steadily deteriorated under this pressure, the trainees' relationships with the state conversely improved. One outcome of the rights training program was often a closer relationship between participants and local government agencies with which they advocated.

For example, one participant was able to successfully mediate a longstanding communications breakdown between his network of CBOs led by men who have sex with men with provincial health officials, thus opening up a new stream of government funding for community-based HIV testing, and in the process ensuring access to testing services for thousands of men. Another participant was able to provide a provincial Center for Disease Control (CDC) with training on voluntary counseling and treatment for HIV (VCT), establishing a channel for communication about other issues arising in the community. Other cohort members partnered with their CDCs to develop joint research and service delivery projects, or formed collaborative relationships with university research projects or national associations, such as a relationship between an LGBT group and the National Association of Psychologists. Still others liaised successfully with policymakers in the National People's Congress and China People's Political Consultative Congress. As Dang, a former Asia Catalyst program manager, commented,

> I would like to think that this is where the program curriculum ... really made a difference for groups to become more strategic: tailoring your message, who do you have in your network that you can approach to carry your message, what opportunities do you have to address and share your message, etc. (Dang 2017)

Likewise, another program participant said,

> We were able to change our approach to communicating with government and change their perception of us. We also placed greater emphasis on collaboration and discovered the benefits of working with local and international organizations, including a better understanding of treatment. In fact, *this collaboration allowed us to sometimes be better informed than local doctors, which meant that they began to see us in a new light.* Eventually, the County Hospital's Director of HIV Treatment and Prevention came to serve as a consultant for our organization. (Lin 2014, 11, emphasis added)

As mentioned above, this shift in subjectivity has a history in the world of HIV and human rights advocacy (Robins 2008). Because of the scientific and technical knowledge required for long-term high-level health rights advocacy, and the relationships of access developed with public health agencies, many long-term health rights activists become deeply embedded in the systems of power they seek to influence.

Activists shift from operating outside the halls of power and begin to position themselves as experts, gaining in confidence and influence (Chan 2015). In her study of global HIV advocacy, Chan describes a "small corps of international civil society elites" who, as longtime advocates who fought for and gained access to UNAIDS, the Global Fund to Fight AIDS, Tuberculosis and Malaria, and other health governance mechanisms, now "cling to power" (Chan 2015, 220–22). But there is a fine line between effective, sustained advocacy and cooptation.

This line may be even harder to navigate in China than in some countries, due to the highly restrictive NGO registration system, which leaves many CBOs operating in a legal gray zone: "Irrespective of registration status, the result is the same: organizations are controlled, making a more independent future unlikely. While the central government's attempt to manage social organizations has not been effective, its overall goals of constraining these groups by closely tying them to the state has been largely achieved" (Hildebrandt 2011, 989).

As mentioned in the introduction, China's new regulations for registration of foreign NGOs have only reinforced these constraints. Eva Pils has noted the challenges for Chinese lawyers of navigating the divide between *tizhinei* (insider) and *tizhiwai* (outsider) positions, and the sanctions attached to the latter (Pils 2014). The same insider/outsider tensions have frequently played out in the right-to-health movement, as noted above in reference to groups accessing health financing. While "insider" positioning may sometimes be available to advocates working on economic and social rights, an issue on which the Chinese government has built its political legitimacy, insider positioning is not always an option available to Chinese advocates working on more taboo civil and political issues, such as ethnic or religious discrimination, corruption by local government officials, police abuse and torture, forced evictions, or arbitrary detention in "black jails."

As Kenneth Lieberthal notes, for the "insiders," China's decentralized "fragmented authoritarianism" model can sometimes leave room for maneuvering and expansion of space by political actors: "Authority below the very peak of the Chinese political system is fragmented and disjointed. The fragmentation is structurally based and has been enhanced by reform policies regarding procedures. The fragmentation, moreover, grew increasingly pronounced under the reforms beginning in the late 1970s" (Lieberthal 1992, 8).

A number of scholars have applied Lieberthal's argument to Chinese civil society, showing how a range of advocates have used fragmented authoritarianism to carve out the needed advocacy space (Mertha 2009; Spires 2011; Wilson 2012; Wu and Chan 2012). As a traditional Chinese saying puts it, *tiangao diyuan*, "Heaven is high and the emperor is far away." In other words, if the emperor can't see what you are doing locally, you can get away with a great deal. The local is certainly the obvious place to begin work for a small community-based organization. In China, it is also a less threatening and less scrutinized space for advocacy than the national or international spheres. In part by grounding their advocacy in deeply local and pragmatic aims, and by carefully avoiding international human rights mechanisms that could trigger brutal state responses (like those suffered by Cao Shunli and the many disappeared human rights lawyers), Chinese right-to-health advocates ensure their continued survival. As a Chinese disability rights advocate observed to Andreas Fulda,

> We must not be pressurized by the government, yet at the same time we must let them know what we are doing so as to avoid suspicion and interference.... [I]t is essential to avoid condemning the government out of hand, otherwise it is impossible to make constructive suggestions. Our aim is not to stand in opposition, but to encourage the government and society to make changes that will really benefit disabled people. (Hallett 2015, 195)

This kind of sophisticated management of government relationships in order to carve out space for advocacy was similarly described by a number of CBO Catalyst participants.

Conclusion

Global right-to-health advocacy, especially for the rights of people living with and affected by HIV, has created space for domestic network-building even in contexts where national-level mobilization is restricted, such as China. Chinese right-to-health groups seek partnership and exchanges with international NGOs, but for the most part their advocacy is deeply localized, focused on engagement with domestic policies and mechanisms.

Participants in the Asia Catalyst capacity-building program formed bonds that linked them to an imagined community of national and international health rights activists. Through training in strategic planning, they developed approaches to advocacy that grounded long-term visions of fulfillment of right to health in measurable, short-term actions and objectives. In some cases, they were able to scale up successful advocacy, especially through building links with more established and officially sanctioned institutions and individuals. The Asia Catalyst discourse linking local advocacy to global movements may have created some encouragement and space for mobilization. But to survive long-term, advocates had to focus on advocating within the local bounds of the permissible, and on relationship-building both within their networks and with government officials.

The example of China raises questions about vernacularization of human rights discourse in highly restrictive societies, where radical challenges risk radical retaliation, and independence may read as rebellion. This example confounds any easy assumptions about what results from the integration of global human rights discourse, funded by bilateral aid, into local advocacy. Chinese activists working on the right to health through this capacity-building program showed pragmatism, sophistication, and reasonable caution in selecting their advocacy targets and tactics, and seized the opportunity to deliver real and measurable gains for their communities: affordable medical care, enhanced sensitivity by healthcare workers, improved funding for community-based health services. At the same time, within the tightly constrained sphere of action that exists in such a high-risk environment, rights-based advocacy cannot always be seen as a fundamental challenge to existing power relations.

Acknowledgments

The authors are grateful for input from participants in the Law and Localization workshop at New York University, and from Joey Lee (commentator) and participants in the Modern China Seminar at Columbia University. Any errors or omissions are the authors' own responsibility.

Note

1. Sara L. M. (aka Meg) Davis founded Asia Catalyst and was its first executive director, from 2007 to 2012. She currently serves on the board of directors. Asia Catalyst was led by an

interim executive director, Andrea Worden, during 2013. Charmain Mohamed took over in late 2013 and served as executive director until early 2016, when she handed over leadership to Karyn Kaplan, the current executive director.

Works Cited

Anderson, Benedict R. O. G. 1991. *Imagined Communities: Reflections on the Origin and Spread of Nationalism*. 1991. London: Verso.
Asia Catalyst. 2011. *Nonprofit Survival Guide*. New York. Accessed May 20, 2016. http://asiacatalyst.org/wp-content/uploads/2015/07/NPSG_EN.pdf.
———. 2013. *Report to State Department Bureau of Democracy, Rights and Labor*. On file at Asia Catalyst.
Asia Catalyst, Korekata AIDS Law Center, and Thai AIDS Treatment Action Group. 2013. *Know It, Prove It, Change It: A Rights Curriculum for Grassroots Groups*. New York, Bangkok, and Beijing. Accessed May 20, 2016. http://asiacatalyst.org/resources/cbo-resources/.
Bob, Clifford. 2005. *The Marketing of Rebellion: Insurgents, Media, and International Activism*. New York: Cambridge University Press.
———. 2009. Introduction to *The International Struggle for New Human Rights*, edited by Clifford Bob, 1–13. Philadelphia: University of Pennsylvania Press.
Chan, Jennifer. 2015. *Politics in the Corridor of Dying: AIDS Activism and Global Health Governance*. Baltimore: Johns Hopkins University Press.
Cheng, Sealing. 2011. "The Paradox of Vernacularization: Women's Human Rights and the Gendering of Nationhood." *Anthropological Quarterly* 84/2: 475–505.
Chinese Human Rights Defenders. 2011. "Chinese Government Must End Persecution of Family Members of Activists." Posted February 12. Accessed May 20, 2016. https://chrdnet.com/2011/02/chinese-government-must-end-persecution-of-family-members-of-activists/.
Chua, Lynette J. 2015. "The Vernacular Mobilization of Human Rights in Myanmar's Sexual Orientation and Gender Identity Movement." *Law & Society Review* 49/2: 299–332.
Cohen, Jerome A. 2016. "A Legal Offense Against Chinese Oppression." *Wall Street Journal*, February 16. Accessed May 20, 2016. http://www.wsj.com/articles/a-legal-defense-against-chinese-oppression-1455645739.
Constitutional Rights Foundation. N.d. "Gandhi and Civil Disobedience." Accessed November 3, 2015. http://www.crf-usa.org/black-history-month/gandhi-and-civil-disobedience.
Crimp, Douglas. 2011. "Before Occupy: How AIDS Activists Seized Control of the FDA in 1988." *The Atlantic*, December 6. Accessed May 20, 2016. http://www.theatlantic.com/health/archive/2011/12/before-occupy-how-aids-activists-seized-control-of-the-fda-in-1988/249302/.
Dang, Gisa. 2017. Email correspondence with former Asia Catalyst program manager, July 17, 2017.
Davis, Sara L. M. 2015. "Measuring the Impact of Human Rights on Health in Global Health Financing." *Health and Human Rights* 17/2: 97–110.
De Feyter, Koen, Stephan Parmentier, Christiane Timmerman, and George Ulrich, eds. 2011. *The Local Relevance of Human Rights*. Cambridge: Cambridge University Press.

De Gaay Fortman, Bas. 2011. *Political Economy of Human Rights: The Quest for Relevance and Realization.* New York: Routledge.

Durant, Gareth. 2017. Email correspondence with the current Asia Catalyst program manager, July 17, 2017.

Eckert, Julia. 2006. "From Subjects to Citizens: Legalism from Below and the Homogenisation of the Legal Sphere." *Journal of Legal Pluralism* 53–54: 45–75.

Economy, Elizabeth. 2004. *The River Runs Black: The Environmental Challenge to China's Future.* Ithaca, NY: Cornell University Press.

Gadsden, Amy E. 2010. "Chinese Nongovernmental Organizations: Politics by Other Means?" American Enterprise Institute Tocqueville on China series, July. Accessed May 27, 2016. http://www.aei.org/publication/chinese-nongovernmental-organizations/.

Goodale, Mark. 2007. Introduction to *Practice of Human Rights: Tracking Law Between the Global and the Local,* edited by Mark Goodale and Sally Engle Merry. Cambridge: Cambridge University Press.

Goodale, Mark, ed. 2013. *Human Rights at the Crossroads.* Oxford: Oxford University Press.

Hallett, Stephen. 2015. "'Enabling the Disabled': The Growing Role of Civil Society in Disability Rights Advocacy." *Civil Society Contributions to Policy Innovation in the People's Republic of China: Environment, Social Development and International Cooperation,* edited by Andreas Fulda, 173–195. New York: Palgrave Macmillan.

Hildebrandt, Timothy. 2011. "The Political Economy of Social Organization Registration in China." *China Quarterly* 208: 970–989.

Human Rights in China. 2015. "Hong Kong's People Heard Their Own Voice: Interview with Han Dongfang." Blog. Accessed May 20, 2016. http://www.hrichina.org/en/china-rights-forum/hong-kongs-people-heard-their-own-voice-interview-han-dongfang-text-and-video.

Human Rights Watch. 2016. "China: New Law Escalates Repression of Groups." April 28. Accessed May 20, 2016. https://www.hrw.org/news/2016/04/28/china-new-law-escalates-repression-groups.

Jacobs, Andrew, and Chris Buckley. 2015. "China Targeting Rights Lawyers in a Crackdown." *New York Times,* July 22. Accessed May 20, 2016. http://www.nytimes.com/2015/07/23/world/asia/china-crackdown-human-rights-lawyers.html.

Levin, Dan. 2014. "Court Sides with Gay Man in 'Conversion' Suit." *New York Times,* December 20. Accessed May 20, 2016. http://www.nytimes.com/2014/12/20/world/asia/chinese-court-sides-with-gay-man-against-clinic-that-tried-to-convert-him.html.

Levitt, Peggy, and Sally Engle Merry. 2009. "Vernacularization on the Ground: Local Uses of Global Women's Rights in Peru, China, India and the United States." *Global Networks* 9/4: 441–461.

Lieberthal, Kenneth G. 1992. Introduction to *Bureaucracy, Politics and Decision-Making in Post-Mao China,* edited by Kenneth G. Lieberthal and David M. Lampton. Berkeley, Los Angeles, and Oxford: University of California Press.

Lin, Shirley. 2014. *2014 Action Assembly Monitoring & Evaluation Memo: China Nonprofit Leadership Cohort: Building the Next Generation of Nonprofit Leaders in China.* Report on file with Ford Foundation and Asia Catalyst.

Mann, Jonathan M., with Sofia Gruskin, Michael A. Grodin, and George J. Annas, eds. 1999. *Health and Human Rights: A Reader.* New York and London: Routledge.

McAdam, Doug. 1986. "Recruitment to High Risk Activism: The Case of Freedom Summer." *American Journal of Sociology* 92: 64–90.

Merry, Sally Engle. 2006. *Human Rights and Gender Violence: Translating International Law into Local Justice*. Chicago: University of Chicago Press.

Merry, Sally Engle, and Rachel E. Stern. 2005. "The Female Inheritance Movement in Hong Kong: Theorizing the Local/Global Interface." *Current Anthropology* 46: 387–409.

Mertha, Andrew. 2009. "'Fragmented Authoritarianism 2.0': Political Pluralization in the Chinese Policy Process." *China Quarterly*: 995–1012.

NSWP (Global Network of Sex Work Projects). 2016. "NSWP Welcomes Amnesty International's Policy on Protecting the Human Rights of Sex Workers." Accessed May 27, 2016. http://www.nswp.org/resource/nswp-welcomes-amnesty-internationals-policy-protecting-the-human-rights-sex-workers.

Oré Aguilar, Gaby. 2011. "The Local Relevance of Human Rights: A Methodological Approach." In *The Local Relevance of Human Rights*, edited by K. de Feyter, S. Parmentier, C. Timmerman, and G. Ulrich, 109–146. Cambridge: Cambridge University Press.

Pils, Eva. 2014. *China's Human Rights Lawyers: Advocacy and Resistance*. Routledge Research in Human Rights Law.

Qin, Amy. 2017. "Liu Xiaobo's Death Pushes China's Censors into Overdrive." *New York Times*, July 17. Accessed July 17, 2017. https://www.nytimes.com/2017/07/17/world/asia/liu-xiaobo-censor.html?_r=0.

Robins, Steven. 2006. "From 'Rights' to 'Ritual': AIDS Activism in South Africa." *American Anthropologist* 108/2: 312–323.

Saich, Tony. 2000. "Negotiating the State: The Development of Social Organizations in China." *China Quarterly* 161: 124–141.

Shen, Tingting. 2017. Email correspondence with a current Asia Catalyst program manager, July 17, 2017.

Shi-Kupfer, Kristin, and Bertram Lang. 2017. "Overseas NGOs in China: Left in Legal Limbo." *The Diplomat*, March 4. Accessed July 17, 2017. http://thediplomat.com/2017/03/overseas-ngos-in-china-left-in-legal-limbo/.

Shieh, Shawn, and Guosheng Deng. 2011. "An Emerging Civil Society: The Impact of the 2008 Sichuan Earthquake on Grass-Roots Associations in China." *China Journal* 65: 181–194.

Simon, Karla W. 2013. *Civil Society in China: The Legal Framework from Ancient Times to the "New Reform Era."* Oxford: Oxford University Press.

Spires, Anthony J. 2011. "Contingent Symbiosis and Civil Society in an Authoritarian State: Understanding the Survival of China's Grassroots NGOs." *American Journal of Sociology* 117/1: 1–45.

Sunstein, Cass. 1996. "Social Norms and Social Roles." Columbia University Program in Law and Economics Working Paper No. 36. Accessed May 20, 2016. https://dash.harvard.edu/bitstream/handle/1/12921744/Social%20Norms%20and%20Social%20Roles.pdf?sequence=1.

Teets, Jessica. 2009. "Post-Earthquake Relief and Reconstruction Efforts: The Emergence of Civil Society in China?" *China Quarterly* 198: 330–347.

Turner, Jennifer L. 2004. "Small Government, Big and Green Society: Emerging Partnerships to Solve China's Environmental Problems." *Harvard Asia Quarterly*: 4–13.

UNAIDS. 2007. "UNAIDS Acts to Strengthen GIPA with New Policy." March 30. Accessed May 27, 2016. http://www.unaids.org/en/resources/presscentre/featurestories/2007/march/20070330gipapolicybrief.

United Nations Office of the High Commissioner for Human Rights. 2016. "UN Human Rights Chief Deeply Concerned by China Clampdown on Lawyers and Activists." Accessed May 20, 2016. http://www.ohchr.org/UN/NewsEvents/Pages/DisplayNews.aspx?newsID=17050#sthash.FFNr21cH.dpuf.

Wee, Sui-Lee, and Stephanie Nebehay. 2015. "At U.N., China Uses Intimidation Tactics to Silence Its Critics." Reuters, October 6. Accessed May 20, 2016. http://www.reuters.com/investigates/special-report/china-softpower-rights/.

Wilson, Scott. 2012. "Settling for Discrimination: HIV/AIDS Carriers and the Resolution of Legal Claims." *International Journal of Asia Pacific Studies* 8/1: 35–55.

Wu, Fengshi, and Kin-man Chan. 2012. "Graduated Control and Beyond: The Evolving Government-NGO Relations." *China Perspectives* 3: 9–17.

Youde, Jeremy. 2009. "From Resistance to Receptivity: Transforming the HIV/AIDS Crisis into a Human Rights Issue." In *The International Struggle for New Human Rights*, edited by Clifford Bob, 68–82. Philadelphia: University of Pennsylvania Press.

Zeng, Jinyan. 2015. "China's Feminist Five: 'This Is the Worst Crackdown on Lawyers, Activists and Scholars in Decades.'" *Guardian*, April 17. Accessed May 20, 2016. http://www.theguardian.com/lifeandstyle/2015/apr/17/chinas-feminist-five-this-is-the-worst-crackdown-on-lawyers-activists-and-scholars-in-decades.

AFTERWORD

Our Vernacular Futures

Mark Goodale

Travel and transformation—these are the two problems in human rights that animate this lively, empirically rich, and consequential interdisciplinary volume. How, when, and why do human rights norms circulate among the quite diverse types of networks that have come to constitute what can only loosely be described as the human rights system? And when these norms circulate, what kinds of transformations follow? Do the norms change in quality and quantity? What about the range of actors who are involved in these circulations? Are they also transformed in some sense? Do they come to think of themselves in different ways? Do they gain in legal, political, or cultural agency? And more broadly, how does a deeper understanding of human rights travel and transformation enlarge ongoing debates about human rights theory and practice at a moment in which the status of human rights remains as "unsettled" (Sarat and Kearns 2001) as ever?

What I want to do here is to provide enough historical and theoretical context to allow us to better appreciate the necessity for this collective intervention, one that is anchored in the lived realities of human rights practice in all of its complexity, possibility, and uncertainty. As we have seen, the attempt to think anew about the practice of human rights through its concepts and categories comes at a turning point in the longer postwar history of human rights. To consider the volume's several key *problématiques* in 2016 is a very different thing than to have done so from the perspective of, say, 1995, or even 2007. It is vital that critical engagements keep pace with the ever-changing landscape of human rights in a world marked by the rise of nationalist and populist movements from Britain to India; growing global inequality and its manifold consequences for health, political stability, and the shrinking possibilities for socioeconomic transformation; and looming yet unpredictable conflicts associated with human-induced climate change.

After framing this context as I understand it, I will make the argument that the chapters in this volume are on what I believe is the more productive side of an important, if subtle, divide in the study of human rights. On one side are approaches to human rights that seek, in one way or another, to use scholarship in order to make legal implementation more effective, claims for institutional legitimacy better grounded, and the lines of political accountability clearer. What unites this side of the divide is a general agreement on the validity of the postwar framework of human rights. The thrust of research and scholarship is to provide the epistemological tools to firm up an international legal and political system that could be made better. There are two dilemmas with research and scholarship firmly rooted on what might be called the *establishment* side of this divide.

First, the scope of analysis is limited by the fact that the form and content of studies are shaped and, at times, predetermined by the purposes to which such studies are undertaken. This makes it difficult to assess establishment human rights scholarship by conventional measures; it would be better, rather, to see work in this mode as akin to internal policy studies that are meant to help an institution function better. And second, establishment scholarship tends to either give scant attention to critiques of human rights, or dismiss them as disingenuous efforts to justify troubling practices or histories in the name of culture, anticolonialism, or normative difference.

The other side of the divide is marked by human rights scholarship that is more open and indeterminate. The content, structure, and meaning of human rights are not taken as given; instead, interventions within what might be described as *alternative* human rights scholarship examine the unsettled status of human rights as a legitimate empirical and conceptual problem. Alternative human rights scholarship tends to be agnostic about the underlying value claims and political aspirations that ground existing human rights activism, yet open to the possibility that critical research might very well point the way toward a radically reconfigured global human rights project. It is not surprising that alternative human rights scholarship often pays close attention to the practice of human rights, since it is in the micronormative details that both the creative possibilities and ultimate limitations of human rights are to be found. And as the chapters in this volume demonstrate, a renewed and systematic focus on the practice of human rights has implications that go well beyond the merely epistemological. There is also a certain urgency to the task in light of historical and ideological developments that seem to forebode the end of what UN Secretary-General Kofi Annan described as the "age of human rights" (Annan 2000).

In the analyses of some critical scholars, the perennially unsettled status of human rights has become something more ominous. As Stephen Hopgood has written, evoking an apocalyptic imaginary,

> we are living through the endtimes of the civilizing mission ... [in which] the prospect of one world under secular human rights law is receding. What seemed like a dawn is in fact a sunset. The foundations of universal liberal norms and global governance are crumbling, creating a vacancy where sovereignty and religion now make dramatic inroads in the post–Cold War world. (Hopgood 2013, 1)

And at much more concrete levels, anthropologists like Lori Allen (2013) and Harri Englund (2006) have given us finely wrought ethnographic accounts of the implementation and promotion of human rights norms that reveal their "rise and fall" (Allen) within ongoing political and legal conflicts, or the way in which the language of human rights can make "prisoners" (Englund) out of those who deploy it. What is notable and challenging about the critical analyses that have emerged from the anthropology of human rights in particular is the fact that they are grounded in often long-term empirical research and a heightened sensitivity to the structural ambiguities that constitute human rights vernacularization. This empirical thickness stands in some contrast to what appear now as the more ideologically infused critiques of human rights and international law, often framed in the rhetoric of postcolonial resistance (e.g., Anghie 2005; Mutua 2001).

More broadly, the fragile structure of the post–Cold War human rights system has come under attack at the level of regional and international political economies with consequences that threaten to undermine efforts to make human rights norms a foundation for progressive change. For example, as different scholars have shown, from Southeast Asia to Latin America, there is often what might be called an intentional gap between legal judgments (for example, those issued by the Inter-American Court of Human Rights) and their influence on ongoing conflicts, particularly those that concern valuable economic resources (e.g., Adcock 2014; Leeman 2014; Medina 2014). What I have described elsewhere (Goodale 2016b) as "state-capital resource assemblages" are created that are meant to financialize human rights legislation and jurisprudence by seeing enforcement as just another form of capital risk management. At the extremes, the enforcement of human rights legislation has led to a boon in the transference of rights over valuable resources to small groups of transnational companies. This is because provisions of national human rights laws require communities to settle conflicts and produce local development plans in ways that, from the perspective of transnational capital, create what the critical development scholars Borras and Franco (2010) have described as a "one-stop shop." In this sense, the threat to human rights comes not from the absence of legal enforcement, but precisely because and in terms of it.

The ongoing conflicts around the International Criminal Court (ICC) underscore even more directly the way in which the momentum of the post–Cold War human rights movement has stalled. The creation of the ICC in 2002 as the world's first permanent international criminal court was hailed at the time as a major triumph in the effort to establish a global framework for the prosecution of major human rights violations (see generally Clarke 2009; Wilson 2011). Yet the influence of narrow national and regional political interests marred the development of the ICC during the first fifteen years of its existence. On the one hand, the nonparticipation of leading global powers has limited the scope of prosecutions. China, Russia, and the United States, all permanent members of the UN Security Council (which plays an important role in ICC jurisdiction), are not parties to the ICC treaty and are—for different reasons—actively opposed to its jurisdictional expansion.

On the other hand, the leaders of countries that have been prosecuted have led a campaign to discredit the ICC as a tool of neo-imperialism. In a 2014 analysis of this anti-ICC campaign by certain African countries, Kenneth Roth, the executive director of Human Rights Watch, worried that this campaign could be "devastating for international justice," since the largest block of members to the ICC treaty is from Africa, and African countries were instrumental in negotiating the treaty and establishing the court. Nevertheless, this broad early support across the continent faded when it became clear that African leaders were the prime (available) candidates for prosecution for gross human rights violations. As Roth put it, "the court's future . . . rests to a large extent on the battle being waged between African leaders with little interest in justice and those Africans, including many activists and victims, who see an end to impunity for mass atrocities as essential for Africa's future." Yet by 2016, it seemed as if this battle was being won by the

"African leaders with little interest in justice." Although not exactly a "mass African defection" from the treaty, countries such as South Africa, Burundi, and Gambia had notified the UN of their formal intention to withdraw from the court at the same time that countries such as Kenya, Uganda, Ethiopia, and Namibia were actively considering similarly abandoning the ICC.

Thus, from the local, discursive level to the level of international relations, the standing of human rights confronts its worst existential crisis since the end of the Cold War. In some sense, the "backlash against human rights," as a leading European human rights center has described it (Venice Academy of Human Rights 2016), was an inevitable response to the failure of the liberal "end of history" to materialize. Instead of the realization of the dreams of a neo-Kantian world of "perpetual peace" grounded in a global culture of human rights, supranational citizenship, and the wide acceptance of universal equality, the world had to come to terms with the sobering realities of Abu Ghraib, growing structural economic inequality (Piketty 2014), the ravages of "savage sorting" (Sassen 2014), Brexit, the illegal military annexation of Crimea by Russia, the sight of little refugee children washing up on the shores of Europe, and the election of Donald Trump. At least some of the sense of human rights in crisis can be attributed to the growing disenchantment with the considerable gap between the promises made during the golden years of the "age of human rights" and the stark, even brutal world of today, one in which identitarian and antihumanist politics flourish, mature democracies flirt with ideological hooliganism, and the so-called Asian Century continues to unfold around ethnic exclusion, resource depletion, and authoritarian command capitalism.

And yet disenchantment alone cannot explain why we supposedly find ourselves in the endtimes of human rights. Other answers are to be sought in the structure of international human rights law itself as it developed during the wilderness years of the Cold War, a system built on top-down treaty creation and the eventual movement to implement and monitor treaties from central nodes in places like Geneva and New York City. The international human rights system emerged within a framework that was highly centralized at both global and regional levels. As its history demonstrates, this orientation built friction and perverse political incentives into its very institutional foundation.

Finally, at a normative level, the largely juridical and declarative form of human rights tended to amplify a certain autopoietic tendency that was present from the drafting of the early foundational documents themselves, a constitutive autoreferentiality that belied later claims that the "international Magna Carta for all mankind" (as Eleanor Roosevelt memorably described the UDHR) was the result of a global, cross-cultural consensus on basic principles. Rather, the normatively closed form of international human rights *law* brought it into structural tension with the much more open, normatively chaotic, and often nonjuridical *practice* of human rights that emerged and developed during the transformative years of the post–Cold War (see Goodale 2016a).

This, then, is the conceptual and historical background, as I understand it, to this collective effort to reconsider the empirical realities of human rights travel and, more important, the potential for different kinds of transformation that these practices and circulations suggest. And as Destrooper and Merry argue in the book's Introduction, attending to these decentralized circulations and appropriations, despite their heterogeneity and ambiguity, is the only way to work our way back to what they describe as the essentially "counter-hegemonic nature" of what might be thought of as actually existing human rights—that is, human rights as an always contested language of everyday ethics that gets put to use within particular struggles with uncertain outcomes. These are the spaces of practice and contestation that often have at most a *connotative* (Goodale 2007) relationship to human rights law, whether in the form of international treaties and declarations or in the form of national legislation whose purpose is to enact domestic treaty obligations.

In their call to be "faithful" to the underlying emancipatory and progressive purposes of human rights, Destrooper and Merry emphasize the critical form of human rights scholarship that seeks to use the study of human rights travel and transformation to effect what Gunzelin Schmid Noerr (2002, 230) has described as a "change in function." What this would mean here is the move toward a much broader, provocative, and confrontational vision of human rights, one in which "socio-economic injustices, exploitation, oppression and inequality" become the central concern well beyond the classically liberal civil and political rights that were the principal focus for institutional and civil society actors for much of the postwar history of human rights. And as new historians of human rights like Steven Jensen (2016) and Christopher Roberts (2015) have shown, what Destrooper and Merry propose is in many ways a contemporary and urgent rediscovery of some of the original impulses that animated early arguments for human rights, arguments that took place both before the UDHR was ratified and which then continued in key centers of postcolonial resistance and theorizing in the Global South.

As the chapters in this volume suggest, an alternative approach to the study of the practice of human rights, one attuned to the deep political economic inequalities that shape this practice, must develop an epistemological framework that both acknowledges the fragile status of human rights and offers a way forward for scholars and policymakers alike. This is no easy task. As Vandenbogaerde's chapter on the UN Human Rights Council shows, the multiple institutional and political layers that form the foundation of the existing international human rights system create the likelihood of bureaucratic resistance to normative innovation from below.

At the same time, as Vandenhole's study of "human rights–based approaches to development" reminds us, a focus on what he describes as "grassroots dynamics" does not ensure greater "local effectiveness" (quoting De Feyter 2011). Rather, as Vandenhole argues, the vectors of influence that shape human rights norms as they travel and circulate can threaten to transform "the very notion of human rights" beyond recognition. In this sense, the concept of the "local" is doubly problematic. On the one hand, particularly when joined to "the global" (another problematic concept) in a neat and tidy conceptual binary, the local as an imagined site of action comes into descriptive tension with the kinds of circulations that actually constitute human rights networks. And on the other hand, "the local" is invested with a certain ideological power in which local actors are assumed to be committed to social justice, willing to sacrifice self-interest for the sake of community, and grateful for the interventions of the much less innocent "justice junkies" (Baylis 2008) with whom they collaborate. But as Waldmüller's chapter on rights experimentation in Ecuador shows, this kind of human rights orientalism, which constructs and sorts human rights actors based on dubious narratives of moral renewal and human goodness, does violence to the actual human and moral complexities that are revealed through a clear-eyed sensitivity to actual practices. Even in places like Ecuador and Bolivia, in which arguably post-neoliberal normative innovation has been pushed to its greatest limits, the "politics of rights always involves the establishment of hierarchies and prioritization of values," as Waldmüller puts it.

The possibilities for normative transformation through human rights travel and vernacularization are challenged even further when case studies are taken into consideration that come from outside the post–Cold War human rights hot zones in which the influence of the "age of human rights" was the greatest. Indeed, it is a particular strength of this volume that it features chapters that reflect meaningfully on the status of human rights in places like China and Vietnam. As MacLean's chapter on domestic responses to police torture in Vietnam argues, the absence of a history of human rights mobilization can mean that justice movements might coalescence around quite different logics of representation and confrontation—in this case, the development of Web 2.0 technologies that were designed to put pressure on the state to punish offenders. Moreover, what he calls the "(non)adoption of human rights discourse" by Vietnamese activists was strongly conditioned by the fact that the country is still very much organized around a "socialist legality" that has little use for what is seen as a bourgeois Western legal import.

The role of China in any debates around human rights transformation and the possibilities for new and expanded human rights practices is absolutely critical. Despite a tradition of "rights hunting" in China undertaken by human rights scholars and activists seeking to prove to the Chinese that human rights norms are in fact more consistent with their legal and political history than they might otherwise believe, these efforts have been largely "misdirected" (Hood 2001). Rather, it is more convincing to understand the relationship between human rights travel and contemporary China in a longer historical framework in which the ideas and values of human rights struggle to form part of a "common heritage" that links distinct philosophical and cultural traditions. Otherwise, as Hood puts it, to make the universalistic argument that Chinese history, and Confucianism in particular, contain a distinct rights tradition "is the same as to suggest that the monarchical regimes of the West knew rights were better but for one reason or another people decided not to claim them" (Hood 2001, 119).

Indeed, as Evan Osnos's (2014) brilliant ethnographic reportage on his five years as a correspondent in China (2008–2013) reveals in such unforgettable detail, China's "Gilded Age" is marked by a series of fundamental tensions between various ideological and philosophical legacies and a more general striving for socioeconomic advancement that has given the individual more potential power and autonomy than at any time in Chinese history. At the center of these pervasive existential crises is a paradox that affects everything from Chinese foreign policy to efforts by ordinary people to find meaning in a society marked by rapid economic development and massive inequalities: the fact that China is both a communist country committed to Marxist-Leninism and "socialism with Chinese characteristics" and, at the same time, the world's most successful capitalist economy, with average growth of 10 percent per year over thirty years and the most billionaires of any country in the world.

Yet as the chapters by Desmet and Davis and Mohamed demonstrate, the role of human rights in mediating contemporary China's "age of ambition" is unclear. In her study of "education-related experiences of social exclusion in the context of internal migration," Desmet shows how both governmental restrictions and cultural expectations combined to limit the extent to which a largely "international" and "hypothetical" language of human rights influenced local conflicts over the education of rural migrant children. Much like MacLean's account of the "(non)adoption of human rights discourse," Desmet urges us to pay attention to what might be thought of as the *nonpractice* of human rights, particularly "in settings where these concepts are not predisposed to play a role."

But when claims that do not involve political, social, or cultural rights are considered, research has shown a modest practice of human rights to have taken root in China. In their study of a health-rights advocacy network focused on government responses to the claims of people living with, or vulnerable to, HIV, Davis and Mohamed argue that health-rights organizations were only successful by respecting the "local bounds of the permissible," which meant emphasizing "deeply localized" approaches to health rights that were not formally linked to global rights movements. Yet it seems clear that health-rights networks in China were allowed to flourish (at least until a crackdown in 2016) precisely because the kinds of claims they engendered worked to reinforce, rather than threaten, the underlying balance between authoritarian—even if "fragmented"—capitalism and one-party rule. Any health crisis that takes potentially valuable workers out of the labor market is bad for business. To allow these health claims to be framed in the language of rights was permissible because, as Davis and Mohamed put it, to do so did not represent a "fundamental challenge to existing power relations."

In light of these research reports, which give us further perspectives on what Rachel Wahl (2016) has described as "human rights from the other side," that is, from the other side of a line that separates clear cases of progressive human rights change from more ambiguous practices and histories, an uncomfortable but necessary question must now be asked: What is the ultimate purpose of a better understanding of human rights travel and transformation? If the objective is to develop innovative scholarship that can also be used by policymakers to address the most critical challenges of our time, an argument can be made that a broader vision of the relationship between law, politics, and action is needed, a vision that finds resonance in this volume. Indeed, as Martínez's chapter on the plight of both *kamaiyas* in Nepal and

Haitian-Dominicans suggests, the use of human rights to frame structural social and economic conflicts can lead to a narrowing of options that can work against progressive advocacy. As his chapter reveals, the implication is that human rights advocates must learn to both understand and even support the (non)adoption of human rights discourse in certain cases and, when it is adopted, to treat its value and relevance with "greater skepticism."

How to understand the nuances of these distinctions will be a key task for the study and practice of human rights in the coming years. The promotion of human rights will need to be modulated to take account of different economic, cultural, and political contexts. Without being able to outline precisely how these modulations should be made, what is certain is that the post–Cold War project to promote human rights as a global value framework with universal application is coming to a close. Vastly different political economies would seem to mark the boundaries between different forms of what comes next.

In countries like Denmark, for example, as Julie Mertus (2009) has shown, human rights are controversial within domestic politics because many people believe that Danish culture offers superior alternative values that are based on community solidarity, consensus, and compromise. In this way, human rights are seen as a framework to be exported into countries that do not enjoy the same economic and cultural advantages. In Mertus's analysis, many Danes feel that their country is too good for human rights. And as Destrooper's chapter on "nonempowering human rights norms" and development in the Democratic Republic of the Congo suggests, we must consider the fact that certain countries, locations, and contexts might not be ready for the imposition of human rights as a basis for socioeconomic transition. Although she is critical of a local health officer's dismissal of human rights as irrelevant to local development that involves the most basic of human needs, I read his stark words somewhat differently. Even if it might be true that rights mobilization for "strategic interests" is an important long-term goal, there is something equally important to be learned when someone working on the very frontlines of human misery explains that "In the end, it's only the [water] pumps that matter."

Despite the many different settings in which the practice of human rights takes place, the response—both academic and policy-oriented—to these demands for fine-tuning our normative sensibilities at the same time that human rights advocacy in certain circumstances is "cut down to size" (Englund 2013) points in one clear direction: toward a reconfigured theory and practice of human rights that is pluralist, decentralized, and perhaps even "de-juridified." This fact gives new meaning to how we understand both the reality and purpose of human rights travel and transformation. To emphasize the necessity for human rights to evolve into new and plural forms is not the same thing as to say that human rights will or should become more localized. As Nesiah's chapter on ICC institutions in Africa reminds us, the notion of the local in the practice of human rights is highly problematic. Rather, it is to give full and even radical meaning to the concept of human rights vernacularization. This is not a way of understanding human rights pluralism that comes simply from the travel of established norms from the global to the local or from the local to the global, or through any other essentially metaphorical variant that attempts to account for the dynamism of existing human rights practices. It is, instead, a way to reimagine the grounding and legitimacy of human rights norms themselves—what they are and what they might be.

Works Cited

Adcock, Fleur. 2014. "Rights through the United Nations: The Domestic Influence of the Special Rapporteur on the Rights of Indigenous Peoples." Paper presented at the American Anthropological Association Annual Meeting. Washington, DC.

Allen, Lori A. 2013. *The Rise and Fall of Human Rights: Cynicism and Politics in Occupied Palestine*. Stanford: Stanford University Press.

Anghie, Antony. 2005. *Imperialism, Sovereignty and the Making of International Law*. Cambridge: Cambridge University Press.

Annan, Kofi. 2000. "The Age of Human Rights." *Project Syndicate*. http://www.project-syndicate.org/commentary/the-age-of-human-rights?barrier=true.

Baylis, Elena. 2008. "Tribunal-Hopping with the Post-Conflict Justice Junkies." *Oregon Review of International Law* 10: 361–390.

Borras, Saturino M., and Jennifer Franco. 2010. "Contemporary Discourses and Contestations around Pro-Poor Land Policies and Land Governance." *Journal of Agrarian Change* 10 (1): 1–32.

Clarke, Kamari Maxine. 2009. *Fictions of Justice: The International Criminal Court and the Challenge of Legal Pluralism in Sub-Saharan Africa*. Cambridge: Cambridge University Press.

De Feyter, Koen. 2011. "Sites of Rights Resistance." In *The Local Relevance of Human Rights*, edited by Koen De Feyter, Stephan Parmentier, Christiane Timmerman, and George Ulrich, 11–39. Cambridge: Cambridge University Press.

Englund, Harri. 2006. *Prisoners of Freedom: Human Rights and the African Poor*. Berkeley: University of California Press.

———. 2013. "Cutting Human Rights Down to Size." In *Human Rights at the Crossroads*, edited by Mark Goodale, 198–209. New York: Oxford University Press.

Goodale, Mark. 2007. "The Power of Right(s): Tracking Empires of Law and New Modes of Social Resistance in Bolivia (and elsewhere)." In *The Practice of Human Rights: Tracking Law*

Between the Global and the Local, edited by Mark Goodale and Sally Engle Merry, 130–162. Cambridge: Cambridge University Press.

———. 2016a. "Human Values and Moral Exclusion." *Ethics & Global Politics* 9 (1).

———. 2016b. "Dark Matter: Toward a New Political Economy of Indigenous Rights and Aspirational Politics." *Critique of Anthropology* 36 (4): 439–457.

Hood, Steven J. 2001. "Rights Hunting in Non-Western Traditions." In *Negotiating Human Rights and Culture,* edited by Lynda S. Bell, Andrew J. Nathan, and Ilan Peleg, 96–122. New York: Columbia University Press.

Hopgood, Stephen. 2013. *The Endtimes of Human Rights.* Ithaca: Cornell University Press.

Jensen, Steven L. B. 2016. *The Making of International Human Rights: The 1960s, Decolonization, and the Reconstruction of Global Values.* New York: Cambridge University Press.

Leeman, Esther. 2014. "Global Discourse, Local Realities: The Paradoxical Outcomes of Indigenous Land Titling Efforts in Cambodia." Paper presented at the Swiss Ethnological Society Annual Meeting. Basel, Switzerland.

Medina, Laurie. 2014. "Law, Jurisprudence, and the Production of Indigenous Land Rights: Maya Indigenous Communities v. Belize." Paper presented at the American Anthropological Association Annual Meeting. Washington, DC.

Mertus, Julie. 2009. *Human Rights Matters: Local Politics and National Human Rights Institutions.* Stanford: Stanford University Press.

Mutua, Makau. 2001. "Savages, Victims, and Saviors: The Metaphor of Human Rights." *Harvard International Law Journal* 42 (1): 201–245.

Osnos, Evan. 2014. *Age of Ambition: Chasing Fortune, Faith, and Truth in the New China.* New York: Farrar, Straus and Giroux.

Piketty, Thomas. 2014. *Capital in the Twenty-First Century.* Cambridge: Belknap Press of Harvard University Press.

Roberts, Christopher. 2015. *The Contentious History of the International Bill of Human Rights.* New York: Cambridge University Press.

Roth, Kenneth. 2014. "Africa Attacks the International Criminal Court." *New York Review of Books* 61 (2) (February 6).

Sarat, Austin, and Thomas R. Kearns. 2001. "The Unsettled Status of Human Rights." In *Human Rights: Concepts, Contests, Contingencies,* edited by Austin Sarat and Thomas Kearns, 1–24. Ann Arbor: University of Michigan Press.

Sassen, Saskia. 2014. *Expulsions: Brutality and Complexity in the Global Economy.* Cambridge: Belknap Press of Harvard University Press.

Schmid Noerr, Gunzelin. 2002. "The Position of 'Dialectic of Enlightenment' in the Development of Critical Theory." In *Dialectic of Enlightenment: Philosophical Fragments,* edited by Max Horkheimer and Theodor Adorno, 217–247. Stanford: Stanford University Press.

Venice Academy of Human Rights. 2016. *Backlash Against Human Rights?* July 4–13. www.eiuc.org/research/venice-academy-of-human-rights.html.

Wahl, Rachel. 2016. *Just Violence: Torture and Human Rights in the Eyes of the Police.* Stanford: Stanford University Press.

Wilson, Richard A. 2011. *Writing History in International Criminal Trials.* New York: Cambridge University Press.

CONTRIBUTORS

Sara L. M. Davis is scholar-in-residence at New York University Center for Human Rights and Global Justice, and a researcher/lecturer at the Geneva Centre for Education and Research in Humanitarian Action. Her research focuses on data, politics, and global health. She was the first senior human rights advisor at the Global Fund to Fight AIDS, Tuberculosis and Malaria. Prior to that she founded and was executive director of Asia Catalyst, an NGO providing management and human rights training to community-based groups in East and Southeast Asia. She earned her PhD at the University of Pennsylvania, and is the author of *Song and Silence: Ethnic Revival on China's Southwest Borders* (Columbia University Press, 2005). Her publications have appeared in *Health and Human Rights, Harm Reduction Journal, Modern China, Wall Street Journal Asia, International Herald Tribune*, and *South China Morning Post*. She has a blog, http://megontheinternet.wordpress.com, and posts on Twitter @saralmdavis.

Ellen Desmet is Assistant Professor of Migration Law at the Law Faculty of Ghent University, Belgium. She is a member of the Human Rights Centre and of the Centre for the Social Study of Migration and Refugees (CESSMIR). She teaches migration law, coordinates the migration law component of the Human Rights and Migration Law Clinic, and co-lectures on legal anthropology. Until September 2016, she was the project manager of the Interuniversity Attraction Pole "The Global Challenge of Human Rights Integration: Towards a Users' Perspective" at Ghent University, and the methodological advisor of the Localising Human Rights research program at the Law and Development Research Group of the University of Antwerp. From 2010 until 2012 she worked as a Senior Research and Policy Advice Officer at the Children's Rights Knowledge Centre. She complemented her law degree with a master in Cultures and Development Studies and a master in Development Cooperation, and holds a PhD in Law from the KU Leuven (2010).

Tine Destrooper is the Director of the Flemish Peace Institute. Before this, she was a Scholar in Residence and Managing Director at the Center for Human Rights and Global Justice at NYU's School of Law and a fellow at the Wissenschaftkolleg, Berlin. She also worked as a postdoctoral researcher with the Law and Development Research Group at the University of Antwerp and at the Center for Governance and Global Affairs at the University of Leiden. She obtained her PhD at the European University Institute, Florence, where she studied the relationship between armed conflict, social movements, and gender. She holds a master's degree in Conflict, Security and Development from University College London and an undergraduate degree from the University of Leuven. She worked for several government agencies in Belgium, as well as for the United Nations High Commissioner for Refugees. Her work has been published in, among others, *Human Rights Quarterly*, the *Journal of Human Rights Practice*, and *Development in Practice*.

Mark Goodale is Professor of Cultural and Social Anthropology at the University of Lausanne and Series Editor of Stanford Studies in Human Rights. He is an anthropologist and sociolegal scholar who conducts research on the cultural dimensions of law and ethics, social change, and human rights. He is the author or editor of thirteen volumes, including *Letters to the Contrary: A Curated History of the UNESCO Human Rights Survey* (ed., Stanford, 2018), *Anthropology and Law: A Critical Introduction* (NYU, 2017), *Human Rights at the Crossroads* (ed., Oxford, 2013), *Surrendering to Utopia: An Anthropology of Human Rights* (Stanford, 2009), *Dilemmas of Modernity: Bolivian Encounters with Law and Liberalism* (Stanford, 2008), and *The Practice of Human Rights: Tracking Law Between the Global and the Local* (coed. with Sally Engle Merry; Cambridge, 2007). He is currently writing a book about revolution, ideology, and law in Bolivia based on several years of ethnographic research funded by the U.S. National Science Foundation and the Wenner-Gren Foundation for Anthropological Research.

Ken MacLean is an Associate Professor of International Development and Social Change, as well as a core faculty member at the Strassler School for Holocaust and Genocide Studies, Clark University. He holds a doctorate in cultural anthropology from the University of Michigan. His research focuses on state-sponsored violence, forced migration, extractive industries, and critical humanitarianism. He is the author of *The Government of Mistrust: Illegibility and Bureaucratic Power in Socialist Vietnam* (University of Wisconsin

Press, 2013). His publications have appeared in *Critical Asian Studies, Focaal: Journal of Global and Historical Anthropology, Political and Legal Anthropology Review (PoLAR), Comparative Studies in Society and History, positions: asia critique, Asian Studies Review,* and *History and Anthropology.* He is currently working on a book manuscript tentatively titled *Search and Destroy: Human Rights Fact Production and Mass Atrocity Crimes in Burma/Myanmar.*

Samuel Martínez is a cultural anthropologist who teaches in the programs in Anthropology and Latin American Studies at the University of Connecticut. He is the author of two ethnographic monographs and several peer-reviewed articles on the migration and labor and minority rights of Haitian nationals and people of Haitian ancestry in the Dominican Republic. He is also editor of a contributory volume, *International Migration and Human Rights* (University of California Press, 2009). In his current research and writing, he brings critical scrutiny to northern human rights solidarity with Haitian-ancestry people in the Dominican Republic, 1978 to 2017.

Sally Engle Merry is Silver Professor of Anthropology at New York University. She is also a Faculty Director of the Center for Human Rights and Global Justice at the New York University School of Law. Her recent books include *Colonizing Hawai'i* (Princeton, 2000), *Human Rights and Gender Violence* (Chicago, 2006), *Gender Violence: A Cultural Perspective* (Blackwell, 2009), and *The Practice of Human Rights (*coedited with Mark Goodale; Cambridge, 2007). Her most recent book, *The Seductions of Quantification: Measuring Human Rights, Gender Violence, and Sex Trafficking* (University of Chicago Press, 2016), examines indicators as a technology of knowledge used for human rights monitoring and global governance. She received the Hurst Prize for *Colonizing Hawai'i* in 2002, the Kalven Prize for scholarly contributions to sociolegal scholarship in 2007, and the J. I. Staley Prize for *Human Rights and Gender Violence* in 2010. In 2013 she received an honorary degree from McGill School of Law.

Charmain Mohamed is a respected and experienced human rights advocate and activist who has lived and worked in Asia for most of the past 15 years. She is currently Advocacy Advisor on Syria for the Norwegian Refugee Council, and she was formerly executive director of Asia Catalyst. She has worked for the UN and Human Rights Watch both in emergency contexts and on long-term issues in countries such as Indonesia, East Timor, Malaysia,

Sri Lanka, and most recently in Palestine. She holds a master's in Human Rights Law from the School of Oriental and African Studies in London and a BA (Hons.) in Southeast Asian Studies and Indonesian Language from the University of Hull. She is fluent in English, Indonesian, and Malay.

Vasuki Nesiah is Associate Professor of Practice at the Gallatin School in NYU. She is a legal scholar with a focus on public international law. Her main areas of research include the law and politics of international human rights and humanitarianism, with a particular focus on transitional justice. Her past publications have engaged with human rights, international feminisms, and the history of colonialism in international law. She has also written on the politics of memory and comparative constitutionalism, with a particular focus on law and politics in South Asia. Her most immediate project includes a coedited volume (with Luis Eslava and Michael Fakhri) on *A Global History of Bandung and Critical Traditions in International Law* (Cambridge University Press, forthcoming). Before entering the academy full time, Professor Nesiah spent over seven years in practice at the International Center for Transitional Justice (ICTJ).

Arne Vandenbogaerde is a postdoctoral fellow at the Law and Development research group at the Faculty of Law. He obtained his PhD in Law at the University of Antwerp (2015) and holds a MA degree in international relations (University of Ghent) and an LLM in International Human Rights Law from the Irish Centre for Human Rights (Galway, Ireland). Previous to his current research at the University of Antwerp he worked with several NGOs and intergovernmental organizations such as the FAO Right to Food Unit. Until recently he was the program coordinator of the Research Networking Programme Beyond Territoriality: Globalisation and Transnational Human Rights Obligations (GLOTHRO). His main research interests include international human rights law, in particular the issues of extraterritorial and transnational human rights obligations as well as research concerning the effectiveness and local relevance of human rights law.

Wouter Vandenhole is an internationally recognized expert in transnational human rights obligations and in human rights and development. He has held the chair in human rights and the UNICEF chair in children's rights at the faculty of law of the University of Antwerp since 2007, and he has headed the Law and Development Research Group since 2013. He serves on the editorial board of several international journals, among which are the *Journal of Human Rights Practice* and *Human Rights and International Legal Discourse*. He has taken up management functions in European research and teaching networks. He has been the lead convenor of an international summer course on Human Rights for Development (HR4DEV, 2012–2015) and of the international training program Sustainable Development and Human Rights (SUSTLAW, 2016).

Johannes M. Waldmüller is a former postdoctoral fellow in Anthropology at New York University and is currently Research Professor at the Universidad de las Americas, Quito. He holds a PhD in Anthropology and Sociology of Development from the Graduate Institute in Geneva (2014) as well as MA degrees in International Development and Intercultural Philosophy from the University of Vienna. By drawing on legal and institutional anthropology, his transdisciplinary work is on the one hand concerned with technologies of governance, human rights, and big data in development contexts (Andes and Sub-Saharan Africa) and on the other with the ethics of transcultural translations and epistemologies by drawing on post- and decolonial readings. He is also co-founder and research associate of Kompreno, a Geneva-based research association working on three continents (www.kompreno.org), as well as co-founder and editor of Alternautas (www.alternautas.net).

INDEX

Abel, Richard L., 186
access, to human rights architecture, 16, 68–69
accountability, in HRBADs, 79–82, 85, 213, 216
ActionAid, 80, 86
African Union, 49
AIDS Coalition to Unleash Power (ACT-UP), 231, 237
Alianza País, 107, 113
Allen, Lori, 253
Alston, Philip, 58
alternative manifestations of rights, 8, 78
Altholz, Roxanna, 140–41
American Convention on Human Rights, 64, 143
Amnesty International, 168, 232
Andreassen, B., 83–84
Annan, Kofi, 253
anthropocentrism, 110, 114
Aristide, Jean-Bertrand, 135
Asia Catalyst, 230, 233–43, 246

Backward Society Education (BASE), 136–40, 142
Balaguer, Joaquín, 135
Bales, Kevin, 144–45
BASE. *See* Backward Society Education
BBC-Vietnam, 166
Berkeley Human Rights Center, 37
Berkeley International Human Rights Law Clinic, 143
Bigombe, Betty, 34
blaming, 186–87, 197–98
Bob, Clifford, 17, 130–32
bonded labor, 21, 133–35, 137–40, 144–45
Borras, Saturino M., 254

Bosico, Violeta, 141–43, 145
Branch, Adam, 43
Brems, Eva, 8
Brown, Wendy, 169
Brucato, Ben, 164
Brysk, Alison, 129
Buen Vivir, 104, 107–13, 115, 121n7

Campaign to Abolish Torture in Vietnam (CAT-VN), 172
Cao, Deborah, 193
Cao Shunli, 230, 245
CAR. *See* Central African Republic
Carruthers, Bruce, 4, 210
cause lawyers, 173–74
CBO Catalyst program, 230, 234–42, 245
Central African Republic (CAR), 29, 48
CFS. *See* Committee on World Food Security
Chan, Jennifer, 244
Chapman, J., 80, 82–83, 86
Chaudhari, Dilli, 137, 142
Chaudhari, Yagyaraj, 139
Chevron-Texaco, 103–4, 111, 116–17
China, 12; children's rights in, 194–95; civil society in, 230, 233, 245; education of migrants in, 183–203; familiarity with human rights concepts in, 191–96; HIV/AIDS activists in, 23, 231–46; refraining from human rights discourse in, 22; repression of human rights advocacy in, 229–30, 233, 242, 244; right-to-health advocacy in, 230–46
Chua, Lynette, 238
CICC. *See* Coalition for the ICC
citizen-journalism, 163–69
Civil Rights Defenders, 171

civil society: in China, 230, 233, 245; HRC and, 67–72; role of, in human rights process, 15–18, 67–72; and Vietnamese torture, 168, 170
claiming, 186–87, 198–202, 223
Clark, Kamari, 49
CMOs. *See* community membership organizations
Coalition for the ICC (CICC), 45–46
Cohen, Stanley, 174
coloniality, 14–15, 149, 151n4
Comaroff, John and Jean, 151n5
Commission on Human Rights, 70
Committee on the Elimination of Discrimination against Women, 91
Committee on the Rights of the Child, 91
Committee on World Food Security (CFS), 71–72
Committee to Protect Journalists, 162
Common Understanding, of HRBADs, 79, 213, 215, 221
community membership organizations (CMOs), 128, 131–36, 138–41, 147, 149–50, 151n1
complementarity, in global-local justice cases, 32–33, 36, 40–41, 43, 47
Confucianism, 202, 204n20, 258
Convention against Torture and Other Cruel, Inhuman, or Degrading Treatment or Punishment (UNCAT), 159–60, 164, 169, 172
Correa, Rafael, 103, 107, 109, 113–15
Crawford, G., 83–84
critical legal studies, 4, 210
cunningness, of human rights claims, 115–20

Dabashi, Hamid, 148–49
Dan Lam Bao (The People Do News) (online news platform), 163
Dan Luan (People Discuss) (online news platform), 164
Darrow, M, 80
Dauphinée, Elizabeth, 158
Davis, Sara, 12, 23, 259
Declaration of the Rights of Peasants and Other People Working in Rural Areas, 19, 61
Declaration on the Rights of Indigenous Peoples, 66

De Feyter, Koen, 8, 93–94, 131–32, 134, 136, 149, 185, 209
De Gaay Fortman, Bastiaan, 9, 81–82
Deguis Pierre, Juliana, 146
democracy, 31, 32, 38, 44–46, 49
Democratic Republic of the Congo (DRC), 12, 19, 29, 39–44, 49; Kongo Central, 22, 211–23
De Schutter, Olivier, 71
Desmet, Ellen, 12, 22, 259
Destrooper, Tine, 12, 22–23, 256, 260
development. *See* human rights–based approaches to development
distributive justice, 47, 130, 144, 149
Dominican Republic, 133–36, 138–50, 151n7
Don, Vo An, 174
Dongjen Center for Human Rights Education, 239
DRC. *See* Democratic Republic of the Congo
Dutch Technical Cooperation, 218
duty bearers, 216–20, 226n15

Eckert, Julia, 133
Economic and Social Council (ECOSOC), 68–69
eco-social rights, 102–4, 107–17
Ecuador, 20–21, 101–20
education, of migrants in China, 183–203; access to education, 189–91; responses to problems with, 196–203
Emil, Antonio Pol, 139
empowerment, in HRBADs, 79–83, 85
ENAMI EP, 103
Engel, Jaruwan S. and Madeline H., 184
Englund, Harri, 253
Ensor, Jonathan, 8, 78, 81, 87, 90
erasures, of local understanding of human rights, 21, 102, 113–20
European Convention on Human Rights, 63–64
European Court of Human Rights, 63–64
European Union, opposition of, to new human rights instruments, 64
extractive industries, 103–5, 114–15

Facebook, 163, 164
Felstiner, William L. F., 186
female genital mutilation (FGM), 91–92

Fletcher, Laurel, 140–41, 143
Food and Agricultural Organization, 20
Ford Foundation, 233
Forgotten Voices (report), 35–39, 51n9, 52n11
framing theories, 22
Franco, Jennifer, 254
Fujikura, Tatsuro, 137, 148
Fulda, Andreas, 245

Gandhi, Mohandas, 237
Gao Yaojie, 233
Gillespie, John, 173
Gledhill, John, 8, 83, 92–93
Global Fund Fight to AIDS, Tuberculosis and Malaria, 232, 244
Global Network of People Living with HIV, 231
Global Network of Sex Work Projects, 231, 232
Godoy, Angelina Snodgrass, 130
Golay, Christophe, 66
Goodale, Mark, 23, 238
Goodman, Ryan, 4
Google+, 163
governmentality, 29, 48, 49
grassroots. *See* local ownership
Greater Inclusion of People with AIDS, 231

The Hague, 33, 34
Haitian immigrants, in Dominican Republic, 21, 133–36, 138–50, 151n7
Halliday, Terrence, 4, 210
Hannerz, Ulf, 224
Hay Bao Ve Nguoi Bao Ve Nhan Quyen (Defend the [Human Rights] Defenders), 168
health, advocacy in China for right to, 230–46; capacity-building for, 235–39, 242; scaling up and managing risk, 241–45; strategic planning for, 239–41; vernacularization in, 236–39
Hemment, Julie, 131
Henan Province Women's Network Against AIDS, 241
Hertel, Shareen, 129
Hinkelammert, Franz, 122n18
HIV/AIDS, 23, 231–46
Hoa Lo Prison, 157
Hood, Steven J., 258

Hopgood, Stephen, 253
HRBADs. *See* human rights–based approaches to development
HRC. *See* Human Rights Council
HRIs. *See* human rights indicators
human rights: actor-centered approaches to, 3–4; benefits conveyed by, to local settings, viii–ix; expanded use of, by social justice activists, 1; as ideals, vii–viii; "light" knowledge of, 217, 222–24; localization of, 3–4; ordinary people's familiarity with, 191–96; scholarship on, 252–53; threats to, 253–55; vernacularization of, viii, ix. *See also* norms and standards for human rights; transformation, of human rights; translation, of human rights; travel, of human rights
human rights–based approaches to development (HRBADs), 20, 77–95; confrontational vs. collaborative approaches in, 86–88; exposure to human rights discourse through, 208–9, 213, 220, 223–24; limits to, 88–94; the local and, 78, 80–82, 86–94; overview of, 79–80; power dynamics in, 82–86, 222; principles of, 80–83, 213, 216–17; Sanitized Villages project as instance of, 212–19; transformation in, 81, 82–86, 88–94; travel of, 77–78, 80–82
human rights bodies, role of, 17–18
Human Rights Council (HRC), 16, 19–20, 57–73; access to, 68–69; Advisory Committee of, 61, 65, 67–68, 70; Chinese intimidation in, 230; establishment of, 70; institutional and political perspectives on, 66–72; and peasants' rights, 60–62, 65–66; and protection gaps, 60–62; review practices of, 170
human rights framework, engagement with, 22–23, 196–203, 215–23
human rights indicators (HRIs), 106–12
human rights instruments: adoption of, 63; Ecuadorian push for, 117–18; opposition to creation of, 64; transnational corporations as target of, 112–13
human rights law, 231, 255
human rights process: institutional and political perspectives on, 66–72; pluralism in, 260–61; role of civil society in, 15–18, 67–72; role of HRC in, 66–72

human rights regime, limitations of, 13–14, 130
Human Rights Watch, 45, 48–49, 158–60, 168

IACtHR. *See* Inter-American Court of Human Rights
ICC. *See* International Criminal Court
ICTR. *See* International Criminal Tribunal for Rwanda
ICTY. *See* International Criminal Tribunal for the former Yugoslavia
Ife, J., 77
IMF. *See* International Monetary Fund
impunity, Vietnamese torture and, 161, 166, 169, 174–75
Informal Sector Service Center, 142
Inter-American Commission on Human Rights, 106, 118, 140–41
Inter-American Court, 64
Inter-American Court of Human Rights (IACtHR), 141, 143, 151n7
International Covenant on Civil and Political Rights (ICCPR), 1, 120, 164
International Covenant on Economic, Social and Cultural Rights (ICESCR), 1, 120
International Criminal Court (ICC), 19, 29–50; and DRC human rights violations, 39–44; legitimacy of, 29, 31–34, 44, 47; local ownership and, 31–34, 40–42, 44–50, 54n29; and sovereignty, 40–44; states' support for, 254–55; and Ugandan human rights violations, 34–35, 38–39, 43; and victim surveys, 37
International Criminal Tribunal for Rwanda (ICTR), 32, 44
International Criminal Tribunal for the former Yugoslavia (ICTY), 32, 37, 44
International Food Security and Nutrition Civil Society Mechanism (CSM), 71–72
International Labor Organization China Office, 241
International Monetary Fund (IMF), 50n1
International Network of People Who Use Drugs, 231
International Tribunal for the Rights of Nature, 118

Jacobson, David, 151n5
Jensen, Steven, 256

Jinks, Derek, 4
Joint UN Programme on HIV/AIDS (UNAIDS), 231–32, 244
juridification, 128–50; dangers of, 16–17, 21, 128–31, 133, 147–50; defined, 151n2; Dominican case study in, 133–36, 138–50, 151n7; Nepal case study in, 133–40, 142, 144–45, 147–50; positive outcomes of, 129; and Vietnamese torture, 173. *See also* lawfare; legal reductionism
justice: distributive, 47, 130, 144, 149; preventive, 159; restorative, 34; retributive, 159, 165; structural, 148; transitional, 35–39, 47, 50
Justice for All, 239

Kabila, Joseph, 43–44
kamaiyas, 21, 133–40, 142, 144–45, 147–50, 152n20
Katanga, Germain, 39–42, 44, 49, 52n16
Kelly, Tobias, 169, 174
knowledge: competing regimes of, 14, 149; decolonization of, 130
Kongo Central, 22, 211–23
Kony, Joseph, 34

law. *See* human rights law; juridification
lawfare, 128, 135, 141–42, 147, 151n5. *See also* juridification
legal mobilization, 186
legal pluralism, 4, 148, 210
legal reductionism, 128, 129, 142–44, 147. *See also* juridification
Levi Strauss Foundation, 233
Libya, 54n29
Lieberthal, Kenneth, 244–45
Liu Xiaobo, 230
the local: conceptions of, 11; power dynamics affecting, 13
localization: bidirectionality of, 131–32, 136, 149, 209–11, 220–21; of human rights, 3–4, 185; postcolonial theory and, 13–15; power dynamics in, 13, 209–10, 223; problems with, 257. *See also* vernacularization
local ownership, 19; conceptions of, 31, 40; HRBADs and, 78, 80–82, 86–94; ICC and, 31–34, 40–42, 44–50, 54n29; role of, in human rights accountability, 29–34;

and Sanitized Villages project, 211–19; transformation of, by universal concerns, 30–31, 33–34, 36, 39, 44–47, 78, 87, 91–93; and Ugandan human rights violations, 34–35; victim surveys as instance of, 35–39
London Charter, 32
Lord's Resistance Army, 34
Lubanga Dliyo, Thomas, 44, 52n16, 53n25

MacLean, Ken, 21–22, 258
Mang Luoi Blogger Viet Name (Network of Vietnamese Bloggers), 168, 170–72
Mariátegui, José Carlos, 130
Martínez, Samuel, 17, 21, 259
Mato Oput, 34
Medina, Carlos, 128
Merry, Sally Engle, 7, 13, 24n2, 78, 88–90, 131, 209, 256
Mertus, Julie, 260
Mexico, 106
Mitchell, Timothy, 49
Mitlin, Diana, 18, 86–87
Mohamed, Charmain, 12, 23, 259
Molyneux, Maxine, 131, 139, 150
Movimiento de Mujeres Domínico-Haitianas (MUDHA), 136, 141–43, 147
Movimiento Socio-Cultural para los Trabajadores Haitianos (MOSCTHA), 136
Moyn, Sam, 131–32
multidirectionality, of human rights travel, 10–13, 80–81, 210
Museveni, Yoweri, 34, 43
MYWO, 91

naming, 186–87, 196–97
National Endowment for Democracy, 233
neoliberalism, 82–83, 132
Nepal, 21, 133–40, 142, 144–45, 147–50
Nesiah, Vasuki, 8, 9, 19, 261
Nghia, Truong Trong, 159–60
Noerr, Gunzelin Schmid, 256
norm entrepreneurs, 10, 24n2
norms and standards for human rights: constraints imposed by, 65–66; core of, 90–93; HRC mechanism for creating, 60, 67–68; HRC responsibility for, 58; ICC and, 29–50; interaction of local and global, 2, 4, 6–7, 29, 33, 35, 40–42, 58,

86–87, 109, 116–18, 185–86, 208–11, 220–24, 257, 260–61; issues in creating new, 64–66; proliferation of, 5, 57–58; protection gaps in, 59–66; translation of, 5–6; travel of, 11–13, 65; upstream vs. downstream approaches to, 62–63

Ocampo, Luis Moreno, 33, 46, 48
Office of the High Commissioner for Human Rights (OHCHR), 79–80, 106, 108–10, 119
open-ended working groups (OEWGs), 68, 69
Open Society Foundations, 233
ordered pluralism, 210
Oré Aguilar, Gaby, 8, 12, 93–94, 185, 201
Osnos, Evan, 258
Overseas Support for the Free Journalist Network in Vietnam, 168

Pant, Shiva Raja, 139
participation, in HRBADs, 79–83, 85, 213, 216–17, 219, 225n4
Patel, Sheela, 18, 86–87
peace, right to, 64
peasants, rights of, 60–62, 65–66, 69
Phu Quoc Prison, 157
Pierre, Sonia, 141
Pils, Eva, 244
police, in Vietnam, 158–75
political opportunity/political process theory, 202
politics: law in relation to, 132–33, 148–49; preemption of, by juridification, 17, 38, 44–45, 128, 130, 151n5
Pong, Myra, 201
postcolonialism, 114–15, 120
postcolonial theory, 14–15
poverty reduction strategy papers, 50n1
power: dynamics of, 11–13; in HRBADs, 82–86, 222; at local level, 13, 209–10, 223; multidirectionality of, 210; power cube model of, 84–85; in transformation, 82–86
preventive justice, 159
protection gaps: addressing, 63–66; application gaps, 60, 62–66; identifying, 59–63; implementation gaps, 60; normative gaps, 59–66
Putnam, Robert, 116

Quan Lam Bao (Officials Do Journalism) (online news platform), 163–64
Quijano, Aníbal, 149
Quynh, Nguyen Ngoc Nhu, 170–71

Radio Free Asia, 166
Ramirez, Javier, 103, 115
Randeria, Shalini, 115
Rankin, Katherine, 138
Refugee Rights News, 41
Reporters Without Borders, 162
responsables (duty bearers), 219–20, 226n15
restorative justice, 34
retributive justice, 159, 165
rights defenders, 140, 147–48, 168, 170, 229
rights subjectivity, 20, 88–90
Rincón, Genaro, 143
Roberts, Christopher, 256
Rome Statute: Article 14, 43; Article 17, 32–34, 36, 40, 47
Roosevelt, Eleanor, 256
Roth, Kenneth, 254
Ruffer, Galya, 151n5

Sanitized Villages project, 22, 211–23
Sarat, Austin, 186
Schaefer, Brian, 165
scholarship, on human rights, 252–53
self-help, 198
self-referrals, 33, 39–44, 54n29
SENPLADES, 108–9
Shack/Slum Dwellers International, 86
Shramik Mukti Sangathan (Organization for Laborers' Liberation), 136
SIIDERECHOS, 108–10
Simmons, Beth, 4
slavery, 134–35, 137, 144–45
social movements: alteration/reformulation of agendas of, 16–17, 21, 130–33, 147–48, 150; emergence and development of, 202; Haitian-Dominican, 138–42; kamaiya struggle as, 136–38
Sousa Santos, Boaventura de, 148–49
Southwick, Katherine, 34
sovereignty, 40–44, 143
Speed, Shannon, 132
standards. *See* norms and standards for human rights
statelessness, 135, 143–44, 146
stealth torture, 169

Steinmetz, Kevin, 165
Stover, Eric, 37–38
structural injustice, 148
sumak kawsay. *See* Buen Vivir
Sundi, Pascal, 214
Supplementary Convention on the Abolition of Slavery, the Slave Trade, and Institutions and Practices Similar to Slavery, 137
Svensson, Marina, 192
Swedish Helsinki Committee for Human Rights, 171
Swedish International Development Assistance, 233

Telesca, Jennifer, 158
Tendetza Antún, José Isidro, 117–18
Thai AIDS Treatment Action Group, 239
Thiem, Bui, 173
toleration, 198, 204n18
Tomas, A., 80
torture. *See* Vietnam, torture in
transformation, of human rights: eco-social and collective rights in Ecuador, 101–20; in HRBADs, 81, 82–86, 88–94; key issues in, 6–8; limits to, 88–94; power as factor in, 82–86; Sanitized Villages project as case study in, 212–13, 219–23
transitional justice, 35–39, 47, 50
translation, of human rights: eco-social and collective rights in Ecuador, 101–20; by hybridization, 89–90; key issues in, 5–7; by replication, 89–90; role of translators in, 88–90; in victim surveys, 36–37; and Vietnamese torture, 173–74
travel, of human rights: concept of, 78; HRBADs and, 77–78, 80–82; key issues in, 5; multidirectional, 10–13, 80–81; of norms and standards, 11–13, 65; Sanitized Villages project as case study in, 212–13, 219–23; upstream vs. downstream, 7–10, 78, 80–82
Treatment Action Campaign, 231
Treaty of Versailles, 32

UDHR. *See* Universal Declaration of Human Rights
Uganda, 19, 34–35, 38–39, 43
UNAIDS. *See* Joint UN Programme on HIV/AIDS

UNCAT. *See* Convention against Torture and Other Cruel, Inhuman, or Degrading Treatment or Punishment
UNICEF, 211–21
United Nations Development Program, 213
United Nations High Commissioner on Human Rights, 230
United Nations Security Council, 47, 54n29
United Nations Social Forum, 70
Universal Declaration of Human Rights (UDHR), 168, 172, 256
Universal Periodic Review (UPR), 21, 170–71, 175
UPR. *See* Universal Periodic Review
Urueña, 210–11
users' perspective, on human rights, 13, 187–88
U.S. Federal Drug Administration, 231
U.S. State Department Bureau of Democracy, Rights and Labor, 233

Van, Tran Thi Bich, 160
Vandenbogaerde, Arne, 16, 19–20, 257
Vandenhole, Wouter, 7, 20, 185, 257
vernacularization: in Chinese right-to-health advocacy, 236–39; concept of, ix, 7–8, 78, 209; eco-social and collective rights in Ecuador, 111; role of translators in, 88–90. *See also* localization
La Via Campesina, 20, 60–62, 65–66, 69, 72
victim surveys, 35–39, 48
Vietnam, torture in, 21, 157–75; digital context for exposure of, 162–65; impunity concerning, 158, 161, 166, 169, 174–75; local-level strategies against, 159, 165–69, 175; obstacles to combating, 162, 169, 173; online documentation of, 164–69; situation analysis of, 159–62; stealth torture, 169; translation issues concerning, 173–74; transnational-level strategies against, 159, 169–73, 175
Vietnam Human Rights Act (United States), 171
Vietnam Reform Party, 163
visibility, strategies of, 157–75
Vivek Pandit, 140, 142
Voluntary Guidelines on the Responsible Governance of Tenure of Lands, Fisheries and Forests, 71–72

Wahl, Rachel, 259
Waldmüller, Johannes M., 6, 13, 20–21, 151n4, 257
Wan Yanhai, 233
We Are One: 2015 Human Rights, Freedom and Democracy for Vietnam Campaign, 171–72
Wheaton, Henry, 192
Women of Zimbabwe Arise, 85, 90–91
Women's Network Against AIDS/China, 241
World Bank, 50n1
World Court of Human Rights, 68
World Summit on Climate Change, 118

Yang Teng, 242
Yasuní-ITT initiative, 109, 114
Yean, Dilcia, 141–43, 145
Yean and Bosico v. Dominican Republic, 141, 143, 145, 147, 150, 151n7
YouTube, 163–65

Zenker, Olaf, 132
Zhongze Women's Legal Counselling and Service Centre, 229

ACKNOWLEDGMENTS

The project out of which this volume emerged benefited from the contributions of many individuals and organizations. We are especially grateful to our colleagues from the Center for Human Rights and Global Justice at New York University School of Law and the Research Group on Law and Development at the Law Faculty of the University of Antwerp, who supported the project in various ways. Philip Alston and Meg Satterthwaite in particular endorsed this project from the outset and gave it an institutional home. Audrey Watne did a magnificent job in facilitating the organization of an expert roundtable that brought together contributors from a wide array of disciplines to engage in a stimulating discussion on the travel, translation, and transformation of human rights. Also Ellen Desmet provided support that was invaluable in bringing researchers from both sides of the Atlantic together to engage in a multidisciplinary and multiregional dialogue. The team from the language service at the Wissenschaftskolleg zu Berlin has been exceptional in providing us with editorial assistance in the last stages of writing, and Carey Harrison's comments and suggestions regarding the language greatly improved the accessibility of the volume, making it relevant for both nonspecialists and specialists alike.

Special thanks go to Koen De Feyter, without whom this expert meeting would not have been organized in the first place. As the head of the Localising Human Rights Project and of the Law and Development Research Group at the University of Antwerp, he stands at the cradle of this initiative, helped refine the focus of the meeting, and contributed a generous amount of time and funding to its organization. His comments during the expert meeting provided many participants with invaluable insights that have significantly shaped the final contributions.

The questions that inspired this initiative stem from the organizers', editors', and contributors' work with "rights users." We have all had the privilege of working with civil society organizations, nongovernmental organizations, community actors, individual rights holders, international organizations, and/or government actors, who often went out of their way to share their time, stories, and insights with us, but who also raised new questions—questions that are at the heart of this volume. Working so closely with these actors helped us to identify those questions that are not only pertinent for scholars and policymakers, but also, and especially, for rights holders and practitioners on the ground.

Our debts continued to accumulate throughout the writing and editing process. Both editors had the privilege of teaching undergraduate and graduate students at the various institutes with which they were affiliated. These students often challenged our ideas and pushed us to further flesh out the logic and argument of the volume. We also owe special thanks to our colleagues who were not involved in the initial roundtable but who provided us with many useful insights from their own (field)work. Special thanks go to Shreya Atrey and to the fellows and staff of the Wissenschaftskolleg zu Berlin, who, during workshops, lunches, and endless coffee breaks shared insights from their own—sometimes seemingly vastly different—disciplines, which helped us to address our argument from different angles. Hours spent in conversation with them convinced us of both the urgency of addressing the issue of how human rights travel and become translated and transformed, as well as the vast empirical, theoretical, and conceptual challenges involved in this endeavor. We try to face these challenges upfront in the introduction, and we are lavishly supported in our quest by the rich empirical analysis throughout the rest of the volume.

We, the editors, are most indebted, of course, to the contributors to this volume, who carved out significant chunks of their time, not just to participate in the original expert meeting but also, and more importantly, to prepare original scholarly papers on the basis of their presentation during the roundtable. Not all contributions to the meeting could be published, but we wish to extend particular thanks to Shareen Hertel, Tyler Giannini, Manisha Desai, Matthew Canfield, Koen De Feyter, Cynthia Soohoo, Maheshwar Singh, Dominique Kiekens, Noemie Desguin, and Lucie White for their participation and contributions, which enriched our understanding of the issues discussed in this volume.